*The Making of a Southern Democracy*

# The Making of a Southern Democracy

## NORTH CAROLINA POLITICS
## FROM KERR SCOTT TO PAT McCRORY

## Tom Eamon

*University of North Carolina Press* CHAPEL HILL

© 2014 The University of North Carolina Press
All rights reserved

Set in Utopia and Gotham types by codeMantra
Manufactured in the United States of America
The paper in this book meets the guidelines for permanence and durability
of the Committee on Production Guidelines for Book Longevity of the Council on
Library Resources. The University of North Carolina Press has been a member
of the Green Press Initiative since 2003.

Library of Congress Cataloging-in-Publication Data
Eamon, Tom.
The making of a southern democracy :
North Carolina politics from Kerr Scott to
Pat McCrory / Tom Eamon.
pages cm
Includes bibliographical references and index.
ISBN 978-1-4696-0697-2 (cloth : alk. paper)
ISBN 978-1-4696-0698-9 (ebook)
1. Political participation—North Carolina. 2. Political culture—
North Carolina. 3. Democracy—North Carolina. 4. North Carolina—
Politics and government. 5. United States—Politics and government. I. Title.
JK4189E35 2014
320.9756—dc23
2013028282

18  17  16  15  14    5  4  3  2  1

*To my editor, David Perry,*

*and to my parents,*

*Floyd William Eamon and Carletta Shaw Eamon*

# Contents

# Illustrations and Maps

# Acknowledgments

The outstanding staff at UNC Press has provided me with assistance far beyond what one might receive from the typical publisher. The staff took a keen interest in the book and made invaluable suggestions. They paid close attention to details in an attempt to achieve perfection. Furthermore, they were unfailingly courteous and welcoming. Some staff members I met and others worked behind the scenes. Caitlin Bell-Butterfield, Paul Betz, Mark Simpson-Vos, Jennifer Hergenroeder, Beth Lassiter, and Regina Mahalek were especially helpful as I wrapped up the project.

John Sanders, one of the leading pioneers in the study of government and public affairs of modern North Carolina, took an interest in my study from the beginning. John is as generous with his time as anyone I know. He reads a manuscript with remarkable attention to detail yet never loses sight of the big picture. He has been a selfless mentor to so many students of North Carolina government and politics.

Political scientist Patrick Cotter of the University of Alabama devoted hours to the manuscript and offered excellent suggestions.

I owe an immense debt of gratitude to Janice Nicholson for typing the initial manuscript. Janice, a longtime family friend, volunteered for the task. She read the manuscript with the keen eye of an individual well trained in the intricacies of English grammar and well versed in North Carolina and American politics. Janice is not only a perfectionist but also skilled in the art of diplomacy.

Copyeditor Ellen Goldlust read the book draft with great commitment and an amazing attention to detail.

My graduate assistants—Kristen Casper, Amanda McGee, and most recently Spencer Anhalt—have contributed immensely to this effort. My 2011–12 graduate assistant, Stefan Haus, devoted hours to the project and was a constant source of inspiration and insight over a period of a year and a half.

As department chairs in recent years, Rick Kearney and Brad Lockerbie were supportive in all respects. In addition, Brad as well as my colleagues Peter Francia and Tinsley E. Yarbrough read portions of the manuscript. Nancy Spalding and Robert Thompson helped me in various ways. And I could not have completed the project without the help of our administrative support team, Sheila Ellis, Kiwana Washington, and previously Violet Blackwelder, Mary Harris, Mary Wesley Harvey, Becky Moye, and Cynthia Manning Smith. Many other colleagues in the ECU Political Science department sharpened my insights in various ways.

So, too, have my students and former students. They have been lively companions with wide-ranging perspectives. While giving full credit where credit is due would take several pages, I must mention several individuals: William Brooks, Michael Carpenter, Jon Dougherty, Daniel J. Fussell, Brent Gaither, Brett Matheson, and Patrick Sebastien.

Other friends who have provided inspiration and insights include Leslie Bailey, Phillip Bailey, Robin Cox, Michael Dunne, David Elliott, Marvin Hunt, Robert Hunter, Mitchell McLean, Bill Mercer, Robert Mills, Bobby Mills, Carmine Seavo, Neil Sessoms, Ray Tyler, Cheryl Warren, Reed Warren, and Willis Whichard. Five friends—Jonathan Brooks, George Hearn, Wayne Holloman, Charles Mercer Jr., and Mary Lynn Qurnell—helped open doors and opportunities for me as I sought interviews as well as offered invaluable suggestions.

My close relatives were supportive all the way, especially my cousin, Jack Shirey, who read much of the manuscript and provided astute comments.

I am indebted to several scholars who have pioneered in the study of modern North Carolina. Political scientist Jack Fleer and historian William Powell led the way. Sociologist Paul Luebke skillfully questioned long-term assumptions related to the state's "progressive" mystique. Historians David Cecelski, Glenda Gilmore, and Timothy Tyson brought to light the tragic developments in the politics of race in the late 1800s and early 1900s and the impact of these events on modern North Carolina politics. Thad L. Beyle, one of my former professors and a mentor to many, has been a leading figure in the study of American state governments. At the same time, he has been a pacesetter in the study of North Carolina politics, and his *Data-Net* and related publications paved the way for all of us with an interest in the subject. Scholar-journalist Ferrell Guillory has worked closely with Beyle and others to keep many projects going. Earlier, Guillory was a distinguished political reporter for the *Raleigh News and Observer*. And I am indebted to several historians who have produced biographies of major political figures and campaigns. The works of Augustus M. Burns III, Karl Campbell, William Link, and Julian Pleasants guided my way. The studies of southern and American politics by political scientists Earl and Merle Black, Michael Bitzer, V. O. Key Jr., Alexander Lamis, Charles Prysby, and Harold Stanley were vital to my work.

North Carolina has produced an able crop of journalists, some of whom have written major books on state politics. In addition to the writings of Ferrell Guillory, I have benefitted from books and articles by Bob Ashley, Ned Cline, Howard Covington, John Drescher, Marion Ellis, and Gary Pearce, the latter a journalist, before going into political consulting.

Rob Christensen, the author of *The Paradox of Tar Heel Politics*, read a number of my chapters. He was enthusiastic and supportive, offering excellent suggestions. Rob is one of the leading interpreters of North Carolina politics from 1898 to now.

I would like to thank Bob Hall of Democracy North Carolina and John Hood of the John Locke Foundation for providing keen insights on the current state of affairs in North Carolina. Equally informative were John Davis's background comments and his newsletter.

The staffs of libraries and archives were invariably helpful. Materials at the UNC-Chapel Hill, East Carolina University, and Durham County Library were especially useful. I appreciate the efforts of Jonathan Dembo and Maurice York at East Carolina's Joyner Library and Lynn Richardson at the Durham County Library.

My editor at UNC Press, David Perry, was an outstanding mentor, and now his friendship is a blessing to me. David offered invaluable advice and encouragement from the beginning. We have met at least once every two months for the last six years, sometimes much more frequently. Near the outset of the project, I lost several relatives who were very close to me, including my mother. Had it not been for David, this book might not have seen the light of day. While the manuscript had to undergo rigorous outside review, as do all UNC Press books, David's help and wisdom were an inspiration all the way through. As an editor and as editor in chief of UNC Press, he has played a key role in the production of many major books on North Carolina history and politics.

This book is dedicated to David Perry and to my parents. My father, Floyd Eamon, is the reason I developed a strong interest in history and politics even before I learned to read. Both he and my mother, Carletta Shaw Eamon, nurtured this interest and so many others as long as they lived. They were stellar parents, and, equally important, they were my great friends and companions, full of wit as well as keen insights.

# Prologue

After the triumph of freedom in World War II, the American South remained entrenched in its old ways. It was a rural and traditional region where white supremacy prevailed even as schoolchildren were taught the words "All men are created equal." North Carolina, a state that had some claim to being the most innovative and progressive in the South, lived in a state of hypocrisy.

This is a book about how and why contemporary North Carolina developed as it did.[1] More broadly, it tells a story of the evolution of American democracy, stressing the period since 1948, the year of the first major election after World War II. It is a narrative of political events. Much of the story is told through the election battles that set the course for the future and the debates that shaped these elections. The North Carolina story is not one producing the nice, neat tapestry of a novel, one where all the threads can be tied together perfectly in the end. Yet, in its own way, it is as compelling as any novel could be.

The first theme is North Carolina's transition from a racially segregated society based on the concept of white supremacy into a state more closely resembling a participatory democracy, where all people have voting rights and fundamental liberties. Well into the era of cars, planes, television, and air-conditioning, almost total segregation permeated North Carolina society. By 2010, blacks and whites patronized the same restaurants and theaters. Interracial dating was not unusual. In 2008, African Americans voted at higher rates than did whites in many locales. Taking the long view, it was a different world.

The second theme is North Carolina's move away from a one-party political order, with the Democratic Party supreme, into a two-party system with stiff competition between Democrats and Republicans.[2] In earlier days, a

1

big-business- and attorney-led faction had the upper hand in the Democratic Party, promoting state support for education and highways as a means of promoting economic development.[3] Toward that end, North Carolina adopted statewide income and sales taxes. The state achieved a progressive reputation even as its political leadership backed white supremacy and resisted workers' rights. By the twenty-first century, North Carolina had become a two-party state. Republicans proclaimed the conservative faith, favoring low taxes, capitalism, and traditional moral values. Many elected Democrats were liberals of some shade but preferred the progressive label. They pushed for expenditures on education, the environment, and transportation. Democrats advocated legal protections for gays, women, and racial minorities. Two-party competition, Democrats versus Republicans, had arrived with a vengeance.

The third theme is that elections matter—often a lot. At times from the 1940s through 2012, political party primaries and general elections took on a sharp ideological tone. While candidates ranging from mildly liberal to mildly conservative prevailed in races for governor, all were fundamentally progressive on education-related issues. A wider range of individuals were elected to the U.S. Senate with center-right and right-wing candidates winning more often than moderates and liberals. Elections reflect the tenor of the times. A few change the course of history, an impact that may not be apparent when the election occurs. They are watersheds.

A fourth central theme is that people make a difference—often a big difference. I believe that individuals influence the course of history as much as do the underlying social and economic forces.[4] The stereotypical great leader is charismatic and has a powerful personality and superior communication skills—Martin Luther King Jr., Franklin Delano Roosevelt, or Ronald Reagan. In North Carolina, Governor Jim Hunt and Senator Jesse Helms, towering figures of the late twentieth century, were effective communicators before cameras and in small group settings. Both did much to shape their political parties and, especially in Hunt's case, the state's agenda. Not all great leaders ooze charisma. North Carolina's governor Terry Sanford (1961–65) lacked the forensic skills of Roosevelt or King, and his down-east drawl was not magnetic. Yet through determination, vision, enthusiasm, and talent at backroom wheeling and dealing, Sanford guided the state through a crucial period in American history. He had an impact.

If the story seems people-centric at times, I make no apologies. As the book moved along, I became more convinced than ever that particular individuals may alter the course of history.

A meaningful study of North Carolina politics must also be mindful of the big national events of the time. A major debate in Washington or an assassination in Memphis may have profound implications for the state. So throughout this narrative, state and national affairs are inextricably linked.

Throughout any comprehensive study of politics, one should also keep in mind underlying population trends as well as cultural factors—the deep-seated or underlying attitudes of a society.

An abundance of books and articles pertaining to the state's history and politics have helped provide us with a better understanding of North Carolina. However, prior to William Link's and Milton Ready's recent books, most general histories stressed specific constitutions, conventions, or battles while giving less attention to the seamier side of North Carolina's political evolution.[5]

Historians David Cecelski, Glenda Gilmore, and Timothy Tyson have offered riveting accounts of civil strife and setbacks for freedom between the 1890s and the 1970s. Their works also attempt to knock major North Carolina heroes, most notably Charles Aycock, from their pedestals. "Progressive" North Carolinians were portrayed as villains or at least deeply misguided.[6] Sociologist Paul Luebke, later a prominent state legislator, argued in a 1990 book that ordinary working-class North Carolinians had gained little as modernizer or progressive-style politicians fought political battles with traditionalist elements.[7] Longtime journalist Rob Christensen presented an incisive account of North Carolina politics throughout the twentieth century, one further enhanced by Christensen's storytelling abilities.[8] Other studies have dealt well with specific aspects of state government and politics such as the nature of political parties and the judiciary.[9]

Yet I have long felt the need for a close look at post–World War II North Carolina politics that focuses on the whys and hows of the state's entry into the modern world. Such a study, I thought, should come from someone with both an academic background and an inquiring spirit, and preferably not someone who was unduly ideological or partisan.

I wanted a study that would focus deeply on elections as well as the politics of major debates on central issues such as race and education. In short, I aimed for a book of record and a serious work of scholarship, one that would be comprehensible not only to professional social scientists but also to interested laypersons and the simply curious. The goals are to explain what happened, how it happened, and why it happened.

I must add with three caveats, however. First, being relatively nonideo-logical or "fair" should never block one from telling the truth, even when it hurts. Second, very few politicians are pure heroes or pure villains. Fairness demands looking at the good and the bad before reaching a final judgment. Third, although I have some degree of objectivity, I also have biases. The most notable is an abiding faith in the possibilities of an American-style democratic republic.

### A VARIED LAND

North Carolina is among the most geographically varied of American states. Southeastern North Carolina is the land of beaches, live oaks, cypress trees, and haunting yet bewitching gray-green Spanish moss, sometimes drooping from the tree branches almost to the ground or the river. This region, especially around Wilmington, resembles subtropical North Florida or the Mississippi Gulf Coast. Boone, in the state's northwest corner, is thirty-three hundred feet above sea level and is a land of majestic autumns and winter gales. Boone's median 29.5° F January temperature is the same as in Providence, Rhode Island, seven hundred miles to the northeast.[10]

The Tar Heel state's three major regions are the *Atlantic coastal plain*, often called the east; the rolling red clay *piedmont* plateau; and the *mountains*, or west. A fourth zone, the sand hills, straddles the southern piedmont and southern coastal plain. In most political discussions including this one, the eastern sand hills around Fayetteville are grouped with the coastal plain and the western sand hills, Pinehurst vicinity, are grouped with the piedmont. Forty-one counties are classified as the coastal plain, thirty-six are in the piedmont, and twenty-three are western or mountain. North Carolina has an area of 53,819 square miles, similar in size to England. (The land area, which excludes Albemarle and Pamlico Sounds, is 48,611 square miles.) The state is oriented on an east-west axis, with a width of 500 miles at some points.

All three regions have been heavily Protestant Christian, befitting a state that until the 1950s was the most Protestant in America. The coastal plain and the northern and southern fringes of the piedmont culturally resembled Deep South states, with large black populations and agricultural economies. Most of the state's cities lie along or near the piedmont's Interstate Highway 85 corridor, roughly forming a crescent. The mountains long suffered from poverty and isolation, but a booming vacation industry has propelled growth since the late twentieth century. Asheville, the region's major city, transformed from a provincial town decried by Thomas Wolfe, a native and sometime New York writer, in the 1920s to San Francisco on the Blue Ridge in the early 2000s.[11]

Eastern North Carolina was overwhelmingly Democratic from 1900 through the 1960s. The piedmont was a partisan blend, with Democrats

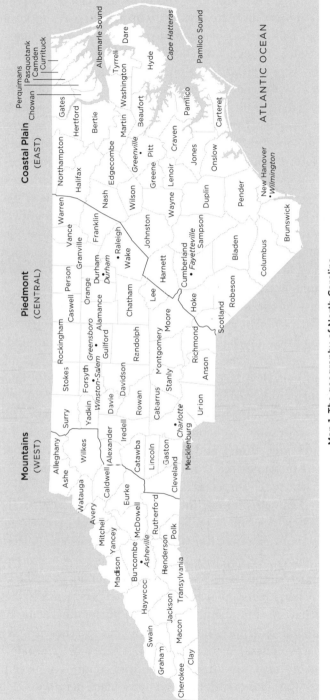

**Map 1. The geography of North Carolina**

having a strong advantage until the 1950s and closer competition afterward. The mountains were divided, with family partisan loyalties going back to the Civil War. A lot of mountain people opposed the state's secession from the Union, believing that secession benefited only lowland planter aristocrats. After the war, those who had opposed North Carolina's decision to join the Confederacy expressed their anger by voting Republican, and many of their descendants still do so today, whether out of belief or inheritance. Mountain Democrats may trace their loyalties to Jefferson Davis or Franklin Roosevelt, but either way, they can be a fiercely partisan lot.

Two North Carolina urban clusters, Charlotte and Raleigh–Durham–Chapel Hill, are among America's fastest-growing. Charlotte is a major banking city and, along with New York and Chicago, one of the country's top financial centers.[12] The financial sector and consequently Charlotte's economy were shaken in the 2008–12 period, yet the area continued its rapid population growth and thrived as a corporate headquarters and trade center. In terms of central city populations alone, Charlotte is bigger than Atlanta, Boston, and Washington, but those cities lie at the centers of gigantic metropolitan areas surpassing Charlotte's. Raleigh, the state's capital, and the nearby cities of Cary, Chapel Hill, and Durham stand at the forefront of a new knowledge-based and creative economy and constitute a major center of research and technology. Another major population center, Greensboro–High Point–Winston-Salem, specializes in finance, commerce, and manufacturing.

Across the state, bleeding industries—largely furniture, textiles, and tobacco—contributed to economic distress. Agriculture suffered as tobacco came under attack and smoking declined. The state boomed and atrophied at the same time. Still, agriculture, including poultry production, remained vital to the state's economy.

For the last half century, social scientists have split southern states into two categories: the Deep South and the Peripheral or Outer South. The Deep South states are Alabama, Georgia, Louisiana, Mississippi, and South Carolina. The Peripheral South states are Arkansas, Florida, Tennessee, Texas, Virginia, and North Carolina.[13] For decades, the Deep South states have had higher percentages of African Americans in their populations than have the Peripheral South states. But for most of the last century, North Carolina's 21–27 percent black population has been higher than that of the other Peripheral South states. Blacks have been the majority in from six to nine of North Carolina's one hundred counties. Between 2000 and 2010, North Carolina experienced a higher black net population increase than all but three states.

The term "Black Belt" or "Black Belt counties" has often been used in explaining southern politics. The term is applied to counties with populations that are 40 percent or more African American. Historically, whites in such counties were resistant to black political activity and voting. V. O. Key Jr. attributed this resistance to whites' fear of losing control.[14] This resistance was notable in North Carolina in the 1950s and 1960s, when the civil rights movement reached its peak. After African Americans achieved full voting rights, the Black Belt counties moved to the left politically. North Carolina's Black Belt counties are mostly in the state's northeastern quadrant, but a few are near the Virginia border in the piedmont, and Anson and Richmond Counties are in the southern piedmont. Just to the east are Hoke and Robeson Counties, where African Americans and Native Americans combine to outnumber Caucasians.

Between 2000 and 2010, North Carolina's Hispanic population grew quickly, reaching almost 10 percent of the total. In 2008, however, Hispanics comprised only 3 percent of state voters, a figure certain to rise in coming years. The Asian population is also growing, especially in the Raleigh-Durham-Cary area.

North Carolinians are often surprised to hear that their state is one of the more rural in the country. Not until 1990 was the state majority urban. However, urban areas now play a much more important role in guiding the state's destiny than was previously the case.

### THE CLEANSERS AND THE SPIRIT OF FIRE

In his October 12, 1933, Founders' Day speech at the University of North Carolina, Robert Winston referred to the revolutionary spirit of his old college friend, Charles Aycock, during their days as students in Chapel Hill in the 1870s: "In a word, he became the leader of the radical Left Wing of the college, a thorn in the flesh of the ultra conservative Right, and the disturber of the peace and quiet of the good old days when every one was supposed to know his place."[15]

Winston's words hinted at the irony in Aycock's life. While serving as governor from 1901 to 1905, Aycock posed as a bold reformer who was trying to make North Carolina better than it had been in his childhood. Aycock's rhetoric and some of his initiatives went against the grain of traditional thinking in North Carolina and the South. Few leaders have spoken more eloquently or passionately for universal public education that at least ostensibly included men, women, blacks, and whites. He tenaciously carried forth his crusade for seven years after his gubernatorial term ended. On April 4, 1912, Aycock addressed a Birmingham, Alabama, group, recalling his commitment to education for all children: "I canvassed the state for four years in behalf of education for the children of the state. Sometimes on Sundays they would ask me down to churches to talk, and I always talked about education."[16]

At that moment, he collapsed and died of a heart attack. Aycock's shadow dominated North Carolina politics for decades to come. Generations of North Carolina schoolchildren were taught that Aycock had been the patron saint of education. North Carolina had no Washington or Jefferson, but it had Aycock. He filled a vacuum for a state that lacked great heroes. Aycock's shadow had a darker side, however. In the 1898–1900 period, he, publisher Josephus Daniels, and Furnifold Simmons formed a triumvirate that led the "Red Shirt" attack on fundamental democratic values, most notably voting rights for blacks. The followers of the movement were called Red Shirts because of the bright red shirts they adopted as their uniform. Similar movements were sweeping the South from Virginia to Texas. Aycock defended "southern womanhood," by which he meant white southern womanhood, a not-so-veiled reference to what whites saw as the ever-present threat of rape by black men. Prevailing prejudices had paved the way for Aycock to be elected governor in 1900. The same year, Simmons was selected as one of North Carolina's U.S. senators, a position he held through 1930. In addition, he became the informal leader of the dominant Democratic faction. He knew well the nuts and bolts of party organization.

Almost a century after Aycock's election, social historian Timothy Tyson wrote, "It was the illegitimate and bloody seizure of power in 1898 that gave birth to the state's moderate posture of white supremacy, but it was the violent and resilient nature of that 'progressive mystique' that preserved white supremacy. The racial paternalism embodied by Governor Charles Brantley Aycock, one of the leading architects and beneficiaries of the white supremacy campaigns, served to consolidate a social order carved out in murder and violence but preserved by civility and moderation."[17] Not only Aycock but all of North Carolina's image as a progressive state was now under assault. Aycock did much to shape the future of a state and its life, and on that his critics and defenders agree.

### THE ESTABLISHMENT REFORMERS

In 1915, the North Carolina General Assembly passed legislation authorizing party primaries. The Democratic Party promptly moved toward choosing all statewide candidates and most county candidates through the direct primary, a process that enabled all registered party members to vote in an election to choose nominees. Ironically, white supremacists promoted direct democracy as early as the 1898–1900 period. Daniels had journeyed to Louisiana to study how that state's Democratic Party used the primary to solidify white control over the electoral process. But with rare exceptions—the Senate contests of 1900 and 1912 featured advisory primaries—North Carolina had not had primaries. By 1915, more than forty states had adopted the primary system in the name of a more pure democracy. Prairie populist William Jennings Bryan, a friend of Daniels, viewed primaries as counteracting the influence of corporations and moneyed interests. Daniels shared this perspective and stressed the benefits of the primary system for the "common man" rather than a racial rationale. All over America, progressives of the time equated the primary with democracy. Since 1900, Democrats had won all of North Carolina's statewide contests, and general elections had less meaning than in earlier times. The primary restored an open election of sorts. North Carolina was a follower rather than a leader in adopting the primary.[18]

In 1916, Attorney General Thomas Bickett won the first Democratic primary and went on to beat his Republican opponent in the general election for North Carolina's governorship. While incumbent Democratic president Woodrow Wilson easily beat his Republican challenger, Charles Evans Hughes, in North Carolina, Wilson barely won the national election. Tax reform was Bickett's legacy. The property tax, which was the state's chief revenue source, had become unwieldy and inequitable. Bickett pushed for a graduated income tax capped at 6 percent, a move designed to decrease (though not eliminate) state reliance on the property tax. The state legislature concurred and submitted the question to the voters, who approved the necessary constitutional change. Many families initially had incomes low enough to escape the new tax altogether.[19] This change put all of the state's resources in the service of all the people and lessened discrimination based on place of residence. In the early 1930s, the state stopped collecting the property tax; subsequently, all property taxes were collected and used by counties and cities. In this respect, North Carolina was ahead of much of the country in moving to share the wealth.

Between 1920 and 1940, two governors stood out: Cameron Morrison (1921–25) and O. Max Gardner (1929–33). Both men sought the governorship in 1920. Gardner was the incumbent lieutenant governor, but the older Morrison prevailed, in part because of his support from Senator Simmons's organization. Critics said that Morrison's forces had stolen the Democratic primary election.[20] Gardner backed women's suffrage. Morrison opposed it. Morrison forces attempted to link the campaign for female voting with a potential drive for African American voting, a specious claim. Shortly after the spring primary, the necessary three-fourths of all states ratified the Nineteenth Amendment, giving women the vote everywhere in the country. North Carolina's legislature had failed to ratify the amendment despite its support from reformers such as journalist Josephus Daniels.[21]

As governor, Morrison was no reactionary. His legacies were a massive road-building program and school improvements. The typical road in 1920 was rutted and bumpy, as hard on the human constitution as on the tires. Morrison persuaded the legislature to levy a gasoline tax of one cent per gallon, to allocate car registration fees to highways, and to borrow fifty million dollars for highway building through the issuance of bonds, earning the nickname the "Good Roads Governor."[22] Despite tremendous progress in building intercity two-lane highways, however, most rural roads remained covered in dirt or gravel. The state legislature also approved Morrison's request for funds to extend the public school year to six months, an unfunded mandate held over from the 1921 legislature. The number of public schoolteachers rose from 16,800 to 22,340. Spending for colleges and universities almost doubled.[23]

Morrison's onetime rival, Max Gardner, won the governorship in 1928. Gardner was unopposed in the Democratic primary but garnered only a lackluster 55.5 percent in his general election race against Republican H. F. Seawell. The Democratic Party that year had nominated New York governor Alfred E. Smith for president. Not only was Smith a Catholic, but he also favored restoring the legal sale of alcoholic beverages, which had been banned since the advent of Prohibition in 1919. Republican Herbert Hoover won a resounding national victory, taking five of the eleven states in the usually Democratic South. Hoover carried North Carolina with 54.9 percent of the vote. Senator Simmons opposed his party's presidential nominee, and many Protestant clergy asserted that the pope would run America from Rome if Smith were elected. Gardner, a loyal Democrat, damaged his candidacy by campaigning for Smith.[24]

Less than a year later, in September 1929, the Great Depression hit. Governor Gardner faced diminished resources and pushed for greater program efficiencies while attempting to protect the core mission of the public schools and higher education. In 1931, he began a successful campaign to consolidate the administration of the University of North Carolina in Chapel Hill with the agricultural and mechanical college in Raleigh and the state college for women in Greensboro. Under the plan, each school kept its own identity and location, and each had a chancellor reporting to the university president in Chapel Hill.[25] The trustees approved Gardner's candidate for the presidency of the consolidated university, history professor and University of North Carolina president Frank Porter Graham. Graham was a humanitarian and a liberal, sympathetic to labor unions and quietly supportive of minority rights. He was charismatic and a first-rate lobbyist. Charles Cannon and other textile executives considered Graham a dangerous radical.[26] Gardner, himself a textile mill owner, antiunion man, and lawyer, was so fond of Graham the educator that he overrode the objectors.

Gardner led the effort to defeat Senator Simmons in the 1930 Democratic primary on the grounds that he had supported the now-despised Hoover. After Simmons's defeat by Josiah W. Bailey, Gardner took control of the business-oriented Democratic machine. For fourteen years after his gubernatorial term ended in 1933, Gardner remained the organization's most influential figure.[27]

The economic depression caused an enormous drop in state, county, and city revenue from income and property taxes. In response, Gardner urged the 1931 legislature to abolish the property tax as a source of state revenue so it could be used exclusively by local governments. To recoup lost revenue, farmers and Daniels, editor of the *Raleigh News and Observer*, called for a sales tax on luxury items. Conservatives advocated a general sales tax, which Gardner protested, saying it would hurt the poor. He persuaded the legislature to raise income taxes and corporate taxes.[28] Gardner is sometimes portrayed as personifying rule by bankers and industrialists. However, his positions on taxation were more in line with what economic populist-style politicians might have advocated. He angered elements of the business community, who felt that they contributed disproportionately to the state coffers and pushed for tax reductions. The dire economic circumstances meant that most of the population still paid no state income tax. Despite their displeasure with the tax situation, most business leaders did not turn against Gardner the man, seeing him as a kindred spirit who sympathized with corporate North Carolina.

In 1932, Democratic presidential nominee Franklin Roosevelt defeated Hoover. Nationally, he achieved a landslide victory in both electoral and popular votes. In North Carolina, Roosevelt led Hoover 497,566 to 208,344. All statewide Democratic candidates won commanding victories. Roosevelt would be reelected in 1936, 1940, and 1944.

Gardner's successor, J. C. Blucher Ehringhaus (1933–37), faced an even more dire fiscal crisis and further pressures from the business community to reduce corporate and income taxes. He proposed modest reductions in income taxes while pushing the legislature to enact a 3 percent sales tax on all nonfood items. In calling for the sales tax, Ehringhaus said, "If it is a choice between the sales tax on the one hand or a decent school on the other, I stand for the school."[29] Ehringhaus said that enacting a sales tax would not only keep the schools open but assure that all schools could achieve the recently mandated eight-month term, a policy not yet implemented in some poor counties. To save money, teachers' salaries and other state services were cut. Ehringhaus might have saved the public schools, but the poor, who could least afford the sales tax, paid a dear price, a price that economic liberals such as Daniels thought should have been borne by the well-to-do.

V. O. Key Jr., a great scholar of southern politics, called North Carolina's rulers during this period "the progressive plutocracy."[30] He believed that business-oriented elites wanted the state to move ahead as long as such progress did not challenge the fundamental order of society. A few leaders, most notably Gardner, were not mere errand boys for the industrialists, kindred though they were. To stay in charge, the state's machine politicians needed to pay heed to the wave of popular protest, which was a reincarnation of economic populism harkening back to William Jennings Bryan in the 1880s and 1890s. The small farmers and working class fueled the movement.

In 1933, Roosevelt launched the New Deal, with programs that included pensions under the new social security program for retired Americans, welfare benefits for the needy, and government employment programs such as the Civilian Conservation Corps (which assisted private contractors in beautifying the Blue Ridge Parkway) and the Works Progress Administration (which built many small bridges in North Carolina). The Rural Electrification Administration and the Tennessee Valley Authority brought electricity to the rural South, a benefit that had been almost totally absent outside the towns and cities. While Governor Ehringhaus and fellow conservatives welcomed assistance from Washington, they were skeptical of federal controls. Tensions developed when Washington funded local programs that potentially threatened state autonomy. State-level politicians feared influence from dangerous radical "troublemakers."[31] The Roosevelt programs marked the beginning of an adjustment in national-state relations. More than ever, the federal government emerged as the dominant partner in this often tense relationship.

In the early 1930s, leftists and rightists camped inside both national parties. With Roosevelt, the national Democrats emerged as the clearly more liberal party, first on economic and welfare issues and later on others. This shift was bound to cause friction between the national party and southern states. The paradox of the New Deal was that it built a stronger Democratic

Party while planting the seeds for a Republican rise from the ashes. But the seeds would not bear fruit until long after the Great Depression.

## FIGHTS FOR DEMOCRACY

With America's entry into World War II following the December 1941 Japanese attack on Pearl Harbor, new North Carolina military bases were established and existing ones such as Fort Bragg and Camp Lejeune were expanded. Much as authorities might have tried to hide or suppress racial tensions, their efforts had little effect. Black soldiers still served in segregated military units but were on the same bases as whites. Black troops—including many from the South—bristled at the sting of segregation and overt white supremacy. The atmosphere was consistently venomous near Monroe in Union County, the home of Camp Sutton, and in the Hampstead–Holly Ridge–Wilmington area close to Camp Davis and the naval installations on the lower Cape Fear River. A race riot broke out in Durham after Booker T. Spicely, a black soldier stationed at Camp Butner, defied local segregation practices by sitting at the front of a bus and was then shot and killed by its driver, Herman Council. A whole block of downtown Durham was gutted.[32]

A few blacks achieved successes in business, sometimes with white patrons but often going it alone. With segregation in death as in life, black-owned funeral homes provided their owners with income and status. Durham had profitable black-owned banks and insurance companies, with blacks among the city's economic elites. The elites did not typically ride buses, so the seating issue generally did not affect them; nevertheless, for African Americans of both high and low status, the constraints of race remained ever-present.

In Durham and Raleigh, African Americans had begun to organize and vote on a small scale in the mid-1930s.[33] Their organizations grew in the 1940s. In 1944, near the time of the D-Day invasion in Europe and the Durham riot, the U.S. Supreme Court ruled in *Smith v. Allwright* that blacks could no longer be excluded from Democratic primaries, which were the only real elections in southern states.[34] For decades, court interpretations had enabled southern state Democratic Parties to exclude blacks from primaries on the legal theory that political parties were private clubs subject to guidelines set by their members—in effect, the white leaders. Long before *Smith v. Allwright*, a few North Carolina communities had permitted a few blacks to register and vote as Democrats. North Carolina's exclusion was more by local interpretation and intimidation than official practice. However, the ruling encouraged supporters of minority voting drives. Such drives were most effective in urban areas, where confident black leaders promoted voter registration. Nevertheless, the old white supremacist order continued to reign in nearly all public and private settings.

After World War II ended in the late summer of 1945, North Carolina's legislature adopted Governor Gregg Cherry's recommendations for a major increase in public education funding, which were not controversial after the freezes of World War II. School attendance was made compulsory up to age sixteen. A new State Board of Education, appointed by the governor, was set up to supervise the expenditure of school funds. The legislature authorized a four-year medical school and teaching hospital in Chapel Hill and a statewide public hospitals program, setting off an unprecedented expansion of medical services across the state.[35] Cherry also promoted corporate well-being, much in the spirit of earlier governors.

Yet rumblings of discontent could be heard among much of the populace. Talented leaders in the Democratic establishment continued to hold sway, and not by organizational skills alone. The most effective governors—Aycock, Morrison, and Gardner—had incorporated some of the earlier economic populist philosophy into their programs. To a lesser degree, other governors did the same. And all of the state's leaders maintained their friendly posture toward big business.

Pressures built for change. Old-style economic populists, mostly whites and Democrats, dreamed of a new order. African Americans dreamed of equality. The boiling point might be near.

## CHAPTER ONE

# Uprisings

It is a well-known genre, especially in the American South—the self-proclaimed economic populist running for office on a platform calling for more abundant lives for struggling, ordinary, hardworking folks. Some of the more strident—Eugene Talmadge of Georgia, Theodore "The Man" Bilbo in Mississippi—were foul-mouthed racists who poisoned the political environments in their states. Others, notably North Carolina's Senator Bob Reynolds (1933–45), provided loud, entertaining rhetoric and did minimal harm.[1]

Immediately after World War II, two committed neopopulists sought the highest positions in their respective states—James "Kissin' Jim" Folsom, who was elected as Alabama's governor in 1946, and Kerr (pronounced "car") Scott, who was elected North Carolina's governor in 1948. Both attracted an almost fanatical following based largely on their rural appeal. Both were rough-hewn and occasionally crude politicians. Both met resistance from economically conservative legislatures wanting to maintain the status quo. Folsom and Scott were racial moderates by the standards of their day, taking segregation for granted while favoring steps that would enhance the economic status of African Americans. But there were differences. Folsom was a heavy drinker and womanizer whose appetites became a bigger story than his forward-thinking policies. Scott was a devout and straitlaced Presbyterian whose vices were tobacco and earthy language. Folsom could find humor in nearly every situation. Scott's greatest flaws were his temper and unforgiving spirit.

## THE CAMPAIGN OF '48

Economic populists had sought the North Carolina governorship earlier in the twentieth century. All were defeated. Scott was a latecomer to the nomination fight. At the campaign's onset, liberals looked to R. Mayne Albright, a young and liberal Raleigh attorney who announced his candidacy in August 1947. A war veteran, he had been the state director of the United World Federalists, not considered a radical organization in the immediate aftermath of the carnage of World War II. Albright proclaimed himself the "antimachine candidate" as he toured the state in a Ford, pulling a campaign trailer. He favored repeal of the state sales tax. Albright was a serious candidate but was unlikely to beat the organization's choice, state treasurer Charles Johnson, a native of the Burgaw area of Pender County in southeastern North Carolina.[2]

Governor O. Max Gardner had named Johnson to head the state treasurer's office when a vacancy occurred in 1932. Since then, Johnson had won election at four-year intervals and so was one of the state's more seasoned officials. The white-haired Johnson possessed an understanding of the intricacies of state government matched by few others, but critics thought him pompous.[3] A majority of the legislators endorsed Johnson, as did myriad state officials, county commissioners, and Democratic Party activists. The state's 1947–48 Speaker of the House, Thomas Pearsall of Rocky Mount, served as Johnson's campaign manager, and he had the support of most business leaders. Among the most prominent were tobacco magnate James Gray of Winston-Salem, textile giant Charles Cannon of Kannapolis, and banker Robert Hanes of Winston-Salem, then the most astute and politically powerful of corporate leaders. Political kingpin Gardner had died early in 1947, just before he was to depart for England to serve as the U.S. ambassador there.[4] The Johnson apparatus, however, was one of the greatest assemblages of former Gardner people ever seen. Johnson was about as close to being a crown prince as any North Carolina politician had ever been.

The hint of another scenario came when Scott spoke at the annual wild game dinner on January 9 at Raleigh's Carolina Hotel, an event sponsored by the state agriculture department. Amid the aroma of cooked rabbit, squirrel, and venison, Scott announced that he would not seek reelection as agriculture commissioner but instead return to tending the two hundred cows on his dairy farm in the Hawfields community of Haw River, just east of Burlington in piedmont Alamance County.[5] In reality, however, he had other plans. At a February 3 appearance in Asheville, Scott delivered a passionate oration calling for paved farm-to-market roads, more extensive rural electric and phone service, and an improved state school system. It sounded like a campaign appeal. At a Burlington press conference three days later, Scott made his candidacy official, adding, "I shall

Governor Kerr Scott on his Haw River Farm, early 1950s. Hugh Morton Collection of Photographs and Films (P081), University of North Carolina at Chapel Hill, Wilson Library, North Carolina Collection Photographic Archives.

resign immediately from the office of commissioner of agriculture because I feel that no man occupying a high state office can serve the people properly while campaigning for the governorship."[6] This statement was a direct swipe at Johnson, who planned to remain state treasurer while running for governor.

Scott's allies cheered, but his outlook was guarded at best. Scott's entry would divide the liberal vote with Albright, although Scott had better personal and political connections than his rival. Accordingly, Albright suggested that Scott was part of the ruling state political organization, an assertion that Scott rejected even as he hoped to recruit organization members who for a variety of reasons did not like Johnson. Furthermore, Scott's call for sharing increased state wealth with rural people resonated in a rural state. Scott possessed a folksy appeal lacked by both Johnson and Albright.

Albright, Johnson, and Scott called for many of the same programs: a teacher pay scale ranging from twenty-four hundred dollars to thirty-six hundred dollars for nine months, state assistance in building local schools, and compulsory school attendance laws. On matters of public education, conservative establishment candidates had often been as progressive as liberals. The campaign of 1948 was no exception.

While Albright opposed the sales tax and Johnson favored it, Scott's position was equivocal. He said that the tax should be removed immediately from restaurant meals—grocery store food items were already exempt—and repealed on other items as soon as was feasible.[7] Johnson called for a one-hundred-million-dollar bond issue to finance rural roads. Scott asserted that Johnson's proposal would line the pockets of bankers and said that the road money should come from unused state monies held in banks.[8] This position eventually came back to haunt Scott.

Both Albright and Scott portrayed themselves as men in the mold of the late, mourned president, Franklin Delano Roosevelt. Albright possessed a polish more akin to Roosevelt's, but Scott, who personified the president's spirit, connected with the voters. Johnson ran as an advocate of fiscal responsibility and a friend of free enterprise and tried to counteract his urbane image by noting that he had grown up on a "dirt farm." Up north he might have been a Republican; in North Carolina, however, he was a conservative Democrat with a few progressive instincts.

## THE OUTCOME

Johnson led in the May 29 primary, but the results did not augur well for him. The count: Johnson 170,141; Scott 161,293; Albright 76,281; and others 15,371. Johnson ran best in western North Carolina, his native southeast, and parts of the Charlotte region. Scott led in rural counties and small towns scattered across the state as well as in the urban counties of Forsyth (Winston-Salem), Guilford (Greensboro and High Point), and Wake (Raleigh). Johnson had carried fifty-one counties and Scott forty-one. Albright took seven counties, mostly in the western coastal plain or nearby areas of the piedmont. These counties, which included the towns of Rocky Mount, Tarboro, and Wilson, had been strongholds for populist-style insurgents of the past.[9] All had large black populations but overwhelmingly white electorates. A Johnson-Scott primary runoff was on.

Albright believed that his bid had been derailed by Scott and refused to endorse either candidate in the runoff, but his state manager, John Barnes, joined Scott's campaign. Indeed, Scott was the logical choice for Albright voters who wanted the state to break with the status quo. One Albright voter who switched to Scott was young Terry Sanford, a former World War II paratrooper and future governor then in law practice in Fayetteville.

Second (runoff) primaries were nearly always nasty. In this one, the stakes were high, and the candidates could not have been more different. Many power brokers—bankers, textile and tobacco executives, and entrenched politicians—feared a loss of access and influence if Scott won. Johnson saw his long and respectable career imperiled. Johnson forces accused Scott of managing his huge dairy farm when he should have been tending to the agriculture department. Johnson also asserted that Scott had built a political machine within the department. Scott called for more open government and a break from business as usual. He portrayed Johnson as a man out of touch with the needs of working people.[10]

One issue not discussed in the campaign was race. In the 1930s and 1940s, candidates were united in their support for segregation. The federal courts had begun to hint that they would look much more closely at the "equal" part of the "separate but equal" doctrine, but they had not dealt head-on with segregation. With Albright out of the race, Scott counted on getting most of the urban black vote, support that could help in a close primary. Outside of a few urban areas, the African American vote was of little consequence. So the campaign bluster was aimed more at whites, with the candidates preaching to their respective choirs and hoping that their supporters would come out and vote.

Scott was a more forceful campaigner than Johnson and knew better how to connect with the voters. Scott understood farmers and talked the way they did. He could be simultaneously funny and bitingly sarcastic when attacking enemies. Late in the afternoon before a night appearance, he might take a ride on a dirt road in the company of his local manager, jotting down the names of people living in the houses. Then in his evening stump speech, Scott would say, "Mrs. Clodfelter, living out on —— road, would love to have her road paved so the dust won't blow on her sheets out on the clothesline."[11] The person named and others wanting paved roads might well be at the rally and hear the remarks. Kerr Scott was adept at personalizing the issues, and he had a penchant for detail that impressed his young driver, Lauch Faircloth, himself a future politician. Many years later, Faircloth recalled, "Kerr had an amazing knowledge down to the precinct level across the state. He could tell you [in advance] who the people would be that you would meet."[12] Scott knew their concerns and what might motivate them to work harder in the campaign.

Scott knew how to use the machine issue. He went so far as to say that machine control put North Carolina in danger of having a "Russian system" in which people might go through the motions of voting but really have no choice.[13] The popular and shrewd Gardner was no longer around to promote organization interests. Moreover, the organization itself was split in the concurrent U.S. Senate race, with some members going for former governor J. Melville Broughton and others for William B. Umstead, the incumbent, whom Governor Gregg Cherry named to fill the seat after longtime Senator Josiah William Bailey died in 1946. Many organization loyalists devoted their energies to that race rather than Johnson's.

After Broughton's 287,901–183,865 Senate win in May, backers of both Broughton and Umstead were able to spend more time helping Johnson, but the hour was late. Furthermore, bitterness from the Senate race lingered, with many in the organization's ranks continuing to believe that Umstead deserved the nomination. New tensions further imperiled unity as well as Johnson's candidacy for governor. Johnson ultimately found the organization's support both an albatross and a blessing.

In the runoff primary, Scott beat Johnson 217,620–182,648. Scott claimed a mandate. The size of his victory surprised nearly everyone. Scott led in the northern coastal plain, partly because he attracted the votes of former Albright backers. Johnson led in his native southeastern coastal plain, a lot of mountain counties, and the Charlotte-Gastonia-Shelby area of the southwest piedmont. Many mountain counties and piedmont Gastonia and Shelby had a history of favoring organization candidates. Scott led in sixty-five of the state's one hundred counties. Except for Johnson's home county of Pender and a few mountain areas, Scott garnered respectable numbers of votes almost everywhere.[14]

Scott's timing was fortunate. His son, Bob, later remarked, "My daddy was a pure populist. The time was right for him to do that. There was a pent-up demand for infrastructure. [Before that time,] the money had gone off for the war effort."[15] Not since the late 1920s had there been such optimism and an ability to pay for new programs. While both Scott and Johnson favored increased spending on education and public works, Scott came across as the candidate of change. During the 1930s and most of the 1940s, the most ambitious initiatives had come from the national government. Now it was the state's turn. A new era had dawned, at least for the moment.

A pattern had emerged in the primary that would become still more pronounced when Scott pursued his populist agenda. Scott understood the phenomenon well. He liked to say that the big shots in the well-heeled urban areas were in his opponent's camp. The proportion of Scott backers increased in small towns and rural areas and grew even further in the backwoods—up the creek or the branch, as a lot of southerners called a small creek. Finally, at the source or head of the branch, the real backwoods, everyone was for Scott. So went the myth. And like a lot of myths, this one had an element of truth to it. Scott called his most fervent backers the "branch head boys," a term that would stick for a long time in Tar Heel politics. Farmers and other rural residents who backed Scott generally came to be known as "branch head boys."[16]

## DISSENSION AND VICTORY

Before Scott could lead the crusade for his rural kindred, there was the formality of a general election, in which everyone assumed that Scott would defeat Republican George Pritchard, an Asheville attorney and past political candidate.

Though Scott was never threatened, the 1948 election saw the development of a deep chasm in the national Democratic Party that had implications for the party's future in southern states. Incumbent president Harry S. Truman had incurred the wrath of many of the party's conservatives as well as its liberals, and when the Democrats convened their convention in Philadelphia, the smell of impending November defeat permeated the atmosphere. Southerners, including most North Carolina delegates, voted for Georgia's brilliant and deeply conservative senator, Richard Russell. The majority of convention delegates, however, seemed ready to go with Truman, though an ignominious loss to the Republican nominee, Governor Thomas Dewey of New York, seemed inevitable. The heat—the kind measured by a thermometer—was intense, and the sweat was only enhanced when a floor fight broke out over the plank relating to African Americans' civil rights. Most white southerners, including North Carolinians, wanted no mention of the issue unless it was to support "separate but equal" facilities or "states' rights." Truman, a racist in his younger days, had evolved on the issue and favored a platform expressing general support for human equality and gradual movement toward racial integration but stopping short of a call for specific actions that would stir the pot.[17] He thought he needed a solid bloc of southern electoral votes to have a chance in the November election.

Truman and his top strategists listened with apprehension when a young, brash Hubert Humphrey, the mayor of Minneapolis, rose to the podium and delivered a ringing oration: "There are those who say to you—we are rushing this issue of civil rights. I say we are a hundred and seventy-two years late!"[18] The convention adopted a civil rights plan calling for an antilynching law, integration of the military, voting rights for blacks, ending the poll tax, and a move toward equal employment opportunities. Southern delegates were nearly unanimous in their opposition. After winning the nomination, Truman embraced the entire Democratic platform. Shortly thereafter, segregationist southern Democrats convened a rump convention in Birmingham, Alabama, to nominate Governor Strom Thurmond of South Carolina as the States' Rights Party presidential candidate and Governor Fielding Wright of Mississippi as his vice presidential running mate. The movement would come to be known as the Dixiecrat Party.[19]

Many of North Carolina's Democratic leaders were unenthusiastic about Truman but still hoped that he and all Democrats would win their state. The party remained united by the bitter memories of Herbert Hoover and the Great Depression. The Hoover era was only a decade and half in the past and the depression's end still more recent. Not just liberals of the Scott ilk but also Democratic establishment conservatives liked to remind voters of those nightmarish years and of Roosevelt the rescuer. He was now the greatest of symbols—maybe not quite a martyr but someone who had died while leading the nation to victory.

Republican Dewey appeared headed toward a comfortable national victory, however. Progressive candidate Henry Wallace, a friend of Roosevelt and enemy of Truman, siphoned left-leaning voters from Truman in close northern industrial states and California. Thurmond was listed on the ballot as the official Democratic Party nominee in Alabama, Louisiana, Mississippi, and South Carolina, and so would likely win in all four states. Truman appeared doomed.

But when all the votes were counted, Truman had 24,105,812 popular votes, Dewey 21,970,065, Thurmond 1,169,021, and Wallace 1,151,172. The electoral vote count was Truman 303, Dewey 189, and Thurmond 39—38 from the four states where he was listed as the Democratic candidate, plus 1 renegade Democratic elector from Tennessee. All other southern states went for Truman, victories more for the Democratic Party than for the candidate. In North Carolina, Truman received 459,070 votes, Dewey 258,572, Thurmond 69,652, and Wallace 3,915. Thurmond ran poorly nearly everywhere in the state but recorded his best showings in counties near the South Carolina border, specifically the Charlotte and Wilmington areas. Even there, however, he trailed both Truman and Dewey. Dewey won the historically Republican counties scattered across the mountains and western piedmont but nowhere else. Truman dominated the Black Belt counties, where Democratic white segregationists stayed with the party. In Bertie County, near the Albemarle Sound, Truman led Dewey 3,034 to 85. Across much of the Deep South, where he was the official Democratic candidate, Thurmond swept the Black Belt counties.[20] Had he been the designated Democratic nominee in North Carolina, Thurmond surely would have done well across the state. But state Democratic leaders across the ideological spectrum resisted the idea, probably fearing that a break with the national party would spell the beginning of the end for Democratic dominance in the state.

Throughout the fall, Scott had pressed forward on the economic populist themes that had won him the nomination. He said that he preferred Truman over the other candidates and consistently urged voters to go for the straight Democratic ticket. But Scott usually avoided mentioning Truman's name in speeches, thinking that doing so might hurt his own campaign.[21] Scott won 570,995 votes to Republican George Pritchard's 206,166. Except for rock-ribbed Republican counties, Scott led everywhere. With a 54 percent primary win and 73 percent general election win behind him, Scott was ready to go forward with his agenda. Old Raleigh hands, including legislators, did not share the voters' affection for Scott and were spoiling for a fight.

### THE "GO FORWARD" AGENDA

Scott's relationship with the state legislature was the most acrimonious of any governor since Republican Dan Russell in 1899 and 1900. Scott and Lieutenant Governor Hoyt Patrick Taylor Sr., the man who appointed Senate committees, disliked one another both personally and politically. The majority of legislators in both the Senate and the House were conservatives who had hoped that Johnson's steady hand would be guiding the state. Many legislators perceived Scott as an erratic liberal who threatened stability and the welfare of business and industry. He was a farmer, albeit a large-scale one, in an office usually occupied by lawyers. Scott also poisoned the atmosphere by displaying public contempt for individual legislators and the General Assembly as a whole.

Given this climate of mistrust, it is remarkable how much Scott and the legislature accomplished. A respectable 60 percent of Scott's recommendations were adopted by the 1949 legislature, giving him a score about average for governors.[22] The output was tremendous: more than one hundred million dollars for state agencies, schools, and institutions; nearly seventy-three million dollars for building projects; a full-fledged dental school at Chapel Hill; and continued salary increases for state employees. As in the Cherry administration, the new programs reflected a backlog of needs resulting from the absence of money during the Great Depression and spending freezes during World War II.

Scott also reversed one campaign pledge. Because he could find the money no other politically feasible way, he promoted a bond referendum to fund both highways and schools. Under this proposal, the state would be authorized to borrow up to two hundred million dollars for road building and twenty-five million dollars for school construction and rehabilitation.[23] School construction is a county responsibility in North Carolina, but the state occasionally has stepped in to help. On road finance, Scott had stolen a major plank from Johnson's 1948 platform, an idea that Scott had attacked. The 1949 session of the General Assembly approved the statewide referendums, although many legislators assumed that voters would reject the proposals.

Scott moved to rally voters behind the bonds, and supporters established a group, Better Roads and Schools. Despite Scott's icy relationship with so many prominent North Carolinians, he gained the backing of progressives and interest groups of various partisan and ideological stripes. The trucking and education lobbies also joined in the effort, as did Scott's 1948 Republican opponent George Pritchard, an influential voice in western North Carolina. Opposition came from petroleum companies that feared the 1 percent sales tax that would come with the bonds. City interests—bankers and politicians—feared that their communities would be shortchanged in the road allocation, a reaction to Scott's consistent emphasis on the need for rural roads, not urban thoroughfares. Scott took to the radio in the days leading up to the June 4 vote, saying that good roads were essential for getting children to school and farm goods to markets.[24]

With little organized opposition, the school construction bonds passed, 273,663–122,420. However, majorities opposed the school bonds in a few urban counties and in a scattering of rural counties where the political leadership disliked Scott. The road bonds vote was closer, but it also passed, 229,493–194,647. The counties containing the four largest cities—Charlotte, Winston-Salem, Greensboro, and Durham—overwhelmingly opposed the road bonds, together casting 42,236 votes against and just 9,867 for. Voters in New Hanover (Wilmington), the most urban place on the coast, cast 3,396 votes against the road bonds and 860 for, but just across the Cape Fear River, then solidly rural Brunswick County voted 2,307 for and 255 against.[25]

In the far western part of the state, rural Mitchell, one of North Carolina's most Republican counties throughout the twentieth century, cast 2,788 votes for and 85 against. The urban-rural divide largely held across the state. The rare exceptions including rural Anson County, the home of Lieutenant Governor Taylor, voted no. In the urban sector, Wake County voted for the road bond issue, probably because part of Wake was agricultural and more than half the county's population lay outside the city of

Raleigh. The county's large contingent of state employees may also have been inclined to support the bond proposals but there is no data to prove that conclusively.

On road building, Scott was a man of his word. Rarely if ever has a capital construction project been implemented so rapidly. In North Carolina, the governor, not the legislature, controlled the highway department and set its priorities by working through key highway commissioners appointed by the governor. By the summer of 1950, the state was in the midst of the most far-reaching road building project ever, and the construction continued for the remainder of the Scott administration.[26] Asphalt machines ventured into the backwoods, beyond the head of the branch.

### LIBERALISM AND REALITY: THE 1950 SENATE RACE

The seemingly healthy Senator Broughton collapsed and died of a heart attack in Washington on March 6, 1949, only a few months into his term. Under state law, the governor was authorized to appoint someone to serve until 1950. The seat already seemed jinxed. When Josiah Bailey died in 1946, Governor Cherry had appointed William B. Umstead, who lost to Broughton two years later. A wide range of names arose in discussions regarding his successor, most prominently Scott allies Capus Waynick and Lennox Polk McLendon, a son-in-law of former governor Charles Aycock, and a Scott foe, former senator Umstead. An Umstead appointment might have smoothed Scott's relationship with the legislature, but the governor preferred someone more in his own political mold. Many such individuals, including Waynick and McLendon, were more liberal than the state's voters. Moreover, McLendon had no desire to serve beyond the 1950 election, and Scott wanted to name someone for the long haul.

According to historians Julian Pleasants and Augustus Burns, authors of *Frank Porter Graham and the 1950 Senate Race in North Carolina*, Scott's wife, "Miss Mary" got the ball rolling for consolidated university president Frank Porter Graham. At her behest, Scott was reading a long list of possible appointees. When he reached Graham's name, Miss Mary said, "Well, you can stop right there. So far as I'm concerned, that's it."[27] Scott, probably for the first time, began serious consideration of Graham. On the same day, Scott adviser and *News and Observer* editor Jonathan Daniels also began arguing on behalf of Graham.

Scott announced the Graham appointment during a banquet at Lenoir Dining Hall in Chapel Hill on March 22. His selection came as a surprise to most people, yet the appointment seemed politically wise. At sixty-two, Graham was among the most highly respected North Carolinians, an active

Presbyterian, inspiring teacher and mentor, effective if slightly unkempt administrator, and able lobbyist. He was a humanitarian—too humane for some people. A lot of the old Gardner crowd loved him as much as or more than did the Scott people. Like nearly everyone of his standing, Graham had made enemies, especially among textile manufacturers and union haters, but the fact that many conservative business leaders admired Graham was a testament to his appeal. Graham headed for Washington as the odds-on favorite to win in 1950.

In 1950, North Carolina was in the unusual situation of having two senatorial elections. Senator Clyde Hoey had completed a full six-year term and sought reelection. The other seat, occupied first by Broughton and now by Graham, was open for a four-year term. After a six-year hiatus, former senator Bob Reynolds wanted to go back to Washington. He initially eyed the Hoey seat, which had been Reynolds's from 1932 to 1944, but decided instead to challenge Graham. Few observers thought that Reynolds, who had been married five times, could win either seat, but he could surely make mischief. Hoey and Graham were predicted to win. Both the Scott forces and organized labor entertained running someone against Hoey. Waynick, a Scott ally and New Dealer, considered running. The conservative Hoey, who had heart problems and was eager to avoid a hard-fought race, offered to "help" the more liberal Graham if Waynick declined to run.[28] The Scott organization decided to direct all its energies toward the Graham race, hoping that in exchange, Hoey would at least remain neutral.

Conservatives were split over whether to mount a serious challenge to Graham. Despite Graham's liberal associations and his ties to Scott, some establishment figures and conservatives planned to campaign and vote for Graham. He had the backing of the Gardner family and bankers and industrialists who admired Graham as a university administrator and a person.[29] But never had someone so socially liberal occupied a Senate seat from North Carolina. By the early 1950s, opposition to the Truman administration was mounting among conservative North Carolina Democrats. And many Democrats—both traditional conservatives and more populist-oriented voters who had backed Scott—grew alarmed about looming pressures to end segregation.

A serious challenge to Graham was almost inevitable. But what viable candidate would take on the task? Umstead thought about it, but he was recovering from throat surgery. The man who replaced Scott as agriculture commissioner, L. Y. "Stag" Ballentine, was mentioned, but he was not interested in giving up his secure post to conduct an uphill race. Nor was Ballentine eager to go to Washington. Raleigh attorney Willis Smith lacked the statewide name recognition of Graham or Umstead, but he had a résumé matched by few other North Carolinians. A graduate of Trinity College (later Duke University) and the Trinity Law School, where he was the top-ranking student in his class, Smith later chaired the Duke Board of Trustees. Smith had been elected president of the North Carolina Bar Association in 1941 and of the American Bar Association in 1945. He had served as Speaker of the North Carolina House of Representatives in 1931, a depression-era session when Gardner was governor. Smith had been active in civic clubs and the state Democratic Party. He knew Scott and had voted for him in the 1948 Democratic primary.[30]

Smith had many friends, but he was no glad-hander. Smith's personality differed from that of the man he was seeking to replace. Graham stopped for chats as he ambled across the Chapel Hill campus. Students, faculty, and visitors could expect a broad smile, firm handshake, and pat on the back. He and his wife, Marian, loved to entertain, hosting Sunday evening open houses that were famous.[31] For all their public contact, however, both Smith and Graham were private individuals. It was difficult to know their inner thoughts. William Friday, who became the head of the University of North Carolina in 1956, later observed of Graham, "No one was really close to him. One couldn't get inside his inner feelings. He was genuine but had to communicate. Interacting with students and community was the oxygen of his life. He was pure, noble."[32]

Graham proved inept as a campaigner, often scheduling just one event a day. In addition, he felt that his duties as senator required him to be in Washington, and he was sidelined by pneumonia for twelve days in May. Though he had grown up in the southwestern piedmont, Graham's campaign was especially weak in Charlotte, a nerve center for the textile industry. *Southern Textile Bulletin* editor David Clark, a longtime Graham critic, led a campaign suggesting that he was a dangerous left-winger. Just to the north, in Cabarrus County, Cannon would not let Graham workers campaign anywhere around his mills.[33]

For someone so adept at lobbying and leadership, Graham was naive. With good intentions, he had played a leadership role in the Southern Conference for Human Welfare. Over time, the organization, like many proworker groups, was infiltrated and influenced by procommunist elements. Even after Jonathan Daniels and other liberals left the organization, Graham continued his association.[34]

Tom Ellis, a young Raleigh attorney, was recruited into the Smith campaign by Bill Joyner, the son of Colonel W. T. Joyner, a prominent attorney and Democratic political wheelhorse. Ellis and the younger Joyner were assigned the task of researching Graham's record. Ellis knew Graham was a liberal but was unprepared for the extent of his leftist associations. He later recalled being "shocked" that Graham "would join or sign a petition for any left-wing organization."[35] Ellis and Joyner's findings paved the way for Smith's campaign to portray Graham as a man out of touch with North Carolina voters. Campaign director Charles Green put together a shrewd publicity team that included Ellis, Joyner, Dunn newspaper publisher Hoover Adams, and WRAL radio news director Jesse Helms. Adams took the lead in transforming the findings of opposition research into campaign ads.[36]

Helms had been on good terms with Scott and liked Graham. Scott had called Helms to the governor's office and, in Graham's presence, asked Helms to serve as publicity director for Graham's campaign. Helms later related that he regretfully turned down the offer, telling Scott and Graham that he admired "Dr. Frank" but did not agree with his political philosophy. Helms told Scott and Graham that he would support Smith if he ran.[37]

Graham selected Jefferson Johnson from Clinton to manage his campaign. Johnson had managed Broughton's successful 1948 senatorial campaign and was also on good terms with Scott.[38] Scott's blessing was a mixed one for Graham. As governor, Scott channeled organizational resources into the campaign and connected Graham with farmers and farm-related business interests. Such contacts were bound to help Graham in eastern North Carolina and parts of the piedmont and mountains.

Also a mixed blessing was the aggressive support Graham received from Jonathan Daniels, publisher of the *Raleigh News and Observer*, son of Josephus Daniels, and a Roosevelt administration veteran. Daniels inherited the economic populist spirit of his father but was more socially liberal. He had not yet endorsed the concept of racial integration but was a strident foe of white supremacist politicians. Daniels was a member of the Democratic National Committee, and he used both his party position and the pages of his newspaper to promote Graham's candidacy. Daniels was a lightning rod for more conservative Democrats.[39]

Smith stressed his anticommunist and anti-labor-union sentiments and his opposition to the Truman administration's liberalism. That strategy did not work. On May 27, Graham led Smith, 303,605–250,222. But Reynolds collected 58,752 votes, while hog farmer Olla Ray Boyd received 5,900. Graham seemed to occupy a commanding position just a few votes short of a majority and with 54 percent of the votes cast for the two major candidates. Smith understood the situation and was skeptical about calling for a runoff. He was urged on by supporters, including Helms, who promoted a public gathering at Smith's house in Raleigh to encourage him to run. These efforts persuaded Smith, and on June 7, he announced that he would call for a second primary.[40]

The only route to victory for Smith seemed to be to play the race card. New Smith campaign ads pointed to the "bloc vote" for Graham in "well known Negro precincts" such as Durham's Hillside High School, where Graham had garnered 1,514 votes to just 7 for Smith. A Smith campaign flier read "Did *YOU* know? Over 28% of the population of North Carolina is COLORED? The SOUTHERN WORKING MAN MUST NOT BE SACRIFICED to *vote-getting ambitions* of *political bosses!*"[41] The message was that racially integrated work sites would lead to white job losses. The most controversial fliers suggested that a Graham victory could lead to interracial marriages. One photograph showed black American soldiers dancing with white women in London during World War II.[42]

For decades afterward, liberals and Graham backers speculated about who had authored the more controversial and graphic racial ads and fliers, with many fingers pointed at Helms and Adams. Smith campaign insiders saw Clark as a leading force behind the racially tinged campaign.[43] There may always be doubt about who instigated the most virulent racist ads. Adams was a leading strategist, and many of the ads reflect his longtime style of writing and use of capital letters, but the most vitriolic might have been the work of Smith supporters in individual counties or undercover campaign workers.[44] Most white North Carolinians were segregationists, and even self-proclaimed white liberals reacted negatively to the idea of racial intermarriage (despite the long southern tradition of extramarital sexual relations between white men and black women). A broad segment of the public was bound to be influenced by a campaign appealing to racial fears. Leaders of Smith's campaign agreed—correctly—that nothing short of a stress on race could rescue their candidate. Half a century later, Ellis reflected that everyone in the Smith camp "had something to do with the racial campaign. There were prejudices all around in the nature of that time."[45]

The U.S. Supreme Court decisions in *Sweatt v. Painter* and *McLaurin v. Oklahoma*, which in effect invalidated segregation in graduate-level education, were handed down on June 5, 1950, two days before Smith called for the runoff.[46] The rulings energized white segregationists and the Smith campaign. Smith also sought and won the endorsement of former senator Reynolds.

Graham maintained advantages. Despite pleadings from the Smith campaign, Senator Hoey remained neutral, although it is not clear whether he did so to keep his promise to "help" Graham or because he believed that sitting senators should stay out of primaries.[47] Whatever his reasons, Hoey's silence was an asset to Graham.

Graham also mounted an aggressive statewide campaign, drawing good crowds nearly everywhere. His allies—though not Graham personally—launched strong attacks questioning Smith's professional integrity. Equally damning and more factual was the charge that Smith had Republican sympathies. From the perspective of national Democrats, Smith's economic views closely matched those of a typical midwestern Republican. Big guns came to Graham's defense. Eighty-year-old former governor Cameron Morrison, whose political career had spanned more than half a century, delivered a radio address urging voters to go with Graham.[48]

Runoff day, June 24, was hot, with temperatures in the mid- and upper nineties except on the Outer Banks and in the higher mountain areas. By early evening, the outcome was clear: Smith defeated Graham, 281,114–261,789. Voting patterns in the mountains, western piedmont, and central piedmont resembled those in the earlier primary, with both candidates maintaining their areas of strength. An exception was rural Allegheny, in the northwest mountains, a county that had often backed segregationist candidates. Graham led there in the first primary, but Smith almost doubled Graham's vote in the runoff. Graham slipped in the eastern piedmont and suffered serious vote erosion in the coastal plain. In May, rural Jones County, in the central coastal plain, had cast 1,142 votes for Graham, 568 for Smith, and 311 for Reynolds; in June, however, Smith received 670 votes, while Graham received 634. Nash County (Rocky Mount), a stronghold for insurgent liberal Democrats from Richard Fountain to Kerr Scott, cast 4,464 votes for Graham, 3,934 for Smith, and 488 for Reynolds in the May primary, but in June, Smith tallied 4,737 and Graham 3,812. Turnout dropped over much of the coastal plain, but nearly everywhere, the raw vote for Smith went up while Graham's went down. Graham won a few eastern counties with long histories of both economic populism and racial friction—Edgecombe, Greene, and Lenoir—but his advantage narrowed. The shift away from Graham in the coastal plain was the key to his statewide loss.

Graham supporters were stunned. Typical was Robert Morgan, at the time a law student at Wake Forest and later a U.S. senator. He had proudly introduced Graham at a local appearance, preparing his remarks with the assistance of his mentor and favorite professor, I. Beverly Lake. Morgan cried when the June 24 results poured in.[49] In a letter to Graham, Lake called the Smith campaign "dishonorable" and accused it of having stirred up "blind, unreasonable racial fear."[50]

In the words of Pleasants and Burns, "Racial segregation was a strongly held belief in white North Carolina in 1950. The consensus supporting it was deep and powerfully felt. Despite North Carolina's cherished reputation as a beacon of enlightenment in southern race relations, that enlightenment had never included the actual ending of segregation—at least not in the immediate future."[51]

Graham, whose views would have placed him on the left end of the political spectrum almost anywhere in the country, would have won the Democratic nomination outright in the first primary if not for Reynolds's candidacy. Though Graham may have lacked political subtlety, he commanded respect for his deep humanity. Distraught Graham backers spoke of writing in Graham's name or voting Republican in the November election. Their talk came to naught. Smith beat Republican E. R. Gavin, 364,912–177,753. Graham received only scattered write-in votes.

The events of 1948–50 set the stage for conflicts that would influence politics for many years into the future. The election foreshadowed the impending civil rights battles. It was exciting. It was mean. It drew a high rate of participation for an election when neither the presidency nor the governorship was at stake. Major political figures of various political stripes cut their political teeth in this race: Tom Ellis and Jesse Helms for Smith; William Friday, Lauch Faircloth, Robert Morgan, and Terry Sanford for Graham. These alliances do not necessarily reflect what modern-day observers might expect. J. Melville Broughton Jr., son of the late senator and a leading conservative in later years, backed Graham. So did I. Beverly Lake Sr., who later built a political career defending racial segregation and states' rights. After William B. Umstead decided not to run, his brother, mildly liberal state representative John Wesley Umstead of Orange County, worked hard for Graham, his college classmate. From a current perspective, Graham was enlightened on race, while Smith was reactionary. The election also featured other themes. Smith emphasized the threat of world communism, then a burning issue. He also mobilized Scott's opponents. In hindsight, the final outcome should not have been seen as a surprise. The election left a legacy of bitterness. It reaffirmed the political and social limits of the time.

## CHAPTER TWO

# The 1950s

The United States has never seen greater change in day-to-day life than it experienced from 1900 to 1950. By 1950, the automobile provided the chief means of daily transportation. North Carolina, though far removed from the leading centers of economic gravity, boasted of direct air service to New York, Washington, Boston, and Atlanta, even if North Carolina's airports resembled converted army barracks with porches. Freeways were a California miracle, but North Carolinians took for granted two-lane asphalt and concrete roads connecting major cities and towns. In the preceding year, television sets had moved from a store window curiosity to a common feature of piedmont living rooms, with new stations in Charlotte and Greensboro beaming in national network variety shows and fifteen-minute newscasts featuring announcers who read from prepared scripts. Dial telephones were ubiquitous. Medical advances, including the use of penicillin, reduced the toll of infections. Stupor-inducing ringworms, hookworms, and mosquitoes were less a scourge than in the past. Yet racial segregation remained almost as entrenched as it had been in the early 1900s.[1]

Much as King Cotton characterized the antebellum South, King Tobacco was crucial for twentieth-century North Carolina.[2] In 1950, tobacco was near its peak. From August into the autumn, the exotic chant of the tobacco auctioneer rang out from tin warehouses. Those markets produced cash that drove the state's lively rural and small-town economies. Tobacco paid the bills. Large numbers of young men and women became the first members of their families to go to college, with tobacco providing the needed cash. While tobacco revenue varied from year to year, a New Deal-era price-support program eased the pain in bad seasons.

Durham, Greensboro, and Winston-Salem were among the world's premier cigarette manufacturing cities. Modern factories replaced more antiquated ones. Duke University in Durham developed a national reputation in the arts, sciences, and medical research, partly through fortunes made in tobacco and in electric power. Wake Forest University relocated from the town of Wake Forest, twelve miles north of Raleigh, to Winston-Salem, where its magnificent new campus was funded by the Reynolds family of Camel cigarette fame. Though Duke and Wake Forest are the best-known examples, most of North Carolina's colleges, both public and private, owed their development at least partly to tobacco. And by 1950, the state was well on its way to distinction in higher education. So tobacco did much to make possible North Carolina's shining cultural temples of the twentieth century. A curse on the human body was a state's blessing.

Despite its industrial might in tobacco, textiles, and furniture, North Carolina was still mostly rural—69.5 percent of the population in the 1950 census, a figure surpassed only by Mississippi, North Dakota, and South Carolina. The United States as a whole was 59 percent urban, and most of the big northern states were between 65 and 80 percent urban. North Carolina had only one city, Charlotte, with its 134,042 residents, among America's one hundred largest cities; Charlotte's 33 percent growth rate in the 1940s and unusually diverse economy by the state's standards suggested a bright future. Winston-Salem, Greensboro, Durham, and Raleigh rounded out the state's top five population centers.

The concept of suburbia came slowly to North Carolina. The outskirts, as populated areas close to the city were called, ranged from islands of poverty to upscale settlements in the mode of incorporated Biltmore Forest near Asheville or the unincorporated Hope Valley subdivision in Durham County. The transition from urban to rural was abrupt, even near substantial cities like Charlotte and Greensboro. The traveler quickly moved from town into a world of tobacco patches, dairy farms, and pine forests. The public associated the suburban idea more with New York and California.

The populace marveled at the wonders of the twentieth century but looked with apprehension toward looming changes overseas and at home. The Korean War broke out in June 1950 and lasted for the next three years. Racial tensions mounted as cases challenging school segregation worked their way through the courts.

### HINTS OF SIEGE FOR A SEGREGATED SOCIETY

The 1950 publication of Raleigh news commentator W. E. Debnam's *Weep No More, My Lady* was a precursor of combat to come.[3] The book was a response to comments that Eleanor Roosevelt, the widow of the late president, had made about the South after a visit to Chapel Hill. In her newspaper column, "My Day," Roosevelt wrote that North Carolina was the most progressive of southern states but then moved on to a frequent theme of her columns, the poverty and racism in the American South. Debnam's rejoinder defended the white South and attacked northern liberalism as personified by the former First Lady. *Weep No More, My Lady* was an enlargement of two radio broadcasts.

The sixty-page paperback published by Raleigh's Graphic Press offered a litany of alleged ills and indignities suffered by the South at the hands of the North from Reconstruction to 1950. Responding to Mrs. Roosevelt's claim of "poverty and unhappiness" in the South, Debnam wrote, "There are signs of poverty and unhappiness just about everywhere. Mrs. Roosevelt doesn't have to come to the South to see these things. Almost from the window of her hotel apartment in New York, she can look out and see what is possibly the greatest cesspool of heaped-up-and-pressed-down-and-running-over poverty and crime and spiritual and moral and economic unhappiness on the face of the earth. We are speaking, of course, of that great Negro ghetto in the heart of New York that is Harlem."[4]

In May, ten thousand copies were printed. The total reached seventy thousand by late September. Each copy sold for fifty cents. The tract was a hit among white North Carolinians restive about the direction being taken by the liberal wing of the Democratic Party. The book's biggest sales occurred in the immediate aftermath of the Willis Smith–Frank Porter Graham Senate race.

Coincidence or not, the book was released during a year when the old order of racial segregation suddenly seemed less secure in North Carolina and in the South as a whole. On June 5, 1950, the Supreme Court announced decisions in three racially charged cases, making the day arguably the greatest since Reconstruction in the eyes of civil rights advocates. In *Henderson v. United States*, the Court ordered railroads to cease segregating blacks from whites in train dining cars, as remained standard practice after trains crossed the Potomac and Ohio Rivers heading south.[5] In *McLaurin v. Oklahoma Board of Regents*, the court dealt with a special brand of segregation in a border state.[6] McLaurin had been admitted to the graduate school of the University of Oklahoma under a court order, but the university had required that McLaurin sit at separate tables in the campus library and the dining hall and at an assigned desk in each classroom. The Court ruled this arrangement to violate both the letter and the spirit of the Fourteenth Amendment, which stated that no state could deny its citizens equal protection under law on the basis of race, color, or previous status as a slave.

For hard-line segregationists, the third case, *Sweatt v. Painter*, was the most ominous, the handwriting on the wall for the practice of state-sponsored segregation. In a unanimous opinion, the Court decided in favor of Heman Sweatt's plea for admission to the law school of the University of Texas in Austin.[7] In 1946, Sweatt, who was black, had sought admission to the state's whites-only public law school. In response, Texas officials rushed to set up a school for African Americans in Houston, 120 miles away. It was a makeshift institution where at first the small faculty commuted from Austin. By 1950, the new school had its own faculty and library, but it remained a pale shadow of the school in Austin. Chief Justice Fred Vinson, a Kentuckian of a segregationist bent, wrote the Court's decision. After outlining the physical gaps between the black and white law schools, Vinson wrote of "intangible" factors making the black school inferior to the state university—the faculty's reputation, the influence of the alumni, and the "prestige" of the Austin law school. His words led to a question that might challenge the old order on all grounds: If prestige were a consideration, could any segregated facility in the American South be equal?[8] The Court refrained from declaring segregation to be unconstitutional. But could such a step be far behind if different institutional prestige levels propelled the Court to declare Texas in violation of the Equal Protection Clause of the Fourteenth Amendment?

In 1942, in anticipation of future challenges on "separate but equal" grounds, North Carolina had established a law school for blacks at the North Carolina College for Negroes in Durham. In 1949, claiming unequal facilities, four African American students filed a suit in federal district court in which they sought admission to the law school at the University of North Carolina at Chapel Hill. Many white North Carolinians, including Jonathan Daniels, liberal editor of the *Raleigh News and Observer*, attempted to differentiate this case from the McLaurin and Sweatt circumstances. Daniels asserted that North Carolina was making a strong effort to achieve true equality in legal education and that the Durham institution was not inferior. However, neither Daniels nor more hostile whites paid adequate notice to the "intangible qualities" phrase in the *Sweatt* opinion. Nor did federal district court judge Johnson J. Hayes when he ruled in October 1950 that facilities at North Carolina College were equal to those at the Chapel Hill law school. The Fourth Circuit Court of Appeals in Richmond overturned Hayes's ruling in March 1951, ordering the plaintiffs' admission by the next academic term. In June, the Supreme Court's refusal to the University of North Carolina's appeal implicitly reinforced doubts about whether separation by law could ever be equal.

Leaders at the University of North Carolina had discussed the possibility of integration over the years and by this time were probably resigned to limited desegregation. In April, the school's Board of Trustees voted in favor of considering "qualified Negro applicants" to graduate programs not available at black schools. Limited minority admissions to graduate programs, including law and medicine, followed.[9]

The state had already moved toward equal compensation for public schoolteachers. A pay system based partly on race was displaced by one based on each teacher's degree earned and years of experience. From 1940 to the 1951 academic year, the average salary for black North Carolina principals and teachers had gone from 73 percent of that for whites to 103 percent. (Black educators had an average of 4.1 years of higher education, compared to 3.9 percent for whites.) Over the same period, the capital outlay per black pupil rose from 30 percent of the amount per white pupil to 93 percent. The number of library volumes per pupil enrolled grew by 47 percent for whites and 100 percent for blacks. Nevertheless, there were still more than twice as many volumes per white pupil (5.4) as per black pupil (2.4).[10]

Overall, North Carolina financed its segregated black schools at a higher level than did other southern states. It is difficult to know how much of the relative gain for blacks reflected a realization of need as opposed to the segregationists' strategy to maintain the status quo. Both phenomena were at work. Lacking hope of immediate integration, African Americans pressed for improvements in their separate schools.

Scott made two appointments that were considered daring at midcentury. He named Harold Trigg, an African American, to the State Board of Education. And never had a woman served as a state trial court justice until Scott appointed Susie Marshall Sharp to a Superior Court judgeship in 1949.

Only 14 percent of Kerr Scott's proposals were adopted during the 1951 legislative session, the worst record of any twentieth-century governor.[11] However, road-paving projects continued at a rapid pace.[12] Scott was never one to give up, whatever the odds against him. Opponents clamored for more cautious and less bombastic leadership.

### CHANGING OF THE GUARD

Former senator William B. Umstead of Durham pursued the governorship in 1952 and won support from business leaders and conservative Democrats. The Scott forces backed white-haired Judge Hubert Olive of Lexington, who had been state commander of the American Legion. Umstead criticized the "Scott machine" and promised cautious but progressive leadership. His policy proposals resembled Olive's. Both men stressed public education and vied for teachers' support. Having served in both houses of Congress, Umstead had the advantage of statewide name recognition, and he defeated Olive, 294,170–265,175. Rural and urban areas were closely divided. Scott's appeal to the branch head boys was not easily transferable to the more polished Olive. Much to Scott's dismay, some of his past political allies defected to Umstead.[13]

For those in the know, the race for lieutenant governor assumed a special significance. Umstead had recovered from major throat surgery. The front-runner for lieutenant governor was Roy Rowe, a legislator from Pender County who had close ties tied to party regulars in both the Umstead and Olive camps. However, corporate leaders, including Robert Hanes of Winston-Salem, sought a fresh face, someone who would be both dynamic and business-friendly. They recruited Luther Hodges, until recently a career executive with the Marshall Field textile company. Born in southern Virginia, raised just over the state line in Rockingham County, North Carolina, and educated at Chapel Hill, Hodges had lived in Leaksville and New York City before retiring from the company in 1950 at the age of fifty-two.

Hodges was ambitious, polished, and an accomplished speaker. He attempted to link his campaign with Umstead's. Umstead, however, brushed aside the suggestion of any connection in the campaigns, viewing Hodges as a prima donna who had not worked his way up through the party ranks.[14] From then on, their relationship was strained. Hodges led Rowe in the primary but did not obtain a majority. Nevertheless, Rowe declined to ask for a runoff primary, making Hodges and Umstead running mates. Both prevailed by huge margins in the November general election. Umstead defeated his entertaining and witty conservative Republican opponent, H. F. "Cousin Chub" Seawell, 796,306–383,329. Seawell had polled more votes than any previous Republican gubernatorial candidate in the twentieth century, but his percentage of the total vote was in line with the anemic showing of other Republicans from 1932 onward and below that of Republican candidates in the 1900–1928 period. Seawell went on to become a prominent conservative media figure, sometimes substituting for Jesse Helms on television station WRAL's "Viewpoint" in the 1960s and early 1970s.[15]

The tide shifted in national politics. Running against "Korea, communism, and corruption," the 1952 Republican presidential nominee, former general Dwight Eisenhower, defeated Democratic governor Adlai E. Stevenson of Illinois, 55 percent to 45 percent. Eisenhower brought a nonpartisan image to the Republican ticket. His thirty-nine-year-old running mate, Senator Richard Nixon of California, thrived on exploiting Democratic vulnerabilities and stressed the dangers of international communism. Republicans captured both houses of the U.S. Congress.

For international political reasons, President Truman had refused to call the Korean conflict a war. The two sides were stalemated, with neither outright victory nor defeat seemingly likely. Eisenhower promised to seek a solution if he won election. Many southern moderate to conservative voters defected to "Ike," as the former general was known. Stevenson, whose vice presidential running mate was Senator John Sparkman of Alabama, carried no state outside the South and border regions. In the South, Eisenhower won Florida, Tennessee, Texas, and Virginia.

Stevenson won North Carolina, 652,803–558,107. Eisenhower's tally represented the second-best showing for a Republican in the state in the preceding half century, trailing only Herbert Hoover's 1928 victory. Eisenhower carried the mountain region and ran almost even with Stevenson in the populous piedmont. Stevenson's cushion had been provided by his two-to-one lead in the coastal plain. Eisenhower won the counties with the state's three largest cities: Mecklenburg (Charlotte), Forsyth (Winston-Salem), and Guilford (Greensboro). Gubernatorial candidate Umstead's strength—almost 70 percent of the vote—shielded candidates for state office, but Eisenhower had some pull in congressional races. Republican Charles Raper Jonas of Lincolnton defeated incumbent Hamilton Jones in the Tenth District. Jonas, whose father had been a Republican member of Congress for one term after the 1928 election, carried Mecklenburg County and the city of Charlotte. Republicans hoped the younger Jonas's victory foretold a new era.

Republicans had reason for long-term optimism. The party's advances had come outside its traditional mountain strongholds. Its best showings were in wealthy white urban precincts, such as Myers Park in Charlotte and Irving Park in Greensboro. But Eisenhower and Jonas had also run strongly in white middle-class areas.[16] In the post–World War II era, the business and professional classes were growing rapidly. Many were economic conservatives, now smarting under the heavy tax burden from the Roosevelt-Truman era. They benefited from federal programs such as subsidized education under the GI Bill but chafed under big government. Nor was Eisenhower's appeal limited to conservatives. He represented change, a breath of fresh air after the tired and worn-out Democrats. Partly as a consequence of the World War II diaspora, the state's population had become more cosmopolitan and open to change.

Blacks, still a weak political force in the state, voted by more than 2:1 for Stevenson. Many African Americans had switched from the Republicans to the Democratic Party during the 1930s because they favored Roosevelt's economic stimulus and social welfare programs. Ironically, a state Democratic Party built partly on white supremacy might soon need black support.

Umstead took office on Thursday, January 8, 1953, a cool, wet day in Raleigh. His program was a bold one—as bold as Scott might have proposed. Umstead wanted to spend heavy sums on public schools, universities, highways, industrial development, and prison reform. His administrative secretary, Ed Rankin, later wrote that a few of Umstead's more conservative backers were "deeply shocked."[17] A bigger shock was still to come. Umstead was exhausted after the usual round of inaugural functions, and on January 11, he was in Durham's Watts Hospital, the victim of a heart attack and borderline pneumonia. For months, doctors limited Umstead's schedule. However, he tried to stay on top of events and had a first-rate team led by Rankin, legislative counsel Frank Taylor, and the governor's brother, state representative John Umstead of Orange County. About half of his legislative proposals were adopted.[18]

In June 1953, Senator Willis Smith succumbed to a heart attack. True to his campaign, Smith had been one of the most reliable conservatives in the Senate. He and Vice President Nixon had developed a personal and political friendship while both were in the Senate. Smith, even more often than his conservative colleague, Clyde Roark Hoey, had joined the informal congressional alliance of southern Democrats and northern Republicans that attempted to block liberal legislation proposed by northern Democrats and the Truman administration. Those interested in Smith's seat included consolidated University of North Carolina president Gordon Gray and state Democratic Party chair John Larkins. Umstead refused to consider Gray because he had voted for Eisenhower in 1952.[19] Larkins was politically close to Umstead and was thought to be in line for the appointment. However, the nod went to state senator Alton Lennon of Wilmington, a respected attorney whose political philosophy was close to Smith's.

Umstead maintained a busy schedule in the fall of 1953 and into 1954 and showed interest in the minute details of government and administration. All the while, school segregation cases from states as diverse as South Carolina, Virginia, Delaware, and Kansas were debated in private conferences and informal discussions among Supreme Court members. Having filed a brief supporting the segregation position, North Carolina officials looked nervously toward Washington.

### JUDGMENT AND RESPONSE

The Supreme Court's decree came from Washington on May 17, 1954, a warm and sunny late spring day across most of North Carolina, hinting of the record summer heat to come. The author of the Court's unanimous decision in *Brown v. Board of Education of Topeka*, Chief Justice Earl Warren, read from the opinion, which managed to be bold and vague at the same time. School segregation was ruled unconstitutional, and the 1896 "separate but equal" doctrine was overturned. The Court declared that state laws requiring segregation violated the Fourteenth Amendment's Equal Protection Clause, which said a state could not "deny to any person within its jurisdiction the equal protection of the law." As a consequence of internal differences on the Court, Warren's determination to have a unanimous decision, and fears of violence in the South, the decision did not say precisely how or when desegregation was to be implemented.[20] The *Brown* case and companion cases presenting similar issues were sent back to the federal district courts for resolution and implementation. The hint of a better day to come for African Americans, the decision was a bombshell for much of the white South, although it could not have surprised observers who had been paying close attention to other legal cases over the preceding four years.

Political elites and journalists immediately began to discuss the decision, though the story did not filter down to the general public for a few hours. People who listened to the afternoon radio newscasts at home heard the outlines of the big decision. Not until late afternoon, when factories, offices, and schools emptied, did the news spread. All the big North Carolina cities had morning and afternoon newspapers, and in smaller cities with only one newspaper, it was typically published in the afternoon. Much of the general public thus learned of the edict from banner headlines in the evening newspapers. In addition, the fifteen-minute network television newscasts at 6:30 highlighted the story.

Across the white South, the reaction to the *Brown* decision was swift and fierce. From the Deep South states of Georgia, Louisiana, Mississippi, and South Carolina came vows of defiance. Even before the decision, Governor Herman Talmadge of Georgia had threatened to use the state militia to prevent school integration. In North Carolina, however, the initial reaction was more tempered. Most of the state officials who ventured opinions stated their opposition with restraint ("I'm disappointed but . . .") or even noncommittal neutrality ("We'll work our problems out the North Carolina way").[21] Umstead's assistant, Ed Rankin, later wrote that the governor was "dumbfounded" by the decision.[22] Umstead, frail though he was, had ultimate responsibility for approving and implementing North Carolina's response. He instructed Rankin to issue a statement in Umstead's name expressing disappointment and promising a detailed response after reading the opinion.

The governor had other items on his plate, including one that required immediate action. On May 12, Hoey had died at his desk in the Senate office building. A sad event for his family and much of the state, it was symbolically exquisite timing. More than any other North Carolina politician, Senator Hoey represented the old order, even more in style than in political philosophy. Hoey would have disapproved of the *Brown* decision, yet in the tradition of North Carolina establishment leadership, he would have burned no crosses. Now Umstead faced pressure to appoint an interim senator quickly.

Not so neatly timed as Hoey's death was the long-scheduled North Carolina Democratic Convention, which opened on May 19. Delegates to the convention, more an ideological mirror of the state's voting population than would be the case in later years, found themselves in a real quandary. Overwhelmingly white and native southerners, most opposed the *Brown* decision. Yet many were reluctant to fan the flames of public outrage by passing a resolution of condemnation. Their keynote speaker was Irving Carlyle, one of North Carolina's most prominent attorneys and civic leaders and a longtime acquaintance of the governor. Some observers thought Carlyle was a top contender for Hoey's seat. His delivery was powerful, even if his message failed to rise above the usual convention banalities. The audience responded with the customary ovations. Near the end of his speech, a hush came over the hall when Carlyle exclaimed, "The Supreme Court has spoken. As good citizens, we have no other course except to obey the law as laid down by the Court. To do otherwise would cost us our respect for law and order, and if we lost that in these critical times, we have lost the quality which is the source of our strength as a state and as a nation."[23]

These words were bold given what was thought to be the tenor of the times. But the audience again responded with thunderous applause, probably more a tribute to Carlyle's courage than to his message. Carlyle never went to the Senate. Whether the ringing declaration cost Carlyle the appointment remains a matter of conjecture. It makes a good story line to portray him as one who sacrificed ambition in promoting a higher belief—a sort of profile in courage. Courageous he was, but there is no firm evidence that he had been Senate-bound prior to the speech. Umstead was seriously considering several people. Carlyle's statement, however, was significant: it was proof that some politically prominent southerners favored acceptance of the *Brown* ruling.

On June 4, Umstead named an old friend, Sam J. Ervin Jr. of Morganton. Ervin's appointment was a surprise, yet his credentials were impeccable.

He was a former state legislator, trial court judge, and member of the U.S. House of Representatives and was currently serving on the North Carolina Supreme Court.[24] More scholar and lawyer than politician, Ervin remained in the Senate for the next two decades, emerging as the legal brain behind the last-ditch effort to prevent or at least stall racial integration. He was also a defender of civil liberties, ready to fight those he saw as a threat to constitutional rights, from Joseph McCarthy in the 1950s to Richard Nixon in the 1970s. While his leanings were conservative, Ervin always maintained a degree of independence.[25]

On May 27, Umstead issued his official statement on *Brown* and the related desegregation cases. The ten-day lapse between the decision and the detailed response reflected both Umstead's cautious nature and the gravity with which he viewed the situation. The key sentences might have come from a more liberal individual such as Kerr Scott. After defending North Carolina's segregation laws, Umstead added, "However the Supreme Court of the United States has spoken. It has reversed itself and declared segregation in public schools unconstitutional. In my opinion its previous decision on this question was correct. The reversal of its former decisions is, in my judgment, a clear and serious invasion of the rights of the sovereign states. Nevertheless, it is now the latest Supreme Court interpretation of the Fourteenth Amendment. Overnight, this decision has brought to our state a complex problem . . . the wise solution of which will require a calm, careful, thoughtful study of all of us. There is no time for rash statements or the proposal of impossible schemes."[26]

For an office-holding southern politician in 1954, this was a conciliatory but not daring statement. Umstead recognized the revolutionary nature of the decision while placing North Carolina in the moderate camp. He issued no call to arms or suggestion of defiance and recognized the ultimate might of a determined federal government, though like other southerners he hoped that Congress and the president would slow the process. For any elected southern officeholder, a pro-*Brown* stance would have been suicidal. Most voices for acceptance were condemned or overlooked. But nearly all blacks—more than a quarter of the state's population—probably wanted at least the right to attend integrated schools. The National Association for the Advancement of Colored People (NAACP) praised the *Brown* ruling. Some whites, not all of them Yankee migrants or sociology professors, urged compliance. L. L. Carpenter, the editor of the all-white Baptist State Convention's *Biblical Recorder*, wrote in the May 29 issue that the decision was "almost inevitable in light of Christian truth, the claim of democracy, and the demands of the world situation."[27] He continued this theme in later editorials. Throughout the 1950s, state Baptist leaders in Raleigh were far in front of their members. In the early 1950s, a liberal Baptist publication, *New Frontiers*, had attacked racial discrimination. Around the state, virtually all Baptist congregations—like those of other white Protestant denominations—excluded African Americans from membership. Colleges and universities such as Baptist-linked Wake Forest and Methodist-linked Duke admitted Asians from the United States and overseas but not black Americans. For American-style apartheid, however, the *Brown* ruling signaled the beginning of the end, though that end would be stretched for decades.

### SCOTT VERSUS LENNON

Governor Umstead had appointed Alton Lennon to fill Willis Smith's Senate seat in 1953; Lennon ran for a full six-year term in 1954. His opponent was former governor Scott, who had not forgotten the fate that had befallen Frank Porter Graham in the 1950 senatorial primary. Scott hoped to beat Lennon with support from farmers, factory workers, the agribusiness community, liberals, and urban blacks. To manage his campaign, he recruited the ambitious and shrewd Terry Sanford, a Fayetteville attorney and former president of the North Carolina Young Democratic Clubs. Lennon would be no pushover. He could count on most Umstead people. Corporate leaders rallied to Lennon, whom they saw as the more fiscally sound candidate. The popular Scott entered the 1954 primary as the front-runner, but narrowly so. Lennon campaigned as a steadfast conservative. He had a booming bass drum voice, which made him sound almost like a white Martin Luther King. Lennon offered a firm handshake and a winning smile. Scott portrayed himself as the people's champion, a progressive in the mold of Roosevelt. By 1954, he had a zeal and campaign organization that old-time conservative party wheelhorses were unable to match.

When the *Brown* decision was announced less than two weeks before the May 31 primary, both candidates immediately made known their displeasure. Scott, however, sought to defuse the situation, saying that it had taken the court more than fifty years to reverse "separate but equal," so fifty more years might pass before desegregation was implemented.[28] In the waning days of the campaign, some county-level Lennon supporters circulated leaflets linking Scott with pro-integration forces. The attacks were milder and more discreet than the ones leveled at Graham four years earlier, however. In the primary, Scott beat Lennon, 312,053–286,703, while Alvin Wingfield received 7,999 votes, and four other candidates collectively had 7,876. As Scott had a bare majority, there would be no runoff. Few voters appeared to have voted on the basis of racial fears, in part because there was little visible difference between the Lennon and Scott positions on segregation.[29]

Conservative columnist Lynn Nisbet, then a leading analyst of state politics, explained that Scott "has a habit of winning just as appointed senators have a habit of losing. It is quite likely that since the death of Clyde Hoey, the best known man in North Carolina is William Kerr Scott of Haw River. When he appears in person or when his name is mentioned anywhere in North Carolina, it is seldom necessary for anyone to ask 'Who is he?' This wide acquaintance among the people plus a canny instinct for knowing who to make mad and when and a political technique developed over 30 years of political activity had more to do with his large vote than anything else."[30]

### TRANSITIONS

Hurricane Hazel slammed North Carolina on October 15, 1954, its damage limited only because of the relative lack of large-scale development along the coast. From Burlington east, Hazel downed trees and power lines. Governor Umstead, who had been in declining health since late summer, responded as best he could, attending meetings and receiving delegations. On November 4, he entered Durham's Watts hospital and was diagnosed with pneumonia. Three days later, he died of congestive heart failure and pneumonia-related complications, the first North Carolina governor since David Fowle (1889–91) to die in office.[31]

Though Umstead's time in office had been short, few two-year periods have been more filled with drama. Despite his frail constitution, Umstead had called the shots. Few governors have maintained such a serious public demeanor. Politically and personally, he came across as a conservative, but one who wanted the state to play a lead role in curing societal ills. To the end, he had been organized and meticulous in tackling administrative challenges.[32]

His successor, Luther Hodges, had a wide range of acquaintances, both in business and politics, but remained an enigma. As lieutenant governor, he was not close to Umstead and had been kept outside the loop; no one knew where he might seek to guide the state. Hodges looked gubernatorial, particularly with the carnation he wore on his lapel each day. His voice was pitched an octave higher than the average man of his age, and some observers thought that he sounded aristocratic. He had in fact known hard work as he was growing up. Whatever insecurities he might have had, Hodges moved with confidence as he assumed the reins of the office. In the early days, he retained nearly all Umstead's office staff and departmental administrators. Rankin became one of Hodges's most influential and trusted advisers, much as he had been Umstead's. More than Umstead, Hodges liked to display his authority and make it clear that he was the man in charge. He carried the mentality of a corporate executive to the governor's office. He stressed efficiency and credentials over political connections and irritated Democratic Party regulars when he appointed nonactive Democrats and occasionally Republicans to posts. But his actions produced a more merit-driven bureaucracy than North Carolina had previously possessed. Hodges named some of the state's most talented attorneys to the Superior Court bench, including two who went on to become federal court judges, J. Braxton Craven and L. Richardson Preyer. Hodges was proud of his independent style; moreover, the special circumstances of his succession meant that he took office without having made any promises about appointments.[33]

### THE RESISTANCE MOVEMENT

On August 8, 1954, Governor Umstead had appointed a nineteen-member Committee on Education, a vague name for a group whose charge was to propose a state response to the *Brown* ruling. He named three blacks to the study group: Hazel Parker, a home demonstration agent from Tarboro; Dr. F. D. Bluford, president of North Carolina A&T State College in Greensboro; and Dr. J. W. Seabrook, president of Fayetteville Teachers' College. Thomas Pearsall of Rocky Mount, the state Speaker of the House in the 1947 legislative session, chaired the committee. After Umstead's death, Hodges asked the committee to continue its work and submit recommendations.

On December 30, 1954, the Pearsall committee presented its report to Hodges. The governor endorsed the report and on January 6, 1955, asked the legislature to adopt its recommendations. The committee worked on the premise that desegregation was neither a worthy nor a practical goal. It recommended that authority over pupil assignment be shifted from the state board of education to the individual county and city school systems. This was a legal stratagem to blunt the effectiveness of a desegregation suit against the state as a whole.[34] Plaintiffs suing for desegregation would have to target the school districts one by one, a far more cumbersome procedure than a single suit against the state board. The legislature adopted the recommendation and established a pupil assignment plan, instructing local boards to make assignments in the "best interests of the child." No specific mention of race was made, but the expectation was that all children would be assigned to segregated schools. Militant segregationists in the legislature proposed stronger bills, including one that would terminate state aid to any local school system that integrated and another that provided state money for private, segregated academies. But the lawyers who led the legislature knew that the militants' approach would not pass constitutional muster. They convinced legislators that the pupil assignment approach without mention of race was better designed to pass federal court tests or at least to delay desegregation. In 1955, the legislature also passed a resolution declaring the mixing of the races to be both impractical and a threat to the state's public schools.[35]

Before adjourning, the legislature asked Hodges to appoint another advisory committee to continue to study the education situation. Hodges reappointed Pearsall as chair but reduced the committee size to seven members, all of them white male and all lawyers or elected officials. Hodges justified his failure to appoint blacks by saying that serving on the committee would put them under too much of a strain. Indeed, the three black members of the former committee, all state employees, had occupied a difficult position. Civil rights advocates wanted them to be advocates for integration. White segregationists did not want them on the committee at all. They had been ineffective representatives of the African American community, yet their presence had probably softened the rhetoric and overt racism of committee deliberations. Hodges was not about to appoint more outspoken civil rights activists, such as NAACP leaders, whom he and other officials labeled "radicals."[36]

The 1954 Supreme Court ruling had left much unsaid. From April 11 to April 15, 1955, the high court heard more arguments from plaintiffs seeking speedy desegregation and southern white attorneys seeking to delay or negate the *Brown* ruling. Assistant attorney general I. Beverly Lake represented North Carolina. Lake had a law degree from Wake Forest, a master's of law from Harvard, and doctorate in law from Columbia, so most acquaintances called him "Dr. Lake." Lake made constitutional arguments against implementation and added that forced racial integration in the schools "would result in such violent opposition as to endanger the continued existence of the schools." On May 31, the Supreme Court issued its decision in *Brown v. Board of Education of Topeka II*. The 1955 ruling declared that conditions might differ from place to place and ordered the states to desegregate with "all deliberate speed," the word "deliberate" hinting that states could move slowly on the matter. The opinion, written by Chief Justice Warren, had been a product of compromise. To southern states, it provided an excuse for delay. Yet the court had reaffirmed its 1954 ruling that state-mandated racial segregation violated the Fourteenth Amendment.

As in the first *Brown* case, the specific cases were remanded to the lower federal courts of origin to determine what was required of the states.[37]

In July 1955, the Fourth Circuit Court of Appeals in Richmond issued an opinion in *Briggs v. Elliott*, the South Carolina case that had been one of the cases the Supreme Court consolidated under the name *Brown v. Board of Education of Topeka*. Chief Judge John J. Parker, a North Carolina Republican who had narrowly failed to win Senate confirmation for a seat on the U.S. Supreme Court in 1930, authored the opinion. Parker wrote that the Supreme Court's decision did not specifically require integration but that it did prohibit the "use of governmental power to enforce segregation." Parker stated that "segregation as occurs as the result of voluntary action was not forbidden."[38] By this time, Parker was a highly respected jurist, so his opinion carried weight. But the ruling, though a defensible interpretation of the *Brown II* ruling, seemed out of touch with the spirit of *Brown I*, which passionately described the harm segregation caused to minority children and was as much a sociological treatise as a legal one. However, Hodges and the other leading North Carolinians jumped on the bandwagon of "voluntary segregation." The NAACP saw it as a subterfuge to maintain total segregation and vowed to press the fight for full and immediate desegregation.

On August 8, Hodges delivered a speech carried by sixty radio stations and ten television stations—all of the state's major electronic media outlets. "North Carolina now stands at the crossroads," he warned. He framed the choice as either segregated public schools or no public schools. Hodges seemed conciliatory when he urged North Carolinians to think as a unified people or citizenry as opposed to separate races. The goal, he said, was to do what was best for *all* children. Hodges never explained precisely how a modest level of integration might destroy the public school system, but unlike more strident southern politicians, Hodges's rhetoric was not of the crass or blatantly racist variety. He hoped his approach would be more effective.[39]

Hodges attempted to gain momentum for his position, appearing before the all-black North Carolina Teachers' Association and later an audience largely consisting of students at North Carolina A&T. The teachers were polite but offered only tepid applause. When speaking at A&T, Hodges used the then commonplace white pronunciations "nigro" or "nigra" (with a short "i")—accounts varied—rather than the standard "Negro." The students in the audience found his pronunciation insulting and started coughing and sliding their feet across the floor. Hodges denied that he had intended a racial slur and considered the students' reaction an act of rudeness. The incident was a good metaphor for the African American response to Hodges's call for voluntary segregation. Civil rights leaders—at that time the NAACP and local political action committees were the most prominent—turned a cold shoulder toward Hodges, calling for immediate and full desegregation. Hodges had failed in his objective of achieving biracial support.

Whites remained the ruling race, and segregation plans moved ahead. The 1956 Pearsall Report urged a continuation of the pupil assignment plan, which required potentially burdensome administrative appeals in state courts for blacks requesting admission to white schools. The committee also recommended a constitutional amendment authorizing state tuition grants for private school attendance for children whose parents did not want them to go to integrated public schools. The amendment included a "local option clause" that permitted any community to vote to close its public schools they were ordered to integrate by a federal court.

Hodges supported the report and called a special session of the legislature to adopt the amendment. Under the North Carolina Constitution, a proposed amendment must be approved by three-fifths of the Senate and the House before being submitted to the voters. If the proposed amendment is subsequently approved by a majority of the voters who cast ballots on it, it becomes part of the constitution. Hodges presented the Pearsall Plan to the legislature on July 23. It was overwhelmingly approved on July 26, though a few ultrasegregationists proposed the outright state prohibition of integrated schools. Hodges and legislative leaders countered that laws requiring any school facing integration to close would be knocked down by the federal courts and make the public schools more vulnerable to immediate racial integration.

Black leaders and the North Carolina Teachers' Association opposed the plan. So did the Parent-Teacher Association (PTA) umbrella group. The local PTA units, more inclined toward bake sales, Halloween carnivals, and other fund-raising events, turned deaf ears to their state leadership. Most voters, black and white, saw the Pearsall amendment as permitting them to take a stand for or against school integration. In later years, liberals, moderates, and even conservative white politicians who had campaigned for the plan asserted that the whole idea was in fact a "holding action," a "safety valve," or a stratagem to permit the orderly and peaceful desegregation of the schools.[40] In 1956, however, the plan was touted as a method of maintaining segregation and "saving the public schools." It was a winning combination. Except for Catholic schools, military base schools, and a few private day schools in cities, all young North Carolinians attended state public schools. North Carolina had among the country's lowest proportions of students in private schools. The amendment was submitted to the voters at a special election in September—the matter was too urgent to wait for the general election in November—and was approved by an overwhelming 471,657–107,757 margin. It carried all one hundred of North Carolina's counties, with the greatest support in rural areas across the state. Greene County in the coastal plan, long defiant in its attitude toward integration, cast 2,707 votes for the amendment and 106 against. Clay, an isolated and Republican-leaning county in the far southwest, voted 772 for and 66 against.

In 1956, segregationist members of the U.S. Congress circulated the Declaration of Constitutional Principles, more commonly known as the Southern Manifesto. The document attacked the *Brown* decision as an abuse of judicial power and an incursion on states' rights. It called for the resort to all lawful means of resistance, with a hint that disobedience was in order. Most southern senators and representatives signed the manifesto, including North Carolina senators Ervin and Scott. Ervin had played a leading role in drafting the document. Nine North Carolina congressmen—eight Democrats and Republican Jonas—also signed. In defiance of political realities, three North Carolina representatives declined to sign: Democrats Charles B. Deane of the Eighth District, Richard T. Chatham of the Fifth, and Harold Cooley of the Fourth.[41] Deane was the longtime recording secretary of the North Carolina State Baptist Convention. His Washington assistant, John Lang, later recalled a conversation in which Deane said he did not want to sign even though he knew that would be a political risk. Lang advised him to sign as a "holding action." Deane replied, "The Lord tells me not to sign it." Lang then said, "Well, I'm not going to be the one to get between you and the Lord."[42] In the May 26, 1956, Democratic primary, challenger Paul Kitchen of Wadesboro, a manifesto supporter, defeated Deane, 23,802–19,658. In the Fifth District, which included Winston-Salem, Ralph Scott of Danbury (no kin to Kerr Scott) challenged Chatham. Chatham was a wealthy and mildly conservative manufacturer who probably could have stayed in Congress for years if he had signed the manifesto. Scott won, 28,335–22,803.

In the Fourth District Democratic primary, conservative radio commentator W. E. Debnam ran against Cooley, then the chair of the House Agriculture Committee and a fighter. Debnam blasted Cooley for not signing the manifesto. Cooley claimed to support segregation but argued that the manifesto did nothing to help the cause but constituted mere grandstanding. After announcing his candidacy, Debnam lost his job with WPTF radio. Cooley portrayed Debnam as a Republican sympathizer, a serious charge in a district that extended from Raleigh into the tobacco country of eastern and piedmont North Carolina. Specifically, Cooley charged that Debnam's book, *Weep No More, My Lady* (1950), had slandered the wife of the "beloved president Roosevelt," although the congressman wisely did not address Debnam's specific charges against Eleanor Roosevelt. Cooley hit at pocketbook issues, pointing out that he was the chief congressional protector of the federal tobacco price-support program.[43] Economic issues and the powers of incumbency ultimately trumped fears of integration, and Cooley won reelection, 34,903–20,650.

In the southeastern Seventh District (Wilmington and Fayetteville), incumbent Frank Ertel Carlyle of Lumberton, a mild segregationist who had signed the manifesto, lost to his more stridently segregationist challenger, former U.S. senator Alton Lennon of Wilmington.

## LIMITED COMPETITION AND ANOTHER DEATH

There was no competitive statewide primary for governor or senator in the second half of the 1950s. Having succeeded Umstead in midterm, Hodges was in the unusual position of being able to run for governor while an incumbent. His most serious challenge might have come from Terry Sanford, the political activist and civic leader who had served one term (1953–55) in the N.C. Senate. Sanford had gone around the state speaking for the Pearsall Plan, which he said would both maintain segregation and keep the schools open. He had a wide circle of friends from the Young Democratic Clubs and Scott organization. Sanford's biographers, Howard E. Covington Jr. and Marion A. Ellis, described a scene in which Sanford was about to walk into the State Board of Election office to file as a candidate for the spring 1956 Democratic primary and then stepped back.[44] A Sanford candidacy would have been daring. He could have mounted a lively challenge, but one unlikely to have prevailed over Hodges's establishment ties, incumbency, maturity, and eloquence. So Hodges coasted along with token opposition. He won the May primary with 401,082 votes to a total of 65,752 for three opponents. In the November general election, Hodges beat Republican Kyle Hayes, 760,480–375,379. In the same year, incumbent senator Ervin, also seeking his first full term, beat Winston-Salem mayor Marshall Kurfrees in the Democratic primary, 360,967–65,512.

In April 1958, four years into his U.S. Senate term, Kerr Scott suffered a heart attack and died. In a decision that dismayed Scott loyalists, Hodges appointed Alamance County textile industrialist Benjamin Everett Jordan of Saxapahaw to the seat. Jordan and Scott were cousins by marriage and onetime allies, but the two men had clashed on internal party matters.

Jordan had become cozy with more conservative Democrats and had supported Smith over Graham for senator in 1950 and Umstead over Scott-backed Olive for governor in 1952.[45]

The old factional Democratic Party competition of business-oriented conservatives versus economic-populist-oriented insurgents seemed to be dormant. Business liked Hodges. With their hero, Scott, gone, the insurgents were not sure where to turn. The leadership vacuum reverberated to the benefit of Hodges and the business classes. However, they had maintained the upper hand throughout much of the period since 1900. And like earlier business-friendly governors such as Cameron Morrison and O. Max Gardner, Hodges had some claim to being a forward-thinking progressive. Any major shakeup would have to wait until at least 1960.

Despite the Democratic monopoly, Republicans showed signs of life. Jonas won reelection in 1954, 1956, and 1958 in the Charlotte-area Tenth Congressional District. Having won four times in a row, he was no fluke. And in 1956, Eisenhower came close to taking North Carolina. The presidential contest was a rerun of 1952, Eisenhower against Stevenson. This time around, Eisenhower won 57 percent of the national popular vote, though Stevenson narrowly took North Carolina, 590,530–575,062. The urban black precincts in North Carolina and across the South voted Republican, the only time this would happen in a presidential race from 1936 through 2012. Stevenson had deemphasized civil rights in his 1956 bid, perhaps believing that if he lost the white southern vote, he would win no states at all. Some blacks feared that the Democrats had taken African American support for granted. Voting Republican was in part an act of retribution toward southern Democrats, the politicians who led the attacks on the *Brown* decision. Moreover, Eisenhower had appointed Earl Warren, the architect of the *Brown* decision, to the Supreme Court.[46] Without his heavy vote from whites in eastern North Carolina, most of them committed segregationists, Stevenson would have lost the state.

## CRACKS IN THE DOOR

As signatures were gathered for the Southern Manifesto, a bus boycott challenged the social fabric in Alabama's capital city, Montgomery. On December 1, 1955, Rosa Parks refused to surrender her seat and move to the back of a crowded city bus. After her arrest, blacks began a boycott that lasted until December 20, 1956, when the U.S. Supreme Court ruled in *Browder v. Gale* that government-mandated segregation on city buses violated the Equal Protection Clause of the Fourteenth Amendment.[47] Martin Luther King Jr., the young, barely known pastor of Montgomery's Dexter Avenue

Baptist Church, was among the boycott's leaders. At first, news of the boycott was consigned to the back pages of newspapers around the country. But when local officials engaged in violent acts against the boycotters, the story moved to the front pages, *Life* magazine, and the television network newscasts. In response to the Court's ruling, North Carolina cities dropped bus segregation, though local authorities and bus companies hoped that most people would adhere to tradition. In Durham, green paint covered the signs that had read, "All white patrons sit from front to back. All colored patrons sit from back to front." Old habits die hard, but blacks began to test the new ruling. They met frowns but no resistance. Times had indeed changed in the twelve and a half years since Herbert Council shot Booker T. Spicely for brashly insisting on the right to sit at the front of a Durham bus. Greyhound and Trailways bus stations, however, remained as segregated as ever: separate waiting rooms, ticket counters, rest rooms, water fountains, and restaurants.

When the 1956–57 school year began, court-ordered desegregation took place in Clinton, Tennessee; otherwise, southern public schools remained segregated. On June 23, 1957, the school boards of the three largest North Carolina cities—Charlotte, Greensboro, and Winston-Salem—convened. The boards and administrators of the three city school systems had informally consulted one another about what they would be doing. At the conclusion of each meeting, officials announced that a limited number of black students would be admitted to formerly all-white schools in September 1957. This was the first voluntary public school integration in the old Confederate states. The boards and superintendents in these three cities favored limited school integration but knew that they were taking a risk, which is why they coordinated their actions. City school boards were to some extent shielded from the political process, as members were appointed to fixed terms by their city councils. Directly elected school boards—the method used by most county boards of education—might not have been so bold. Direct democracy was no friend of racial equality.

City leadership (and more discreetly state leadership) also had strategic motives for accepting applications from a few black students. Voluntary integration might persuade the federal courts to allow local officials to control the process. All three cities wanted to grow and attract outside business. A major race flare-up would harm their prospects. Business and political leaders believed, probably correctly, that locally mandated integration would be better received by the white public than would court-ordered integration. All three cities had wealthy and powerful hierarchies whose members thought that at least token public school integration was inevitable. When they united behind a plan, it usually succeeded. These power brokers—some openly, others quietly—supported the boards.[48]

In September 1957, bedlam and violence erupted when Arkansas governor Orval Faubus and segregationist militants resisted court-ordered desegregation at Little Rock Central High School. For days, it was the big national news story. Black students secured admission to the high school, but only after President Eisenhower reluctantly ordered federal troops into the city to quell the disturbance. The national media contrasted North Carolina's voluntary and "peaceful" integration with the defiance of Little Rock. In fact, however, the North Carolina cities experienced serious tensions. The most trouble came in Charlotte, where "small-scale" violence occurred.[49] There and to a degree in the other cities, black students sometimes received the silent treatment in school and bullying on the nearby streets afterward. Teachers ranged from welcoming and empathetic to glaringly hostile. But a big step had been taken. The principle of school integration was established. A few other school systems had followed by 1960. For the time being, North Carolina's reputation as the most progressive of southern states remained intact.

### THE MARKETING IMPRESARIO

Hodges was a pacesetter who re-created the office of governor. On economic development, he initiated a model for governors around the country. Hodges envisioned an office that would recruit business and industry from other parts of the United States and from around the world. Until the 1950s, most governors sought to protect existing businesses and industries but traveled out of state more for political events, vacations, or rare trade missions. Hodges approached industrial recruitment with a missionary zeal. As past governors had seen education as the key to moving the state onward and upward, Hodges looked to the holy grail of outside capital.[50]

In 1957, Hodges persuaded the legislature to modify tax laws to benefit multistate corporations. The proportion of corporate income subject to North Carolina taxes was reduced. Whatever revenue might be lost in lower taxes and franchise fees, Hodges believed would be more than offset by the increases in factories, workers, economic stimulation, and consequently tax receipts. North Carolina advertised aggressively for new business and emphasized its "good labor climate," a well-understood euphemism for weak or nonexistent unions. Industries beyond the traditional big three—textiles, tobacco, and furniture—settled in the state. As early as 1955, Hodges had looked toward a joint effort of government, business, and universities to establish a research center to develop medicines and technologies for the future. Key planners in the earliest stages included bankers Robert Hanes, Archie Davis, and George Watts Hill and university presidents William Friday of UNC and Hollis Edens of Duke. Davis led a fund-raising drive to buy the five thousand acres of pine forest, tobacco land, and cornfields near where Durham, Wake, and Orange Counties came together, with most of the immediately developable property in southeastern Durham County. Hodges and other promoters stressed the proximity of the proposed Research Triangle Park to the research universities and laboratories in Chapel Hill, Durham, and Raleigh.

By the end of Hodges's term in 1961, the land had been purchased. In September 1961, eight months after Hodges stepped down, *Harper's* magazine ran a piece on the research and economic boom propelled by the proximity of universities in two locations—Route 128, a circumferential highway around Boston, and the Pacific peninsula between San Francisco and San Jose (later known as Silicon Valley). The article cautioned that few places had the special chemistry required to duplicate Boston and the Bay area but pointed to North Carolina's fledgling research park as a place that might blossom because of its ambience and excellent academic institutions.[51] Such ideas remained more vision than reality until 1964, when Chemstrand Corporation built a four-hundred-employee research center and the U.S. Forest Service established a laboratory at the park, a good place for it since the surrounding forest was almost as thick as ever. But the Park's days of glory and traffic jams loomed ahead.

Hodges seized every opportunity to advertise North Carolina businesses. Superficially the stateliest of governors, he was also a great showman. On one occasion a team from *Life* magazine, then one of the largest circulating in the United States, visited the governor's mansion to highlight Hodges's role as a business promoter. The picture essay told what Hodges was doing and included a number of revealing shots. In one, Hodges, fully clothed in suit and tie, stood in a gushing bathroom shower to illustrate the durability of North Carolina–made fabrics. In still another photo, Hodges posed in his North Carolina–made undershorts as his trousers dropped down. The photo was captioned "Tar Heel Briefs."[52] Mrs. Hodges, who learned of the stunt when the magazine came out, was horrified. Smooth-talking recruiter, publicist, or avuncular male model, Hodges did what he thought it took to foster business-driven prosperity.

### THE SPIRIT OF A DECADE

Luther Hodges reflected the overriding attitudes of the 1950s. He believed that the American destiny was greatness and economic abundance. Since the Civil War, the capitalist system had propelled growth. Earlier North Carolina governors had close ties to business and industry, but they were attorneys. Hodges knew the corporate world from the inside and had faith in what it could do for society. Americans have had a love-hate attitude toward big business. They admire its ingenuity and to a point its cold efficiency. They look to business captains with a combination of awe and envy. At the same time, citizens blame big business (along with big government) for a host of ills—greed, gross inequality, impersonal bureaucracies or service departments, and lack of sensitivity to the day-to-day struggles of the average citizen. Economic populism arises from these resentments. Such attitudes had propelled the Franklin Roosevelt presidency, still wildly popular in North Carolina. North Carolina retained a latent strain of economic populism throughout the 1950s, but after Scott, it remained under wraps. Much as in the 1900–1948 period, mildly conservative business leaders and attorneys dominated the Democratic Party and the state. Ten years after V. O. Key Jr. published his epic *Southern Politics in State and Nation*, what he had called the progressive plutocracy still governed North Carolina.[53]

The *Brown* rulings and early civil rights movement reignited the flames of racism. Many North Carolina whites demanded the racial status quo, the preservation of segregation. Hodges got the message and manned the wall, but only to a point. Then he let change occur—gradually.

Hodges was both a hard-nosed realist and a dreamer. He possessed a puritanical streak and a sense of self-righteousness. He was an active Methodist who could be found regularly in a church pew. He was impatient with the political system even as he used it well.

Hodges made his mark as an industrial recruiter, but during his gubernatorial administration, race emerged as the most tormenting issue for domestic American politics, including North Carolina. Twenty-first-century optimists may argue that economic modernization and increased national wealth inevitably would have led to racial equality. Such optimism is dubious. Whites in the Black Belts—the heavily black counties—were no more eager to relinquish political control in 1950 than they had been in 1920. These counties still had economies based on agriculture, with mechanized farm equipment, electric lights, cars, and television providing the modern touches. Attitudes had not changed. The cities and mill towns supported segregation and white supremacy. The textile industry was rigidly segregated, and if anything, the tobacco industry had moved backward since earlier days.

Historian John W. Cell has argued that industrial barons were leaders in perpetuating the separation of the races during the first sixty years of the century.[54] But the powerful business oligarchy had a lot of company. By the 1950s, support for segregation had softened among whites, but not enough to bring about appreciable change. The typical voter—the small-town insurance agent, the hardware dealer, the barber, the school principal, the one-hundred-acre farmer—resisted change. Maintenance of segregation was one of their abiding principles. Many were deeply racist and used "nigra" rather than the then standard "Negro." They voted, and they would have wielded their stinging whip on any candidate so bold as to advocate true racial equality. Racism was far more than a conspiracy of a self-centered group of millionaires or of mill hands. It penetrated all layers of white society, from the lowest to the middle and to the most privileged.

New and revitalized forces challenged the old order: a federal court system more committed to a literal interpretation of the Fourteenth and Fifteenth Amendments, a growing and politically vocal African American community in major northern states that pushed for more racial equality in the South and North, and an insecure but increasingly aggressive cadre of black leaders in southern states that was willing to challenge the existing order. Seasoned civil rights advocates still thought that court action provided their best hope, but many were tired of waiting. A more aggressive mode, such as the Montgomery Bus Boycott, looked appealing to the young and restive.

For the white American middle classes, probably few times have been so imbued with a spirit of optimism as the late 1950s. True, a small-scale recession hit late in the decade, and some farmers were hurting. But the god of technology and scientific advance seemed poised to solve almost any problem. People were no longer quite so nervous about a nuclear attack from the Soviet Union. Except in a few urban outposts and universities, a comfortable conformity had set in. Church pews were packed, and civic clubs went about their good deeds. North Carolina and a few other parts of the American southland were forging more than ever into the new world even as they clung to a racial caste system more akin to that of South Africa. The signs of prosperity were all around: televisions, automatic washing machines, high-powered sports cars, and Cadillacs with enormous tail fins. There were still roads to conquer, all part of the inevitable path toward progress. There remained what whites called the "Negro problem" or "colored situation" and blacks called "the long struggle for equality." And there remained the fact that only small numbers of blacks—such as former baseball star now turned businessman Jackie Robinson and a few Durham banking and insurance executives—had come close to achieving the

American dream. A growing black middle class felt the sting of segregation almost every day but built bonds through churches, schools, and fraternal organizations. A revolution was coming, one that would extend down the southeastern crescent from Virginia and North Carolina to Louisiana and Texas. The 1960s beckoned.

## CHAPTER THREE

# There's a New Day Coming

Seldom does history bend itself to the human calendar. But barely into the new decade, dramatic events unfolded. They started in Greensboro on February 1, 1960, when four young men from North Carolina A&T State College, an all-black public school, quietly seated themselves on lunch counter stools in Woolworth's five-and-dime. The demonstrators were met with icy stares, and the lunch counter closed for the day, but larger numbers of students came on subsequent days.[1] Greensboro liked to think of itself as one of the most progressive cities in the South, a place with many colleges, a humanitarian streak brought on by its Quaker legacy, and bustling commerce and industry. It was also one of the region's first cities to implement small-scale integration in the public schools. Still, it remained a segregated city. The sit-in movement that started in Greensboro galloped across North Carolina and the old Confederacy. A new day was dawning, but it was fraught with risk and a potential for violence.

Residents of piedmont North Carolina enjoyed sunny, mild weather on February 12, even if Abraham Lincoln's birthday was little more celebrated than Groundhog Day. However, the next morning, in a break from the generally soft southern winters of the 1950s, they awoke to surprising sleet and snow. The rest of the month was wintry, and people shivered as the civil rights demonstrations continued. March came but did not bring the usual golden forsythia, purple thrift, flowering cherry trees, and new green growth on the weeping willow trees. The piedmont, mountains, and even parts of the coastal plain had snowstorms on the first three Wednesdays in March. The election season had come. Contenders and would-be contenders vied for public notice. Until more balmy days in late March and the explosive riot of spring in April with its succession of dogwood and azalea blossoms, the candidates in waiting and an incipient social revolution took back seats to the long, late winter.

A small number of North Carolina political contests had stood out for their bloodletting: the general elections of 1898, 1900, 1928, and the Democratic primary for senator in 1950. The gubernatorial primary of 1960 turned into a pivotal event in the development of modern North Carolina politics. Journalist John Drescher's sharp and balanced analysis of the primary argues that Terry Sanford's campaign set the stage for the type of progressive appeal that successful southern Democrats would offer for forty years to come.[2] It did, but the campaign also left wounds that still have not fully healed.

For a front-runner, Sanford's public service background was modest. A state senator from Fayetteville (1953–55) and an attorney, his greatest accomplishments were in Democratic Party activities. As a paratrooper in World War II, survival had been a major achievement. Sanford made valuable connections when an undergraduate in Chapel Hill before the war and a law student afterward. He was meticulous about political detail and built possibly the widest network of friends of any young man in the state. Through strong support for public education and occasional opposition to racial segregation in the Methodist Church, Sanford developed a progressive reputation. He was elected president of the North Carolina Young Democratic Clubs in 1949. He managed former governor W. Kerr Scott's 1954 U.S. senatorial campaign. That alliance provided Sanford with inroads into the Scott wing of the party, but it created potential problems for him with the state's business-oriented conservatives.[3] Through Jaycee activities, Sanford had established links with younger businesspeople.

In 1956, in the name of support for the public schools, Sanford campaigned for the proposed Pearsall Plan, which the state's leaders had sold as a means of protecting segregation and public education. Sanford later described the proposal as a "safety valve" and said that even in the 1950s, he had favored a quick movement toward racial equality.[4] Friends verified that Sanford was critical of segregation in private discussions, but in keeping with the times and his ambitions, he was publicly coy on the subject. Prior to running for governor, Sanford discreetly established links with key black political figures. He was hoping for a 1960 campaign in which integration would not be discussed in any public forum and in which he would receive the quiet backing of African American voters, who comprised 10–12 percent of the primary electorate. Sanford knew that liberals became endangered when race became the dominant issue. Any hopes for a campaign free of overt racial conflict were quickly dashed, however, and the 1960 contest became one of the most racially charged in the state's history. A national campaign for black civil rights erupted, and at the last minute North Carolina's most prominent segregationist, Dr. I. Beverly Lake, announced his candidacy for governor.

In his February 4 opening statement and throughout the first primary campaign, Sanford stressed the themes of educational progress and economic development. He endorsed the program of the United Forces for Education, a public school lobby, which called for a 21 percent salary increase for teachers and a massive increase in spending for other school programs. Sanford said that he would push for the program even if it required a tax increase, a risky move. But in the early 1960s, the antitax fervor was not what it would be in the last quarter of the twentieth century.[5]

Moderate to conservative North Carolina political activists and business leaders looked for a safe candidate who would be a moderate segregationist in the mold of current governor Luther Hodges and, like Hodges, a promoter of economic growth. Lake, a strident segregationist and vocal Hodges critic, was out of the question. That left two contenders, John Larkins and Malcolm Seawell. Larkins, a nine-term state senator from the small Jones County town of Trenton, announced his candidacy on January 20. He had built contacts as chair of the state Democratic Party in the early and mid-1950s, and he gathered support from local-level party activists across eastern North Carolina and in some mountain counties. He ran as a fiscal conservative who would hold the line on taxes while providing teachers with a 15 percent across-the-board salary increase. Larkins was a racial moderate, expressing support for segregation while avoiding fiery rhetoric. He hoped for Governor Hodges's support, though he and the governor had developed a mutual distrust.[6]

The silver-haired Seawell was from Lumberton, in the southern coastal plain, and currently occupied the attorney general's office. He was a fiscal conservative and outspoken opponent of labor union militants and the black sit-in movement. He was also a critic of the Ku Klux Klan (KKK) and the bitter-end segregationists, and he supported token integration in the schools as the most reasonable response to the *Brown* ruling. Seawell and Lake had split over the state's position in segregation cases. Lake saw Seawell as an agent of appeasement, and Seawell's entry into the race increased the likelihood of a Lake candidacy. Partly because of his behind-the-scenes support from Hodges, Seawell attracted money and other support from many of North Carolina's prominent business and professional leaders.[7]

Lake had for months talked of running as a champion of segregation and states' rights. Nevertheless, his campaign was a long shot. Lake's campaign had little money, and he was a former academic not accustomed to the rough-and-tumble of primary campaigns. Furthermore, Lake and Larkins had been friends since their years as classmates at Wake Forest Law School.

Lake, the son of a Wake Forest College science professor, was a popular law professor at his alma mater. An ardent critic of big utility companies, he had some economic populist instincts. In the 1950 senatorial primary, Lake supported liberal Frank Porter Graham over victorious conservative Willis Smith, though Lake's position may have reflected a lingering personal dispute with Smith.[8] Lake had criticized Smith's campaign for inflammatory racial rhetoric while suggesting that Graham might be better able to maintain the racial status quo.[9] Lake considered himself a champion of "cordial" race relations, but he vociferously opposed the *Brown* rulings and had represented the state before the Supreme Court when the second *Brown* case was argued. Lake emerged as North Carolina's most articulate advocate of segregation. As a state deputy attorney general, he specialized in civil rights cases in the mid- and late 1950s, with his opposition to compromise fueling a feud with Hodges and Seawell. Lake then left his position with the state and became a law partner of Raleigh's A. J. Fletcher, a noted patron of both the arts and conservative causes and an emerging media magnate.

Lake decided to enter the race after a meeting with prospective financial and political backers in Rocky Mount. Those present included Dr. Clarence Bailey and his son, Jack, who later became a conservative Republican activist, as well as Robert Morgan. Members of the Bailey family made major financial commitments to Lake. Morgan, then a senator from Harnett County and former law student and admirer of Lake, was named his campaign manager. Morgan had economic populist instincts and would have backed Sanford if Lake had not joined the race.[10]

When Lake announced his bid for the governorship on March 1, 1960, picketers protesting lunch counter segregation in Raleigh were visible from his office. Lake said that the preservation of the social order and segregation would be his campaign theme. A day earlier, Lake had traveled to New York to defend segregation on Dave Garroway's nationally televised *Today* show.[11] He blasted the sit-ins and proclaimed that any restaurant or store owner should have the right to determine who would be served in the establishment. Other planks in Lake's platform promised school improvements and an equitable tax distribution between individuals and corporations, with the suggestion that individuals should get better treatment.[12]

Race eclipsed all else. The media often identified him as "segregationist" I. Beverly Lake instead of the "gubernatorial candidate" label used for Larkins, Sanford, and Seawell.

In many respects, Lake defined the contest. The other three contenders would have preferred to avoid the race topic altogether except for generalized support for harmony, goodwill, and voluntary segregation. Lake's presence made them uncomfortable. Candidates might say that the big issue was education or economic progress, yet both they and the voters knew that race was the undercurrent.

In the 1950s, most segregation battles had been fought in the courts, with the National Association for the Advancement of Colored People (NAACP) as a plaintiff. Civil rights activists had for the most part acted within the law. Except for the Montgomery Bus Boycott, these activists had focused on school segregation and voting rights. In 1960, however, their tactics and goals were changing. The sit-in movement had spread across much of the American South, creating a climate that was ripe for what would later be called a white backlash. For Lake, the coincidence was fortuitous. As the campaign progressed, the sit-in deadlock continued. Governor Hodges, other state leaders, and all the candidates denounced the demonstrations, but Lake seemed to relish such attacks.

Nearly all political strategists assumed a Sanford lead in the first primary. Larkins and Seawell, who thought they were fighting each other for a position in the runoff, were critical of Sanford. Sanford, in contrast, offered only mild attacks on Lake, Larkins, and Seawell, presumably in hope of gaining the support of the candidates who failed to make the runoff. Sanford's campaign saturated the state with a commercial that featured a song announcing, "The man on the go for the state on the go! That's Terry Sanford! There's a new day coming, so for your next governor, vote for Terry Sanford!" When the song ended, Sanford spoke briefly—in his strong North Carolina accent—in support of "quality education."[13] Lake asserted that only he had taken a clear and straightforward position on segregation; the other candidates, including Sanford, responded by criticizing the NAACP.

Polls were cruder and rarer than they are today, although national pollster Louis Harris, a friend of Sanford, conducted a poll for his campaign—the first commissioned for a state-level campaign in North Carolina. Harris and other pollsters erred in failing to predict a big Lake vote. His rallies attracted ever-larger crowds, and his audiences seemed to be more enthusiastic than those of the other candidates. When Lake expressed "goodwill" toward people of all races, there was silence. But when he launched into an attack on civil rights demonstrations and those who would oppose the "southern way of life," there was loud applause.[14]

Even those astute political observers who had detected a surge for Lake were generally unprepared for his solid second-place finish. In the May primary, Sanford received 269,463 votes, Lake 181,692, Seawell 101,148, and Larkins 100,757. Sanford's organization had performed well, but he fell far short of a majority. Larkins and Seawell supporters were stunned by their failures to reach the 20 percent level.

Lake and his supporters knew from election night that they would stay in the race and seek to topple Sanford. However, no runoff announcement was made until early the next week. Many of Larkins's supporters were conservatives from eastern North Carolina, and Lake hoped to win them over by appealing to their concerns about Sanford's liberalism. Would principal figures in the Larkins and Seawell camps line up with Sanford as the almost certain winner? Race remained the wild card.

### THE POLITICS OF RACE AND PERSONAL DESTRUCTION

The Lake-Sanford runoff was one of the most boisterous affairs in North Carolina political history. In announcing his second primary bid, Lake's tone was civil enough. Calling Sanford a friend, Lake commended his opponent's ability and "excellent character." Lake said, "I like him, but I am opposed to his economic policies and program, and I am opposed to the mixing of white and Negro children in our public schools."[15]

Lake's kickoff statement stressed support for a sound conservative fiscal policy and described Sanford's program as "spend, spend, spend and tax, tax, tax." Because Lake was a blend of economic populism and social conservatism, his introductory emphasis on fiscal conservatism was likely strategic. Much of the state's business community, he thought, would be up for grabs, and fiscal conservatives would feel threatened by the possibility of greatly increased taxes. Lake sought endorsements and financial support from former Larkins and Seawell supporters, acknowledging that his campaign was running on a "financial shoestring." Yet fears of Lake's "radicalism" on race, combined with the perception that Sanford would prevail in the end, diminished Lake's prospects for big-business support.

The opening statement quickly turned to race, the subject that most interested the media as well as many voters. Lake reiterated his opposition to the NAACP and his pledge to resist the NAACP "program"—presumably its advocacy of school desegregation—"at every step." Lake suggested that he could create a climate against integration in North Carolina, not at the time a daunting task. While race was Lake's campaign trademark, he was sensitive to the possibility that some North Carolinians might find his rhetoric extremist or frightening, so he attacked Sanford and his supporters for suggesting that Lake's approach would result in the closure of public schools. Lake argued that North Carolina governors did not have the legal or constitutional power to shut down the public schools and said that he would strive to keep the schools open: "I shall continue to fight the NAACP, and with your help, we shall keep your schools open, equal, and separate."[16]

Lake suggested that the 1957 clash over school desegregation in Little Rock, Arkansas, had resulted from the city board of education's attempt at voluntary token integration. Such efforts, he said, could lead to similar fights and animosity in North Carolina. While Lake was correct in saying that moderates dominated the Little Rock board, he failed to mention that integration there occurred under a court order and that Governor Orval Faubus had inflamed the situation. Yet Lake appeared to be subtly disassociating himself from such firebrands as Faubus, perhaps to deflect the charge that his policies might result in school closures. The bitter experience of Prince Edward County, Virginia, which had closed its public schools in 1959 rather than integrate, cast a shadow over North Carolina. Lake's statement was carried live over Raleigh's one television station, WRAL, owned by Fletcher, Lake's law partner. Many news-oriented radio stations, including Raleigh's WPTF, also provided live coverage.

Sanford demanded and got equal time, firing back with a vengeance that forever poisoned his personal relationship with Lake. "Let's get this straight right now on the race issue. . . . I have been and will continue to oppose to the end domination or direction by the NAACP. Professor Lake is bringing on integration when he stirs this up. I don't believe in playing race against race or group against group. Let's use our brains instead of our mouths." Sanford asserted that the real issue was how well North Carolina's children would be educated. North Carolina, Sanford said, ranked poorly in education and needed to improve. He charged that Lake's race-based campaign was a diversion from the real issue.[17]

Sanford's follow-up broadcast on WRAL and other stations surprised friends and foes alike. His usually mild-mannered—some would say boring—public persona turned to one of belligerence. He said that this runoff had the potential to be the most bitter in the state's history. While calling for restraint, Sanford mounted a political and personal attack on Lake. Professing "shock" over Lake's remarks, Sanford said that Lake was using the race issue to set up a "straw man." Strictly on issues and qualifications, Sanford asserted, he would beat Lake with ease. Consequently, he argued, Lake was trying to win by poisoning the state's racial climate. With more force than sincerity, Sanford asserted that he, too, opposed integration and that he could control the integration threat, while Lake could not. "Professor Lake yells about mixing the races, about NAACP domination, and he is appealing to blind prejudice for the pure and simple purpose of getting a few votes. I did not grow up in an ivory tower of a college campus as the professor did. I was raised around the cotton patches and tobacco fields of Scotland County, and I know how to handle the racial situation better than a theoretical college professor."[18]

Sanford declared that Lake's opposition even to limited integration might lead the federal government to mount an all-out assault on segregation in North Carolina. Citing the Little Rock experience and invoking Prince Edward County, Sanford raised the specter of closed public schools and federal troops occupying the streets of North Carolina. He portrayed Lake as a dupe for those who might favor massive integration in the state and his programs as leading "to bloodshed and integrated or closed schools."[19]

Frank Graham's shadow also hung over the campaign. Sanford believed that Graham had lost to Smith's segregationist campaign in 1950 because Graham was too gentlemanly in his behavior.[20] Sanford did not err on the side of gentility. His attacks on Lake's professional background touched on demagoguery. Sanford continued this approach for the next three weeks while continuing what he called a "positive campaign" stressing quality education. A stunned Lake stepped up his personal attacks on Sanford. More than ever, race colored every aspect of his effort.

Lake, the conservative, was an innovator. At the suggestion of Fletcher and former Lake student John Burney of Wilmington, WRAL began airing Lake's campaign rallies live, the widest use to date of television in a North Carolina campaign. As in later years, North Carolina's conservatives used television more effectively than did the state's moderates and liberals. Lake grew much more comfortable as a campaigner, both before large groups and on a more personal level. He never adjusted to the role of professional politician in the Sanford mode, but he was appealing, especially to those who shared his beliefs. He was a more articulate speaker than Sanford. He could not and perhaps never wished to match Sanford's ability to come across as a folksy down-home boy.

In this campaign as in the runoff campaign of 1950, the "Negro bloc vote" was a point of contention. Lake and his campaign charged that blacks had voted en masse for Sanford in the first primary, producing precinct results from Charlotte, Greensboro, Raleigh, and Winston-Salem. Sanford well remembered how the Smith forces used the "bloc vote" issue to weaken Graham in the 1950 Senate race. Anticipating this line of attack, Sanford had indirectly encouraged the Durham Committee on Negro Affairs, the city's leading black organization, to endorse Seawell in the May primary. It did so. In Asheville, evidence indicated that a majority of African Americans had voted for Larkins. Sanford pointed to those figures. Moreover, he asserted that the black vote in rural Iredell County north of Charlotte had gone for Lake, though Lake disputed this charge. While Iredell County did go for Lake, precinct analysis suggests that Sanford won the black vote there. Sanford himself later admitted that he might have altered the facts to goad Lake and weaken his campaign.[21]

Seawell endorsed Sanford in the runoff. Governor Hodges did not make a formal endorsement but met secretly with Sanford, raised money for him, and urged his business allies to work for Sanford. Larkins offered no endorsement. Some of his top workers went with Sanford and others with Lake. Larkins later revealed in his memoir that he voted for Lake but explained his choice as resulting more from their longtime friendship than from political philosophy.[22]

Sanford won the June 27 runoff handily, garnering 352,133 votes to Lake's 275,905. Sanford carried all of the state's major metropolitan counties except Durham, where racially conservative white textile and tobacco workers provided the votes to give Lake a narrow lead. Sanford won overwhelmingly in most mountain and foothill counties. Moving eastward, Lake's strength generally increased, a pattern not surprising, since the whites in areas with large black populations were acutely sensitive to racial issues. Lake's support slightly surpassed Sanford's in counties where African American populations exceeded 30 percent, most of which were located in the coastal plain and eastern piedmont. By 1960, some blacks were registered voters in all these counties, but whites remained a large majority. Sanford nevertheless won in parts of eastern North Carolina, where he had two advantages. First, Sanford built superior organizations. His political operatives in the east were adept at playing the white racist version of the race card. "Sanford's okay on the colored issue," was an oft-heard refrain. Second, Sanford lived in Fayetteville and had grown up in Scotland County, giving him hometown appeal in two areas with large black populations and many segregationist whites.

Sanford carried multiple advantages into the runoff. He had a head start of at least three years. He had developed a superior statewide organization that gave him an edge in much of the state and made him competitive even in difficult areas. Sanford cultivated the interest groups. Teachers'

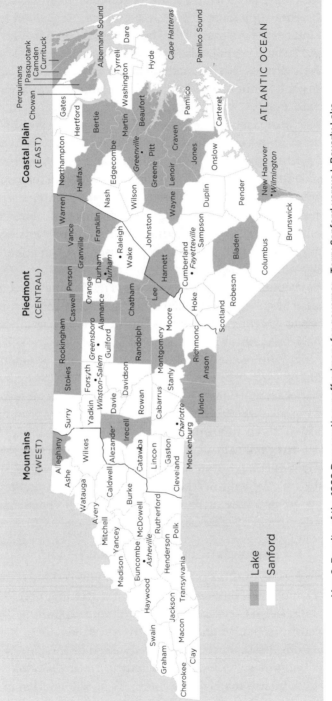

Map 2. Results of the 1960 Democratic runoff primary for governor—Terry Sanford versus I. Beverly Lake

associations were a de facto arm of the Sanford campaign, as was much of the broader education lobby. The Parent-Teacher Association leadership helped formulate the program of the United Forces for Education that Sanford plugged so hard. Sanford also courted Democratic activists, organized labor, lawyers' groups, Jaycees, and big businesses—Charles Cannon, the head of the giant Cannon textile empire and a union hater, announced his support for Sanford early on.[23]

More surreptitiously, Sanford sought out religious leaders, both black and white. He appealed to the state's psychology. Political folklore suggests that North Carolinians liked to think of themselves as progressive. At the same time, their underlying social instincts were often conservative with an undertone of racism. Sanford proudly ran as a progressive but attempted to avoid being labeled a racial liberal in the Graham tradition. Furthermore, Sanford stressed his rural North Carolina roots and church connections. Many top business and professional people feared that a Lake victory might damage the economic climate and therefore backed Sanford the second time around. Sanford had made valuable connections as manager of Scott's 1954 senatorial campaign, giving him organizational links to the party's economic populists and probably delivering some rural support that would otherwise have gone to Lake. Finally, the still small but growing African American vote was near 100 percent for Sanford in the runoff primary.

Sanford was a tough politician, willing to do almost anything to win. He was also a moralist who felt his people deserved a new Age of Enlightenment. The 1960 Democratic primary proved to be a high point of Sanford's long and stormy political career. On the day after the runoff the *Raleigh News and Observer* ran a front-page editorial written by publisher Jonathan Daniels. In "A Free Governor," Daniels argued that Sanford's broad mandate would give him a free hand to carry out a progressive agenda.[24] But Sanford's struggle was far from over.

### THE DAREDEVIL AND THE CATHOLIC

After celebrating his primary victory, Sanford plunged into controversy. The 1960 Democratic National Convention was coming up in July. Most delegates from North Carolina and the South were supporting Texas senator and majority leader Lyndon Johnson. However, Senator John Kennedy, a Catholic from Massachusetts, was now viewed as the party's probable presidential nominee. Sanford met secretly in North Carolina with Robert Kennedy, who was managing his brother's presidential campaign, and made a tentative commitment to back Jack Kennedy. Word of the meeting was leaked to columnist Drew Pearson, who wrote a piece hinting that Sanford had been paid off by the Kennedy forces for a promise of support. Sanford immediately responded, "It's a damn lie." Pearson later retracted the charge, but the damage had been done.[25]

Sanford refused to announce whom he was supporting before the convention. The Kennedy forces had asked him not to make public his choice before the convention, thinking that an endorsement there might influence some wavering southern delegates. When Sanford finally made his announcement, it generated an uproar. Governor Hodges and Senator Sam Ervin were furious, as were many Lake supporters and Protestant clergy. This anger intensified when Sanford gave a speech seconding Kennedy's nomination. Reflecting Sanford's stance, Kennedy got more support from North Carolina than from neighboring southern states. Kennedy received 6 votes (half a vote each from 12 North Carolina delegates), while Johnson received 27½. Other North Carolina delegates called the Kennedy supporters the Dirty Dozen.[26]

The liberal platform adopted at the Democratic Convention—specifically the plank calling for a stronger federal stand on civil rights for blacks—generated discord in the state. Ervin delivered one of the speeches opposing the plank. But nearly all the delegation rejoiced when Kennedy tapped Johnson as his vice presidential running mate.

In August, the Republican National Convention nominated Vice President Richard Nixon for president and Henry Cabot Lodge of Massachusetts, the American ambassador to the United Nations, for vice president. Lodge, the grandson and namesake of the senator who had blocked U.S. entry into the League of Nations in 1919, was socially liberal. The Republicans adopted a "moderate" platform: vigilance against communism, support for free enterprise, and a generalized commitment to equal rights for Americans of all races. North Carolina delegates were pleased with the Nixon nomination but less than thrilled about Lodge, who was an outspoken civil rights supporter.

Seasoned political observers thought that Kennedy would have an uphill race in North Carolina, and Sanford, too, suddenly seemed to be in trouble in the general election. This time a primary victory might not be "tantamount to election," the phrase typically used by the media to indicate that state-level Democratic nominees always won general elections. A few midlevel Democrats and Sanford primary boosters abandoned ship. Still, most party leaders declared their support for Sanford and Kennedy after the convention, and Governor Hodges became a leader for Kennedy's statewide campaign. But deep scars remained.

Robert Gavin, the Republican gubernatorial nominee, was from the town of Sanford in Lee County. He and Terry Sanford had been acquainted since their undergraduate and law school days in Chapel Hill. Gavin had served as a U.S. attorney from 1957 to 1958 before returning to private practice in Lee County. For the first time since 1928, the Republican candidate for governor was not to be taken lightly. At the Republican National Convention in August, Gavin was tapped to deliver one of Nixon's seconding speeches, a direct if symbolic swipe at Sanford. Both Democrats and Republicans got the message that Gavin was a serious candidate. Gavin was a moderate conservative, closer to Sanford than to Lake on race issues. While saying that he would not make race an issue in the campaign, Gavin criticized the national Democrats' support for new civil rights laws, a position he shared with most leading white North Carolina Democrats as well as Republicans. Gavin asserted that Sanford was a pawn of the liberal national Democratic Party and organized labor and hinted that Sanford could not be trusted in the aftermath of his "secret deal" with the Kennedy forces. Gavin argued that Sanford was not honorable in the sense that earlier Democratic governors had been.[27]

Lake had pledged to support Sanford when the two shook hands on the night of the June primary, but the defeated candidate's support ended there. He stressed that his conservative principles were "eternal." When making rare appearances at Democratic rallies, Lake criticized the direction of the national party. His mood was sullen if not defiant. He believed that Sanford had conducted a vicious primary campaign and represented an alien philosophy. In contrast, Lake's former campaign manager, Robert Morgan, campaigned for Sanford and personally introduced him at many eastern North Carolina's political events. Morgan also spoke out on behalf of Kennedy. Hodges, who hoped for a cabinet appointment as secretary of commerce if Kennedy won, worked hard for both Kennedy and Sanford. U.S. senators Sam Ervin and B. Everett Jordan also fell in line and spoke at rallies, though both privately remained wary of Sanford.[28]

The outcome, with hard-fought victories for Kennedy and Sanford, is a gripping chapter in American political history. Kennedy's razor-thin national popular vote margin of 119,000 out of more than 71,000,000 cast is the stuff of legends. The electoral vote edge was a superficially more secure 303–219. North Carolina provided Kennedy with a surprisingly strong if still close win, a 58,000 edge in the popular vote for 52 percent of the total. Sanford led by 131,000 votes with 54.3 percent of the total votes. He counted himself lucky, though his performance was anemic for a state-level Democrat.[29]

Several questions stand out. First, how did Kennedy win the national election, and what special role did North Carolina play in his victory? Concurrently, how did Kennedy, a Catholic and a liberal in name if not always in practice and spirit, put together a winning coalition in North Carolina, a state that had nearly supported the Republican candidate for president in 1956? Why was Sanford's margin so unimpressive, at least by historical standards? And on what foundation was his shaky coalition built?

The 1960 election marked a turning point in the strategic nature of American presidential campaigns. Journalist Theodore White, who revolutionized the way that election campaigns were covered, argued that Kennedy's national campaign permanently altered American politics.[30] Kennedy and his strategists applied the techniques of polling, television persuasion, and media manipulation in ways that later came to characterize campaigns on both the national and state levels. Over time, the new strategy paved the way for more expensive campaigns in which the old-time political organizations wielded less influence, ironically even as old-time machines in Chicago and South Texas did much to cement Kennedy's victory.

Kennedy won by combining electoral-vote-rich states in the Northeast and Great Lakes regions with victories in his running mate's home state of Texas and some states in the Old South—a coalition of the most Catholic and least Catholic states. On the northern flank were states where active politicians were, by standards of 1960, ardent proponents of civil rights for blacks. In the South, Kennedy's support came from states whose politicians opposed the mildest federal intervention for equality and where segregation remained the way of life, even if the faintest cracks had begun to appear. Immediately after the election, public attention centered on Kennedy's narrow and controversial leads in Illinois and Texas. Opponents accused the Democrats of widespread vote fraud, though whether such efforts might have determined the result in either state will always be a matter of conjecture. Without Illinois, Kennedy would have still had 276 electoral votes and a slim win. But subtracting Texas, he would have dropped to 252, below the required 270. Less populous Kennedy states such as Delaware, Nevada, and New Mexico had been perilously close. At the time, North Carolina had fourteen electoral votes, the highest figure in the South except for Texas and the tenth-highest electoral vote of any state. The Kennedy forces rightly considered North Carolina a pillar in building victory. Furthermore, their North Carolina win was built on a solid foundation that could have withstood any postelection challenge despite the possibility that a bit of vote tampering occurred in a few Democratic-controlled counties in the generally Nixon-leaning mountain region, tampering more designed to help local Democratic candidates than Kennedy.

For all the talk of chicanery and fraud, Kennedy won the presidency largely because he conducted the more skillful campaign at a time when much of the citizenry was willing to return to its Democratic political roots. Eisenhower's victories in 1952 and 1956 had exposed the vulnerability of the old Roosevelt New Deal–based Democratic coalition, but now Ike's parade had passed. Kennedy exuded intelligence and possessed good looks, a suntan, grace, charm, and a distinguished war record. And he wrote books: *Profiles in Courage* had been a bestseller. For Catholics, by 1960 a major force in the big northern electoral vote states, the Kennedy victory brought hope of full citizenship and social acceptance. Kennedy's image had been enhanced by a campaign that realized the power of television, now in most homes.

Had Kennedy not possessed all these strengths, defeat rather than a shaky victory would have been the outcome. This might have been a mortal wound to the Sanford campaign. Gavin might have become the first Republican governor in sixty years, though he would have been paralyzed by a conservative but partisan Democratic state legislature.

The outcome in North Carolina reflected both national trends and dynamics unique to the state. Social strictures and general tolerance remained narrow, but southerners in general and North Carolinians in particular retained many of their loyalties to the Democratic Party based on economic populism and support for the Roosevelt New Deal. The Great Depression had not faded from memory. The Democrats thus had an edge over the Republicans in national party registration and declared affiliation. In the South, this legacy provided the Democrats with a powerful advantage even while relations with the national party had become strained.

Another reason for Kennedy's victory in North Carolina, as elsewhere, involved the images and personalities of the candidates themselves. Nixon was not an attractive candidate, despite his résumé and keen mind. Good marks for hard work as Eisenhower's vice president never fully erased the perception that he was a master of smear. Many voters saw him as "Tricky Dick," a man who could not be trusted.[31] His discomfort before the camera was difficult to conceal. Nixon might win a race based on intelligence and experience, but not on charm or lovability.

While the television debates, the first seen in a presidential contest, emphasized Nixon's weaknesses, they were ready-made for Kennedy. Makeup enhanced his physical attractiveness and concealed his often sallow complexion. Kennedy's eastern New England accent sounded a bit strange, but he was articulate, charming, witty, informed, and sufficiently tough. Unlike Nixon, Kennedy knew how to look directly into a camera. Television brought a handsome, likable Bostonian into the living rooms of North Carolina. Barriers fell.[32]

Yet North Carolina had its own concerns, which it did not necessarily share with America as a whole or even with the South. Understanding why Kennedy carried the state requires placing eastern North Carolina—the forty-one-county coastal plain region—under the microscope. The coastal plain delivered the state for the Boston Catholic, casting just under 30 percent of North Carolina's vote but with decisive impact. Without the area's vote, North Carolina, like Tennessee and Virginia, would have gone for Nixon. In the east or coastal plain as a whole, Kennedy garnered 68.7 percent of the votes, massive by any standard except the performance of Sanford and the rest of the Democratic ticket, whose levels surpassed 70 percent. Counties that had voted for the segregationist Lake in the spring primaries were now among Kennedy's best in the state.

Greene County, in the heart of the region, was one of the most rural counties in this rural region, and tobacco was king. As in most of the coastal plain, Baptists reigned supreme. A few years later, Greene developed a reputation as a hotbed of Ku Klux Klan activity. Though almost 50 percent of Greene's population was black, its electorate remained overwhelmingly white in 1960. Lake had won 63 percent of Greene's vote in the June run-off, but in November, Kennedy received 87.3 percent of the county's vote. State-level Democrats did even better.

While Kennedy carried much of the rural South, nowhere but in parts of rural Georgia and machine-dominated Hispanic counties of South Texas did he run as well as he did in eastern North Carolina. No major region of the country voted more solidly for him. The 68.7 percent figure in the coastal plain topped even what Kennedy took in his home state of Massachusetts (60 percent of the vote) and in New York City (63 percent), both of which had large Catholic and Jewish populations, considered to be the bedrock of the Kennedy victory. Even in Brunswick, Carteret, Dare, and Sampson, the coastal plain counties where Eisenhower had won or come close in 1952 and 1956, Kennedy had comfortable margins.

Why did Kennedy run so well in an area that seemed so culturally incompatible with his background? True, eastern North Carolina was historically yellow dog Democratic country, but the same held true for many other areas across the South where Kennedy ran less well or even lost. In the aftermath of the strong segregationist campaign for governor the preceding spring and the civil rights movement's ongoing demonstrations in

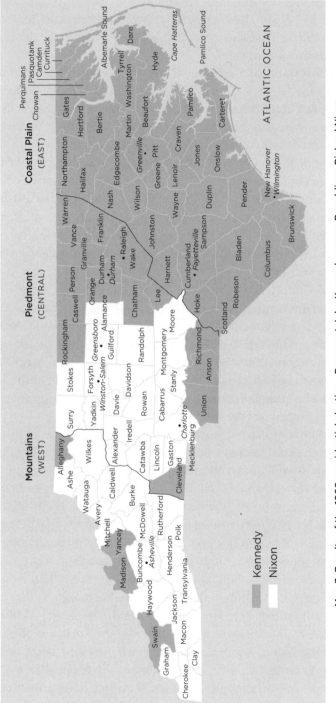

**Map 3. Results of the 1960 presidential election—Democrat John Kennedy versus Republican Richard Nixon**

North Carolina, tensions were high. Kennedy professed a broad if not always specific commitment to racial equality, though so did Nixon in more muted language. At this point, white North Carolinians still made little distinction between the national parties on racial issues.

Tobacco and agricultural issues were major themes in the region. As the world's leading tobacco producers, eastern North Carolinians were acutely sensitive to any risk to the New Deal's tobacco price stabilization program, which generally prevented the price of tobacco from falling below certain levels. Congressman Harold Cooley from Nashville, on the western edge of the coastal plain, chaired the House Agriculture Committee. Cooley, a highly partisan Democrat with a populist streak, warned voters that the Republican hostility to federal price supports might one day threaten the tobacco program. Voting Democratic was seen as a way of protecting the program and the area's lifeblood, a theme on which the Democrats hammered. Nixon had expressed support of this particular program while opposing other subsidies, but many farmers were suspicious of the Republican Party and its free-market philosophy. And even if tobacco subsidies survived, Republicans had targeted other programs that affected North Carolina's farmers.[33]

In addition, Eisenhower's presidency was less popular in the eastern part of North Carolina than it was in urban parts of the state or in much of the rest of the country. His agriculture secretary, Ezra Taft Benson, an ardent free marketeer, incurred the wrath of many farmers. Farmers in eastern North Carolina and elsewhere had seen a recession in the mid- and late 1950s. Agriculture was a stepchild not sharing in the national prosperity. While many forces contributed to the slowdown in the agricultural sector, farmers blamed Eisenhower and Benson. In this already Democratic part of the country, more than a few voters thought the administration needed a figurative punch in the nose.

Moreover, economic populism had long been a theme in the coastal plain, and the Populist Party had had pockets of strength there. In the 1930s, insurgents Richard Fountain and Ralph McDonald scored well in much of the coastal plain though they did not win their bids for the governorship. Unlike in parts of the piedmont and mountains, the term "Republican" was still an epithet. Both Kennedy and Sanford rode the tailwind from the past.

But statewide strength for Republicans Nixon and Gavin offered evidence of a party poised to become a force. For three presidential elections in a row, the Republican candidate had been competitive in North Carolina, carrying the three largest urban areas and much of their hinterlands.

In 1960, Gavin had become the first Republican gubernatorial candidate since 1928 to mount a serious challenge. He attempted to tie himself to Nixon and attacked Sanford's Kennedy connection. However, Gavin's inexperience led him to commit several major gaffes. In the spring, he had endorsed new taxes, if necessary, to implement the United Forces for Education program, a position almost identical to Sanford's. By the fall, however, Gavin denied that he had ever supported new taxes. The more politically astute and experienced Sanford, who had already shown that he could go for the jugular, pounced on Gavin's inconsistency.

Sanford's electoral coalition was shaky. In November, he lost the populous western piedmont and much of the mountain region, the same areas that had provided much of Sanford's winning margin over Lake in the second Democratic primary. Aside from his home region, fanning out from Fayetteville and Laurinburg on the southern coastal plain, Sanford's highest general election percentages came from former Lake strongholds of northern coastal plain and northeast piedmont. The area was indeed the state's Democratic heartland, but the Lake vote suggested that it was also an area on the brink of a major white backlash. In November, the potential dissidents had stayed with Sanford, more for his party label than for enthusiasm over his sweeping reform proposals and despite his racial moderation. Some voters in the east and other Lake strongholds might have supported "quality education," but they had no love for Sanford. He nevertheless prevailed by attracting nearly all of the voters who went for Kennedy, plus a few others.

Losing the piedmont and mountain regions, Kennedy nevertheless had improved on Stevenson's showings there in 1952 and 1956, in part as a consequence of the growing African American vote in the larger cities from Raleigh to Asheville. In 1956, Eisenhower had won the urban black vote in North Carolina and much of the South, an uncharacteristic result for a Republican candidate. In 1960, nearly 70 percent of black voters chose Kennedy, perhaps influenced by his attempt to get civil rights leader Martin Luther King Jr. out of jail in Georgia and the perception that the Democrat offered more hope on bread-and-butter issues than did Nixon. Kennedy lost the three biggest cities—Charlotte, Winston-Salem, and Greensboro—but, thanks to black voters, not by overwhelming margins. He easily carried Durham and Raleigh, with African Americans providing a firm cushion.

As Sanford campaigned for himself and against Herbert Hoover and the Great Depression, the gubernatorial candidate also spoke up for Kennedy. Sanford believed that a united party front was necessary for victory on all levels. Ironically, though Sanford had been wounded by his association with Kennedy, their fates were linked, and the unified effort saved both. Not considered a likely winner, Gavin had minimal financial assistance from the national Republican Party. Yet he had won a psychological victory and hope for a resurgent GOP.

Old habits die hard. After the contentious 1960 election, the Democrats held a 48–2 edge in the N.C. Senate and a 105–15 margin in the N.C. House, not their record but still impressive. The Democrats had an 11–1 edge in the state's U.S. congressional delegation. With redistricting after the 1960 census, however, the state would lose one of its seats in Congress because North Carolina's population had grown more slowly than the national average over the preceding decade.

When inaugurated on January 5, 1961, Governor Sanford looked forward with as much confidence as if he had won the overwhelming Democratic victory so common in earlier years. He vowed to push for his entire campaign platform, with an emphasis on education and economic development. In looking to the future, Sanford recalled the state's legacy: "There is a new day in North Carolina! . . . It is here because Charles Brantley Aycock had a great heart and dauntless vision and because he made North Carolina believe in universal education in an uncertain, uneasy, and difficult day. . . . Gone are the shackles. Gone are the limitations. Gone are the overwhelming obstacles. North Carolina is on the move and we intend to stay on the move."[34]

### CRUSADE FOR THE PEOPLE

"Sanford forced issues on the state," observed William Friday in an interview more than forty years after Sanford's stormy but extraordinarily bold and creative term as governor had ended.[35] Other figures have been more charismatic, superior speakers, and maybe more politically astute, but no major state official so aggressively pushed North Carolina toward new frontiers—frontiers that many people had no desire to cross. Sanford envisioned a state that would lead the way in education and economic development. Like most white southerners and Americans of his time, Sanford's initial vision of racial equality was less bold. But events catapulted him into the position of broker as the longtime racial order came under attack. Sometimes daringly, at other times discreetly or even haltingly, North Carolina's new governor moved out in front of other southern political leaders on matters of racial justice. His steps simultaneously fueled momentum for the movement and an angry reaction.

Sanford was both a larger-than-life figure with a moral compass and a crafty politico who knew how to make a deal. Former state supreme court justice and Campbell University Law School dean Willis Whichard remarked, "Sanford was a very engaging extrovert. . . . His vision in life was to help people. He had a huge ego. Of all people I've known in politics, he had the strongest focus on government being there to make life better for the people. He was very optimistic—probably too optimistic at times. Optimism might have been innate in his generation, especially males who fought in World War II and lived. If you could survive World War II, you could survive anything."[36] The American South of the early 1960s was riddled with political minefields. Now in command, Sanford faced obstacles that could shatter his promised initiatives for the state and maybe his political career.

Sanford was a leading force in the transition from an older South where segregation defined a social order and cotton, tobacco, and the textile industry dominated the economic sphere into a new South where modernization was the mantra of the day. In some respects at least, this transition heralded a more civilized South. Many more of its native daughters and sons eventually would choose to remain in their home states, and the region would become a magnet for outsiders. But first the South and North Carolina had to face the 1960s, politically the most unsettling decade for the region since the 1890s. Many leaders of the time—Governors George Wallace in Alabama, Lester Maddox in Georgia, and Ross Barnett of Mississippi, to name several of the most fiery—led the charge against change with the fervor, if not the intellect, of a reborn John C. Calhoun. Sanford, in contrast, preached the gospel of a bright future of prosperity and economic opportunity. In spirit and technique, he owed much to earlier North Carolina governors as well as to idealists in the mold of Frank Graham. He borrowed from both big-business-friendly progressives Cameron Morrison and Max Gardner and neopopulists, most prominently his mentor, Kerr Scott. Sanford lacked Gardner's political finesse but was nonetheless a talented and shrewd politician. He believed in himself and his cause. Sanford equated his own success with the well-being of the people.

As a campaigner and later in assembling much of his staff, Sanford went for talented outsiders—younger elements in the business community, the legal profession, and academia. Typically, governor's staffs were populated largely by campaign workers. But for wheeling and dealing, Sanford chose old pros such as Ben Roney, a shrewd but hard-drinking veteran of the Scott administration.[37] Sanford's main goal was to push a program through the legislature, whose members ranged from neopopulists to ultraconservatives. At the center of power in the N.C. House of Representatives were mildly conservative attorneys, business owners, and persons who identified themselves as farmers but who often were large landholders more adept at managing balance sheets than scattering seeds. These men—and nearly all the legislators were men—were hardly reactionaries, but they believed that responsible decisions on public issues could best be made by those who had met payrolls. Most legislators had little respect for the theoreticians found in universities and government—the kinds of people who gathered around Terry Sanford and national Democratic leaders. Such academics, they thought, should remain in Chapel Hill or Cambridge while sound men ran the government. Sanford had assembled one of the most brilliant staffs of any state executive, but he also understood the legislature. He let the members of his staff do what they could do best, generate ideas and specific policy proposals for him, while he was personally respectful to more seasoned political leaders.[38]

To promote the sweeping program of the United Forces for Education—huge salary increases for education professionals, new libraries, and almost surely new taxes—Sanford turned to experienced political hands. Legislators were not necessarily hostile to Sanford's program, but they had to be convinced that it was feasible, not simply a pie-in-the-sky proposal. Furthermore, it had to be accomplished in ways that would cause minimal political damage among constituents, many of whom had no love for Sanford. Wanting a cautious, effective conservative as his legislative lobbyist, Sanford persuaded former senator William Copeland from rural Black Belt Hertford County, in the northeastern quadrant of the state, to act as the administration's legislative lobbyist. As a legislator, Copeland had been the floor manager for Governors William B. Umstead and Luther Hodges. He was a skillful vote counter. While the education lobby had not considered Copeland a friend, the choice was a smart one.[39]

Sanford felt a kinship with the new lieutenant governor, Cloyd Philpott, a furniture executive from Lexington and a man of progressive instincts who eyed a future bid for the governorship. Philpott, like other lieutenant governors prior to 1989, appointed the chairs and members of N.C. Senate committees and influenced the flow of business in the Senate. Philpott suffered a fatal heart attack shortly after the session ended. Speaker of the House Joe Hunt, a cousin of Sanford's campaign college coordinator, Jimmy Hunt, was a hard-nosed and pragmatic politician. Sanford moved to form a close political bond with the speaker, who not only appointed committees but had strong control over the House agenda. In lining up his forces, the forty-three-year-old governor acted with the skill of a longtime capital wheelhorse. At least at the beginning of his term, he had the goodwill of the legislative leadership. A few prominent legislators were natural

Sanford allies and personal friends. Notable in this group was Senator Ralph Scott of Alamance County, the brother of the late governor and a pragmatic, shrewd dairyman of neopopulist instincts.

In the abstract at least, the program put forth by Sanford and the United Forces for Education had a strong appeal to the public at large. The challenge was to find the money to finance it. North Carolina's corporate and income taxes already stood at higher levels than those of most states, and more than a third of states imposed no income taxes at all.[40] Property taxes were entirely the domain of North Carolina's counties and cities. Some states would likely have raised their debt levels and hoped that an expanding economy would bring extra money in the future. North Carolina ran a much tighter budgetary ship. The leading watchdogs, state auditor Henry Bridges and state treasurer Edwin Gill, were conservative men, proud of the state's fiscal integrity and skeptical of major spending initiatives. Attorney General Wade Bruton and the members of the North Carolina Supreme Court were sticklers for following proper procedures and were much more conservative than Sanford. If Sanford was to fulfill his campaign promises, the risk of higher taxes had to be taken. He and legislative leaders soon concluded that a sales tax expansion should be proposed. North Carolina already levied a 3 percent retail sales tax on most items, but store-bought food was exempt. Ending that exemption could raise a tremendous amount of new revenue. Whatever else they might sacrifice in hard times, people had to buy food. An alternative might have been a luxury tax on such products as tobacco and soft drinks, but many North Carolinians saw those products as sacred, so taxing them at much higher rates than other goods was out of the realm of serious discussion. Nor was an income tax increase politically feasible. Sanford decided to go for a 3 percent sales tax on food items.

The idea of a food tax presented difficult questions, both moral and political. Sanford's base supporters—blacks, labor unions, and liberals—considered it to be the most sinful of taxes. The poor already struggled to eke out a living. To tax them for nourishment was a low blow; a levy of 3 percent might not mean a lot to the rich or even the middle class, but it would cut into the day-to-day living needs of the needy. Could Sanford propose such a tax with a clear conscience? And wherever his conscience might guide him, would the legislature and public accept a food tax? Sanford quickly overcame any moral reservations about the food tax and moved ahead at the end of February. Few North Carolinians knew precisely what Sanford would do until a joint legislative session took place on March 6, 1961.

The General Assembly received Sanford's proposals politely, but many legislators privately declared the idea of a food tax dead on arrival. The press and liberal allies thought there must be a better way. Specific counterproposals were few and far between, however, though the *Greensboro Daily News* suggested raising the general sales tax from 3 percent to 4 percent but keeping the food exemption.[41]

Rather than calling the new levy the "food tax," Sanford referred to it as the "school tax" and mounted a campaign rivaling his recent run for governor. He maintained a whirlwind schedule, meeting with civic and school groups while constantly courting state legislators. Sanford placed the political burden on critics to come up with a better way of financing the program. He invited legislators to the governor's mansion for breakfast. Sanford's constant attentions won legislators' affection, and some of them contrasted his gregarious personality with that of his more aloof predecessor, Luther Hodges.[42] Many critics of the new tax, including major newspapers and many liberals, grudgingly came to accept the idea when it became clear that without it, the ambitious education scheme would be trimmed. Protax forces offered still another, more sinister assertion to pacify traditionalists: The food tax was the fairest because everyone would have to pay. The message, expressed more bluntly only in private, was that poor blacks and whites would be caught by this tax and no other.[43] The assertion was uncharitable but effective. To the last minute, Copeland and the Sanford forces saw a close vote. The resounding victory for sweeping new education expenditures and the food tax made what had been a fierce battle seem a cakewalk: the levy passed 42–8 in the Senate and 85–31 in the House. Conservative political columnist Lynn Nesbit called Sanford's effort "the most astute salesmanship campaign ever conducted by a chief executive of North Carolina," adding that "the majority of those who voted for his bills did so not because of promises or threats, but because they had been convinced that it was the right thing to do."[44]

The legislative session was the most reform-oriented since the Republican-Populist alliance of the 1890s. It increased the minimum wage to seventy-five cents an hour, imposed tighter regulations on small loan companies, and threw a loaf to the old and disabled by increasing their welfare payments, in part to compensate for the new food tax. Sanford hailed the legislature's courage. He had won his second great political battle; he also incurred the everlasting antipathy of a slice of the population, not so much the poor, who were most hurt by the tax, as the white working and lower middle classes. The name "Food Tax Terry" would stick for years.[45]

The education lobby was delighted with the entire package but especially the part providing a 21.8 percent salary increase for schoolteachers and slightly higher raises for some administrators. Public colleges and universities benefited from a similarly generous package, and the foundations for a major community college system were laid. (A rudimentary technical college system had been begun under the Hodges administration.) For the direct beneficiaries of the Sanford program, the food tax was a small price to pay.

Sanford's success reflected his boldness and his assessment of political realities. The first reality was that major new taxes or an expansion of existing taxes were required if he was to keep his campaign promises on education. The second was that private corporate leadership had the power to block any major tax initiative presented to the legislature. That combination of circumstances led to the food tax proposal, which was the least objectionable to corporate North Carolina as a whole. Retail grocers and wholesalers opposed the idea, but they were no match for the big manufacturers, the banks, and the utilities. Much of the corporate elite remained neutral or tepidly supported the Sanford program. The third reality was that the legislature was essentially a conservative body on the matter of taxes, reflecting both its members' economic interests and the attitudes of the folks back home. Tying progress and the welfare of a future generation to a tax "everyone will have to pay" was brilliant political strategy, whatever the implications for social justice.

Sanford and more directly some legislators paid a political price for their actions. Many North Carolinians were angry about new taxes of any kind. The 1961 legislative session proposed ten capital improvement projects to be presented to the voters in a bond referendum. The projects included buildings for educational institutions, port facilities, mental institutions, and cultural facilities. Voters resoundingly defeated all ten items in November 1961. A year later, Republicans increased their legislative strength, going from 15 to 23 in the N.C. House, although Democrats maintained their 48–2 edge in the N.C. Senate. In the same election, the number of Republicans in the state's U.S. House of Representatives delegation rose from one to two after a fumbled attempt to gerrymander the popular Charles Jonas out of a seat. Democratic legislators put Jonas's home county, Lincoln, and his voting base, Mecklenburg (Charlotte), in the Eighth District, which was represented by conservative Democrat Paul Kitchen of Wadesboro in Anson County. Despite Democrats' confidence in Kitchen, Jonas won handily. In the Ninth District, immediately to the north and west, Republican James Broyhill, the scion of a prominent furniture family, defeated incumbent Democrat Hugh Q. Alexander.

Voters in 1962 did approve major court system reforms designed to make the system more efficient and more consistent statewide. The same year, Sanford appointed Superior Court judge Susie Marshall Sharp to the North Carolina Supreme Court, making her the first woman to serve on the state's highest tribunal and one of very few women to serve as justices in any high U.S. court.[46]

After the 1962 elections, Sanford was down but undeterred. He believed that his tax package had put North Carolina on sound footing to enter a modern, dynamic world. In his 1966 book, *But What about the People?*, Sanford wrote, "Governor J. C. B. Ehringhaus, whose courage I have always admired, insisted on a new tax structure, the first in the nation. 'If it is a choice between a sales tax on the one hand and a decent school, I stand for the school,' he told the General Assembly."[47] If Sanford could applaud the adoption of a sales tax in the midst of the Great Depression of the 1930s, he would have had few qualms about removing the exemption for food in the more prosperous 1960s.

New taxes were not on the table in the 1963 legislative session. Nor were new revenues needed, as state government benefited from the food tax revenue and a national economic boom. While the public schools received still more money, Sanford went for more creative programs in education and the arts. With legislative approval, the state established an Advancement School in Winston-Salem for able but underperforming high school students. Sanford's son attended the school for a while. More iffy was a proposed public residential school for the performing arts in Winston-Salem. With exceptions, legislators cared more about business ledgers and college athletics than ballet or opera. The United States had no freestanding public college of the arts, but Sanford and Roney won over wavering legislators with some old-fashioned logrolling, offering appointments and roads in exchange for support for the arts school. More attuned to legislators' local concerns was Sanford's continued push for technical schools with the long-term goal of turning them into a community college system.

Knowing that he had already pushed the legislature to its limits, Sanford sought Ford Foundation support for programs aimed at fighting poverty. He slyly told foundation officials he was seeking not money but their advice on how to lift poverty-stricken youth from their dire straits. When Ford expressed interest in funding a specific program, Sanford put his recently recruited "ideas man," John Ehle, on the project. The Ford Foundation was in the early stages of funding a "gray areas" program designed to help minority residents in northern cities. Over time, the discussions led to the creation of the North Carolina Fund, heavily financed nationally by the Ford Foundation and locally by the Mary Reynolds Babcock and Z. Smith Reynolds Foundations. The fund's efforts led to grants for team teaching and teacher aides and helped provide a model for Project Head Start, the centerpiece of President Lyndon Johnson's efforts later in the decade to assist impoverished children via preschool programs.[48] Another North Carolina Fund program encouraged communities to come up with proposals to fight poverty in their own neighborhoods. Eleven programs were funded, including day care facilities and job training. This program, too, influenced later federal efforts to fight poverty.[49]

At the same time, Sanford worked assiduously to attract new business and industry to the state. Partly as a political payoff for Sanford's support, President Kennedy awarded a new environmental research center to the fledgling Research Triangle Park between Chapel Hill, Durham, and Raleigh. The new facility later became the Environmental Protection Agency, and it provided a major boost in jobs and prestige for the new research park, whose successes to that point had been limited.[50]

Sanford had proved himself a reformer with a creative and entrepreneurial spirit who maximized the benefits of the political process. He blended the probusiness progressivism of earlier governors such as Hodges and Gardner with Scott's economic populist spirit. Simultaneously, however, Sanford faced an impending racial crisis in which assurances of goodwill were not enough.

### FROM SCARED NEIGHBORS TO GOOD NEIGHBORS?

When Sanford took his oath of office in 1961, North Carolina's racial order had changed little from 1910. Segregation remained entrenched. Despite the introduction of token integration in a few urban school systems and the state colleges, 99 percent of the state's black public school students attended racially separate schools. The federal courts had ruled against the legality of segregation on buses and trains, but station facilities remained rigidly segregated, as did hotels, motels, restaurants, theaters, public parks, and beaches. In the case of eating and sleeping establishments, "segregation" usually meant that blacks were banned outright except from places that served blacks only.

Though the black proportion of registered voters exceeded the low levels of pre–World War II days, whites still constituted 90 percent of the registered electorate. Nonwhites (a category that also included Native Americans and Asians) comprised nearly 25 percent of the population. A study by the federal-government-sponsored North Carolina Advisory Commission on Civil Rights estimated that in 1961, 90.2 percent of the potential white electorate was registered, compared to only 31.2 percent of the potential nonwhite voters. In the state's major cities—Charlotte, Durham,

Greensboro, Raleigh, and Winston-Salem—black registration was heavy enough to influence some election outcomes. In rural and small-town counties, especially those of the coastal plain and the eastern piedmont, black voting was discouraged and remained low.[51]

*Raleigh News and Observer* editor Jonathan Daniels had counseled Sanford to make a bold statement on racial equality in his 1961 inaugural address, but Sanford incorporated only one sentence on the subject: "We are not going to forget as we move into the challenging years ahead, that no group of our citizens can be denied the right to participate in first class citizenship."[52] Still, from a southern governor in 1961, such a statement signaled a break with tradition. In addition, Sanford's daughter, Betsee, and son, Terry Jr., were enrolled in the "integrated" Murphy School (which had one black student) near the governor's mansion rather than in a private school. North Carolina and national newspapers noted the symbolism of the decision.[53]

Both Sanford and John Kennedy, who assumed the presidency on January 20, 1961, saw economic reform and new government social programs as their road to building a legacy. Both viewed the impending racial crisis as political dynamite and a diversion from their main agendas. However, both also soon found themselves drawn into the maelstrom of racial conflict. Initially hesitant to confront racial inequality head-on, Kennedy and, more discreetly, Sanford emerged as leading white advocates for change.

Sanford had nervously watched the lunch counter sit-ins when he campaigned in 1960. In 1961, demonstrations continued, though the focus of the civil rights movement shifted further south, providing North Carolina with a brief respite. In the interim, Sanford and his director of conservation and development, Hargrove "Skipper" Bowles, moved to desegregate state-owned parks. Parks had been segregated by administrative regulations rather than formal statute, so a new policy could be enacted without a bruising and very public legislative fight. With the cooperation of parks supervisor Thomas C. Ellis, a Sanford loyalist, park desegregation was enacted on an incremental basis and attracted minimal public attention. In the spring of 1962, a policy directive approved by Sanford stated, "It is now the policy that no colored person shall be denied the use of any facility in any state park nor shall any employee by words or action make the impression that their use is not permitted."[54] While the administration took this action in part to avoid rumored lawsuits, both Sanford and Bowles thought it was the morally proper thing to do. Moreover, they acted a year before the Kennedy administration proposed requiring similar standards throughout the United States.

In 1962 and 1963, Freedom Riders, many from outside North Carolina, targeted segregation in bus station waiting rooms, restrooms, and dining rooms as well as chain restaurants—notably S&W cafeterias and Howard Johnson's restaurants. The atmosphere became heated as hundreds and then thousands of North Carolina students and other sympathizers joined in the biggest social protests seen yet. No longer was it so easy to blame the movement on "outside agitators." Bus stations in North Carolina, more often than further South, began grudgingly to accept desegregation where the issue was forced. Owners of independent restaurants resisted, not merely because they opposed integration but also because they feared the reaction of their white patrons.

Unlike many white leaders of the time, Sanford was acquainted with many black business and political leaders. He brought Durham bank executive John Wheeler into interracial discussions. Wheeler publicly prodded Sanford to take bolder steps toward integration but also offered vital links to more militant younger people whom Sanford did not know. On one occasion, Sanford held a private meeting with James Farmer, the national head of the Congress of Racial Equality, and the group's second-ranking official, Durham's Floyd McKissick. The two men promised temporarily to suspend the demonstrations after one more big push to give Sanford a chance to work from the top. If he could not produce results, however, the demonstrations would resume with increased furor.

Sanford stealthily urged local officials and business owners to accept some desegregation in restaurants and public facilities. Durham businessman R. Wensell Grabarek, who was elected mayor with strong black support in 1963 and who wanted a quick end to the huge demonstrations in his city, moved with dispatch. Grabarek, in cooperation with local business leaders, including the economically powerful Hill family, pushed hesitant white restaurant proprietors to drop their rigid segregation policies. Sanford and other urban leaders argued that ending formal racial barriers would promote peace and a good business climate.[55]

To accept change was portrayed as an act of local patriotism. Otis Kapsalis, the co-owner of Durham's Palms restaurant, a downtown establishment catering to business and professional people, families, and Duke students, later said that he came under pressure from banker George Watts Hill to integrate or have his mortgage called in.[56] Around the same time, Thomas Pearsall of Rocky Mount, who had chaired the commission on school segregation in the 1950s, quietly integrated the Howard Johnson's restaurants he owned along Highway 301 in one of the most hardcore segregationist parts of the state. Pearsall, who combined an inbred conservatism with a progressive spirit, was close to Sanford as well as to his predecessor, Hodges. Pearsall and his wife, Elizabeth, were touched when they observed that when military buses stopped at the Pearsalls' restaurants, black soldiers had to eat outside while whites partook inside.[57] The fears of Sanford and key white business and political elites—and in Sanford's case at least some sympathy for the civil rights cause—brought substantial restaurant desegregation to North Carolina a year before it was required by federal legislation. The national media saluted Sanford's initiatives, which reached fruition at around the time that Birmingham, Alabama, public safety director Eugene "Bull" Connor turned fire hoses and police dogs on black demonstrators seeking to end segregation. By that standard, Sanford was an "enlightened" southern leader. But for a while at least, most small-town restaurants and many less visible urban establishments stayed rigidly segregated, as did nearly all of the state's hotels and motels.

Largely in response to events in Birmingham, President Kennedy proposed sweeping national civil rights legislation in the summer of 1963. With Congress considering a measure that required an end to racial segregation in government-owned facilities as well as an end to segregation in privately owned facilities serving the general public, a long period of hearings began.

In September 1962, Sanford had proposed the establishment of the North Carolina Good Neighbor Council to forge better racial relations and economic opportunity. In a speech to the Methodist Men of the Gastonia area, the governor was vague and seemed to go little further than Governor Cameron Morrison's Commission on Interracial Cooperation in the 1920s. But Sanford was serious about racial change. Further pursuing the idea in a Chapel Hill speech to the North Carolina Press Association on January 18, 1963, he proclaimed, "The American Negro was freed from slavery one hundred years ago. . . . Now is a time not merely to look back to freedom but forward to the fulfillment of its meaning." Sanford added that employment discrimination against African Americans held back the nation and concluded that discrimination needed to end "because it is honest and fair for us to give all men and women their best chance in life."[58]

On the same day, Sanford issued a statement setting up the biracial North Carolina Good Neighbor Council to improve employment opportunities. He asked that county commissioners establish similar local councils, a step some of them soon took. Sanford was the first high elected official in the American South to declare racial equality the official state policy. Knowing the sensitivity of the state's elites to the North Carolina

(above) Civil rights demonstrators in front of a High Point, North Carolina, movie theater shut down to prevent integration, 1963. Capus Waynick Papers (#421), East Carolina Manuscript Collection, J. Y. Joyner Library, East Carolina University, Greenville.

(below) Counter-demonstrators and police, High Point, North Carolina, 1963. Capus Waynick Papers (#421), East Carolina Manuscript Collection, J. Y. Joyner Library, East Carolina University, Greenville.

image and the entire population's stake in economic prosperity, he linked this action to self-interest. But Sanford stated courageously and emphatically that employment discrimination and by implication overt racism were wrong. Perhaps this time, Sanford's conscience played as big a role as political calculation or the need to respond to an explosive situation. As Sanford negotiated with conflicting parties in 1962 and 1963, he suffered politically, but his legacy was solidified. His enemies watched in amazement and anger and marshaled their forces for battles to come. But no one anticipated the shots that would echo around the world.

## CHAPTER FOUR

# The Unsettled Society

Rare are the days that capture the collective consciousness of a nation: November 11, 1918, when church bells pealed across the land to signal the end of the "war to end all wars"; December 7, 1941, after the Japanese attack on Pearl Harbor; April 12, 1945, following the radio bulletin reporting the death of the seemingly immortal President Franklin Delano Roosevelt; September 11, 2001, with its crashing buildings; and the day President John F. Kennedy was shot, November 22, 1963. After such events, more often ones of trauma than joy, generations of people remember where they were and what they were doing at the exact moment the news came. In 1963, little time elapsed between the first news flash of the bullets in Dallas and the confirmation of the president's death at Parkland Hospital. A long period of mourning and reflection began Kennedy, part glamorous and heroic chief and part carefully cultivated image of a new media age, took his last flight back to Washington.[1]

Kennedy's finest hours had come in times of national and international crises. Tributes flowed from Americans of nearly all political persuasions. North Carolina governor Terry Sanford said, "With a passionate concern for all people from both sides and from behind, President Kennedy set his strength determinedly for human understanding and world peace, remaining always resolute in his faith, always undaunted and unafraid. The valiant soldier of freedom is dead. All mankind is less."[2] Nearly the entire country watched with rapt attention the arrival of the body at Andrews Air Force Base, John Jr.'s poignant salute to his father's coffin, the Monday mass at St. Matthew's Cathedral, and the dirge at Arlington National Cemetery.

North Carolina had been a key state in Kennedy's 1960 election victory. But as in all the American southland, his groundbreaking racial initiatives—the dispatching of more than fifteen thousand federal troops to secure James Meredith's admission to the University of Mississippi in 1962 and the proposal for sweeping civil rights legislation in the late spring of 1963—had taken a toll. In the declining days of late autumn, Kennedy had seemed well positioned to win reelection the following year against the increasingly probable Republican nominee, the unapologetically conservative and blunt Barry Goldwater. Indeed, Democrats spoke confidently of an impending Kennedy landslide, based on unprecedented party strength in the Northeast, Midwest, and Pacific Coast regions. Kennedy strategists had written off much of the South but still hoped for victories in North Carolina and Vice President Lyndon Johnson's home state, Texas.[3]

North Carolina politicians had needed no polls to know that Kennedy's odds in the state were at best even. The Democratic bastion—the coastal plain—was restive about race. Many of its whites were upset with the president and outraged over the pro-civil-rights stance of his younger brother, Attorney General Robert Kennedy. White Democratic loyalists felt a sense of betrayal. They resented outside interference. On November 27, when the new president, Johnson, a vain man wearing a cloak of humility, passionately, even eloquently, called for the passage of the Civil Rights Act as the "most fitting memorial" to the slain president, the North Carolina response was muted.[4] At that moment, it did not seem proper to rail against that which was associated with a fallen hero. Hard-core segregationists held their ammunition for a later time—several months later.

Governor Sanford was a lame duck. At the time, regular legislative sessions were held every other year, and the 1963 legislative session had ended. Most appointments had already been made. Would-be candidates for governor recognized that anti-Sanford currents might sweep them to victory. But for Sanford, nothing was quite so devastating, personally or politically, as the loss of his spiritual kinsman, John Kennedy. Their backgrounds had been different, yet they viewed each other as leading society to a new era. Both men had seen combat and survived in a war against tyranny. Sanford was the Kennedy brothers' favorite southerner. Now Johnson, a man with a long memory, occupied the White House. He could never forget the 1960 Democratic National Convention, where Sanford stood out starkly among the generally pro-Johnson southern delegates. North Carolina's senators, Sam Ervin and Everett Jordan, and a few members of the congressional delegation now provided the state's closest links with Washington.[5]

Sanford was not one to make public display of his gloom. He redoubled his efforts to recruit industry, still eager to surpass the stellar six-year record of his predecessor, Luther Hodges. Somewhat incongruously, given his past willingness to take risks, he said he opposed the proposed Civil

Rights Act, though he never worked against it. Sanford thought its goals admirable but insisted that action should come on the state level. While his record shielded him from charges of hypocrisy on the matter, he had to know that without federal action, the pace of racial progress in much of the South would be glacial. Sanford remained governor for just over thirteen months after the Kennedy assassination.[6] But the glory days were extinguished forever with the volley of bullets in Dallas.

## THE VOTERS' REVOLT

By late 1963, the next year's Democratic primary for governor—still considered the real election despite signs of growing Republicanism—began to take shape. I. Beverly Lake was the consensus choice of the vocal segregationists. Well-known and articulate, he would immediately command broad support in a primary where noncandidate Sanford was to many voters a pariah. Racial tensions had escalated even from 1960 levels. The sweeping civil rights bill, which mandating an end to segregation in private businesses serving the general public and in state government facilities and cut off federal funds for state agencies that discriminated against blacks, seemed headed for passage in Washington. As forceful as ever in his defense of states' rights and criticism of demonstrators, Lake softened his earlier calls for a fully segregated society, but he held back no venom in going after the proposed civil rights act. Many moderate to conservative business and political elites—leading bankers, industrialists, and people in the camps of Senators Ervin and Jordan—sought a candidate who would slow down what they considered Sanford's breakneck forward pace. However, they also feared Lake.[7]

Dan K. Moore sought their support. Moore, a former state superior court judge, currently served as legal counsel for the Champion Paper Company and lived in Canton, an industrial town west of Asheville. He was smart and well connected in political circles and had legislative and judicial experience. Moore was not a gifted speaker, but he conveyed both charm and sincerity in personal conversations. Yet he possessed a winning, if vaguely plastic, smile and a firm handshake. Most important, many members of the Democratic Party's old guard—admirers of such leaders as O. Max Gardner, J. Melville Broughton, and William B. Umstead—moved toward Moore as politically sound as well as untarnished. They looked at other possible candidates as well. William Friday, by then the state's most prominent academic administrator but not part of any campaign, recalled that after one meeting, he was called across the room by Durham banker and deal maker George Watts Hill. Moore and Thomas Pearsall (also well connected and regarded as a possible candidate) were standing together. Hill jovially said to Friday, "I'm trying to decide which one of these men to run for governor." After a bit more banter, he pointed to Moore as if it were a done deal.[8] The Hill family and the Holdings (the family that controlled First Citizens Bank, based in eastern North Carolina) and most veterans of the 1960 Larkins and Seawell campaigns fell in behind Moore. In fact, Moore's candidacy was the product of discussions that had gone on for months at Democratic fund-raising events and in corporate conference rooms. This time, people in the tradition of former governor Hodges—self-proclaimed progressive conservatives—were determined to maintain a united front. Furthermore, it remained the custom to rotate the governorship between eastern and western North Carolina, and it was the west's turn.

Ironically, Sanford might have gone along with the moderate conservatives if they had tapped Pearsall, with whom the governor had become close. But Moore was more aggressive about running than Pearsall, so he won the support of Hill and other key players. After extended discussion, federal judge L. Richardson Preyer (pronounced "prior") of Greensboro, a gentleman intellectual and scion of a wealthy drug-industry family, was recruited as the Sanford organization candidate. He resigned from his lifetime judgeship to run. His economic proposals were more cautious than Sanford's had been. Preyer asserted that new taxes would be unnecessary and that he planned to stress education.[9]

Both the Sanford apparatus and Preyer knew that a candidate closely associated with the current administration would start out with two strikes against him. According to Bob Scott, Preyer slipped into a meeting of Sanford people disguised in a trench coat, the uniform of a spy.[10] Preyer's campaign sought endorsements from business leaders not closely identified with Sanford and painted the candidate as a cautious moderate. Former governor Hodges, now the U.S. secretary of commerce, had privately indicated a preference for Preyer, but he never extended a public endorsement, probably because most of his political friends backed Moore.[11]

Sanford's coalition, including teachers' organizations, labor unions, and blacks, fell in line for Preyer. The state public schoolteachers' and principals' lobbies constituted a de facto arm of the campaign, much as they had for Sanford's 1960 bid. Moore moved to establish himself as the centrist. He advocated new spending for education and public works without a tax increase. Some of his proposals were more ambitious than Preyer's. Moore attacked the leftward drift under the Sanford administration and castigated the Johnson-backed civil rights act, by that point on the verge of congressional approval. While he disassociated himself from militant, bitter-end segregationists, Moore criticized civil rights demonstrators and "outside agitators," whom he accused of inflaming the atmosphere of what he called a peaceful, racially tolerant state.

Moore's goal was to run well enough to make the almost certain run-off primary. As the candidate in the middle, he hoped to be the choice of the voters who favored the candidate eliminated, whether it was Lake or Preyer. To finish second required all the resources that Moore could muster.

In the May primary, Preyer received 281,430 votes, Moore 257,872, and Lake 217,172. Lake had carried more counties than he did in his strong 1960 bid. He once again scored well in counties that were more than 30 percent black, even though blacks now comprised a slightly higher proportion of the electorate in those counties than had been the case four years earlier. County and precinct voting returns suggested white support for Lake that was as great or greater than in 1960. He led the field in the coastal plain region. Further west, Lake took a plurality of votes in his home county, Wake (Raleigh), which he had lost to Sanford in both of the 1960 primaries, and Lake repeated his win in then-industrial Durham County. Preyer led in the largest cities of the western piedmont—Charlotte, Winston-Salem, and his home, Greensboro. He ran second to Lake in much of the coastal plain, reflecting the growing black vote. He was second to Moore in the mountain region. Preyer's mountain strength came mainly in a few counties where local Democratic organizations had strong ties to Sanford. Overall, Moore's lead in his native mountain region was commanding. Without it, he would have trailed Lake. Moore, however, recorded respectable third-place finishes in both the piedmont and east. Furthermore, his supporters there included many of the powerful and wealthy as well as other whites who saw themselves in the state's mainstream.

Despite his first-place finish, Preyer instantly became the underdog for the June runoff.[12] Moore announced that he would call for a second primary. He stepped up his attacks on the Sanford organization—"the machine." Moore and his team also called for a large turnout to combat the "bloc vote," a reference to the near unanimous support for Preyer in predominantly black urban precincts. More than any time since the 1950 Willis Smith–Frank Porter Graham primary, the specter of the solid black vote became a campaign issue.[13]

The Preyer camp hoped that a campaign focus on economic populism—the needs of working people—would appeal to some Lake voters and maybe to Lake himself, who might have been more an economic populist at heart than either Moore or Preyer. Preyer blasted Moore's associations with corporate North Carolina, specifically singling out First Citizens Bank and the Holding family. However, Preyer's effort to come off as the champion of the worker was a loser from the start. Preyer was not a Gray, Reynolds, or Duke, but in North Carolina's social order, he was an aristocrat. While to a nonsoutherner, Preyer's enunciation sounded distinctly southern, it sounded just a little alien to good-old-boy types, especially when Preyer pronounced the personal pronoun "I" more like a Yankee than in the softer, flatter southern manner. Whatever Moore's diction problems, no one could question his genuine down-home touch.

The best Moore television ads were those where he said nothing. The candidate was known as the "mountain man," and the Moore media campaign turned the label to his advantage. With mountains in the background, Moore came across as independent and self-reliant, vaguely hinting of Daniel Boone or Davy Crockett. Media and television commercials featured the jingle "Dan K., Dan K. Moore, He's our choice for '64." On the tube voters saw a beaming Moore who conveyed both sincerity and a common touch.

Two attorneys high up in the Preyer campaign, Phil Carlton and Nat Townsend, called on Lake at his Wake Forest residence, located on a charming tree-lined street near the Baptist seminary that now occupied the old Wake Forest College campus. As was typical for him, Lake greeted them cordially, almost effusively, expressing delight at their visit. As a pre condition for a possible endorsement, Lake asked that Preyer promise not to appoint Terry Sanford or Bert Bennett, the Winston-Salem oilman who had masterminded Sanford's 1960 victory, to the U.S. Senate if either Ervin or Jordan should die or retire midterm. While he requested no appointment for himself, Lake asked for a commitment from Preyer to name Lake people to one-third of all state government appointments. The Preyer forces informally agreed not to appoint Sanford or Bennett but rejected the idea of naming so many Lake allies to government positions, and the meeting ended on a pleasant note but with no false illusions.[14]

But Lake could never forget the 1960 primary and what he regarded as personal attacks by Sanford. Reflecting on the situation more than forty years later, Phil Carlton expressed doubt that even a Lake endorsement could have thrust Preyer into the position of front-runner.[15] The typical Lake voter, more than the typical Moore supporter in the first primary, disliked Sanford.

There was no assurance that Lake's grassroots voters would turn out in large numbers for anyone in the runoff. While things looked good for Moore, what he most coveted was a public endorsement from Lake himself. Lake didn't know Moore well but saw common ground on the all-important states' rights debate. By endorsing Moore, he might gain both retribution against Sanford and influence inside the new administration.

Top Moore and Lake operatives secretly met in the furnished basement of WRAL television executive Jesse Helms's Raleigh home. While Helms had no official capacity in the campaigns, he saw urgency in defeating the Sanford-Preyer forces. Joe Branch, a prominent Halifax County attorney and Moore's state campaign manager, initially negotiated with Allen Bailey of Charlotte, Lake's 1964 manager and one of North Carolina's greatest trial lawyers. Branch found Bailey's approach off-putting and demanding. With negotiations at a standstill, Branch thought of Robert Morgan, who remained close to Lake but had not managed the 1964 campaign because Morgan was running for the N.C. Senate. According to Morgan, "Joe Branch called and asked me to come up to Raleigh. Bailey was making blunt demands. 'We want this and this position.' They asked me to replace Bailey in negotiations."[16] Branch, Morgan, Moore, and Lake knew that a deal was well within reach. However, Lake needed assurances of real influence in an upcoming regime.

As the consultations wrapped up, Lake agreed to make a public endorsement of Moore. Now present to seal the deal, Moore said to Lake, "How might I improve my campaign?" Lake replied, "In your speeches, you give the impression that you are just as surprised as the audience when you turn the page. Read the speech first." Moore smiled wanly and said he would try.[17]

According to Morgan, Moore made only one specific promise: "There will be no difference between Moore people and Lake people if I am elected."[18] Lake and Morgan were convinced of the candidate's sincerity and believed that a Moore administration would treat the Lake forces kindly in making appointments as well as consult them when making key policy decisions. There remained a campaign to be fought, but Preyer's fate had been sealed. Still, neither camp acknowledged that the game was over. Moore's troops intensified their assaults on "the machine" and the "bloc vote," interests that they said would prevail unless ordinary, hard-working North Carolinians—code language for white voters—turned out in full force on primary runoff day. If dispirited, Preyer and his legions put on a bold public face. Their attacks on Moore's corporate backers rose to the highest pitch yet. The Preyer team also charged that Moore had the support of the Ku Klux Klan, an accusation Moore denied, though he refused to attack the Klan. Teachers' lobbyist Claude Ferrell held meetings with educators around the state, warning that a Moore victory might doom Sanford's innovative initiatives, a claim not buttressed by a reading of Moore's platform.[19]

In an election-eve television appearance, Sanford revealed what nearly everyone knew—that he was supporting Preyer as the candidate who would continue his programs. Joining Sanford in the endorsement were Greensboro civic leader Major Lennox Polk McLendon and Thomas Pearsall of Rocky Mount, who had been runner-up to Moore when the business forces chose their candidate and the chief author of the 1950s pupil assignment plan.

The number of total voters rose from 773,294 in the May primary to 774,293 in June, the first time votes had increased between two primaries in a statewide race since 1920. Decreases in the number of candidates between the two primaries and in the number of offices up for grabs as well as the onset of the summer doldrums usually meant that the number of voters dropped. Moore's total vote climbed from 281,430 in May to 480,431 in June, while Preyer's total rose from 281,430 to 293,863. With 64 percent of the vote statewide, Moore had carried all three major geographic regions: 65 percent in the coastal plain, 58 percent in the piedmont, and 71 percent in the mountains. Thanks in large part to Lake's support, Moore had moved from second-place finisher in May to landslide winner in June.

Moore had benefited from an anti-Sanford backlash and as well as good campaign strategy. Many voters saw him as the safe candidate in the middle. Change seemed assured in an impending Moore administration, but it was likely to be change in tone and personnel rather than a fundamental reversal in direction from the previous decade's pattern. The primary voters had staged a revolt, but those looking for a sweeping rollback of Sanford's programs were bound to be disappointed if, as seemed probable, Moore prevailed in the general election.[20]

Neither a populist nor an old-time southern demagogue, Moore reigned as a business-friendly governor with a progressive streak, in keeping with the North Carolina tradition. Economic conservatives for whom segregation was a secondary consideration looked for a steady hand in the governor's mansion. Whites in general hoped that a period of calm lay ahead. Blacks and racially liberal whites—what few there were—looked to Washington.

Liberal elements could find solace in the victory of Robert W. "Bob" Scott in the race for lieutenant governor, hoping that he would be a liberal reformer in the mold of his father, Kerr Scott. In fact, young Scott had run as a centrist. The thirty-five-year-old Scott had held no elective or other public office but had served a term as master of the state Grange, a leading farmers' organization. Scott's name and political talents were enough to give him an advantage over two more seasoned but less colorful politicians in the race, Clifton Blue and John R. Jordan. In the June runoff, Scott defeated Blue, a former Speaker of the House, 373,027–359,000. This race had a life independent of the governor's contest, with Scott attracting support from some people in both the Moore and Preyer camps. Sanford-Bennett forces hoped that Scott's pedigree would make him one of their own. But tensions began to build as Bob Scott and other old Scott hands thought the Sanford people had "gone uptown" and lost touch with the branch head boys.[21]

### DREAMS OF THE FUTURE AND SHADOWS OF THE PAST

The summer of 1964 was tense yet full of promise. Race riots broke out in Rochester, New York, and in New York City, signaling mounting tensions in the urban North. Civil rights workers disappeared in Mississippi, leading to a long search that ultimately found their bodies. North Carolina experienced a lull in demonstrations, a calm brought on by state moves toward limited integration and the expectation that the proposed civil rights act would pass. Southern Democrats, with Senator Ervin among their leaders and master strategists, waged a filibuster to keep the measure from coming up for a vote.[22] Proponents of the legislation mustered the two-thirds vote necessary to cut off debate and consequently to quash the filibuster. By summer, the Civil Rights Act of 1964 won overwhelming approval from Congress with the votes of most nonsouthern Democrats and Republicans. The North Carolina congressional delegation unanimously opposed the bill. The new law cut off federal funds for state agencies operating on a racially discriminatory basis and mandated an end to segregation in public facilities such as courthouses and parks as well as in most privately owned businesses, including restaurants and motels.

One of the bill's few opponents from outside the South was Senator Barry Goldwater of Arizona. Ironically, Goldwater, of Jewish ancestry but a practicing Episcopalian, had long been an outspoken foe of racial discrimination. He asserted that he would have voted for the bill except that he objected to the provision telling private business owners whom they must serve. Goldwater was an early libertarian, skeptical of any government interference with private enterprise. There was probably also a bit of political calculation. He was running for president in 1964 and hoped to carry the southern states, since his chances elsewhere were slim. Goldwater captured the Republican nomination at a rowdy convention in San Francisco, where the party's right wing ran roughshod over moderates, liberals, and the media. Republicans and renegade Democrats from the Deep South cheered Goldwater on. In North Carolina, Republicans were cautiously optimistic about Goldwater's prospects; Democrats were nervous. However, few observers thought that Goldwater could win the national election.

At summer's end, the Democratic convention delegates gathered in Atlantic City to nominate Lyndon Johnson for president and liberal Minnesota senator Hubert Humphrey as his running mate. The convention was really more of a coronation than a nomination, as a variation on the title song from the current Broadway hit, *Hello, Dolly*, rang out: "Hello, Lyndon." Johnson outlined plans for a "Great Society" in which more Americans would share in the national abundance. To a man, North Carolina's congressional Democrats had voted against the civil rights act, yet all to varying degrees expressed support for their party's nominees. Whatever happened in North Carolina and the South, Johnson appeared headed toward a national win of avalanche proportions, in part because many voters feared that Goldwater would dismantle the Roosevelt safety net, including social security, and that he might dramatically step up American involvement in a far-off Asian war or be a little careless with the nuclear trigger.

A high-profile convention dispute centered on the attempt of a black "Freedom Democratic Party" delegation from Mississippi to be seated in the place of the regular, white, conservative party delegation. With Johnson's quiet backing, the convention credentials committee gave the nod to the regulars, people who were unlikely to vote for Johnson in the fall election. The convention decision was strategic. Democrats knew that they would lose Mississippi and Alabama in November but hoped that seating the regulars would signal moderation to wavering whites in Tennessee, North Carolina, and other southern states that were competitive. Blacks, Johnson knew, would vote for him anyway.[23]

Moving into the autumn campaign, North Carolina Democrats anticipated an easy Moore victory over the repeat Republican challenger Robert Gavin. Moore himself was more guarded, to the extent that he omitted naming Johnson when he promoted the Democratic ticket at rallies and other public appearances. The president, Moore feared, would be a drag on the state ticket. Moore also did not want to offend his primary backers, some of whom were now supporting Goldwater. Senators Ervin and Jordan, who knew both Johnson and Humphrey well, and Sanford campaigned hard for the national ticket, as did key members of the congressional delegation such as House Agriculture Committee chair Harold Cooley. The Democrats told wavering farmers that Goldwater would end all agricultural subsidies. Leading politicos warmly greeted the First Lady, Lady Bird Johnson, when her southern train tour, the Lady Bird Special, crossed North Carolina. Near the end of the campaign, Moore bowed to pressure from fellow Democrats and spoke Johnson's name as he plugged the state Democratic ticket. Reading the tea leaves, Moore concluded that Johnson would win North Carolina with or without his endorsement. Johnson, barring assassination or a recurrence of heart illness, was certain to continue to be the president. Moore had little choice in the matter.

Gavin mounted an energetic campaign, behaving as a seasoned pro. He cautiously appealed to moderates and liberals who had backed Preyer in the primary. Gavin attacked the status quo—longtime Democratic rule—while emphasizing that he was a progressive conservative. He also gained support from white supremacy groups. Gavin needed Republicans who were planning to vote for Goldwater as a base. His only chance was to ride the coattails of the Republican presidential nominee while picking off a few votes from disenchanted Democrats in the Sanford-Preyer mold.[24]

On Election Day, Johnson took 61 percent of the national vote, the highest popular vote percentage recorded by any twentieth-century presidential candidate. Goldwater did, however, win fifty-two electoral votes and six states: Alabama, Arizona, Georgia, Louisiana, Mississippi, and South Carolina, with Alabama, Georgia, Mississippi, and South Carolina supporting a Republican presidential candidate for the first time since Reconstruction. Johnson registered 56 percent in North Carolina, a proportion as high as Moore's. Johnson received 800,139 votes, while Goldwater took 624,844; Moore got 790,343, while Gavin got 606,165. Activist Democrats of the Sanford ilk jubilantly pointed out that Johnson's votes had exceeded Moore's. The president led from the mountains to the sea. His 61 percent in the coastal plain reflected a 7 percentage point fall from Kennedy in 1960, but like Kennedy, Johnson took all of its forty-one counties. Johnson led in the piedmont and in its three big urban counties that had earlier gone for Republicans Dwight Eisenhower and Richard Nixon: Forsyth, Guilford, and Mecklenburg. In another reversal from the last three elections, Johnson won the mountain region and the majority of its counties. Moore held 67 percent in the coastal plain and a strong 54.7 percent in his home mountain region. His 52.4 percent in the piedmont was close to Johnson's, but conspicuously Gavin carried two of the state's three most populous counties: Guilford (Preyer's home) and Forsyth. He lost the state's biggest county, Mecklenburg, by a mere eighteen votes. A few counties went for both Goldwater and Gavin, but they were historically Republican or counties that for years had been trending Republican.

North Carolina's white vote had split almost evenly in the presidential and gubernatorial contests. Black voters, a stronger presence than in 1960, went nearly 95 percent for Johnson and almost as solidly for Moore despite the ill feelings from the primary. Johnson's minority support was a jump from Kennedy's in 1960, estimated to have been near 70 percent.[25]

Aside from Johnson's Texas, North Carolina gave the Democratic presidential ticket the strongest support in the South. Why? Much of the answer could be found at opposite ends of the state. In the coastal plain, tobacco was still king, and many people—not just farmers—feared that Goldwater's free market and antisubsidy policies would harm the region's economy. Furthermore, the imprint of economic populism and memories of Roosevelt's New Deal reforms remained firm. Eastern North Carolina was the only region of its kind in the South—lowland rural with a large but historically shut-out black population—to vote for Johnson over Goldwater. The Roosevelt legacy also lured mountain voters. The Tennessee Valley Authority had brought government-subsidized electricity to area's hills and hollows during the 1930s and 1940s. Goldwater proposed selling the TVA to private owners. A popular anti-Goldwater bumper sticker in the mountains exclaimed, "Sell TVA? I'd sooner sell Arizona!" Across the entire southern Appalachian region, normally Republican voters moved to Johnson and the Democrats. Johnson was the first Democrat since Harry Truman to carry North Carolina's mountains. Moore's local roots also helped Democratic get-out-the-vote efforts in western North Carolina.

The bigger cities across the state, moving this time in a Democratic direction, followed a pattern seen in urban areas across much of the Outer South from Virginia to Tennessee to Texas. Wealthy and middle-class white precincts still went Republican but did so by smaller majorities than in 1952, 1956, and 1960. Reflecting an attitude that swept much of the country, the Republican deserters saw Goldwater as an extremist or as too radical. Heavy black support for Johnson in the cities was enough to overcome the smaller white majorities for Goldwater.[26]

In North Carolina as in nearly all America outside deepest Dixie, the martyrdom of John Kennedy probably aided the Democratic ticket. But in the aftermath of Johnson's triumph, most observers failed to notice an important milestone: For the first time, North Carolina had voted less Democratic than the United States as a whole, 56 percent compared to 61 percent.

Promising to protect and expand the Roosevelt-inspired welfare state, Johnson was the candidate of stability—the safer choice—for many voters. His was a victory for old-fashioned economic populism at a time when social or cultural populism seemed ready to take off. A lot of whites were angry but nevertheless afraid to cast their lot with Goldwater. A nervous public hoped for peace, growth, and prosperity.

However, the national election of 1964 was also a referendum on civil rights. Race had been the biggest national issue during the Johnson administration and the last eighteen months of the Kennedy administration. A majority of voters had signaled approval of or at least acquiescence to the new laws. Racial unrest continued, but for the immediate future, Johnson hoped to focus on advancing the social welfare state inaugurated by Roosevelt. In February and March 1965, civil rights forces led by Martin Luther King Jr. waged protests in South Alabama. A chief target was sheriff Jim Clark of Dallas County (Selma). Clark, with the backing of Governor George Wallace, sought to keep African Americans from registering to vote. Violence flared.[27] This propelled Johnson to propose the Voting Rights Act of 1965, designed to end discrimination in voting.

### HIGHER EDUCATION WARS: GROWTH BREEDS CONFLICT

In the mid- and late 1960s, many of North Carolina's hot-button issues touched on higher education. Until the end of World War II, college education had largely been reserved for the privileged or the ambitious. Most high school students went straight to work after graduation. Now, demographic trends and intense promotion from within had made state colleges and universities one of the new growth sectors. From 1958 to 1965, enrollment in North Carolina's institutions of higher education more than doubled, climbing from thirty thousand to near sixty-seven thousand. A big jump in births had occurred during and after World War II, resulting in a bump in college admissions starting in 1960. North Carolina State College in Raleigh, Appalachian State College in Boone, and East Carolina College in Greenville had administrations bent on expansion and outreach. Longtime teacher training colleges, including Appalachian, East Carolina, and Western Carolina College at Cullowhee saw themselves more and more as champions of regional development. Institutions that had historically served racial minorities, such as North Carolina College in Durham and Pembroke State College, wanted to remain true to their original missions as well as add programs appealing to Caucasians. They saw more integration as both an opportunity and a peril.

As Moore fought to win the governorship in 1964, the first wave of the still bigger post–World War II baby boom spent its junior and senior years in high school. Their impact on higher education would dwarf anything seen before. Public and private colleges prepared for a deluge that would overshadow the one of the 1958–65 period. Terry Sanford, always the visionary, had tried to prepare the way when he appointed the Carlyle Commission in 1961. Its chair was Irving Carlyle, who had daringly urged compliance with the *Brown* desegregation decision in 1954. With Sanford's blessing, the commission in 1962 proposed a three-tiered system of higher education. The top tier, the existing three-campus consolidated university, would stress graduate programs and research while boosting long-standing undergraduate programs. Chapel Hill stood informally at the top of the pyramid, though North Carolina State College would enhance its already strong research role in applied science and agriculture. Greensboro's Woman's College was to become coeducational and looked toward more graduate programs. On the second level were the undergraduate comprehensive colleges that performed a lot of the bread-and-butter work of teaching, with limited graduate degree programs—the former teachers' colleges and minority institutions. On the third level were the post-high-school technical schools and new community colleges, which would offer two-year associate degrees and feed the upper level of the comprehensive colleges.

The commission report became state policy, ostensibly with the blessings of most college leaders.[28] Whatever differences Moore might have had with the Sanford administration, he approved of the Carlyle Commission framework. Furthermore, the new governor believed that higher education expansion would be one of the great legacies of his administration. Moore dearly loved his own alma mater in Chapel Hill, despite his wariness of some of its professors.

Moore had accepted an invitation to speak at the annual Farm City Week on November 19, 1965, an event held at the North Carolina State University Faculty Club. When he had to cancel at the last minute, his emergency replacement was Leo Jenkins, the president of East Carolina College since 1960. Jenkins usually made good copy and had in recent years aggressively promoted East Carolina's role. Moore's cancellation provided Jenkins with a forum to propose a great leap forward. Jenkins hailed East Carolina as "the shining beacon" for a region wanting to shed the yoke of poverty. He told his audience that East Carolina College should assume full university status with graduate school and doctoral programs and added that its existing graduate offerings already made the school much more than a college. Thus began a battle that preoccupied state leaders for years to come but ran much of its course during the Moore administration. Jenkins had been a member of the Carlyle Commission but now ripped into its framework.[29]

Jenkins's speech and the follow-up campaign for university status put him in direct conflict with powerful interests in the piedmont and the state

Terry Sanford, "the education governor" (right), with East Carolina University president Leo Jenkins, 1961. Daily Reflector Negative Collection (#741), East Carolina Manuscript Collection, J. Y. Joyner Library, East Carolina University, Greenville.

university hierarchy. Leading power brokers, most notably banker George Watts Hill and attorney Victor Bryant, both of Durham, saw Jenkins's posture as an attack on Chapel Hill and the consolidated university Board of Trustees, where both Hill and Bryant wielded enormous influence. Major urban newspapers blasted Jenkins as a power grabber trying to push a "mediocre college" into the big leagues, whatever the consequences. William Friday, a major player in the Carlyle report, adroitly moved forward to protect the interests of the consolidated university.[30]

Friday and Jenkins shared a few traits but were primarily a duo in contrasts. Friday was the product of a middle-class Gaston County family and as a young man had worked briefly in a cotton mill. For years, however, he had been comfortable with members of the elite such as Gordon Gray, the patrician former consolidated university president. Coming from a wealthy Winston-Salem family, Gray had difficulty relating to his social inferiors. Friday, his administrative aide, had been Gray's ambassador of goodwill. Later, as Gray's successor, Friday had the ability to put people at ease whatever their status. He often sat in a chair directly facing visitors, not behind the protective barrier of a desk. He was soothing yet forceful when he needed to be. Many years later, state senator Billy Mills, a strong East Carolina booster, recalled Friday as one of the most powerful and effective lobbyists he had ever known, arriving early at every committee hearing so that he could greet and chat with arriving legislators, often about family or personal matters rather than university business. His formal remarks to committees were concise and well reasoned.[31] Friday understood power as well as anyone in the state, and he exuded a reverential air when he referred to "the University," an institution and concept that he loved. A progressive Democrat, Friday carefully avoided direct involvement in primaries or general elections. His undergraduate degree was from North Carolina State, but he felt a special kinship to Chapel Hill, where he had attended law school and had for many years lived.

Jenkins, the new symbol of eastern North Carolina, grew up in a working-class neighborhood in Elizabeth, New Jersey, within the metropolitan orbit of New York City. Fiercely loyal to friends, Jenkins was direct, sometimes brusque. Introduced to club presidents, he would say, "When are you going to invite me to give a speech?," occasionally uttering these words before even saying "Hello." A Marine major in World War II, Jenkins had displayed in the public area of his house a photo of a Japanese soldier being beheaded. He once seemed oblivious when members of a visiting Japanese delegation looked at the photo in astonishment. Jenkins proudly proclaimed himself a New Deal Democrat, regularly attending state and local Democratic functions and occasionally speaking at local and regional gatherings. He understood the levers of power as well as Friday and built close ties with conservative Democrats and Republicans. WRAL's commentator Jesse Helms admired Jenkins, partly for his educational mission and partly for his gall. To some, Jenkins symbolized a battle against a snobbish and elitist university in Chapel Hill that needed to be put in its place. While Jenkins at times seemed aloof, he was amazingly accessible. It was not uncommon for him to receive drop-in students, alumni, or passersby in his office almost immediately. But he also spent a lot of time on the road, playing the role of academic populist.

Jenkins had majored in political science at Rutgers University in New Brunswick, New Jersey, and briefly taught political science at New Jersey

State Teachers' College in Montclair. He possessed a master's degree from Columbia and a doctorate in education from New York University. He was no intellectual in the classic sense, but like Terry Sanford, Jenkins was a visionary, passionately pursing the advancement of his institution and adopted region.[32] His immediate goal was to lobby for the bill before the 1967 state legislature that would make East Carolina a university.

Always respectful of one another in person, Friday and Jenkins were formidable foes who believed in the righteousness of their respective causes. A top Jenkins ally in the N.C. Senate was Robert Morgan, an East Carolina alumnus, the chair of the school's Board of Trustees, and by now one of the state's leading politicians. He and Jenkins saw the need to form alliances with mountain political interests wanting to boost Appalachian and Western Carolina Colleges.

All three had an interest in acting quickly. The east and west were stagnant in population, but the piedmont was growing. In a 1962 case, *Baker v. Carr*, the U.S. Supreme Court had ruled that state legislative seats must be distributed based on equal population per legislator, not counties or the traditional considerations benefiting rural interests.[33] A federal court in North Carolina weighed changes to comply with the ruling. To date, rural easterners and to a degree westerners wielded enormous influence in the legislative halls, yet their clout was bound to diminish soon. The battle lines were drawn.[34] To counteract Jenkins's geographic strategy, the consolidated university interests moved to embrace the state college in Charlotte, then in the process of transforming from a junior college into a four-year program, as a fourth campus, something Moore had promised to Mecklenburg County during his 1964 campaign.[35]

In April 1967, the N.C. Senate defeated the bill to make East Carolina a university, 27–23. Moore had lobbied heavily against the bill, calling it a recipe for "chaos." The governor's stand poisoned the atmosphere within the Democratic Party, which was disproportionately dependent on voters from eastern North Carolina. As governor, Moore was the titular and symbolic head of the party, and eastern political interests believed they had been crucial in cementing his 1964 primary victory. ECU booster Morgan was a member of Moore's "kitchen cabinet," which offered advice on appointments and political issues. As a leading architect of the East Carolina bill, Morgan was miffed at a governor he had often supported. Hoping for a resolution, Moore urged the East Carolina trustees to petition for membership in the consolidated university. Jenkins declined. Moore's proposal would have put him directly under the control of his adversaries.[36]

In 1967, Senator John Henley of Fayetteville, hitherto a consolidated university loyalist, introduced "An Act to Provide for Regional Universities and the Establishment of the First University, East Carolina University." This proposal originated with former governor Sanford, who was on good terms with both Jenkins and Friday. At the time, Sanford was attempting to build political goodwill and support in the east for a possible run against Senator Ervin in 1968. The bill declared that other state colleges that had awarded master's degrees for ten years or more would be eligible to apply for regional university status. Appalachian State in Boone and Western Carolina in Cullowhee were considered the most likely candidates. Lieutenant Governor Bob Scott, a North Carolina State graduate deeply skeptical of the consolidated university board, put his full weight behind Henley's bill. Scott's support added momentum to the effort, as he was widely regarded as the front-runner in the 1968 gubernatorial race. In addition, Jenkins had hinted that he might run for governor. Scott hoped to head off such a candidacy, which had the potential to diminish his support in eastern North Carolina.

Moore expressed opposition, restating his position that an aspiring East Carolina should aim for inclusion in the consolidated university.[37] The State Board of Higher Education sought to kill the legislation through a stratagem of urging all state colleges to apply for university status. Its plan would have amended the Henley bill to permit any state college to be called a "university" if it requested that status. Sanford opposed the amendments, saying the idea behind his proposal was a gradual evolution into an expanded system. With the support of East Carolina's leading legislative backer, Morgan, the regional university bill was amended to give immediate university status to Appalachian, Western Carolina, and North Carolina A&T. The amended bill passed. In 1969, Wilmington College and Asheville-Biltmore entered the consolidated university as UNC-Wilmington and UNC-Asheville, respectively.[38]

The fight had revolved around clashing visions of higher education and outsized egos. Even without Jenkins, the newer state colleges—which had started as teacher training institutions—would have demanded and likely won a bigger slice of the pie. The nation was on the cusp of an explosion in higher education enrollments, much too big for the system to absorb in its present state. But the alliance of Jenkins, Morgan, and others from upstart colleges speeded the process. Higher education was to thrive thereafter.

Moore inherited a vexing problem from the Sanford era that Sanford had found himself unable to solve. Near the end of its session, the 1963 legislature had quickly enacted a measure that became known as the Speaker

Ban Law, which directed that no state-funded college or university could let its facilities be used by a speaker who "is known to advocate the overthrow of the United States or the State of North Carolina; [or] has pleaded the Fifth Amendment of the Constitution of the United States in refusing to answer any question with respect to Communist or subversive connections, or activities."[39] Senate President Pro Tem Clarence Stone of Rockingham County, an unreconstructed southerner but a personal and political friend of Sanford, sponsored the bill. In the brief Senate floor "debate" over the bill, Stone, who was presiding at the time, refused to recognize opponents of the legislation. Only after its passage did Stone call on Senator Luther Hamilton of Carteret County, who asked to speak on a point of personal privilege. Hamilton, one of the oldest members of the chamber, delivered an impassioned talk on the sanctity of freedom of speech. Hamilton had hoped to give the speech during the debate, but Stone had refused to recognize him even though he was sitting on the front row and in clear sight of the podium.[40] Stone and many legislators used the bill to take a punch at leftists and proponents of racial integration in Chapel Hill and at North Carolina State, although the law applied to all state institutions of higher learning and made no mention of race.

Sanford lacked the veto weapon. Furthermore, he knew that the legislature would be unreceptive to amending or repealing the Speaker Ban Law so soon after its passage. Late in his term, Sanford did not want to see his other initiatives threatened by a sure-to-fail effort against the Speaker Ban Law. The average North Carolinian probably thought the new law reasonable and proper. Most academic administrators around the state, including Friday and Jenkins, immediately spoke out against the ban. Professors and liberal students stridently opposed what they saw as an assault on academic freedom. Opponents of the act quietly approved when the Southern Association of Colleges and Schools threatened to lift the accreditation of all North Carolina's colleges, a threat that they thought would be a powerful argument for repeal of the ban.

Moore had expressed mild support for the speaker ban in his 1964 campaign but now feared for the well-being of state higher education. Furthermore, key Moore backers George Watts Hill and Victor Bryant opposed the law. Moore appointed a nine-member commission chaired by his trusted friend, state representative David Britt. The commission held four days of televised hearings in the late summer of 1965. Without specifically criticizing the law, the commission recommended a "modification" that would give trustees of each school control over decisions about inviting speakers. Moore endorsed the report, which was almost precisely the recommendation for which he was quietly hoping. He called a special legislative session for November 15, and the legislators quickly approved the Britt Commission report and returned control of speakers to campus boards. So by the end of 1965, a crisis that promised large student demonstrations and the stain of an accreditation battle had been averted. But the dispute continued at specific universities, most notably UNC–Chapel Hill. Trustees and administrators knew that legislators were watching closely and consequently refused to approve requests from groups wanting to host controversial speakers. With the conflict in Vietnam escalating, small but visible antiwar protests took place on college campuses, feeding the legislature's and general public's anger about what they saw as campus radicalism. Finally, in 1968, a federal court invalidated the original 1963 Speaker Ban as a violation of the Free Speech Clause of the First Amendment. Behind the scenes, Friday had encouraged UNC student body president Paul Dixon to initiate the lawsuit that led to the ruling.[41]

## PUBLIC SCHOOL SEGREGATION: CRACKS AMID RESISTANCE

Like the colleges and universities, the elementary and secondary public schools grew as a younger wave of baby boomers entered the school system. Politically, the issue of racial integration eclipsed growth and expansion. More than a decade had passed since the *Brown* desegregation ruling. In 1957, Charlotte, Greensboro, and Winston-Salem had won praise for their voluntary moves toward token integration. Still, in the 1964–65 school year, only 1.42 percent of all black students enrolled in the state's public schools attended "integrated"—previously all-white—schools. In September 1965, the better mobilized African American community and the newly empowered federal government increased the pressure for desegregation. In the fall term, black registration in desegregated schools rose to just above eight thousand, nearly twice what it had been the previous year.[42]

More significant for the long term were two pieces of recent federal legislation, the Civil Rights Act of 1964 and the Elementary and Secondary Education Act of 1965, passed in the spring. Title VI of the civil rights bill mandated that there be no racial discrimination   a term meant to target segregation— in any state or local program getting federal aid. The law directed federal agencies to take steps against any such discrimination and provided that as a last resort, federal funds could be withheld from any discriminating state or local agency. The biggest state agency or program was public education. The education act boosted federal financial aid for state school systems from near 5 percent of their budgets to the 10–11 percent range. North Carolina had already received federal aid for schools in "impacted areas"—a designation for schools near military installations—and for special programs promoting the sciences. While the new legislation provided money for all jurisdictions, it would be crucial for poorer districts—just the kind of school districts found across much of North Carolina and the South.[43]

A Washington bureaucracy, the Department of Health, Education, and Welfare (HEW) inherited the role of chief enforcer of the new legislation. Its expanded Office of Equal Educational Opportunity acquired broad powers. That office had supervisory authority as the approval agency for all integration plans and thus controlled the federal purse strings. Recalcitrant districts risked losing crucial federal dollars, potentially jeopardizing their ability to operate. This was a politically difficult time to be a county commissioner or local school board member, for much of the white voting public remained as skeptical as ever of full-scale racial integration. Without federal funds, the county commissioners, who in North Carolina made local spending and taxing decisions, faced the dilemma of increased taxes or unpopular program cuts. Either option could stir public anger and retribution in the voting booth. (Primary funding responsibility for public school operations remained with the states.)

The 1966 elections approached. North Carolina Democrats were nervous. Senator Jordan was the odds-on favorite over his Republican opponent, John Shallcross: Senator Ervin shouted at rallies, "Shallcross shall not cross the River Jordan."[44] In the Fourth District, Harold Cooley of Nashville, the aging lion who chaired the House Agriculture Committee, faced a stiff challenge from Republican Jim Gardner of nearby Rocky Mount, who had made his money through the Hardee's fast-food chain. In this district that straddled the western coastal plain and eastern piedmont, Cooley would normally have been the favorite, but Gardner blasted the aggressiveness of HEW and the Johnson administration and linked them with the "liberal" Cooley. And indeed, Cooley had a liberal voting record on issues other than race. Even on civil rights, he was a moderate, having refused to sign the Southern Manifesto in 1956. Cooley talked with Johnson, who urged the agency to take a less aggressive posture, at least for the duration of the campaign. But HEW's long-term goals stayed the same, and Gardner defeated Cooley in the 1966 midterm election. The Democratic edge in the N.C. Senate dropped from 49–1 to 43–7; in the N.C. House, the Democratic advantage fell from 106–14 to 94–26. Jordan, as expected, was reelected.

## THE WHITE FIREWALL

No one really knew the numbers, but anecdotal evidence suggested that the Ku Klux Klan had grown immensely in North Carolina between 1960 and 1966. The Klan leadership, like that of more benevolent organizations, including churches, was prone to overstate its membership but remained secretive about most activities. Huts, lodges, and "hunting clubs" known to be Klan buildings turned up on the edges of swamps and small towns. Klansmen also thrived in larger towns and cities. The Klan occasionally held large public rallies in farm fields or vacant lots just outside towns. At some of these rallies, they welcomed visitors, whether potential members or the merely curious. The KKK's presence was especially notable in Greene and Johnston Counties in the tobacco belt east of Raleigh and Iredell and Rowan Counties north of Charlotte. The Federal Bureau of Investigation estimated the Klan's dues-paying membership at six thousand at its 1960s peak, a figure that, even if accurate, greatly understated Klan support and influence. Large numbers of North Carolina whites sympathized with some or all of its agenda.[45]

Originally founded after the Civil War, the Klan diminished in importance after the end of Reconstruction but experienced a second surge in the aftermath of World War I. The Klan was a self-proclaimed Christian organization that espoused both nativism and southern pride. In the 1915–28 period, Catholics, Jews, and immigrants as well as blacks had been Klan targets. But in the 1960s, as it had a century earlier, attention focused almost entirely on blacks. Now, however, most Klan leaders were plebeians, not former Confederate officers. J. Robert "Bob" Jones of Granite Quarry in Rowan County was the Grand Dragon (state leader) of the United Knights of the Ku Klux Klan in North Carolina in 1966.[46]

The Klan reached its post–World War II zenith in the 1966–68 period. The KKK in North Carolina was less openly violent than Klan groups in Alabama, Georgia, and Mississippi, but their presence created a climate of fear among blacks and racially liberal whites in many communities. While much of the white civic and political leadership looked down on the organization, the safest course of action was to avoid attacking it head-on. Governor Moore, however, began to move more aggressively, announcing the establishment of a Law and Order Committee in January 1966: "Because of the extremist nature of the Ku Klux Klan, the committee will give special attention to any potential law violators and fomenters of violence within this organization."[47] During the 1967 legislative session, Moore pushed for the passage of a law that made cross burnings on private property without permission of the owner a felony. In response to a racially motivated burning of houses in Anson County, a new law specifically provided imprisonment for such offenses. The new law was partly symbolic, as existing laws provided for stiff penalties for burnings or other attacks on private property.

The more respectable White Citizens' Councils criticized lawlessness and violence but sought to prevent integration through legal means. The Councils spoke out for states' rights and voluntary segregation in the schools. Partly as a result of their efforts, private all-white academies began to crop up all over North Carolina. They did, however, mobilize opposition to desegregation and provide momentum for a 1968 George Wallace presidential campaign.

The growth of the Klan and Citizens' Councils and the more generalized anger among many whites had come in the aftermath of some of the biggest civil rights advances in U.S. history, including the Civil Rights Act of 1964. A year later, at the behest of President Johnson, Congress had adopted the Voting Rights Act of 1965, which suspended the literacy test, a device that had been used to block blacks from voting in many parts of the South. White resistance had been unable to block the change.

### MOORE THE MODERNIZER

Amid the conflicts and turmoil of the mid-1960s, dynamism and innovation could be easily overlooked. This was a prosperous time in American history. Job opportunities expanded as cities boomed. In North Carolina as in much of the United States, suburbs grew as never before while rural areas lost population. The revenue from Sanford's earlier tax increases helped translate big ideas into reality without further tax boosts. Both the 1965 and 1967 General Assemblies adopted record budgets. Indeed, the 1967 legislature passed a $2.8 billion budget while that included a modest $23.5 million income tax cut. Salaries for schoolteachers went up by 10 percent in 1965 and 20 percent in 1967–68.[48] Moore subsequently accepted an invitation to address the convention of the North Carolina Education Association, which had ferociously fought him in the 1964 Democratic primary. Departing from his typical tact, Moore told the school personnel that despite their opposition to his candidacy, his administration had provided one of the biggest salary increases ever. The salary increases under Moore equaled those of the Sanford period.[49]

Moore and legislative leaders pushed hard for court reform. At the same time, voters approved the establishment of a new intermediate appeals court between the superior court (trial court) level and the supreme court, resulting in a state court organizational plan more akin to the federal court system and taking some pressure off the overworked state supreme court.

By any traditional yardstick that measures success by new programs and improved infrastructure, Moore should rank as one of North Carolina's most successful governors.[50] Nonetheless, many opinion makers—academics, newspaper editorialists, and outside observers who chronicled progress in the state—offered restrained or only mildly positive assessments of his administration. Why? Moore had entered office under a dark cloud from the standpoint of promoters of a brave new South. He not only had resoundingly defeated the reputedly more progressive Richardson Preyer in the Democratic primary but had done so in a campaign tinged with racism. Moore's predecessor, Sanford, while not a magnetic speaker, had won the hearts of liberal reformers by going further than any leading southern politician of his time to break down old barriers and build a modern twentieth-century society. During the campaign, Moore had attacked Sanford and by implication his programs and spirit.

As governor, Moore staffed his office and other top positions with moderate to conservative Democrats, often people who had been prominent in the Umstead and Hodges administrations or, even more to liberals' dismay, the Lake campaign. And Moore had so little charisma that he made Sanford seem almost Rooseveltian. Finally, Moore had close ties to the manufacturers and bankers who had long held sway in the state. In a way, therefore, he seemed to be a throwback to business as usual, part a result of image and part reality.

Nonetheless, Moore's legacy is solid. When asked in a 2007 interview what North Carolina governor of the twentieth century was the most underrated, Friday unhesitatingly named Moore.[51] Robert Morgan and Bob Scott, both of whom sometimes had differences with Moore on big issues, commended him as a good listener and man of sound judgment.[52] Behind the scenes, Moore had attempted to build consensus on controversial matters. He was among the most successful of governors in getting his programs through the legislature, even though he lost on a few high-profile issues, most notably the reorganization of higher education. Under his stewardship, North Carolina pressed forward despite fears and high tension. But moving into 1968, the tensions showed no sign of abating.

## A GREAT SOCIETY?

Lyndon Johnson, wanting to resurrect the spirit of Roosevelt and the New Deal, moved to broaden the reach of the federal government in almost every sphere. He persuaded the heavily Democratic 1965 Congress to adopt government health care (Medicare) for people old enough for full social security benefits, an idea previously proposed by Kennedy.[53] A hallmark of Johnson's 1964 campaign had been a declaration of war against poverty. In Johnson's view as in Roosevelt's, the South offered the greatest challenges and opportunities. During the first months of 1964 and the subsequent presidential campaign, Johnson focused on poverty in Appalachia, a big slice of which lay in North Carolina. This hauntingly beautiful but scarred region had for years been a backwater of the American economy. Parts of it had a big coal mining business, but not in North Carolina. Its population remained largely Caucasian, with Native Americans the largest minority in a few counties and African Americans in the others. Young men and women left in huge numbers to work in the factories of Detroit or Ohio. Johnson spoke incessantly of Appalachia and took a number of excursions there. Politically, Appalachia made a good symbol for the antipoverty crusade. Because it was mostly white and stretched from Alabama to southern Ohio and southern New York, Johnson could stress that poverty knew no ethnic or racial boundaries. Johnson knew that he was indelibly linked in the public mind with the crusade for black equality. The same public associated poverty with the Black Belt South and growing minority ghettos in northern cities. Johnson had no wish to reinforce further his identification with poor African Americans, a group still disdained by many whites in the South and elsewhere. Emphasis on white Appalachia was a way to break out of that box and still push one of his most cherished goals.

When implemented in 1965 and afterward, the poverty programs plunged into controversy. The most visible fights came in North Carolina cities far from Appalachia and spilled over into the persistent racial animosity of the time. The antipoverty programs were based on the premise that needy people—not elected state and local officials—should decide how to spend the funds allocated to the new community action projects. The federal Office of Economic Opportunity (OEO) established links with community action programs led by individuals wanting fundamental political and social change. Friction between white local officials and community activists, many of whom were black, was constant. The activists saw local officials as part of the problem. Local officeholders saw OEO programs as a threat to the status quo. In their eyes, federal seed money was going to fund a revolution. The programs bogged down in controversy as time passed. For Johnson, the War on Poverty became secondary to the war in Vietnam.

The antipoverty effort simmered on the back burner, without a real chance to prove whether it could work. Overall, Johnson left a deep imprint: Medicare, massive federal involvement in education on all levels, and civil rights. However, the War on Poverty was more a dream than a reality. But from 1964 to early 1968, the war in Vietnam had expanded from a sideshow barely in the public consciousness to one of the major wars of the twentieth century.

The mid-1960s were a time when federal and southern state priorities collided in ways not seen since the Reconstruction era of the 1860s and 1870s. Resistance to change was the big political theme. Yet the stage was set for the most fundamental economic and social change in a long time. Swedish economist and sociologist Gunnar Myrdal had spoken in the 1940s of "an American dilemma."[54] Myrdal referred to the lack of full democracy and racial equality, especially in the South. At last, a nation and a region had been forced to confront that dilemma head-on. Time would tell, but a new society might be emerging after all. More immediately, bloodshed loomed both at home and abroad.

## CHAPTER FIVE

# Dirges in the Dark

Beginning in the mid-1960s, a small group of students, left-leaning intellectuals, and Quakers stood like sentinels at such locales as the sidewalk outside the Chapel Hill post office. Their anti–Vietnam War protest was a lonely one. Then, in 1968, antiwar sentiment began to spread even in conservative North Carolina. But 1968 would be the least peaceful of years.

Peace groups organized and grew on college campuses. The more privileged sons of North Carolina—the ones who could afford to go to college and thus gain long-term student draft deferments—began to feel threatened as the war expanded.[1] So far, the war had been fought disproportionately by youth from the working class. They, their families, and North Carolina's large military community felt a sense of betrayal when reading of or witnessing on the screen the loud protestations from Chapel Hill or California. North Carolina elites, corporate and political, also seethed. But many of their college-age sons and daughters inched toward sympathy for the demonstrators, fearing that they or their loved ones might be drafted to fight in an ever-expanding tropical hell.

By late 1967, Minnesota senator Eugene McCarthy began what at first seemed a quixotic presidential campaign opposing Lyndon Johnson and the war. Then came a major American setback as communist forces mounted the early 1968 Tet Offensive in Vietnam. McCarthy made a strong showing in the first primaries in New Hampshire and Wisconsin.[2] Claiming the torch of his brother, Robert Kennedy entered the presidential race in April 1968, running against both Johnson and the war. Johnson withdrew from the race. On the night of April 4, while standing on a Memphis motel balcony, Martin Luther King Jr. was assassinated. Riots broke out in Chicago, Washington, and other cities.[3] Large North Carolina cities were placed under states of emergency, night curfews, and National Guard control for a few days, although violence occurred on only a small scale. North Carolinians held peaceful marches and candlelight vigils for King. Most marchers were black, but a few whites, including ministers, participated. In Wilson, a young attorney, Jim Hunt, then president of the North Carolina Young Democratic Clubs, joined a march and church service.[4] Not quite two months later, on June 3, Sirhan Sirhan assassinated Robert Kennedy as Kennedy celebrated his California primary victory in a Los Angles hotel.

With the most passionate of leaders gone, political convention time grew nearer. In Johnson's place, the fervent liberal vice president, Hubert Humphrey, now a pariah to many liberals because of his unswerving support for the Vietnam War, became front-runner for the Democratic nomination. McCarthy and a late entry, Senator George McGovern of South Dakota, gained delegates, but they possessed neither the insider status nor the drive to prevail in the caucuses and backrooms where large numbers of delegates were selected.

McCarthy supporters had packed precinct caucuses and county conventions in North Carolina's cities and academic centers. They made headway and won control of the party apparatus in Orange County (Chapel Hill). But party regulars of a more conservative bent would choose most of the state delegates to the national convention in Chicago.[5]

Since 1916, North Carolina had held party primaries to choose nominees for governor and other state offices, but presidential primaries with the possibilities of a more democratic selection process did not come until 1972. The party caucuses and state conventions chose nominees to the state convention. The incumbent governor (still Dan Moore) traditionally wielded strong influence on delegate selection.

Candidates for state office nervously eyed national trends. Most were unenthusiastic about all of the possible Democratic presidential nominees, fearful that their liberalism would hurt the state ticket. Closer to home, the candidates were worried about the social unrest, black protests in the streets, and campus protests. Candidates feared a voter backlash that would hurt the state Democratic ticket.

### THE LAW-AND-ORDER PRIMARY

Since 1964, Bob Scott had been the favorite for the 1968 Democratic gubernatorial nomination. He had the name and impeccable connections with agricultural interests. As the son of former governor Kerr Scott, Bob Scott had links to the liberal wing of the party. However, the younger Scott never warmed to the Sanford administration and its intellectual brain trust.

Scott had been peripherally involved with the Sanford campaign in 1960. He attended an early strategy session to promote the 1964 gubernatorial campaign of Richardson Preyer.[6] Instead, however, the thirty-five-year-old Scott had embarked on a run for lieutenant governor. His most serious opponent in 1968 was J. Melville Broughton Jr., the son of the former governor and senator. Broughton had ties to the conservative wing of the party and business interests but had not held public office. Charlotte dentist Reginald Hawkins, the first African American to seek the governorship, ran to Scott's left. Hawkins provided excitement but was never able to expand his support beyond blacks and a few of the most liberal whites.

While Scott campaigned on the usual progressive Democratic themes of improved education and infrastructure, he was nervous about the perception that he was part of the Sanford organization.[7] North Carolina voters were moving rightward politically, partly as a response to bedlam in the streets related to the growing antiwar movement and black protesters. Scott wanted to make a break from the liberals, at least on social issues. He decided on the place and time: Dunn in the late winter of 1968. Dunn was a conservative town on the western edge of the coastal plain and the home base of the conservative newspaper publisher Hoover Adams. The setting was a Kiwanis Club meeting. The theme was law and order, a code phrase among conservative politicians attacking not only criminal elements but militant young blacks, street protesters, and the emerging mainly white hippie culture. Scott's address was the most sensational event of the campaign. He told the crowd that he would come down hard on protesters. Violators of the law, especially spoiled college brats, would be shown no mercy. His audience erupted into applause, and the liberal press denounced his speech as demagoguery. Terry Sanford privately called the remarks "deplorable."[8] In a 2006 interview, Scott recalled the speech as a key event of the campaign:

> I knew I was perceived to be a member of the progressive wing of the Scott-Sanford ilk. Mel Broughton was from the conservative wing of the party. Obviously, Reginald Hawkins was liberal. The middle of the road was pretty narrow. I needed to widen that middle. I needed to break the glass prism that saw me as a member of the progressive wing. I had to do that in some way. I wanted a law-and-order speech. Ben Roney [Scott's special assistant and political adviser] put Robert Redwine on it. He was a speechwriter for Kerr Scott. He was a great writer but could achieve greatness only when he was drunk. He wrote a fireball speech on law and order. Both Ben Roney and I thought it needed to be toned down.

So we softened it some. . . . There were several purposes. I was trying to broaden my appeal, but I didn't want to get in a ditch with conservatives. I wanted to marginalize the opposition. I wanted to show I had the same heritage as the typical North Carolinian.[9]

With 337,368 votes to Broughton's 223,924 and Hawkins's 129,802, Scott received just shy of a majority in the May primary. He had run first in most counties and all regions. In a runoff primary, Hawkins supporters were likely to vote for Scott as the less unacceptable choice or not to vote at all. Seeing the futility of a runoff, Broughton endorsed Scott.

On the same day, Jim Gardner of Rocky Mount, the U.S. representative who had unseated veteran Harold Cooley in 1966, won the Republican nomination for governor. Gardner was young, glib, and photogenic. He beat John "Jack" Stickley of Charlotte, the choice of many traditional western North Carolina Republicans. Stickley, too, was a polished speaker and regular on the civic club circuit but lacked experience in public office. Gardner's victory signaled added clout for eastern North Carolinians in the Republican ranks. Scott still had the edge. But with chaos mounting in the national Democratic Party, Gardner hoped to mount a competitive challenge, in which he portrayed himself the law-and-order candidate.

In addition to the governor's race, one Democratic primary race attracted major attention. Robert Morgan opposed incumbent Wade Bruton for attorney general. The conservative Bruton lacked charisma. Morgan still exuded the aura of youth, and he was a tireless campaigner. Though he had managed I. Beverly Lake's 1960 segregationist campaign for governor, Morgan was friendly with Sanford and many moderate to liberal Democrats. In his campaign, Morgan promised to transform the attorney general's office into one that aggressively watched out for the public interest on matters such as consumer protection while also aggressively enforcing the law. Even colorless incumbent members of the Council of State (state-level offices below governor) usually won reelection, but in this case, Morgan prevailed over Bruton.[10]

### KNOCKDOWN BATTLE

The Republican National Convention in Miami Beach went smoothly, with former vice president Richard Nixon beating New York's liberal governor, Nelson Rockefeller, for the nomination. Nixon tapped Maryland governor Spiro Agnew as his running mate, largely because Agnew had not accumulated battle scars. At the same time, Agnew had the potential to play the role of hatchet man, a valued quality in vice presidential nominees.

Without renouncing his past support for minority rights, Nixon quietly hinted that he would not stress further racial integration. South Carolina senator Strom Thurmond, who had switched from the Democratic to the Republican Party in 1964, backed Nixon for the nomination and promised to campaign hard for him in the South. Nixon hoped to attract moderate white southerners who found both Humphrey and Wallace too extreme for their tastes. But Nixon initially wanted to minimize controversy. The Democrats seemed in a self-destructive mode. A cardinal rule of politics is not to interfere when the opposition is bent on suicide.

At the Democratic National Convention in Chicago just before Labor Day, Mayor Richard Daley's police took the battle against demonstrators into the streets. Police riot units bloodied protesters and even a few reporters in Grant Park. Inside the convention hall, pandemonium erupted when Daley attempted to restrain the large contingent of antiwar delegates. The coup de grâce was a police raid—ostensibly a drug search—on the headquarters of the defeated McCarthy on the morning after the convention.[11] Vice President Hubert Humphrey, the happy warrior and longtime civil rights crusader, received the Democratic nomination for president. Humphrey, who as Johnson's loyal aide-de-camp had relentlessly defended the Vietnam War, now found himself a quisling among his former liberal allies. In one of the great ironies of American political history, many old conservative southern segregationists joined with party regulars and Johnson loyalists to provide Humphrey the nomination. He was the least of the evils in a nomination fight where the chief opponents were McCarthy and McGovern, the latter having inherited many of the dejected Robert Kennedy delegates.

Among the North Carolina delegates, UNC–Chapel Hill political science professor Alden Lind and soft drink dealer Jim Johnson, appointed state Democratic chair by Bob Scott, voted for McCarthy. Scott and other members of the delegation supported Humphrey with their votes if not their enthusiasm. Humphrey had never been popular in North Carolina. Running on a Democratic ticket with Humphrey was a daunting prospect in North Carolina, as it was in all of the South. Aside from Herbert Hoover in 1932 and Barry Goldwater in 1964, few presidential candidates had taken to the campaign trail with more scars. Humphrey carried heavy baggage: Johnson, Daley, and national exhaustion from all things political. Nor could conservative white southerners forget his brash racial liberalism. Almost as much as Martin Luther King Jr., Humphrey had personified the long battle for black racial equality. In an atmosphere of racial animosity and general anger, North Carolinians welcomed the vice president as they once might have the boll weevil. White southerners had resigned themselves to recent civil rights legislation, but its chief proponents—aside from the now martyred John Kennedy—were not viewed favorably. Humphrey's prospects were so bleak that North Carolina Democrats shunned mention of his name. No major Democratic candidate endorsed Nixon; indeed, most said they would vote a straight Democratic Party ticket. But when a statewide radio commercial proclaimed, "Ten good reasons to vote the state Democratic ticket," it named Bob Scott, lieutenant governor candidate Pat Taylor, and the eight Democrats running for Council of State positions, such as attorney general and insurance commissioner. Humphrey was a conspicuous omission.

Nixon was thought to have the edge in North Carolina, but George Wallace, running on the American Independent ticket (called American Party on the North Carolina ballot), was a serious force. He later toned down his rhetoric, but there was no denying that Wallace tapped white prejudices and racial fears. More broadly, however, he attracted people who were fed up with campus agitators, faceless bureaucrats, and federal judges tampering with old ways. His craving for attention seemed to border on the erotic. While Wallace's greatest appeal was to the white working class, he also drew backing from middle-class ranks. Cunning, narcissistic, and just plain angry, Wallace relished his role as defender of ordinary, hardworking folks. Near the campaign's end, the ebullient Humphrey and his popular vice presidential running mate, Senator Edmund Muskie of Maine, rebounded in much of the Northeast and Midwest but made little headway in North Carolina. The national election outcome suddenly was in doubt as Humphrey's aggressive appeal brought New Deal–style and economic-populist-style Democrats and social liberals back to the party fold.

In the end Nixon prevailed, outpolling Humphrey 31,785,480–31,275,166. Nixon's electoral vote lead was a more commanding 301–191, yet slight shifts in a few big Nixon states—California, Illinois, Ohio, New Jersey—would have put Humphrey above the magic 270 votes and into the White House. In North Carolina, Nixon received a 39.5 percent plurality with 627,129 votes. Wallace finished second with 31.25 percent (496,188), and Humphrey third with 29.25 percent (464,113), a drop of more than 26 percentage points from 1964. Nixon led in the piedmont with 43 percent of the vote and in the mountains with 49 percent. Wallace led in the coastal plan with 41 percent, finished second in the piedmont with 29 percent, and third in the mountains with 22.5 percent. Between 1964 and 1968, the Democratic presidential vote share dropped from 61 percent to 32 percent in the coastal plain, from 53 percent to 28 percent in the piedmont, and from 54 percent

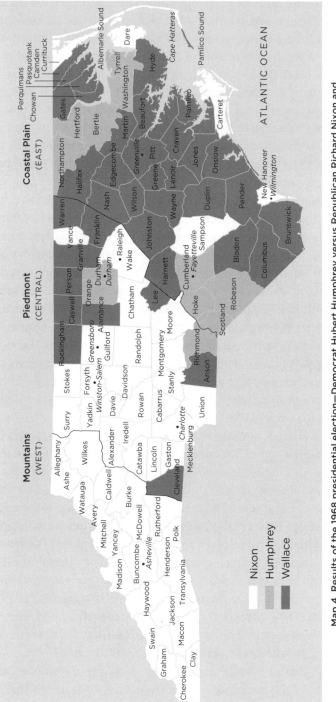

Map 4. Results of the 1968 presidential election—Democrat Hubert Humphrey versus Republican Richard Nixon and American Independent George Wallace

to 28.5 percent in the mountains. Humphrey took a few Black Belt counties where the Voting Rights Act of 1965 had increased the percentage of African American voters. Humphrey also led in Durham and Chapel Hill, where many former McCarthy and Kennedy backers unenthusiastically voted the straight Democratic ticket. Otherwise, he was shut out across the state. The Democratic collapse occurred despite the party's huge edge in voter registration (a nearly 4:1 advantage over the Republicans). And in a 1968 public opinion survey, 60 percent of North Carolinians still called themselves Democrats, whereas only 21 percent called themselves Republicans.[12]

The biggest Democratic drop had come in eastern North Carolina, where Wallace, not Nixon, was the beneficiary. Indeed, the Republican presidential vote there dropped from 39 percent in 1964 to 32 percent in 1968, returning to its anemic levels of 1952, 1956, and 1960. Wallace had advantages in this historically Democratic but socially conservative region. He was a southerner and nominally a Democrat, even as he ran under the American Party label in this election. People not wanting to vote for a Republican could protest by voting for Wallace. They were making a psychological break from the straight Democratic ticket while still supporting a kindred spirit. The phenomenon was not entirely clear at the time, but Wallace's candidacy provided some voters with a bridge from the Democratic Party to the Republican Party. Once voters had made the break from the party of their forefathers, it would be easier to do so again, and maybe the next time, they would mark Republican ballots.

More immediately, Wallace represented and led a growing mass movement fueled by anger over black protesters, student radicals, the hippie culture, and rising crime rates. Wallace was the archetypical southern social populist demagogue. He knew how to fuel the flames of resentment, a strategy historian Dan T. Carter has called "the politics of rage."[13] Wallace said before the cameras what many whites were saying to their friends and kindred. Voters, especially males, admired Wallace for his gall. Years earlier, voters had been most concerned about their economic security. Now they were angry at social forces unleashed in the land. Former supporters of Franklin Roosevelt and John Kennedy turned in anger and frustration to Wallace. Most of the counties that backed Wallace in 1968 had voted for Kennedy in 1960. In 1968, voters in eastern North Carolina and to a lesser degree other parts of the state followed Wallace, who voiced their emotions.

For all Wallace's emotional appeal, it was Nixon who benefited electorally from the rising anger. Nixon said he would appoint judges who were "strict constructionists" of the Constitution. This was an indirect signal that his potential court appointees would not push school integration any faster than was absolutely necessary. The 1968 election marked the biggest fracture yet in the national Democratic Party. On the presidential level, it signaled the end of Democratic supremacy in North Carolina.[14] The old Roosevelt coalition seemed to be on its deathbed. Republicans saw a new day coming.

Two new Republicans, both conservative, were elected to Congress, leaving North Carolina Democrats with only a 7–4 edge among U.S. representatives. Former major league pitcher Wilbur "Vinegar Bend" Mizell took the Winston-Salem–area Fifth District, and Catawba College dean Earl Ruth won the southern piedmont Eighth District. Liberal Democrats celebrated the victory of Democrat L. Richardson Preyer for an open seat in the Greensboro-area Sixth Congressional District. Traditional Democrats were buttressed by the reelection of Senator Sam Ervin. Republicans captured 12 of 50 seats in the N.C. Senate and 29 of 120 in the N.C. House, their highest levels since the 1928 election. Democrat Henry Frye of Greensboro won a seat in the House, making him the first African American candidate to win election to the state legislature since 1898.

Led by Scott, the Democrats won all major state offices. Nevertheless, Scott's margin of victory was the smallest of any Democrat gubernatorial candidate to date in the twentieth century. He took 821,232 votes (53 percent) to Gardner's 737,578. Scott had continued to stress progressivism, state services, and law-and-order themes. Gardner tried to link Scott with the liberalism and alleged permissiveness of the national Democratic Party. Gardner took a neutral stance toward the contest between Nixon and Wallace. Insisting that he still was a loyal Republican, Gardner said that either a Nixon or Wallace victory over Humphrey would be a good outcome. He hoped to gain a lot of votes in eastern North Carolina, a goal that required him to pick up a large number of Wallace voters. Gardner carried a scattering of eastern counties, but Scott took in the region as a consequence of his vigorous campaign, his late father's popularity, and perhaps memories of his law-and-order speech at Dunn. Republicans and some independent voters in the mountains and piedmont disliked Gardner's flirtation with Wallace voters.[15] Gardner might well have won the election if he had been more emphatic in his support for Nixon. However, that theory presupposes that he would have still picked up a lot of Wallace voters in the coastal plain and eastern piedmont.

After one of the most turbulent elections in modern history, Scott and other Democrats faced the prospect of governing a fractured North Carolina. Despite campaign bows to the cultural conservatives, Scott's specific policy proposals had stressed greater funding for education on all levels and transportation improvements. His stance hinted at his father's economic populism but offered a stronger scent of the growth-oriented progressive model personified by Charles Aycock and Terry Sanford. The tensions of the time threatened to divert Scott from his main goals.

## THE AUDITION

Hardly had Scott been inaugurated when a dispute broke out over wages and benefits for cafeteria workers at the University of North Carolina at Chapel Hill. Workers dissatisfied with wages and general conditions went on strike. The Black Student Movement (BSM), a radicalized version of the former student chapter of the National Association for the Advancement of Colored People (NAACP), took up the cause of the workers under their top leaders, Preston Dobbins and Reggie Hawkins, son of Scott's primary opponent, Reginald Hawkins. As the crisis brewed, Scott warned that he would not tolerate any action obstructing classroom activities or the normal functions of the university. He seemed ready for a fight.

Taking up the challenge on March 4, the Black Student Movement and the protesters' white supporters staged a cafeteria serving line "stall-in" at Lenoir Dining Hall, now staffed by replacement workers. President Friday and UNC chancellor Carlyle Sitterson said that they would reopen the facility but also negotiate with protesting students, and the two men expressed sympathy for the workers. Scott demanded that Lenoir Hall be opened in time for breakfast on March 6. Friday and Sitterson said they needed more time, but on March 6, Scott sent state police in riot gear to occupy Lenoir Hall—ironically, the spot where Scott's father had announced consolidated university president Frank Porter Graham's appointment to the U.S. Senate in 1949. The police also moved across the quadrangle between South Building and the Wilson Library.[16] A national guard unit stood by in Durham, twelve miles away. Scott's action caused an uproar on the campus. Most administrators, faculty, and the more vocal students expressed anger toward Scott. However, he had the backing of some conservative students, many trustees, and, he believed, most of North Carolina's white population.

The legislature was in session at the time. On March 20, the governor expressed support for legislation introduced by his uncle, Senator Ralph Scott of Alamance County, who was a liberal on good terms with UNC administrators, to raise the state minimum wage to $1.80 an hour. As a prelude, Ralph Scott had arranged a meeting between the governor and one of the cafeteria strikers, Mary Smith, who had known the Scott family in Alamance County.[17] The minimum wage bill passed. Tensions remained, but the threat of serious violence subsided.

Most accounts of the dispute portray Bob Scott as mercurial and often shooting from the hip. Even staunch defenders conceded that he had a temper. However, in private conversations and negotiations, Scott could also be reasonable and conciliatory. He was a good listener and also had a feel for what was and was not politically possible. More than his legendary father, he was capable of reconciling with former adversaries.[18]

Scott reflected thirty-five years later, "The civil rights movement and the antiwar movement required a lot of attention when I was governor. I think of what all we might have accomplished if that had not taken up so much of our time."[19] Scott was thinking of an ideal that he associated with such governors as his father and Terry Sanford: a major thrust forward in education, services, and transportation. In fact, however, Scott did have a broad agenda, and he persuaded the legislature to adopt 77 percent of his proposals, a success rate that placed him in the upper range of governors.[20] While not a visionary in the Sanford mold, Scott had strong ideas about where the state should go. He inherited his father's populist instincts but had a closer relationship with business and industry. He had seen the fruits of the industrial recruitment efforts undertaken by Hodges and his successors.

In keeping with his disdain for sacred cows, Scott was willing to take on the tobacco industry. The 1969 legislature adopted a $3.5 billion budget, the largest to date. The budget required tax increases. For the first time, special taxes were levied on cigarettes (two cents a pack) and soft drinks (one cent a bottle) and syrup for soft drinks (one dollar a gallon). While the tobacco tax was one of the lowest in the country, Scott displayed audacity in pushing it through a reluctant legislature. No product had maintained sacred status for so long. State residents began to see bumper stickers proclaiming, "Let's put the ax to the cigarette tax." Less controversially, existing taxes on alcoholic beverages were boosted, and the gasoline tax more than quadrupled from two cents to nine cents a gallon. Scott displayed an interest in environmental matters, with money appropriated for the protection and acquisition of coastal estuaries, the breeding grounds for the state's abundant seafood crop.

Record spending included a big boost for education. Public school-teachers won a 12 percent salary increase, while college faculty received an 8 percent salary increase. But the major thrust came in huge capital expenditures for higher education expansion. In addition, 1969 saw five predominantly minority colleges named as regional universities: Elizabeth City State, Fayetteville State, North Carolina Central in Durham, Winston-Salem State, and historically Native American Pembroke State. Thus, every degree-granting public institution of higher education except the School of the Arts was now a university. Like his predecessor, Moore, Scott dealt with record college enrollments brought on by the baby boom generation. Years later, Scott recalled higher education as the greatest legacy of his administration. Scott could not have had so much success with his policy initiatives without the backing of legislative leaders such as Senator Kenneth Royall of Durham, a conservative with vision and the legislature's budget wizard. Among other key budget writers were Sam Johnson of Wake and Phillip Godwin of Gates, a Democratic leader and then Speaker of the House. Another major figure in the leadership cadre was Scott's uncle, Ralph Scott.[21]

State government reorganization was another legacy of the Scott administration and the 1969 legislature. In the name of accountability and efficiency, the 1969 legislature had proposed a constitutional amendment directing the General Assembly to reduce the number of state departments and agencies from more than three hundred to no more than twenty-five principal departments by July 1975.[22] Voters approved the amendment in 1970. The 1971 legislature and Scott began its implementation.

The 1971 session further expanded state programs, including a pilot project for state-supported kindergartens. Kindergartens were part of the public school system in some states but never had been so in North Carolina. Bigger towns had private kindergartens, but the great majority of children started school in the first grade at age six. Scott wanted the program expanded, but the legislature had already adopted a record $4.3 billion two-year budget, including 10 percent salary boosts for public school and college teachers and state employees.[23]

Attorney General Robert Morgan also commanded headlines. To this point, the attorney general's office had focused on representing the state on legal matters, law enforcement, and the issuance of advisory legal opinions. Morgan, however, believed that his office could be a major force in reshaping and democratizing the state. He forged a close relationship with fellow attorneys general across the country and built bonds with Scott and the legislature. While paying heed to law enforcement, Morgan transformed the office into the people's advocate. The consumer protection division achieved a high profile as it investigated complaints and offered advice to the public. Morgan used the power of the office to rein in utility rates. He was an economic populist and the brightest new star in the Democratic Party.

## THE MULTIUNIVERSITY

The thorniest legislative issue in 1971 related to a proposed reorganization of the state's higher educational system. Competition among state colleges and universities had raged for years. Individual college presidents spent a lot of their time lobbying the legislature. The new regional universities—both the historically black and the historically white—believed that they had been shortchanged. The big schools of the consolidated university feared that the demands of the rising regional universities posed a potential threat to their own strong research programs. And three urban schools that until recently had been two-year colleges had been brought into the consolidated university fold, though their missions remained uncertain.

Now Bob Scott jumped into the fray. A graduate of North Carolina State in agricultural husbandry, he was deeply skeptical of the flagship university in Chapel Hill and what he saw as its privileged position within the consolidated university and the state. Scott had a special disdain for the small executive committee of the one-hundred-member consolidated university Board of Trustees. He believed that the system was dominated by Victor Bryant and George Watts Hill of Durham, Virginia Lathrop of Asheville, Wachovia bank chair Archie Davis of Winston-Salem, and state senator Thomas White of Kinston. Despite fierce disagreements over the food workers strike of 1969, Scott had respect for Friday's ability but also saw him as too close to the powerful executive committee. Scott came to believe that establishing a superuniversity system, modeled after California's multiuniversity system, would result in a fairer distribution of resources as well as rein in the power of what he saw as a clique running the consolidated university.[24]

Not all leaders of the consolidated university were hostile to the idea of a supersystem. Some saw it as a way to restrain Leo Jenkins and the other politically strong presidents of regional universities. Furthermore, states all around the country were adopting such multiuniversity structures. Friday expressed generalized support for a new structure, but he to protect the special position of the consolidated university.

Throughout much of 1970 and 1971, a stalemate existed. Scott preferred a transition board that would give Board of Higher Education interests and the regional universities at least equal weight to the consolidated university, a frightening prospect for UNC interests. The regional universities continued to fear a system dominated by Chapel Hill and to some degree North Carolina State. The matter was deferred to a special legislative session to be held in October 1971. Scott wanted a thirty-two-member governing board for the new system, fearing that power would gravitate to a small group if the board were larger; he also wanted to appoint some of the board's members. Consolidated university leaders favored the existing one-hundred-member board. The legislature decided on thirty-two.

For the transition board, Scott wanted fifteen members from the consolidated university, fifteen from the regional universities, and two from the State Board of Higher Education. Representative Ike Andrews of Chatham County, a few miles south of Chapel Hill, mounted a successful legislative effort to have sixteen members each from the consolidated university and other schools, with two temporary nonvoting members from the State Board of Higher Education.[25] The change meant that the old consolidated university could not be outvoted by a coalition of the regional universities and State Board of Higher Education.

Scott won the battle for reorganization. But at least for the near term, the old consolidated university interests won on the details. Scott had reservations about making Friday the new system's president, but the other stakeholders saw Friday as the obvious choice, and the board named him to head the system. By that time, Friday had a national reputation in higher education circles, and in hindsight, Scott recalled, "I thought Bill Friday was the only one who would know how to run it."[26]

Few at the top thought that old-style turf fights among the university campuses would end. Though the new administration in Chapel Hill was now the official lobbyist for the whole system, individual university chancellors were well connected and knew how to lobby through their supporters, many of whom were influential legislators. And the legislature would have the broad power of the purse over the new system. The university budget was subject to legislative approval. Some of the biggest institutional fights were still to come, but the reforms worked overall.

### PROTESTS AND REACTIONS

In 1968, a cultural shift took place on college campuses in North Carolina, especially the major state and elite private universities and colleges. The shift had occurred earlier at the University of California at Berkeley, Columbia University, and San Francisco State, and the changes in North Carolina paralleled those occurring across much of the country. At first, the changes were subtle and manifested themselves through student interest in peace movements, the McCarthy campaign, and the Robert Kennedy campaign. Many students had been more liberal on political issues than their parents, but until the late 1960s, social conformity was the rule.

But 1969 saw a massive transition. For a period, a general, calculated sloppiness ruled. Hair not only grew longer but became a source of messy creativity. Faded blue jeans proliferated. As alcohol had been to earlier generations, marijuana and to a degree other drugs were to the new college crop. Rock-and-roll music had reached a new creative high with the Beatles,

Rolling Stones, and Bob Dylan in the mid-1960s. Their lyrics and those of other talented groups such as the Animals and the Doors dominated the charts for the rest of the decade. The new artists sang of peace, love, and a freedom from sexual constraints. While college campuses had rarely been sanctuaries of Puritanism, birth control pills facilitated new levels of sexual experimentation.

Many citizens, including parents of college-age students, looked on with horror and disgust. Never in the twentieth century was the tension between university communities and the general public as high as it was in the 1969–72 period. The student culture of the time contained coexisting strains of burning idealism and self-destruction. But by 1971, a sense of foreboding was also creeping in. The war had raged in Southeast Asia for years. Violence had occurred in the streets at home. Despite the presence of a law-and-order advocate in the White House and other high-level political offices, crime rates skyrocketed. And young people were busted for drug possession or in rare cases died of drug overdoses.

For evening entertainment, liberal students in piedmont North Carolina watched WRAL television commentator Jesse Helms, who spoke for vast numbers of older North Carolinians as he excoriated societal permissiveness, lawbreakers, and radicalism on college campuses. Many students laughed at and jeered a man they saw as a buffoon. More than ever, campuses were breeding grounds for protest.

On April 30, 1970, American planes bombed Cambodia. From a purely military standpoint, an incursion into Cambodia might have been plausible, as it was a staging ground for communist troops going into Vietnam, and President Nixon was pursuing plans for a big withdrawal of U.S. troops from Vietnam in the next year. Nonetheless, Nixon's action suggested that a seemingly endless war was expanding further. By now, many Americans wanted to get out—and quickly. Antiwar students protested all across the United States, sometimes running afoul of local regulations.

On May 4, members of the Ohio National Guard sent to Kent State University by Governor James Rhodes shot and killed four nonviolent student protesters. As never before, huge numbers of students—and not just liberal ones—exploded in anger and dismay. Like many of their contemporaries across the country, North Carolina's students demonstrated and called for a class boycott. Student protesters marched on Raleigh, where they pressed state officials to oppose an "immoral war." In Chapel Hill, protest leaders asked professors and graduate teaching assistants to call off classes. Classes officially went on, and administrators told state officials, legislators, and the media that the learning process continued. But in reality most teachers in the social sciences and humanities suspended their classes. The semester was nearly over. Students were informally allowed to take their present grades without having to take final exams or finish other coursework. The state's other schools experienced less disruption than did Chapel Hill and Duke, yet many had students join in antiwar demonstrations and marches.[27]

On May 11, 1970, a twenty-three-year-old black Vietnam veteran, Henry Marrow, walked into Robert Teel's grocery store in Oxford, a community thirty miles north of Durham. An altercation occurred, with Teel claiming that Marrow had offended the honor of the store owner's daughter-in-law, Judy. Marrow ran from the store. In full view of witnesses, Teel and his sons beat Marrow and shot him to death. Teel was a rough-hewn but successful merchant who belonged to the Ku Klux Klan. Sporadic violence occurred in coming days, and on May 24, angry African American protesters returning from a march on Raleigh set afire Oxford's Chapman Lumber Company; the building's combination of wood, paint, and turpentine led to an explosion that rained debris over the town.[28] Scott had received a delegation of antiwar protesters in his office but refused to meet with blacks from Oxford wanting to express their grievances. Oxford's prominent whites looked down on the Teels but bristled over the rioting and burning, and the governor wanted no hint that he had softened on law-and-order issues.[29]

Protest marches and riots occurred overnight on May 25–26, with looting, arson, and firebombings. Parts of the Oxford business district burned, and Scott sent in the National Guard.[30]

Few times have been so tense in North Carolina as the late 1960s and early 1970s. By law and even in practice, the society had achieved a modicum of racial equality. Racial barriers had dropped at bus stations and in many restaurants. But serious school integration was just beginning. Interracial groups in restaurants still raised eyebrows. Most churches remained rigidly segregated. Militant white groups prepared for a racial war. Many blacks, especially the young, began to think that violence might be the answer.

The port town of Wilmington experienced a long period of unrest. Although the city had a lively beach, industrial, and trade economy, it was probably at its twentieth-century nadir, with businesses having departed over the preceding twenty years and parts of the city barely hanging on to their shabby charm.[31] Like its sister cities to the south, Charleston and Savannah, Wilmington hovered somewhere between an illustrious past and a dynamic future. However, in 1970, there was no assurance of a better day to come.

The Ku Klux Klan had infiltrated the New Hanover County Sheriff's Department. A more open and violent group, the Rights of White People (ROWP), also defended the status quo. A leadership vacuum emerged as public officials hesitated to become involved in a potentially explosive situation.[32] Anger built among blacks as well as whites. Among Wilmington's new militant leaders was Ben Chavis, a member of a longtime Oxford family. Before moving to Wilmington, Chavis had emerged as a leader in the Oxford protests. The Reverend Leon White, a member of the United Church of Christ and longtime civil rights leader, took Chavis under his wing and offered him ordination and a clerical collar. Chavis worked with the Gregory Congregational Church. Chavis and other church leaders wanted to negotiate with the local board of education, which was attempting to slow down court-ordered school desegregation, but local officials were in no mood to deal with Chavis. Chavis soon opened his own storefront church, the Church of the Black Madonna. During this time, neither black nor white militants showed much restraint and perpetrated acts of violence. Chavis's rhetoric, if not his physical acts, fanned the flames.[33] Chavis could point to history, claiming that major events in human history had been propelled by violence, not moderation.

On the afternoon of February 6, ROWP members shot a local black minister who was attempting to calm the situation. Cars and trucks of ROWP forces sprayed bullets into the Gregory Congregational Church, where Chavis and some of his allies had taken refuge in the basement. Subsequent events are somewhat murky, but members of the Chavis contingent were charged with burning a nearby grocery store, and fires broke out across the city. The Highway Patrol and later members of the National Guard blocked off the church. Chavis and nine others in the church were arrested.

Thus began the case of the Wilmington Ten. The defendants were portrayed as violent racist revolutionaries by their enemies and as persecuted freedom fighters by their allies. The key prosecution witnesses gave conflicting testimony in the police investigation, a fact not revealed to defense attorneys.[34] A climate of hostility to Chavis and his cohorts prevailed locally and in Raleigh. Chavis was sentenced to between twenty-nine and thirty-four years in prison, and his codefendants also received lengthy sentences that reflected the hostile political climate. The ROWP was at least as culpable as the Wilmington Ten in the February 6 violence and bore more of the blame for the underlying poisonous climate, but the fury of the state came down on Chavis and his band of young militants. The case haunted the state for years to come. Chavis remained in prison until 1979. In December 1980 a federal appeals court overturned the convictions.

The federal-court-driven move to integrate North Carolina's schools peaked between 1969 and 1971. In the mid- and late 1960s, the U.S. Department of Health, Education, and Welfare had pushed hard for integration, but as late as the 1968–69 academic year, most students attended schools predominantly of their own race. Civil rights lawyers such as Charlotte's Julius Chambers of the NAACP's Legal Defense and Education Fund kept up the pressure. Chambers, one of the few blacks to attend the UNC Law School before the mid-1960s, ranked first in the class of 1962 and later received a master's degree in law from Columbia University.

In 1965, he and associates had filed briefs in a case that came to be known as *Swann v. Charlotte-Mecklenburg Board of Education*. James Swann and black students from nine other families had been denied admission to predominantly white schools in a system that kept racial mixing to a minimum long after its first official integration in 1957. Chambers's plaintiffs won in a case heard by U.S. Federal District Court judge James McMillan of Charlotte. McMillan, who informally consulted with local black and white leaders, concluded that because of housing patterns, large-scale busing of students that would put an end to the traditional neighborhood school would be the only means of achieving full school desegregation.[35] In 1971, his general plan was upheld by the U.S. Supreme Court.[36] The ruling approved mandatory busing as a tool of integration in areas with a history of past discrimination. With the neighborhood schools of the past, full-scale desegregation was almost impossible, as most urban neighborhoods were mainly of one race. The ruling provided the Supreme Court's stamp of approval for an affirmative commitment to racial integration in the schools of North Carolina and the rest of the South.

Integration advanced in ways not seen before, with mixed results. Proponents hoped that resources would be poured into all public schools and would no longer be based on students' class or race, a goal that was reached in many districts. But on achievement tests, schools serving proportionately more students from well-to-do backgrounds continued to outperform schools serving poor populations, whether urban or rural. Students now attended schools that more comprehensively represented the cities and counties where they lived. On the negative side, many students, both black and white, did not want to be taken from the comfortable environments of their old schools. Interracial fights were rampant. In hallways and school yards, segregation prevailed, imposed not by the state but by hostile peer groups. Parent-teacher organizations continued to thrive in some schools but went downhill in others.[37] The role of the school as a community center declined. While interracial bonds were built among schoolteachers, hostilities arose in instances when both black and white teachers and administrators believed that they had been deprived of their positions or transferred to other schools because of their race. But North Carolina and the other southern states had seen one of the greatest attempts at social transformation in twentieth-century America.

Fearing declining educational standards and violence, a (mostly white) slice of the population fled the public schools. Private, tuition-supported academies began to flourish across much of piedmont and eastern North Carolina. Some grew into distinguished institutions, while others withered on the vine after the initial anguish over school integration faded. With the growth of private schools, public educators feared that the state's commitment to the public school system would decline. Such was not the case, and most students continued to attend state-supported schools. However, any politician campaigning against "forced busing" attracted a following.

### SEEDS OF CHANGE IN A SPLINTERED SOCIETY

By 1972, hotels, restaurants, public schools, and a few civic clubs and churches took for granted the presence of members of different races. Under the law, if not in reality, all races were equal. Yet the level of racial tension remained as high as or higher than it had been in 1962.

The 1970 U.S. census confirmed that a few North Carolina cities— Charlotte, Raleigh, and military towns—had grown in population and wealth during the 1960s. Much of the textile belt held its own, with many people employed but at modest wages. Agricultural areas lost population or grew slowly as blacks and whites sought higher income or security in urban North Carolina or in other parts of the country. The brightest spot had been the rapid growth in education at all levels. The turbulent universities might yet provide the basis for a prosperous future, but they depended in part on a solid system of elementary and secondary schools.

Duke, a private university with mostly out-of-state students in its ranks, had experienced student protest and labor turmoil in the 1968–70 period. President Douglas Knight at times felt imprisoned in his office and house. By 1969, he had begun carrying a pistol in his pocket on late-night inspections of the campus. In the winter of 1969, around sixty black students had seized the registrar's office in the Allen Building and labeled it the Malcolm X School of Liberation. Their demands included abolition of the Scholastic Aptitude Test for black student admission, a black studies curriculum, and a black student union. At Knight's request, Governor Scott dispatched the state highway patrol to Duke. The campus was in turmoil, but the occupiers slipped out of the Allen Building before patrol units moved in. Knight, who many trustees and alumni felt had lost control of the university, re-signed.[38] Over the next few months the committee looking for his replace-ment turned its attention toward a man with a reputation as an innovator, troubleshooter, and master politician—Terry Sanford. Sanford took over as Duke's president on April 2, 1970, just a month before the Kent State shoot-ings. In the coming weeks, he built good rapport with both his board of trustees and students, thus passing a crucial test. Sanford had at least two major objectives: building the already wealthy and distinguished Duke into a still greater institution, and winning the U.S. presidency. Sanford's biographers, Howard E. Covington Jr. and Marion A. Ellis, later called him a man of "outrageous ambitions."[39] More specifically, he pursued his ambi-tions with the same vigor as he had demonstrated in earlier days.

Probably at no time in the twentieth century was the United States more splintered than in the 1968–72 period. Despite the challenges still to be met, the 1950s had seen high hopes for the future that persisted even after John Kennedy's assassination. Growing economic abundance diverted attention from underlying social problems. Then came war abroad and anger at home. Calls for law and order did nothing to contain exploding urban crime rates. Cynicism abounded, and dreams turned to nightmares. In 1971, Don McLean's song, "American Pie," became a hit. In it, McLean re-called the death of the early rock-and-roll idol Buddy Holly in a plane crash on February 2, 1959—"the day the music died." But the ten-minute-long song captured the mood of the time when it was written. Its lyrics—"We sang dirges in the dark / The day the music died"—were appropriate for the late 1960s and early 1970s.

New advances in American democracy had transformed North Carolina and the broader American South more than other sections of the country. A decade and a half earlier, racial segregation had remained in place from the lunch table to the movie theater to the schoolhouse. Rural blacks voted with difficulty when at all. Now, however, they could contemplate public office. With a shove from southern advocates of equality, most of whom were black, and from Washington politicians and bureaucrats, segregation as a legal doctrine had been wiped off the map. Big problems remained, but it was a different world from 1954. And by the end of 1971, the neces-sary three-fourths of all states had ratified the Twenty-Sixth Amendment, lowering the voting age from twenty-one to eighteen.

North Carolina had made huge strides in education under governors Sanford, Moore, and Scott. But the dividends seemed slow in coming. North Carolina's position relative to the country and the South had not improved. Infant mortality and illiteracy rates remained high. The poor remained a big segment of the North Carolina population, a situation that increased spending on schools had done little to change. However, new public school programs and an admired university system provided the basis for the largest expansion yet in the black and white middle classes. Educational advances increased the state's appeal to new and growing industries, research operations, and banks. North Carolina became more cosmopolitan as Asians and northerners moved in. Despite the unrest of the 1968–71 period, the state had been building with an eye to the future.

## CHAPTER SIX

# The Storms of '72

The bitterest races, the ones that can tear a party asunder, do not always involve sharp ideological or issue differences. Ego sometimes eclipses grand ideas. The 1972 Democratic primaries for the U.S. Senate and governorship ripped the North Carolina party apart in ways that could not have been foreseen. Major debates over political philosophy would have to await the general election in the fall.

With incumbent Richard Nixon their certain presidential nominee, Republicans hoped for the best party showing to date in the nation and possibly in North Carolina. Nixon combined public piety with a private strategy of political vengeance. He dreamed of a new Republican majority built on a base in the long-Democratic South.

## THE SKIRMISHES

Senator B. Everett Jordan wanted another term, not an unlikely prospect in the current order of things. Jordan and his more senior colleague, Sam J. Ervin Jr., had served together for fourteen years, each initially by appointment after the death of an incumbent. Jordan made few waves. He chaired the Senate's committee on Rules and Administration. With midrange ratings from both liberal and conservative Washington-based ideological groups, Jordan was about as close to moderate as anyone in the Senate.[1] In addition, political impresario William McWhorter Cochrane, a shrewd and scrupulous practitioner of politics as the art of the possible, served as Jordan's administrative assistant. Few grasped the ways of Capitol Hill or North Carolina better than Cochrane. Under his direction, Jordan's office excelled in constituent service. Jordan's public persona was bland and colorless, not always a handicap for North Carolinians in Congress. At times he came across as worn out and ready for retirement, a view reinforced when he had cancer surgery. Still, had it not been for Nick Galifianakis, a son of Greek immigrants who projected youth and vibrancy, Jordan would likely have coasted to renomination.

From 1961 until his election to Congress in 1966, Galifianakis had been a Durham member of the N.C. House. His congressional district, stretching across the north central piedmont and diverse with white conservatives and academic liberals as well as a large and well-organized black constituency, was not easy to represent in contentious times. Facing a shaky political situation after reapportionment, Galifianakis saw 1972 as a good time to run for the U.S. Senate. He hoped that voters would go for a younger, more dynamic man who embraced not only Roosevelt's New Deal but also the free enterprise principles. His voting record in Congress resembled Jordan's, so Galifianakis was no radical.[2] His name might sound alien to North Carolina voters, but Galifianakis made jokes about it and pointed to his Greek descent and his family's successful climb as a fulfillment of the American dream and then said, "Just call me Nick."[3]

The Jordan forces initially viewed Galifianakis's Senate bid as more an affront than a serious challenge; however, the campaign took a bitter and more personal turn in its waning days. Jordan's supporters, who were representative of the party's old-time wheelhorses, could not quite swallow the results of the first primary, in which Galifianakis took 377,993 votes to Jordan's 340,301, with a few minor candidates receiving enough votes that Galifianakis did not get a majority. The challenger then won the June runoff primary, 333,558–267,997. Younger Democrats and those of a reform bent envisioned a bold new era in politics. Galifianakis may have been a bit more conservative than they would have liked, but he did represent change and a generational transition. Even his name and background were assets. Maybe the Old South was yielding to the New.

Yet white conservatives together with white supremacists could still influence Democratic primary outcomes in North Carolina, a reality made clear in the May 1972 Democratic presidential primary, in which George Wallace overwhelmed former governor Terry Sanford by a vote of 413,518–306,014. A third candidate, Representative Shirley Chisholm of Brooklyn, the first black to make a serious bid for the nomination, received 61,723 votes. While the combined Sanford-Chisholm vote was short of Wallace's, white activists of a liberal bent and newly enfranchised African Americans were emerging as a force in party affairs. By 1972, their presence was more keenly felt both in the party caucuses and in primaries.

With Bob Scott ineligible for another term, the governor's race attracted big names. The slight favorite among top officials and party activists was

Lieutenant Governor Pat Taylor, who knew the ropes in Raleigh and state politics. Not an eloquent speaker, he was nevertheless a good storyteller and mixer. But he lacked that lean and hungry look so often seen among politicians of his rank. Off the record, some associates thought him to be on the lazy side. Taylor sometimes spoke of how tired he was getting of the whole process.[4] He enjoyed golf even in the heat of a campaign. Taylor unquestionably had the proper résumé and pedigree, with service in the legislature. His father had been lieutenant governor (1949–53), generally conservative on economic affairs, and the nemesis of the late governor Kerr Scott. Paradoxically, the elder Taylor and his wife had quietly raised a young African American almost as a member of the family.[5]

The younger Taylor was friendly with Governor Bob Scott and had helped Scott with his legislative program. The Taylor clan came from Wadesboro in Anson County, a locale almost as far west as Charlotte though culturally more akin to the Black Belt of eastern North Carolina. While Pat Taylor did not speak out boldly against racism until later, he did privately and publicly make known his opposition to segregation and inequality in the 1960s and early 1970s.[6] Taylor was the model of a calm and reasonable politician. The times were passionate.

Taylor's strongest opponent might have been Attorney General Robert Morgan, elected in 1968 after stints as a state senator. I. Beverly Lake's campaign manager in 1960 and chair of the East Carolina University Board of Trustees, Morgan had built ties with North Carolina politicians across the political spectrum. A pioneer in turning the attorney general's office into a leading advocate of consumer protection, Morgan appealed to farmers, industrial workers, and some labor unions as well as middle-class followers of national consumer advocate Ralph Nader. Morgan was a scrapper for the causes in which he believed. In 1970, he came under pressure from a wide range of party activists, especially from eastern North Carolina, to seek the governorship in 1972. He declined.

Four major considerations influenced Morgan's decision. First, he liked being attorney general and had come to regard it as the state's most powerful office. Furthermore, occupants of this and other Council of State positions could, unlike the governor, stay in office beyond one term. Second, Morgan saw the governor's office as leaving its occupants with legions of enemies among disappointed office seekers. Third, Morgan, not one to bow easily to pressure, tired of the relentless attempts at persuasion from others to enter the race. Finally, knowing that age and temperament might induce Senator Ervin to retire in 1974, Morgan cast his eye toward Washington.[7]

Two active candidates who had little chance added spice to the donnybrook. Reginald Hawkins, the Charlotte dentist who had made history in 1968 as the first African American to mount a serious campaign for the governorship, was back. Bumper stickers imprinted with red letters on a black background promoted him as the "candidate for hope and progress."[8] However, his 1972 effort lacked the spark and excitement of 1968. The main question was how many votes from blacks Hawkins might get and where those votes would go in a runoff.

In part the lack of enthusiasm over Hawkins reflected the entry of longtime state AFL-CIO activist Wilbur Hobby. Hobby had been on the left fringe of state politics and had evolved into a racial liberal who believed that "civil rights are the human rights of every American citizen."[9] In 1969, on his fourth attempt to win the presidency of the North Carolina AFL-CIO, Hobby prevailed. Now a man who had grown up under hardscrabble circumstances in one of Durham's poorest textile precincts sought the state's top political prize. While lacking polish, Hobby had a good wit and was something of a bon vivant. Of modest height, he was a rotund man, and health problems were setting in. Hobby's gravelly voice detracted little from his eloquence in defending the poor and downtrodden. His campaign slogan was, "Keep the big boys honest," a reference to the state's wealthy, especially the corporate leaders. Hobby had borrowed the slogan from Henry Howell, who had a run a strong but unsuccessful race for the Virginia governorship in 1969.[10]

Hobby's passion was matched by a man of the political center. Hargrove "Skipper" Bowles was a natural-born salesman and crusader who had for years eyed the governorship. Now seemed to be his time.

While political oddsmakers were betting on Taylor, Bowles carried powerful armor into the campaign. He had great wealth and was willing to spend a slice of his fortune to win the governorship, which then paid $38,500 a year. As finance director for Sanford's 1960 gubernatorial campaign, Bowles had developed ties with people who would be generous toward a progressive centrist candidate. He had public office experience, both as director of the state Department of Conservation and Development under Sanford and later as a member of the N.C. House and Senate representing Guilford County.[11] With a political base in Greensboro, Bowles expected a big "friends and neighbors" vote from what was then North Carolina's second-largest county. A big booster of the University of North Carolina at Chapel Hill, Bowles maintained a first-name cordiality with many of the state's business and professional leaders. Bowles and Governor Bob Scott were not close, but even that seemed advantageous for

Bowles. With his bluntness and bold new tax initiatives, Scott had left a trail of enemies. Bowles could and did distance himself from the Scott administration. While the natural heir to much of the old Sanford organization, Bowles cultivated other factions. Morgan, who was friendly with Taylor, remained neutral in the race. But significant numbers of Morgan people in eastern and piedmont North Carolina lined up with Bowles. With an eye toward the runoff, Bowles quietly sought goodwill among blacks. Though he promised to hold the line on any tax increase, Bowles highlighted the need for a greatly expanded community college system and technical education as the key to prosperity.

The Bowles campaign proved to be a watershed for North Carolina politics. In the spring of 1972, old-style campaigns were still the rule, with candidates driving from country store to country store, giving speeches at civic clubs, visiting mills at shift changes, and taking out printed newspaper ads and circulars. Bowles and his campaign team, which included political scientist and public opinion wizard Walter De Vries, saw a new and more sophisticated world. From that time forth, North Carolina's campaigns blended survey research with emerging technology. The Bowles operatives used focus groups, opinion polls homing in on the cutting-edge issues, and slick television commercials.[12] The Taylor forces were stunned when Bowles won the May primary, garnering 367,433 votes to Taylor's 309,919. Bowles's margin was broader than the totals suggested: He led in the coastal plain, piedmont, and mountains and in every major urban county.

Hobby, the champion of the working class, managed a plurality in only one North Carolina municipality, the very non-blue-collar Chapel Hill. Hawkins again drew support from African Americans, but so did Bowles and Taylor. Hawkins and Hobby together attracted a lower combined percentage of the primary vote than Hawkins alone had in 1968.

Taylor called for a primary runoff, which became bitter and personal. While old loyalties going back to the Sanford-Lake competition were alive, they had little bearing on the 1972 competition for governor. This time, the forces of education were split. The community college and technical school interests, which sometimes seemed to be the stepchild caught between the powerful lobbyists for the elementary and secondary schools on the one hand and universities on the other, had reason to be enthusiastic about Bowles and his unrelenting emphasis on technical education. Public school personnel and their professional group, the North Carolina Education Association, liked Taylor's specific commitments for salary increases and backed his candidacy. Among party regulars, many old Sanford hands inclined toward Bowles, but Taylor, too, had former Sanford backers. Scott loyalists beat the bushes for Taylor.

Bowles had the momentum, and he never lost his front-runner status, taking the June runoff, 336,035–282,345. The jubilant Bowles forces moved to cement their position in the Democratic Party. An organization long controlled by Scott now saw leadership posts go to Bowles backers. A postprimary step toward more influence for the party's gubernatorial nominee had been customary, but feelings seemed more bruised than usual. Both Scott and Taylor allies were dejected. Bowles made modest moves toward reconciliation, but the atmosphere chilled when perhaps in jest he remarked that his supporters would, after victory in November, "get the white meat" of the chicken and supporters of other Democratic primary candidates would "get the dark meat." Bowles's quip did not go down well among Taylor people.[13]

Less in the limelight, the simultaneous Republican primary for governor was as heated as the Democratic race. Historically, Republican primaries in North Carolina were small affairs, largely ignored by the media and the public at large. The stakes were low, as defeat in the general election seemed likely. The GOP often completely skipped primaries in favor of choosing candidates at conventions. The old pattern was about to change, however. The trend lines were clear. Over the preceding decade and a half, Republican strength in gubernatorial races had risen from one-third or less of the total to more than 47 percent in 1968. Republican representation in North Carolina's delegation in the U.S. House of Representatives climbed from none in the 1940s to four after the elections of 1968 and 1970. Leaps in Republican strength typically occurred in presidential election years—specifically, those when the Republicans had potent presidential candidates. While still too early to know for sure whom the Democrats would nominate for president, Nixon looked strong in North Carolina.

Encouraged both by the possibility of long Nixon coattails and party growth, two high-profile Republicans sought their party's nomination for governor. Jim Gardner, a former member of Congress from Rocky Mount, thought that his strong race against Scott in 1968 merited another shot. Among many traditional Republicans in the western half of North Carolina, however, Gardner was persona non grata. That he had run well in 1968 was undeniable. But his de facto neutrality between Nixon and George Wallace was unforgivable, leading a few Republicans and pro-Nixon independents in western and urban counties to refuse to vote for Gardner in the 1968 general election. Another Republican with respectable credentials and a record of service to the party would be more to their liking.

Jim Holshouser, the minority leader in the N.C. House of Representatives, was a shade young and untested. He would turn thirty-eight just before the 1972 general elections and had no experience chairing a legislative committee. Moreover, his hometown, Boone, was tucked away in the remote far northwestern corner of North Carolina. Getting there involved a tortuous winding climb up a mountain. Leaning Republican, Watauga County had been isolated from the mainstream of state politics. Holshouser was likable and politically savvy. But could he win the general election if other pieces of the puzzle should fall into place? And did he possess that overriding ambition, the fire in the belly, often needed to win the state's top office? Holshouser later remarked, "I was not one who grew up planning to run for governor. It's just something that developed."[14] But Holshouser's mild demeanor concealed other traits: determination, focus, and a daring spirit.

Holshouser was a Davidson College graduate and Presbyterian in a state where Presbyterians have done well politically despite their minority status. He earned a law degree and made friends in Chapel Hill and later served on the Board of Directors of the UNC Alumni Association. Over the years, Holshouser assiduously but diplomatically promoted the interests of the Republican Party, first in Watauga County and then in the state, and he became the chair of the state party.

If Gardner was the scrappier and more media-oriented of the candidates, Holshouser was a master of the numbers game within the Republican primary. "Things were very predictable," he said. "We could go by the past pattern. Fifteen counties had half the vote. We would target the heavily Republican counties: Avery, Mitchell, Davie, Yadkin, Wilkes (all rural or semirural counties in the mountains or western piedmont), Mecklenburg (Charlotte) because of its big population, Forsyth (Winston-Salem), Guilford (Greensboro), and Henderson, just south of Asheville. I had represented Avery and Mitchell in the legislature, so I knew a lot of people there. There were not many Republican primary voters in eastern North Carolina, as the Democratic registration lead was overwhelming. Piedmont and mountain party organizations were well established."[15]

The new age of persuasion utilizing the electronic media was imminent, as the Bowles campaign was showing, but in a Republican primary, major television and radio advertising was impractical. The photogenic and smooth-talking Gardner had excelled in using the electronic media in beating Representative Harold Cooley in 1966 and scaring Bob Scott in the 1968 gubernatorial race. The immediate Republican primary challenge, however, lent itself to the tactics of the 1940s, not the emerging, glossy media-driven campaigns of the late twentieth century.

Gardner and his strategists were veterans and hardly naive. He was confident of good margins in eastern North Carolina. While few registered Republicans lived in any single eastern county, the region as a whole had enough votes to influence a primary outcome, especially if Gardner's overall regional percentage was overwhelming. The party chairs and other activists in the coastal plain were often recent recruits to the party, people who had been motivated by the 1964 Goldwater campaign. What they lacked in seasoning, they made up for in enthusiasm and a commitment to conservative causes, and Gardner was seen as the more conservative candidate in this race.[16] Moving into the piedmont, Randolph County had a large number of Republican registrants and thus the prospect of a big primary vote. It had been part of Gardner's congressional district in 1967 and 1968. Gardner also made a major effort in what should have been Holshouser strongholds such as Wilkes County in the northern mountains and built respectable support networks in the larger piedmont cities. The result was an ultrathin victory for Gardner in the initial primary, 84,906–83,637. Two minor candidates combined for 2,040 votes. Holshouser exercised his prerogative to call for a runoff primary.

Fewer votes were cast in the second primary—138,050. Even more than in the first primary, the key to victory was turning out the faithful. The voting pattern was much as expected, with Holshouser leading in the cities, most mountain counties, and parts of the piedmont. Gardner maintained a good base nearly everywhere. Still, his edge in eastern North Carolina, while substantial, was not massive enough to overcome Holshouser's lead elsewhere. Holshouser's plodding strategy now resulted in a 1,782-vote victory.

The Republican senatorial primary attracted little attention in an environment where other races seemed more exciting. Early on, it was thought even less likely to produce a general election winner than the Republican primary for governor. Tom Ellis urged Jesse Helms to enter the primary. Both Ellis and Helms had changed their registrations from Democratic to Republican, with Helms making the switch on September 17, 1970, partly in anticipation of seeking political office as a Republican. Before taking the plunge, Helms wanted clearance from his boss, A. J. Fletcher, the owner of WRAL and the Capital Broadcasting Company. Fletcher viewed Helms's prospects as bleak, but he assured Helms that he could have his old job back if he ran and lost. According to Ellis, "Fletcher thought it was a crazy idea but was willing to go along with it if that's what Jesse wanted to do."[17]

Helms faced primary opposition from Jim Johnson, a member of the N.C. House of Representatives from Cabarrus County, northeast of Charlotte.

Johnson was loquacious and politically more liberal than the typical North Carolina Republican. With a strong showing in eastern North Carolina, urban areas, and parts of the west, Helms crushed Johnson, 92,496–45,303. A third candidate had only 16,032 votes, so Helms was nominated. Establishment Republicans had accepted Helms, but they were not enthusiastic. The Holshouser and Helms campaigns cast wary eyes at each other. Except for official Republican functions, they avoided alliances.

The fact of lively Republican primaries for governor and U.S. senator was significant. Though the state's Democratic identifiers still greatly outnumbered Republican identifiers, the GOP nomination was now seen as worth something. In the three most recent gubernatorial elections (1960, 1964, 1968) Republican candidates had polled respectable shares of the vote—between 45 and nearly 48 percent. Democratic senators Ervin and Jordan had won their most recent elections (1968 and 1966) without difficulty, but their Republican opponents had polled more than 40 percent.

And change was occurring within the Republican Party. Through the mid-twentieth century, neither the Republican nor Democratic parties of North Carolina had been ideologically based. Party identification was passed down from one generation to another and often resulted from family loyalties going back to the Civil War. But since Roosevelt's New Deal, the national Democratic Party had been moving to the left on economic issues. And by the 1970s, the Democrats were the more liberal party on social issues, most notably civil rights. Many southern whites began to loosen their Democratic moorings. And a few, including Ellis and Helms, switched their party registrations. They, along with Jim Gardner, hoped to make the GOP a vehicle for conservative causes. In 1972, Gardner had lost and Helms had won primary contests. Yet both contests were precursors of things to come.

Many other primaries were held, most of them in the Democratic Party. Of special significance were the primaries for the reapportioned Second Congressional District and for lieutenant governor. In the Second District, Howard Lee, mayor of Chapel Hill since 1969 and an African American, challenged the entrenched conservative incumbent, L. H. Fountain of Tarboro. Fountain managed a 60 percent victory in the twelve-county district, with Lee taking only his home county of Orange. But Lee's surprisingly good 40 percent finish hinted of a bright political future.

Margaret Harper, who published the *Southern Pilot* newspaper with her husband, Jim, ran for lieutenant governor. She earned respect although she was introduced nearly everywhere as "the best looking candidate in the race," a line invariably followed by light laughter.[18] Harper ran a strong third in a five-candidate field, polling a respectable 151,819 votes. She trailed Scott administration conservation and development director Roy Sowers Jr., who had 177,016 votes, and Wilson political activist and attorney James Baxter Hunt Jr., who polled 329,727 votes. Though Sowers could have called for a runoff, he bowed to the inevitable and withdrew. The Harper campaign offered a degree of hope and inspiration for women, who were still largely shut out of top public office. Hunt emerged as a star, offering hope for a political party not quite sure what the long-term future held.

### DEMOCRATIC TREMORS AND A RISING STAR FROM THE EAST

Governor Bob Scott had six months remaining in his term. He maintained a strong hold on state government and chaired the North Carolina delegation to the 1972 Democratic National Convention in Miami Beach, a rowdy if earnest affair where prior to adjournment near 4:00 A.M. on July 14, Senator George McGovern of South Dakota delivered his acceptance speech to the delegates. This was the first national convention for more than 80 percent of the delegates and for many from North Carolina. Under newly mandated national and state Democratic party rules, more blacks (15 percent), women (38 percent), and young people (13 percent under twenty-five and 33 percent under thirty-five) were among the delegates. Fewer were officeholders than in past conventions. The Illinois delegation, headed by Chicago's legendary boss, Mayor Richard Daley Sr., was expelled from the convention and replaced by a reform delegation.

McGovern, a dignified and sartorially impeccable presence, and his running mate, Missouri senator Thomas Eagleton, were spoiling for the fight against Nixon and Vice President Spiro Agnew. Then the public learned that Eagleton had received psychiatric treatment for clinical depression, a chapter in his running-mate's life that McGovern was unaware of. Suddenly, Eagleton became the victim of the deep-seated fear of mental illness, which was still spoken of in hushed tones, much as AIDS would be in the 1980s. McGovern bowed to the public will and dropped Eagleton. A special meeting of the Democratic National Committee on August 8 named Sargent Shriver, the former Peace Corps director and brother-in-law of John Kennedy, as the vice presidential nominee. Shriver possessed perhaps the finest gift that a man of his current calling could have possessed, a keen and self-deprecating wit.

Not all was gloom and doom for North Carolina's Democrats, who remained cautiously optimistic about retaining the U.S. Senate seat and confident about the governorship. Whatever those outcomes, the Democrats also had a rising star in Jim Hunt, their nominee for lieutenant governor.

At thirty-five, Hunt anticipated a dynamic political future, almost a divine calling to public life, though he was too smart politically to acknowledge anything beyond a possible interest in the governorship after a four-year stint as lieutenant governor. Hunt's climb had already been meteoric. His parents were part-time farmers, while his mother taught English and his father was a soil conservation official. Hunt, a past president of the student body at North Carolina State College, always seemed a man with a goal. He held a master's degree in agricultural economics from State and a law degree from UNC–Chapel Hill. Hunt failed the state bar examination on his first try but passed when he retook the exam two years later. In the interim, he and his wife, Carolyn, spent two years in Nepal, where Hunt served as an agricultural adviser to the Nepalese government under a Ford Foundation–sponsored program. The experience enhanced Hunt's knowledge not only of the world but also of agriculture, knowledge that he might one day put to use back home.[19]

Returning to Wilson, Hunt began to practice law and to engage in civic and political affairs. Striving to build establishment credentials, he could also be daring, as when he participated in a parade mourning the assassination of civil rights icon Martin Luther King Jr. in April 1968. Hunt served a one-year term as president of the North Carolina Young Democratic Clubs, then a major way station on the path to state public office. By the early 1970s, Hunt was running hard for lieutenant governor. He was enthusiastic and had an intensity surpassing that of the average politician-climber. His hair was short and well oiled, an outdated look for a young person by the late 1960s. Both his appearance and his earnest demeanor set him apart from the crowd.

Working party activists had not been surprised by Hunt's 1972 primary win, but his background was not conventional. Lieutenant governors, whose chief constitutional duty was to preside over the Senate, historically were former legislators. Bob Scott and Luther Hodges were exceptions. However, Scott possessed one of the best-known names in North Carolina politics. Hodges, who had the bearing of an eminent personage, was aided by big-business backing and luck. Hunt, never in the legislature, offered superior political talents, and when civic or Democratic activities provided him with the opportunity, he cultivated relationships with more conservative businesspeople. Most important, through past labors for the Sanford organization, Hunt had developed close ties with some of the party's best political brains.

Sanford's forces saw Hunt as one of their own. Hunt's shrewdest move was the recruitment of Bert Bennett of Winston-Salem, the brilliant if controversial mastermind behind Sanford's 1960 victory, as his campaign director. After his setback as director of the Preyer campaign of 1964, Bennett was ready for another battle. While state legislators in Raleigh discussed among themselves who might be the next lieutenant governor, Hunt was out on the hustings, gathering commitments and financial aid. Though lacking a political legacy, legislative experience, and personal financial resources, Hunt was poised to be a key player in state government and party affairs.

### THE FURIES OF AUTUMN

Rarely has there been a North Carolina general election campaign with such high levels of friction within the parties as that of 1972. Except for the most tacit of endorsements, Democrats avoided McGovern much as they might have a leper. As Galifianakis's campaign for the Senate seemed to falter, the Bowles forces saw more wisdom in a go-it-alone strategy. When asked three decades later how he would describe the relationship of the Helms and Holshouser campaigns, Helms strategist Tom Ellis said, "There was no relationship. They didn't want to have anything to do with us."[20] However, Helms and Holshouser maintained a surface cordiality, and the pull of each man would indirectly benefit the other.

The national Republican Party did not place North Carolina's races near the top of its priority list. At the outset, the national party saw neither Helms nor Holshouser as likely winners. What resources it did throw in went mainly to Holshouser, who had better connections with the national apparatus. Still, his campaign was money-starved. The entire staff shared a Raleigh apartment. However, their semiprofessional polls showed a steady climb in the race against Bowles.[21] The Helms campaign went deeply in debt on its way to outspending Galifianakis by a 6:4 ratio. It managed to be professional, polished, and stinging.

On November 7, 1972, heavy rain fell as the Democrats heard the bad news from their Sir Walter Raleigh Hotel headquarters. Projections of vote outcomes were still a fairly new endeavor for the national networks, but early on election night, they declared Helms the winner. For the Democrats, hope remained in the tight governor's contest, but before midnight the trend was clear. Tired and dejected, Galifianakis and Bowles acknowledged defeat.

Republican spirits were high. In North Carolina, Nixon had gone from a 39.5 percent plurality win in 1968 to 69.5 percent majority win in 1972. On the national level, Nixon's 61 percent ranked along with the victories of Roosevelt in 1936 and Johnson in 1964 as one of the most resounding of the twentieth century. McGovern took the electoral votes only of Massachusetts and the District of Columbia. The magnitude and uniformity of the Republican sweep of North Carolina can be seen by comparing the state's three major regions: the coastal plain, piedmont, and mountains. Nixon took between 69 and 70 percent in each, an unprecedented uniformity. Republicans often did well in the piedmont and mountains, but never had they come close to this level. Yet the magnitude of the shifts there paled by comparison to what had happened in eastern North Carolina, where the Eisenhower national Republican landslides of the 1950s had made little dent. Nixon took 69 percent plus of this region, where twelve years earlier against Kennedy he struggled for 31 percent. Of the state's one hundred counties, McGovern led in only two—Northampton, which was 62 percent African American and had a well-organized Democratic organization, and Orange, where the liberal academic precincts of Chapel Hill outvoted the county's more rural central and northern precincts.

More than 80 percent of black voters had supported McGovern, so a heavier black turnout would have enabled him to run better in parts of the state. Even then, he would not have topped one-third of the total vote, and North Carolina would still have been one of McGovern's weaker states. The white Democratic exodus was the big story.

Thanks in part to the anti-McGovern phenomenon, 1972 made an indelible imprint on North Carolina and southern politics. Helms (55.5 percent) and Holshouser (51 percent), graciously accepted congratulations but let it be known that the voters' verdict marked an end to business as usual. Helms, the voice of conservative despair for so many years, might now be a force in Washington. Holshouser, the softer-spoken but steadfast proponent of accountable government and two party politics, offered a breath of fresh air in a state capital that many voters thought was due for a shake-up. In their own ways, both men would have an impact for years to come.

In the aftermath of the election, neither the victorious Republicans nor the despondent Democrats had quite reconciled themselves to what had happened. There had been little intraparty unity in either strategy or spirit, but overall, the Democrats had suffered more. While some Democrats promoted the entire slate, the fallout from bitter primaries had lingered. More than a few Jordan and Taylor backers sat on their hands or even talked down nominees Galifianakis and Bowles. While both Galifianakis and Bowles had realized early on that they had serious and determined opponents, both Democrats felt that history was on their side. By October, though, the Galifianakis forces had known he was in trouble. To them Helms still seemed a polarizing figure in a state that might be conservative but was not mean-spirited.[22] They failed to recognize the extent to which people might like the message of the hard-hitting man of the Right.

Bowles's forces, cognizant of the vulnerabilities of the Greek American senatorial candidate and the McGovern albatross, pretty much ran their own show. After all, their candidate and his primary campaign had demonstrated the possibilities for success of sharp strategists backed up by the best tools in the trade and an enthusiastic cadre of supporters. Bowles and his staff labored tirelessly as polls showed a tightening race, but he made only a minimal effort to shore the rift with Governor Scott, who had both political smarts and loyal supporters, or with Lieutenant Governor Taylor. Bowles had been on top of North Carolina's political world after his primary win. He reasonably expected to prevail in the general election with a high-powered media campaign saturating the airwaves. The Scotts had long been known for charity toward their friends and for getting back at their enemies. In this close race, Bowles might have won by building more bridges with rival Democrats. Instead, both the white and the dark meat were shared at the Republican feast.

Any Republican celebration had the potential to be short-lived. Even during the successful fall campaign, the Helms and Holshouser forces largely ran their own shows. Helms, more than most active politicians of his day, comprehended the power of electronic media, and he knew how to use those media with maximum effect. To him, the message came first, even if it put the messenger at risk. But he knew how to deliver his message with stunning impact. He had still another weapon—Richard Nixon. Despite his flaws, white southerners saw him as representing a caution and stability in uncertain times. For many, Nixon stood as a bulwark against the forces they saw as running amok in the America of the early 1970s. Helms billboards proclaimed, "Nixon needs Jesse Helms." Together, they might restrain the seemingly relentless slide toward some unknown but fearsome abyss.

A candidate for governor does not usually stake his fortune too heavily on a presidential candidate, even a popular one. The demands as well as the political milieu that they face may differ markedly. But like Helms, Holshouser was delighted to be running on the Nixon team. More precisely, he saw early on the damage the McGovern nomination was likely to inflict on the Democrats, and he united with Nixon and Helms under the big Republican tent.[23]

Holshouser led in much of the mountain and western piedmont regions, where Republicans often did well. He also led in the Charlotte, Winston-Salem, and Raleigh areas. Bowles carried most eastern North Carolina counties, though Holshouser carried the Wilmington area.

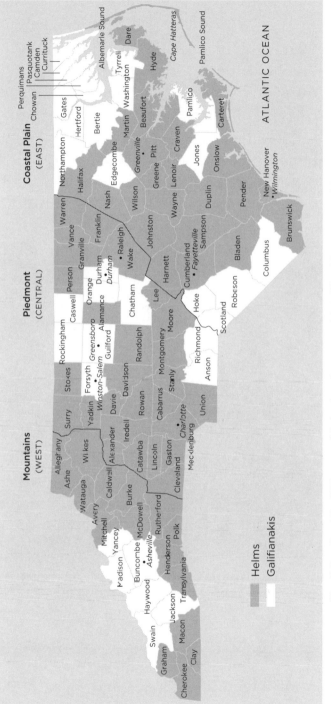

Map 5. Results of the 1972 senatorial election—Democrat Nick Galifianakis versus Republican Jesse Helms

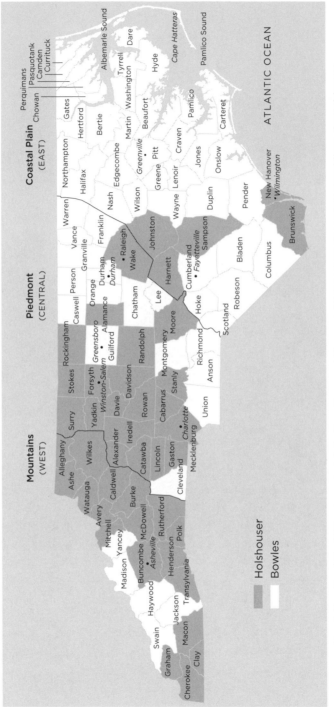

Map 6. Results of the 1972 gubernatorial election—Democrat Hargrove "Skipper" Bowles versus Republican Jim Holshouser

The resounding Helms victory left little room for what-ifs. He won the Charlotte and Raleigh areas. Among urban counties, Galifianakis mustered a large majority in his home base of Durham and narrowly took Forsyth and Guilford. In the piedmont region and mountains, Helms matched Holshouser's strong performance. Eastern North Carolina, where Bowles and the state Democrats had easily prevailed, pulled its partisan rug from under Galifianakis. Enough of the coastal plain's counties were swept by the anti-McGovern/Galifianakis tide to give Helms a solid edge in what had hitherto been one of America's most Democratic regions. Galifianakis carried some but not all of the counties where blacks were one-third or more of the voters and a few that had powerful local Democratic machines. He did best in a blanket of thinly populated counties in the state's far northeast, places in the Norfolk, Virginia, media market where exposure to the Helms's media campaign and earlier television editorials would have been thin. Aside from his newfound comrade, Nixon, Helms was the first Republican to carry the coastal plain in the twentieth century. While Helms had run behind Nixon there, his victory cannot be attributed strictly to Nixon's long coattails, for the voters were splitting their tickets and in the process showing that they could and would mark the Republican ballot even while holding on to their Democratic roots in other state and local races.

## THE MAN AND THE HOUR

So how did Helms, a Republican whom opponents and even some Republicans had dismissed as an extremist, run so well, even in areas historically hostile to the Republican Party? The reasons were many, some related to timing and some to Helms's personal attributes.

Helms was in many respects a logical successor to George Wallace. Like Wallace, Helms was ambitious, bold, crafty, and outspoken, often thriving on the enemies he had made and the feathers he had ruffled. Both Helms and Wallace knew how to demonize their enemies to maximum advantage, citing their remoteness from the lives of hardworking citizens and their hostility to the great American nation. Hippies might favor love over war, but they inspired neither peace nor love in the souls of ordinary folk. In 1968, Wallace had carried eastern North Carolina and had run respectably in other areas. In May 1972, he won the North Carolina Democratic presidential preference primary. Helms now filled part of the void.

Helms was a man of principle and causes. Some of these causes, most notably his fierce opposition to the civil rights movement, went against the flow of history and evolving standards in human relations. But much more than the average politician, he had a firm set of ideas about where his country should and should not go. When Helms spoke, there could be little doubt that he believed in what he said. His liberal critics, from the groves of academia to the temples of organized labor, often failed to grasp his appeal to a lot of voters, even some who disagreed with Helms on a wide range of issues. Those near Helms saw a man who was personally honest even as he might pursue enemies with an unmatched zeal using every trick in the book. So, too, did many voters. Furthermore, on a personal level, he could be a man of great charity and compassion.[24] While in certain respects an heir to Wallace, Helms rose to levels of rectitude and dignity rarely seen in the Alabamian. Helms drew a broader range of support in 1972 than Wallace did in 1968.

White racial insecurities worked powerfully for both Wallace and Helms, but their ideologies had developed from different core beliefs. In the 1930s and 1940s, Wallace had been an economic liberal. As a state legislator, he was about as left-leaning as any elected Alabamian. His racial stance was a response to the poisoned Alabama climate of the 1950s—it was the road to higher office. Helms's original conservatism, which developed under the tutelage of his father-in-law, Jacob Coble, and A. J. Fletcher, was more rooted in an abiding religious faith, capitalism, individualism, and anticommunism.[25] Helms attracted both money and enthusiastic support from North Carolina's corporate leadership, especially in furniture, tobacco, textiles, and banking. He possessed a respectability that Wallace lacked. Wallace always sought the limelight. Helms sought to change the course of history.

Moreover, Helms possessed a real macho image, though he did not fit the Hollywood stereotype of that image. His bearing was strong and masculine. He possessed a radio announcer's deep, well-modulated voice, not the sometimes high-pitched shrillness of Wallace. Helms also lacked the bouncing gait that Wallace had possessed prior to being paralyzed during the 1972 campaign, a gait that can be highly effective in person but is sometimes less so on television. Wallace might have been the maestro, but Helms was the rock. To his backers, Helms was a bulwark for the country of their ancestors.

Helms communicated powerfully. Few North Carolina politicians had better grasped the power of television and radio. He lacked the captivating smile and good humor of a John Kennedy or Ronald Reagan, but he knew well his supporters and others who might be receptive to parts of his message. He was a master at tapping their emotions.[26]

Helms had worked at WRAL since 1960, making him one of the most familiar voices in an area fanning out about eighty miles to the east, north, and south of Raleigh and forty miles to the west. People in this broad expanse of territory might love or loathe the viewpoints expressed by Helms just before the national news each evening, but he was difficult to ignore at a time when the regional and national network newscasts had huge audiences. Except for Galifianakis's Durham–Chapel Hill base, the Helms message had over the years attracted more adherents than critics in the hinterland spreading out from Raleigh. Yet this area had also maintained a strong history of voting Democratic in state and national elections prior to 1968. Four years later, the Republican Party nominated a senatorial candidate with a familiar face and well-known views—opposition to mandatory school busing for integration, war protesters, and heavy social spending. He entered the race with far higher name recognition than many long-established Republicans would have had.[27]

In 1972, Helms carried county after county in this culturally conservative region, the same region that had voted so strongly for Democrats from Franklin D. Roosevelt to Lyndon Johnson. In the piedmont as well as the coastal plain, Helms scored well in the urban millworker precincts and in the rural communities where Wallace in 1968 and Lake in 1960 and 1964 had done so well. In the Senate and presidential contests, the state's Democratic base had collapsed. Social issues trumped the old economic populism.

By then, segregationist white southerners might have recognized the inevitability of racial integration. They had little choice but to acknowledge defeat in the long war against civil rights. But a significant portion of this cohort retained deep resentments. The civil rights battle was an assault on their deeply ingrained racial prejudices, which they denied even as they asserted African Americans' intellectual and moral inferiority. For whites of more marginal circumstances, self-pride might have been at stake, with blacks now rivals for both jobs and social status. Previously, the white day laborer could maintain the myth that he was socially superior to the black bank president. But the laws that made such claims possible had been swept away by recent federal civil rights legislation and court rulings.[28]

But there was still Jesse Helms. From his podium, Helms offered a defense of the old southern values when he could, citing common sense and the Constitution. And when that position became untenable, Helms attacked the agents of change for their meddlesome ways, immorality, and hostility to America. He stated what others thought but might have been afraid to say outside their circles of family and friends. Old-fashioned American patriotism and discipline seemed under attack. Helms decried "anti-American" activities, his voice reaching a crescendo in the 1972 campaign.

All the time, he saw himself as the white knight in shining armor, defending obedience to the law, patriotism, and basic decency. Unlike so many politicians, Helms's public message and private views were the same.

The campaign slogan, "Jesse Helms: He's one of us," implied that Helms, not Galifianakis, was the true North Carolinian in the Senate election. That idea resonated with many voters. The heritage of the white majority targeted by that message was largely English, Celtic, or German. But the name Galifianakis sounded alien. Helms was a safe North Carolina name going back for generations.

### THE NEW POLITICS

Only a few elections truly represent major turning points in the history of a state or nation. For North Carolina, 1972 was such an election, though political analysts may not have realized its significance at the time.[29] An era of two-party competition was on the horizon. The Democrats were not about to disappear, but now, more than in 1928, the Republican Party stood on a solid rock in the American South. And nowhere was this more true than in North Carolina, where it seemed a new day had dawned.

A battle had ended, but the war continued. Partisans and ideologues on all sides were not about to surrender. The Democrats had won the consolation prizes: continued dominance of the state legislature, albeit with the lowest margins so far in the century (now 35–15 in the Senate and 85–35 in the House); control of all state executive offices other than governor; and symbolically most satisfying, Jim Hunt's 56 percent of the vote in the lieutenant governor's race, giving him an overwhelming victory over Republican Johnny Walker.[30] Hunt, now sporting a more up-to-date if not modish look, had remained as focused as ever and as cool as a cucumber during one of the state's most tense campaign seasons since 1900. Walker's main marks had been his bibulous name and his bouncy campaign theme song, "Walk right in . . . vote for Johnny Walker." Walker's respectable tally reflected the growing Republican base in North Carolina elections, an indicator of long-term trends in state and regional politics. But Hunt's win gave the Democrats hope of a coming savior, a leader who might one day be the kingfish of North Carolina politics, a kingfish ruling through hard work, persuasion, flattery, and the politics of inclusion rather than through attacks and brute force.

CHAPTER SEVEN

# Transition in the Shadow of Watergate

On three occasions in the first three-quarters of the twentieth century, national political tides reversed with a vengeance: the 1930–32 descent into economic despair; the late 1960s and early 1970s, when many whites grew weary of social protest movements; and from 1973 to 1976 in the shadow of Watergate.

The 1972 campaign shenanigans first entered the public consciousness after operatives from President Richard Nixon's campaign conducted a "third-rate burglary" on the Democratic offices in Washington's Watergate complex. After Nixon sailed on to victory in the 1972 general election, media scrutiny of Watergate set off a chain of events leading to the appointment of a special U.S. Senate committee to investigate alleged abuses.

To chair the panel, the Democratic Senate leadership tapped North Carolina's Sam J. Ervin Jr., a conservative Democrat respected for his high ethical standards and erudition on legal matters. The conspicuously folksy and homespun Ervin achieved fame when the investigation uncovered the extent of the abuses by the Committee to Re-Elect the President (soon known by the acronym CREEP) and Nixon's attempts to hide the truth. Facing impeachment and certain removal from office, Nixon resigned in August 1974. The man liberals loved to hate was gone.[1]

Nixon had quietly assured southern whites that he would rein in federal bureaucrats who aggressively pushed racial integration. Still, the first massive school integration occurred on his watch, although it was propelled by a shove from a few federal judges. Nixon and young political strategist Kevin Phillips promoted an emerging Republican majority built on an appeal to social conservatives—Anglo-Saxons in the South and formerly Democratic Central and Southern European ethnics in the North.[2] From 1968 to early 1973, the vision advanced down the road to reality. All was torn asunder by Watergate, or so it seemed. But ringing in the year 1973, few imagined how suddenly national events would unfold. North Carolina's Democrats faced the prospect of sharing power with the Republicans. The Democrats hoped for a revival while fearing a continued slide downward.

Gerald Ford, a less contentious figure, assumed the presidency after Nixon's resignation. He offered an olive branch to nearly everyone. Even his autumn "advance pardon" of the depressed Nixon might have been an act of mercy. While Ford sought national healing, a wary public saw a big-time crook escaping any chance of legal consequences. For many Democrats and independents, Ford's act was incendiary. It figuratively ignited the torch at the front of Democratic victory marches.

Meanwhile, in North Carolina both parties faced the responsibilities of governing the state. The Democrats did not quite know what to make of a situation where they lacked a governor to provide party direction. Republicans saw new opportunities and perils. One of the perils was deep party division.

### THE AFTERMATH OF '72: SAILING UNCHARTED WATERS

The 1972 election left a leadership vacuum. It was not a vacuum in the conventional sense, because many people were willing to fill it, but neither voters nor leading politicians were sure who had the legitimacy, much less the mandate, to lead. Jim Holshouser was the governor, but he had been narrowly elected, and Democrats and Republicans alike considered his win a fluke. Furthermore, North Carolina governors' power had resulted more from political smarts and connections than from the state constitution. Governors often drove the state's agenda, but they could do little without the legislature. As a former legislator, Holshouser knew the political reality. He moved to build bridges across party lines. He and leading Democrats such as Senate leader Gordon Allen and Speaker of the House James Ramsey already liked one another.[3] Holshouser and Ramsey had been law school classmates. Allen, Ramsey, and Lieutenant Governor Jim Hunt—all hoping to one day be governor—headed off a legislative attempt to reduce Holshouser's powers. Ed Rankin, a former top aide to Governors William B. Umstead, Luther Hodges, and Dan K. Moore, spoke against tampering with the governor's prerogatives.[4]

Within the Republican Party, Holshouser had a shaky base. Jesse Helms and his allies looked toward taking over the state party. Only Holshouser and established western Republicans such as the Broyhill family stood in the way. Holshouser controlled many state-level appointments, had good connections with the Nixon and Ford administrations, and for the moment dominated the state Republican organization. Several years passed before the conflict between the Holshouser and Helms forces played out, a situation that contributed further to the uncertainty about who had the legitimacy and clout to lead.[5]

Centrist and liberal Democratic activists saw Jim Hunt as a natural party leader, and he moved to consolidate his position. As lieutenant governor, Hunt presided over the N.C. Senate, appointed its committees, and directed the flow of legislation. With influence came risks. A stumble might cripple a political career. As early as November 1972, Hunt was the front-runner for the Democratic nomination in 1976. Attorney General Robert Morgan had admirers among Democrats, but he and Hunt had reason not to go after one another. Morgan liked his current role but was eying the U.S. Senate, considering a challenge to the aging Ervin. After flirting with a 1972 run for governor, Morgan leaned against seeking that office. Many Morgan supporters were also Hunt people. One of the most prominent was Charles Winberry, a former president of the Young Democrat Clubs who had practiced law in Wilson and Rocky Mount. The rotund Winberry was shrewd, talented, and a confidante of both Hunt (his kinsman) and Morgan. Hunt and Morgan allies saw Winberry as an able strategist for rebuilding the party. Ervin was not deeply concerned with state party affairs, and most of his energy and intellect were turned toward investigating suspected wrongdoings in the Nixon administration.[6]

Following tradition, gubernatorial nominee Skipper Bowles had named the top Democratic Party officers in 1972. The chair was New Bern attorney James Sugg. Sugg found himself in a unique position for a Democratic chair: He had a claim to being the party's real leader. Past Democratic Party chairs had followed the governors' directives on party and policy matters. Sugg had no governor to provide guidance, though he and Bowles remained allies. A smart political operative, Sugg knew that after the election, the party had many power centers. In 1973 and 1974, Sugg and the State Democratic Executive Committee, which had representatives from every county, wielded enormous influence. They set out to rebuild a party in shambles. Inevitably, tensions arose between the Sugg forces—many of whom were former Bowles people—and the forces loyal to Hunt and Morgan. But in 1973–74, Sugg won plaudits from political activists for rebuilding a party that had only recently seemed a wreck.

The Republican Holshouser led the state much in the spirit and tradition of earlier Democratic governors. In a 2006 interview, Holshouser said that the state's residents had historically wanted their chief executive to govern from the center, to be a pragmatic can-do person rather than an ideologue.

As a legislator, Holshouser had opposed Scott's tax proposals, but the new governor acknowledged that his efforts to expand state services including public schools, universities, and the budding statewide kindergarten program were enhanced by the revenue from the Scott administration's tax hikes.[7] He worked with the legislature and Hunt to pass a groundbreaking coastal area land management act (CAMA), designed to prevent or at least control rampant development on the Atlantic Coast. For the time, it was a bold piece of legislation. In a place where the ethos of private property rights reigned, the passage of a mild land control act applying to rural areas constituted a major accomplishment.[8] Many of the legislation's goals were later stymied under pressure from local officials and developers, but Holshouser and legislative promoters such as state Democratic representative Willis Whichard of Durham had shown foresight and political skills in forging a bill that could win passage.

Higher education battles loomed. The most controversial issue revolved around East Carolina University chancellor Leo Jenkins's dream of a four-year medical school at ECU. Holshouser, many piedmont interests, and William Friday, the president of the sixteen-campus state university system, opposed East Carolina's bid, saying that it would be inefficient and a drain on state finances. In 1973, the state legislature had approved a two-year medical school at East Carolina after previously establishing a one-year school. The school was underfunded and riddled with problems.[9] Its opponents argued that rural health care could be provided more efficiently if existing four-year state and private medical schools were expanded. As part of that expansion, rural regional health centers were to be established. Under the university reorganization act of 1971, the Board of Governors of the public university system would have made the decision on any new medical school.[10]

Lieutenant Governor Hunt endorsed a four-year medical school at East Carolina and argued that it was a basic health matter, not simply one of higher education. He said that the legislature, not the Board of Governors, should make the decision. Helms urged fellow Republicans and conservative Democrats to support the four-year medical school. With four of the state's shrewdest politicians—Hunt, Helms, Jenkins, and Attorney General Morgan—going to bat for ECU, that train became hard to stop.

The decision to adopt a four-year school was delayed, but there seemed little doubt that it would soon come. The 1975 budget was tight—so tight that teachers and state workers faced a salary freeze—but in June the state legislature funded a four-year medical school at East Carolina, with Pitt County Memorial Hospital in Greenville as its affiliated teaching hospital. Once the school was inevitable, Friday supported a high level of funding and backed

Combatants and shapers of modern higher education in North Carolina:
East Carolina University chancellor Leo Jenkins and University of North Carolina
system president William Friday, late 1960s or early 1970s. Chancellor Jenkins and
President Friday, 1970–1975, 55-01-1676, Visual Materials Collection (UA55),
University Archives, East Carolina University, Greenville.

the hiring of William Laupus, a talented medical administrator from Virginia, to supervise the gargantuan project.[11] Jenkins and Friday now had a common goal: building a first-rate medical school and teaching hospital. The school went on to perform much of its intended mission, providing health care for both down-at-the-heel and soon-to-be prosperous coastal plain counties. To pacify UNC–Chapel Hill interests, the area health centers under their control were expanded. And state subsidies were provided to students attending existing private medical schools—Duke in Durham and Bowman-Gray at Wake Forest University in Winston-Salem. The entire process was driven by politics. The cost was high—indeed, exorbitant—in lean budget times. But decades later, few wanted to turn back the clock.

Holshouser and Hunt also united to support the Equal Rights Amendment, a proposed amendment to the U.S. Constitution specifying that women had equal political rights with men in all spheres. Opponents, including Helms backers, conservative Democrats, and Senator Ervin, asserted that the amendment could require same-sex bathrooms and threaten marriage and motherhood.[12] Despite strong efforts from backers of the amendment, the North Carolina Legislature narrowly defeated the measure, and it never received the approval of the required three-quarters of the states for adoption.

Whatever else, North Carolina had been true to its past in the 1973–75 period, forging ahead, but with limits. Issue debates transcended party and ideological differences. But around this time, critics were focusing more and more on the state's shortcomings. Citing North Carolina's high infant death rate, low per capita expenditures on welfare, and school dropout levels, journalist Jack Bass and political scientist Walter De Vries wrote a book, *The Transformation of Southern Politics*, in which they called North Carolina "the progressive myth." According to Bass and De Vries, many North Carolinians were oblivious to their state's problems even though it was falling behind much of the rest of the South as well as the nation.[13]

All the while, North Carolina's tax burden remained higher than that in many other states, though its reliance on corporate and income levies was more "equitable." Citizens chafed under these taxes and the more recent sales tax expansion. Good leadership had not paved the streets with gold and was having enough difficulty just filling the potholes.

### A REVERSAL OF FORTUNES

The 1974–76 period brought Democrats in North Carolina and other parts of the United States gains not imagined in the aftermath of Richard Nixon's 1972 electoral avalanche. A series of events—some, such as the Watergate scandal, national in scope, some reflecting a new racial calmness in the South, and still others unique to North Carolina—conspired to bring a pronounced if temporary reversal of what appeared to be the Republican tide in southern politics. The state Democratic Party, which had for a few years seemed a lumbering giant—still the majority party but on a down-ward slope—achieved a domination of offices not seen since the 1950s. For Republicans, the national nightmare of Watergate had powerful local reverberations after Nixon resigned amid scandal.

In November 1974, the number of Republican-held seats fell from 15 to 1 in the 50-member N.C. Senate and from 35 to 9 in the 120-member N.C. House. Republican strength in North Carolina's U.S. House of Representatives delegation dropped from 4 to 2. Stephen Neal, a publisher of small, locally oriented newspapers, ousted Wilmer "Vinegar Bend" Mizell in the Fifth District, around Winston-Salem, and W. G. (Bill) Hefner, a radio station owner and country gospel singer, beat Earl Ruth in the animal-shaped

Eighth District, running from the foothills east to the sand hills. Both were upsets even in what had promised to be a good Democratic year.

In the 1974 race to succeed the retiring Ervin, Morgan prevailed over Republican N.C. House member William Stevens, 633,725–377,618. Morgan had flexed his political muscle in the spring Democratic primary, when he won a clear majority in a ten-candidate field that included former congressman Nick Galifianakis and Henry Hall Wilson, a prominent businessman with national political connections. The icing on the cake for the Democrats was Rufus Edmisten's 618,046–390,626 victory over Republican attorney general William Carson, whom Governor Holshouser had appointed to fill the temporary vacancy when Morgan resigned as attorney general to campaign for senator. Republicans had hoped that this appointment would give Carson the edge in the November election. Some Democrats had been privately worried, citing Edmisten's long de facto residence in Washington and his playboy image. But they and Republicans had failed to grasp Edmisten's tremendous political skills, folksy personality, and general attractiveness as a candidate as well as the extent of the anti-Republican backlash. The Republican foothold on the Council of State level was swept away after only a few months. That James Martin in the Ninth District and James Broyhill in the Tenth had retained U.S. House seats for the GOP attested to their personal popularity more than it did to Republican strength in their areas. Their victories offered small consolation to the Republicans.

Republican governor Holshouser still had two years left in his term. It was tempting to liken his dilemma to that of the last Republican governor, Dan Russell, elected in 1896. Two years later, his party suffered a stunning defeat at the polls, and its prospects for the 1900 elections looked bleak. Russell still wore the crown but was impotent and despised. Yet Holshouser's position was distinctly different. He remained popular with many Democratic legislators and leaders in the business community. The strained state budget of 1975, more than partisan bickering, limited new initiatives. The biggest political quarrel with Holshouser and his forces came not from the Democrats but rather from Reagan/Helms-style conservatives within the Republican Party. While Helms and Holshouser maintained a courteous but distant personal relationship, the Helms allies were out for blood— if not Holshouser's, then surely that of his faction of the party. That struggle continued into 1976, further weakening the GOP in its time of peril.

### NOMINATION BATTLES

On the national level, the political cauldron boiled with implications for 1976. A weakened Republican Party had suffered casualties in the 1974 election. Its numbers dropped from 42 to 37 in the U.S. Senate and 192 to 144 in the U.S. House. When Gerald Ford assumed the presidency following Richard Nixon's forced resignation in August 1974, the new chief executive initially won bipartisan praise for his gentler style of governance. But the scars of Watergate and the Nixon pardon had overcome any empathy for Ford by the time of the 1974 midterm elections.

Ford's most immediate challenge came from a man who was ambivalent about Nixon's fate but determined to rescue America from what he saw as a leftward drift and lack of zeal in the struggle against communism. Former California governor Ronald Reagan found his fellow Republican Ford wanting in the fight for national survival. Reagan's transformation from grade-B movie actor to political superstar was now well under way. Yet for all his charisma, Reagan's effort to win the Republican presidential nomination seemed doomed when he lost to Ford in the early New Hampshire and Florida primaries. His campaign might have ended but for the North Carolina primary. The state's Democratic-dominated state legislature, with the explicit goal of increasing the state's influence in the party's selection process, had approved holding a March presidential primary, two months earlier than the traditional May date. The presidential primary was moved to March, ostensibly to increase the state's influence in the process, but also to provide a boost to former governor and current Duke University president Terry Sanford's planned bid for the Democratic presidential nomination. However, Sanford's prospects had faltered in the cold winter blasts of New Hampshire, and he withdrew from the race, citing chest pains.[14]

As other Democrats brought their campaigns to North Carolina, a bigger drama was unfolding in the Republican primary. With the Reagan campaign seemingly all but dead after a loss in Florida, conventional wisdom held that Ford would win the Tar Heel primary and that Reagan was near his political end. Senator Helms and the Congressional Club were not intimidated. Helms, though nervous about the political consequences of bucking the tide and an incumbent president, campaigned for his ideological soul mate, Reagan. Over the preceding several years, the most conservative wing of the party had moved from upstart or outside status to the controlling force, at least in organizational matters. While Governor Holshouser and long-established party forces were sympathetic to Ford, seeing him as a more likely general election winner than Reagan, they were outgunned by Congressional Club strategists Tom Ellis and Carter Wrenn. North Carolina breathed new life into the Reagan campaign when he defeated Ford, 101,468–88,897. Reagan's campaign picked up national momentum and remained alive through the summer's national convention.

At the ensuing state Republican convention, the Helms wing of the party called the shots. Neither Holshouser nor the state's Republican members of Congress, Broyhill and Martin, were elected delegates to the national convention. Ellis later said that Holshouser and Martin asked for his support, but neither would meet his condition for support—a switch from Ford to Reagan.[15]

On the same day that North Carolina Republicans resurrected the Reagan campaign, Democrats faced off in their own multicandidate presidential preference primary. Most attention centered on Jimmy Carter and George Wallace. After winning the New Hampshire primary, Carter had gone on to beat Wallace in Florida, which had provided a big boost to Wallace in its 1972 primary. The Wallace of 1976 was a different man, mostly confined to a wheelchair, frail, and often motionless except for a visible shake. His voice was still distinct, but the passion seemed lacking. Arthur Bremer's bullets at the Maryland shopping center in 1972 had weakened a body and wrecked a political soul.

With North Carolina's Sanford no longer an active candidate, whether as a result of chest pains or of faltering political prospects, all eyes focused on a match between the two voices from the Deep South. With them came the obvious story line, Old South versus New South. Wallace no longer had a chance for the presidency, but a North Carolina victory might keep his campaign alive at least in the southern and border states. Carter had the opportunity to administer the coup de grâce to Wallace in the sense that a politically wounded man's campaign would be snuffed out. If Wallace could not win in North Carolina, a culturally more southern state than Florida, his campaign was over.

In the March primary, Carter beat Wallace, 324,437–210,166, a defeat that was as sweeping as his victory had been in 1972. The county-level voting testified to its magnitude. Carter led in eighty-five counties, some of them former Wallace strongholds. Wallace pluralities were mostly restricted to a few old segregationist bastions where both he and Lake had done well in the past. Even allowing for the possibility that the most partisan and committed Democrats turned out at a higher rate than others in the special presidential primary, Wallace had suffered another stinging blow. Defeating Wallace in a major southern state provided Carter with needed momentum. The party hoped to cast aside the Wallace albatross and restore its former North-South electoral coalition.

How did what might have been a forgotten presidential campaign emerge from its Georgia base to capture North Carolina, the South, and ultimately a convention? Carter grasped southern politics and its blending with national politics in ways matched only by Lyndon Johnson among earlier candidates. In 1976, personal demeanor counted for a lot. Carter knew how to connect. His voice was determined but soft, a characteristic that served him well in small-group meetings and on television. Carter was a product of the Deep South and, best of all, a small southern town. His livelihood was agriculture and agribusiness. Carter's ads portrayed him as a farmer. Many rural dwellers as well as townspeople identified with the village and the farm. Carter was a Sunday school–teaching Southern Baptist in a region where Protestants predominated. North Carolinians welcomed the symbolism of a God-fearing man walking out of a small-town Baptist church on Sunday morning, a candidate of faith and deep abiding morality.[16] Whatever ruckus might occur on the floor of the Democratic National Convention, a fellow Christian would be there to calm the waters.

Carter experienced small bumps on the road to the nomination, notably when California governor Jerry Brown entered the race. But Carter won primaries in Pennsylvania and other key northern states and never lost his front-runner status after the boosts from New Hampshire, Florida, and North Carolina. In June he picked up endorsements from Chicago mayor Richard J. Daley and the vanquished Wallace, cementing his nomination.

When the New York convention opened, Carter was at the pinnacle of his political career. Following an easy first-ballot nomination, Carter was joined on the podium by a bevy of luminaries that most poignantly included Wallace and Pastor Martin Luther King Sr., the father of the slain civil rights leader. Holding hands, the Democratic elites and former adversaries led the convention hall in a rendition of the old civil rights anthem, "We Shall Overcome." The words rang out across the hall and the land. No twentieth-century convention witnessed a more touching moment, filled with symbolism and promises of a new and more enlightened world.[17] Like most miracles, the miracle of Jimmy Carter could not sustain itself for long. But the delegates, especially those from such southern states as North Carolina, left New York with enthusiasm for a candidate who could carry their home states and put a formerly outcast region into the national mainstream.

The subsequent Republican convention was a suspense-filled gathering where tooting horns created an almost surreal atmosphere. The platform committee, on which East Carolina University political science professor John East exercised strong influence, adopted planks more in line with Reagan's brand of conservatism than Ford's moderate positions. Since his victory in the North Carolina primary, Reagan had been competitive. Ford garnered 1,187 votes to Reagan's 1,070, the first time since 1952 that a

Republican convention presidential ballot had been close. Ford and his running mate, Robert Dole of Kansas, embarked on a campaign with long odds.[18]

The legislature's decision to move up the presidential primary was also influenced by a desire to protect candidates for state and local offices from having to choose sides in the presidential primary. No one had greater reason to be concerned about that scenario than gubernatorial candidate Hunt, a man closely tied with the Sanford crowd but now striving to win votes across the ideological fault lines. Hunt also had the best organization of any likely candidate for governor, and with his support, the 1975 legislature had also moved the state-level primaries to August, with runoffs to be held in September if necessary. The change shortened the state's traditional five-month campaign season, and a short general election campaign usually benefits the best-known candidate, since the opposition has less time to make mischief. Furthermore, a primary in the summer dog days might draw fewer voters, also a benefit to the best-known and best organized candidate—Hunt.

Politically well-placed figures, including Speaker of the House James C. Green, considered challenging Hunt for the governorship. Hunt and Green had clashed on many issues, most emotionally, the Equal Rights Amendment. Green claimed neutrality on the question but in fact had worked to kill the amendment in the N.C. House.[19] Hunt and Green also fought over spending levels for education. While both professed support for public schools, Hunt supported higher spending. After reflection and fearing he could not stop the Hunt juggernaut, Green sought the lieutenant governorship. Gordon Allen and James Ramsey of Person County, longtime leaders in the Senate and House, respectively, had thought of running for governor but concluded that challenging Hunt would be a futile exercise. Ever since his narrow 1972 defeat, Skipper Bowles had told friends that he would make another run, but Hunt had already cornered many veterans of the earlier Bowles campaign. Nonetheless, a Bowles entry would have been a real hindrance to Hunt, as both drew support from Sanford and Morgan backers. Citing heart problems, Bowles announced in March that he would not pursue the race.

As Hunt surveyed the scene, he had more reason than ever to be upbeat. He had covered nearly all bases in the party. With Bert Bennett still a strategist and the backing of talented friends from Wilson County, most notably campaign chair Joe Grimsley, Hunt built one of the ablest campaign organizations ever assembled in North Carolina. Hunt had been too liberal for veteran conservative legislators, but he had also taken stands that opened doors on the right. An aide said at the time, "Jim is paranoid about being labeled a liberal."[20] Hunt backed the reinstitution of capital punishment, a penalty provided for by North Carolina law but suspended by the U.S. Supreme Court from 1967 to 1976. Knowing Wallace's popularity among many North Carolinians, Hunt courted the Alabama governor's backers and had a friendly conversation with him when he stopped off in North Carolina. Hunt stressed his own religious faith and eschewed alcohol and profanity, at least in public.

Social populists—persons believing in core Christian values and obedience to the law and opposing rapid social change—could find much to admire in Hunt. So could economic populists when Hunt spoke about the pain of high energy costs and utility rates. Many voters blended faith in God and country with a skepticism of the big shots in society. Hunt appeared to share that viewpoint. All the while, he astutely courted big business, stressing that he thought business-friendly tax policies and minimal regulation— where feasible—would ultimately create jobs and prosperity for the state.[21] He was more a classic North Carolina progressive than economic populist. As with Sanford, elements of economic populism became part of Hunt's progressive message. Democratic members of the legislature increasingly looked to Hunt for leadership, wanting to be in good standing with the probable governor. Hunt played up to their egos and policy interests.

Hunt drew three serious opponents: Ed O'Herron of Charlotte, George Wood of rural Camden County, and Tommy Strickland of Goldsboro. O'Herron, chair of the board of the huge Eckerd's drugstore chain, ran as a fiscal conservative and social moderate, supporting the Equal Rights Amendment. He saw himself as the logical choice of people who had previously backed Hodges and Moore. With carefully coiffed gray hair and a body befitting a former Marine and boxer, O'Herron looked like a governor. He hoped to build on a big hometown vote. Wood, a farm owner and businessman who had represented a geographically large Senate district in sparsely populated northeastern North Carolina, ran to the left of Hunt, opposing tax loopholes and favoring a 20 percent salary increase for teachers over a two-year period. He hoped to attract liberal voters disenchanted with Hunt's "wishy-washy" philosophy. Wood picked up endorsements from Skipper Bowles and the liberal *Raleigh News and Observer*. Political scientist Walter De Vries, the public opinion wizard who advised Bowles's 1972 campaign, presented Wood with data suggesting that Hunt was strong with Democratic activists but that a challenger might capitalize on Hunt's fuzzy image among voters in general. Wood's official campaign manager was former North Carolina State University president John Caldwell, one of the most articulate and highly respected educators in mid-twentieth-century North Carolina. Caldwell's backing of Wood was a blow to Hunt, who saw North Carolina State people as his natural constituents. Strickland, a veteran legislator and evangelical Christian, backed George Wallace and opposed the Equal Rights Amendment. He favored increasing state financial assistance for private colleges.[22]

Hunt had been informally running for governor since 1972. While other potential candidates legislated, made money, or slept, he sought political goodwill. For years, Hunt had showered black civic and religious leaders with attention, surpassing even Sanford in developing a rapport with the African American community. Teachers' leaders, feminists, and organized labor were appreciative when the lieutenant governor sought their counsel and confidence. He convinced most of these groups that his heart was in the right place but that political reality might prevent the immediate attainment of "our goals." After Wood entered the race, Hunt moved to the left on a few issues, specifically stressing that he too favored closing tax loopholes for the wealthy.[23] But he also heaped praise on business leaders for their efforts to build the state. Seeing Hunt as the likely winner, they responded with checks and offers of public support.

With the possible exceptions of Terry Sanford in 1960, Furnifold Simmons in the early twentieth century, and O. Max Gardner in 1928–46, Hunt had built the largest network of political loyalists that North Carolina had seen. Like Sanford's supporters, Hunt's backers came from myriad backgrounds: people who had known him as a teenager in the Future Farmers of America, fellow college politicos, Jaycees and former Jaycees, preachers, attorneys, and party activists. Hunt regularly reminded all these individuals that they were very special.

Hunt looked both friends and potential supporters in the eye as he pumped their hands and told them, "We are counting on *you* to help us build a new day in *North Carolina!*" He had a special way of pronouncing "North Carolina." First, there was a strong emphasis on the "North." The "i" in "Carolina" was pronounced more as the sharp "i" in Midwestern American speech than in the softer southern dialect. However, Hunt's usual tone and enunciation were southern, a refined and distinct southern. By 1976, Hunt seemed much more polished and confident than he had in the early 1970s. Professional politicos might laugh or wink at his style, but many longtime friends and new acquaintances found him both charming and sincere. He was the master.

In the August primary, Hunt took 362,102 votes (53 percent of the total), O'Herron 157,815, Wood 121,673, Strickland 31,338, and the lesser known J. Andrew Barker 5,003. This was 53 percent for Hunt and 47 percent for the combined opposition. Hunt was strong nearly everywhere. O'Herron took his home county of Mecklenburg, but not convincingly. Wood led in scattered counties near the Dismal Swamp and Albemarle Sound, the area he had represented in the legislature. Strickland swept his home county of Wayne but ran a poor fourth in most places.

The total of 677,931 votes was below the Democratic primary turnouts between 1964 and 1972, even though the total state population and number of registered Democrats had increased. The summer timing surely depressed the 1976 numbers and aided the well-organized and better-known Hunt. Still, he would have likely won big whenever the primary was held.

Despite bleak November prospects, two well-known Republicans sought their party's nomination for governor. David Flaherty had served as secretary of human resources in the Holshouser administration after a stint representing Caldwell County in the N.C. House and after building his career as an executive with Broyhill Furniture. Flaherty had also chaired the state Young Republicans. His Republican primary opponent, the Reverend Coy Privette, headed the Christian Action League. Privette was the most vocal opponent of legal liquor sales in North Carolina, a big issue at the time. Privette's ideas on social issues were close to those of Jesse Helms, but Helms and his organization were deeply involved in the Reagan drive for the presidency and chose not to become entangled in the race for governor.[24] Flaherty won the primary.

There was still the formality of a general election, but no Democrat since Hodges in 1956 had looked toward November with as much confidence as Hunt had in 1976. And this time the Democratic presidential nominee would not be a drag on the ticket. The general election was still two and a half months off, but Hunt was the presumptive governor-elect.

### THE MAN FROM LITHONIA

Ten years earlier, the idea of an African American seeking a top state office would have met with scorn from many white voters. Even people sympathetic to change might have seen the whole effort as a bit wacky, but Howard Lee mounted a serious challenge for the lieutenant governorship in 1976. The office, viewed by aspirants as a stepping-stone to the governorship, had many seekers including Board of Wake County Commissioners chair Waverly Akins; Buncombe County representative Herbert Hyde, a moderate widely regarded as the wittiest member of the state legislature; and gifted attorney-lobbyist John R. Jordan, a Raleigh insider. Most formidable was Speaker of the House Jimmy Green. Green, a tobacco warehouseman, was variously described as "crusty," "sly," or a "gentleman of the old school." He came from Clarkton, in Bladen County, and emerged as the first choice of many down east Democrats. His voice was slightly high pitched, sometimes raspy, but his words were carefully chosen. A native of south-central Virginia, Green had attended the elite Washington and Lee University. Green's dress was sharp but conservative. A political conservative, he had a pragmatic streak and quietly reached out to political centrists and state employees.

Howard Lee grew up in rural Lithonia, Georgia. Georgia of the 1950s was rigidly segregated, even by southern standards. After earning a sociology degree from Fort Valley State College in 1959, Lee worked as a juvenile probation office in Savannah. Frank Spencer, a local white shipping executive of progressive instincts, hosted a reception for the seventy-two-year-old Frank Porter Graham and invited Howard Lee and his wife, Lillian, to attend. Eyebrows were raised when they arrived. Graham heard of Lee's plan to pursue graduate studies in social work and urged him to apply to Chapel Hill. Graham then used his influence to secure a hefty scholarship package for Lee. After finishing his master's degree, Lee joined the social work faculty at nearby Duke, but the Lees wanted to live in progressive Chapel Hill. White real estate agents initially refused to show houses outside all-black neighborhoods. After months of effort and despite threats, the Lees bought a house in the all white Colony Woods subdivision. Lee and a band of progressives lobbied the city's Board of Aldermen to adopt an open housing ordinance. Meeting a wall of resistance, the progressives decided to run one of their own for mayor.[25]

A consensus developed for Howard Lee. He ran hard and in 1969 won the prize.[26] Lee defeated Roland Giduz, the candidate of the Chapel Hill business establishment. Giduz was no reactionary but rather a business-oriented moderate conservative. Lee called for more open, responsive government and won admiration even from a few people in the business community. His timing was fortunate. At the spring 1968 county Democratic convention, forces backing the presidential candidacy of Eugene McCarthy had won control of the Orange County Democratic Executive Committee. The new majority immediately began to focus on local politics and voter registration. Lee's respectable but unsuccessful 1972 challenge to incumbent Congressman L. H. Fountain had provided further statewide name recognition.

Lee stood out in a crowd, and his bass voice propelled an oratorical style superior to that of run-of-the-mill politicians. He drew widespread support from Democratic activists. Hunt's forces stayed zealously neutral in the lieutenant governor's race, but some of them quietly hoped for a Lee victory, thinking that he would be an ally in governing and that Green would not. However, Democratic tradition suggested that Lee's race and liberalism might make him a drag on the whole ticket. Akins, Hyde, or the more conservative Green might do more for election unity. Lee believed that many old Wallace supporters—people with an antiestablishment and economic populist streak—should be his natural allies and thought them more likely converts to his cause than business-oriented moderates inclined toward Akins or Jordan.[27] Anecdotal evidence suggests that Lee gained backing from a few Wallace people but far from enough to make a big difference.[28] Lee led Green by a sliver in the August primary, 177,091–174,464. Jordan, Akins, and Hyde together had 224,381, with three other candidates totaling 63,585 votes. Green called for a runoff primary.

The candidates shunned overt racial language in their campaign statements, but predictably, race was the major undercurrent. In private conversations, it was a leading theme, along with the candidates' backgrounds and characters. The media focused on the historic implications of a black winning a top office in a southern state. Green had experience and seasoning in state politics, but his image as an old-time politician did not play well with some young and urban white voters. Green ads consistently showed pictures of both Green and Lee, presumably to remind voters of Lee's race. Green's appeals urged a heavy turnout to keep a "small segment" of the population from determining the outcome.[29] Lee's campaign worked to boast the turnout among blacks and liberal whites, arguing that his positions on state development and education resembled those of Hunt.

Turnout dropped about 20 percent between the first primary and the runoff, and Green prevailed, 282,362–229,195. Despite Green's victory, Lee showed that an African American could win a lot of white votes in the former Confederacy. He had been a serious contender. That in itself was a victory for the advocates of greater racial equality and expansion of the American Dream.

Despite the changes that had taken place, North Carolina in 1976 still had many characteristics of the Old South. Only fifteen years earlier, segregation and white supremacy had been the order of the day. If African Americans had turned out to vote at a significantly higher percentage than whites, Lee could have won the 1976 runoff.

THE GENERAL ELECTION OF '76: A SOUTHERNER TRIUMPHS

Carter led throughout the presidential campaign, but he committed blunders along the way. Like underdog Democrat Humphrey in 1968,

Republican Ford in 1976 came close to snatching victory from the jaws of defeat. Or perhaps more accurately, Carter came close to snatching defeat from the jaws of victory.

Carter suffered little damage among fellow southerners for his running mate selection, liberal Senator Walter "Fritz" Mondale from Minnesota. In the presidential debates, Carter committed no faux pas. Nor did Mondale in his debate with GOP contender Bob Dole. Carter was more glib than Ford, who was not comfortable before cameras and inclined to verbal slips, however solid he might be as a person.

Yet Carter stirred lingering doubts. North Carolinians—usually those who had backed Eisenhower and Nixon—said over and over, "I'm afraid of Carter." For all his southernness and down-home style, something seemed just a little odd about the Georgian. In the end, doubts about Carter made the national race close, even if they never put North Carolina's final outcome in question. The most puzzling incident, raising eyebrows among voters, especially in the South, occurred when Carter consented to an interview with *Playboy* magazine. The interview was conducted shortly after the Democratic National Convention but was not published until much closer to election time. Carter admitted that he had sinned by lusting in his heart, and he used the word "screw" in a sexual context.[30] If nothing else, the *Playboy* interview reinforced a widespread view that Carter was a bit strange.

In retrospect, it is hard to understand how Carter could possibly have lost. He was a more aggressive and agile campaigner than Ford, much quicker to go for the kill. More important, the Republican Party was split and dejected. Nixon had let them down. People of all ages and persuasions were angry. Tom Fetzer, later a leading Republican activist and two-term mayor of Raleigh and state GOP chair, had delivered an enthusiastic speech for Helms when he was a student a Sanderson High School in 1972. By 1976, Fetzer was eligible to vote, but he "was jaded and cynical over the whole process. I didn't vote until 1980. I'm not sure who I would have voted for in 1976."[31] Young Fetzer's idealism had been shattered. More broadly, many Republicans, especially Reagan enthusiasts, sat on their hands or made only tepid efforts for Ford. Jimmy Carter was no George McGovern. Just maybe, Carter would be preferable to Ford. Ronald Reagan, thanks to his impressive convention showing, might still have his day in the sun.

Nationally, Carter received 40,830,763 votes (50.1 percent) to Ford's 39,147,793 (48.0 percent). Although the results were by no means the closest popular vote ever, Carter had still come close to losing. In the Electoral College, he took 297 votes to Ford's 240. A shift of a few thousand votes from Carter to Ford in Mississippi and Ohio would have given Ford those states and the presidency, though Carter would have retained the lead in the popular vote.

Carter won every southern state except closely fought Virginia, most by large margins. His 55.2 percent in North Carolina was his ninth-best in any state, tenth when including the District of Columbia. All of Carter's top ten states except Massachusetts and Rhode Island were southern or border states. More than in any election since 1916, the South had been the main building block of a Democratic victory. Close wins in New York, Pennsylvania, and Ohio put Carter over the top. He was weak in the West, losing all the Pacific states except Hawaii, all the Rocky Mountain states, and much of the Great Plains region. Carter also lost the megastates of Illinois, New Jersey, and Michigan, the latter Ford's home. So Carter was now president thanks in large part to a region that supported a native son but whose long-term loyalty to the national Democratic Party seemed shaky.

Carter's North Carolina support was broad. He managed majorities of 53 percent both in the mountains and piedmont, near the levels received by Lyndon Johnson twelve years earlier and far surpassing what Democrats Adlai Stevenson and John Kennedy had received in 1952, 1956, and 1960. Both regions had many counties that had majorities of Democratic registrants but for years had been Republican strongholds in presidential elections. Like Johnson in 1964, Carter won small pluralities in the cities of Charlotte, Greensboro, and Winston-Salem, where middle-class white voters had already abandoned the Democrats in droves. Ford usually led in the middle- to high-income white areas, but Carter often got between 25 and 40 percent of this vote. Ford carried the traditionally Republican upland counties but often by 3:2, not 2:1 or 3:1 ratios. Carter had a 62 percent majority in the coastal plain, taking all counties except Lenoir (Kinston) and Wayne (Goldsboro). While this showing trailed Kennedy's 68 percent in 1960, it represented a 34 percent Democratic rise from McGovern's results in 1972. In precinct after precinct that had gone for Wallace in 1968, Carter beat Ford.

The big North Carolina winner both in breadth and depth was Jim Hunt. He won 65 percent of the popular vote and defeated Flaherty in ninety-six counties, including four that had been longtime Republican bedrocks—Henderson, Randolph, Wilkes, and Yadkin. Four factors contributed to the Hunt romp: the anti-Republican trend in the wake of the Watergate scandal, many southerners' affinity for Carter, Hunt's superior organization, and Hunt's immense stamina and political skills. The Hunt-Carter coattails were long, with Democrats doing well on all levels. Republicans picked up 3 seats in the N.C. Senate but still trailed the Democrats, 46 to 4. In the N.C. House of Representatives, the Democratic total rose from 111 to 114 of the 120 seats. As in 1974, Republican congressmen Martin and Broyhill won reelection.

While a repudiation of the Republican Party, the 1976 election was not a victory for any particular ideology. Hunt wanted to be identified as a centrist Democrat, one for whom both conservatives and liberals could comfortably vote. Yet his early heroes were Franklin Roosevelt and Kerr Scott. Hunt hoped to be a transformative governor and to shake up government and the society in which he lived. Former state supreme court chief justice Burley Mitchell said that Hunt "had the foresight, the vision, and the uncanny ability to know where the state needed to go. Also, he knew you can't take the people where they don't want to go." Few have been as consumed by the political process as Hunt, but unlike the stereotypical ambitious politician, Hunt seemed to care as much about governing as he did winning office. Whatever his goals, he pursued them relentlessly. Mitchell added, "Hunt is the most focused person I've ever known other than Bill Clinton."[32] Hunt wanted North Carolina to lead the nation, not just the South. Speaking objectively, such a goal was unreasonable at the time. But without such a bold vision, stagnation might have set in.

Despite the forceful leadership from recent governors, the raw statistics indicated that North Carolina was losing whatever edge it might have had. Historically somnolent or backward southern states, notably Georgia and Virginia, were beginning to move ahead. Growth in leading metropolitan areas did not compensate for economic bleeding across North Carolina. While attention focused on the depopulation of the coastal plain, many mountain and piedmont counties also faced bleak outlooks. The textile industry was still centered in the Carolinas, but its days of rapid expansion were gone. The state's unemployment rate was among the highest in the United States. In North Carolina as elsewhere, gasoline shortages posed a constant threat to economic growth. With inflation and recurring unemployment, the 1970s provided the severest economic challenges since the 1930s.

Yet North Carolina was better positioned to seize available opportunities than many other states. Much of the Northeast and Midwest faced factory closures and population exodus. Whites and—in a dramatic reversal of long-term trends—blacks began to seek economic opportunity in the South.[33] Economic and social changes offered new growth opportunities.

There was less risk of a racial explosion. Blacks moved ever so tentatively into the mainstream of society, prodded on by the effects of the 1960s civil rights legislation. By 1977, most middle-class homes were equipped with air-conditioning. Furthermore, the interstate highway system moved closer to completion, providing quick access to major Atlantic and Great Lakes population centers. As a trucking and distribution center, North Carolina drew the attention of more and more manufacturers. Hunt recognized that his state could build on old strengths.

In January 1977, Jim and Carolyn Hunt and their four children moved into the governor's mansion. A nonstop campaign at last yielded the whirlwind of leadership. Hunt pushed his staff to crowd more activities into his schedule than they thought wise. In a 2008 interview, his press secretary and special assistant Gary Pearce said, "Hunt was not a demanding boss, but he was an exacting boss. We would try hard because he tried so hard and we wanted to be part of it."[34] Ironically, he had so much that he wanted to do that the governor's office was not quite as open to the general citizenry as it had been under previous governors. More would-be visitors were shunted off to other staff members. Yet no governor had ever been any more in the tune with the temper and feel of the general public than Hunt. He visited factories, farms, hospitals, and schools. He followed up with letters and phone calls that both praised past actions and encouraged future ones. Political allies—those who thought they could get away with it—sometimes took their phones off the hook to avoid potential late-night interruptions from the governor. In short, he was the same Jim Hunt as in earlier days. But now he had power. Whatever Hunt's excesses, he seemed never to have been corrupted by the power and prestige of the office. His personal tastes remained simple. Hunt moved to master the bureaucracy as much as possible without stirring up a hornet's nest. Pearce, patronage director Joe Pell, and budget director John A. Williams handled the messier details and unpleasant confrontations.[35] Yet Hunt was in on all the major decisions. He micromanaged in a manner rarely seen among North Carolina governors.

Hunt's seven-member cabinet was a blend of natural talent, political smarts, and diversity, with some individual members combining all three traits. Howard Lee became secretary of community development and natural resources, the first black to serve in a top state-level executive position. In a milieu still dominated by white males, two white women now held cabinet posts: Sarah Morrow, who replaced Flaherty as secretary of human resources, and Sarah Hodgkins, the new secretary of cultural resources. Two other appointees brought both extensive business and political experience: former Raleigh mayor Tom Bradshaw, the transportation secretary, and the wily land developer/hog farmer Lauch Faircloth, who had labored in the political vineyards for both Scotts, Graham, and Sanford and was now secretary of commerce. To oversee the Department of Corrections, a ticking time bomb, Hunt selected a professional, Amos Reed from Florida. Campaign manager Joe Grimsley took over the Department of Administration. Grimsley, devoted to forwarding Hunt's political career, had long inspired trust and confidence among his associates. He was the opposite of an in-your-face politician and had keen political instincts. Grimsley's highly influential assistant secretary was Jane Patterson, a native of Columbus County and later resident of Greensboro who had ardently supported liberal causes, including minority rights, at a time when doing so was risky. She had a burning drive and intense loyalty to Hunt.[36]

The administration, like its predecessors, tried to fill midlevel bureaucratic positions with political allies. Conflict inevitably arose as some career state employees were shoved out of the way or pushed into less desirable positions. North Carolina had never maintained a professional civil service system for upper-level employees in the mold of the federal government, but longtime state workers thought of themselves as career people. Any definition of which positions were political and consequently subject to change from one administration to another created tensions, which reached new heights under the Hunt administration.[37]

Like his predecessors Charles Aycock and Sanford, Hunt wanted education to be his hallmark. He pushed the legislature to adopt statewide competency testing for high school students as a means of improving learning and establishing accountability. The North Carolina Association of Educators opposed Hunt's proposal, fearing that the new tests might smear the reputations of individual teachers as well as the profession as a whole. Hunt counseled the educators' association, one of the key groups in his election coalition, that the tests were about improving school quality, not evaluating teachers. The educators softened their rhetoric but remained suspicious. Black civil rights organizations also fought the tests, arguing that standardized tests contained inherent cultural biases. They, too, softened their opposition as Hunt stressed his commitment to improving educational opportunities for minority students.[38] The legislature adopted the high school competency test, launching a still-ongoing debate over the effectiveness of such testing.

With a push from Hunt, the legislature enacted a program to provide teacher aides and instructional supplies for the first through the third grades at an initial cost of roughly fifteen million dollars. Hunt also obtained legislative approval to test students in those grades on their reading and math skills. At least some educators found the new record-keeping burdensome, but Hunt saw a need for greater accountability.

Hunt persuaded the legislature to pass the Community Schools Act, which encouraged the development of the public schools as centers of community activity. Under the plan, people of all ages would be encouraged to look to nearby schools as places for meetings, social gatherings, and perhaps even classes for adults. The concept was admirable, reflecting Hunt's populist instincts. With long-distance school busing for racial integration, the connection between neighborhoods and schools had often broken down. Hunt's plan seemed a way to restore that connection, but the program had limited impact. School administrators were unenthusiastic, with principals often feeling proprietary about their schools. Outside groups might inflict property damage, and utility bills would increase with the addition of after-hours activities. Someone—usually the principal—had be on call from early morning to late at night to open and close the schools and keep the keys. At a time when smoking was still common, the fear of fire was a constant threat. School bureaucracies quietly did what they could to minimize Hunt's community schools initiative. Nevertheless, the idea was a good exercise in public relations and a boost to Hunt's goal of becoming the "people's governor."

Hunt began to lay the groundwork for a public high school that would teach mathematics and science to some of the North Carolina's ablest youngsters. His vision called for a special school with the highest standards of teaching, learning, and creativity. The concept of a public high school that would admit only the top echelon of students was controversial among both educators and legislators. The North Carolina Association of Educators fought the idea, but Hunt argued that the school would have a mandate to seek out students from all over the state and if necessary go out of its way to find talent in isolated mountain and coastal counties. Hunt also asserted that its graduates would boost a state wanting to forge ahead in technology.

Following narrow legislative approval, the state acquired the old Watts Hospital building site in northwest Durham, and the North Carolina School of Science and Mathematics opened its doors to eleventh- and twelfth-graders from throughout the state in 1980. Its students have subsequently performed at levels equivalent to those of the nation's top private academies. Few governors of any state would have promoted such a concept, and almost nowhere would pragmatic, budget-conscious legislators have adopted it without prodding from on high. Hunt, like Sanford, who had pushed for a School of the Arts over a decade earlier, was a dreamer and innovator. The new high school may have provided Hunt with few votes, but more important, it boosted the state's educational quality and garnered national recognition.[39]

For years, North Carolina's leaders had considered permitting the governor to seek reelection, but the idea went nowhere. The change would have necessitated amending the state constitution, which would have required approval by three-fifths of both chambers of the state legislature and then approval by a majority of the state's voters. North Carolina remained among the small number of states where governors could not serve two successive terms, and the last governor to leave office and then win reelection was Zebulon Vance, who held the post from 1862 to 1865 and from 1877 to 1879. Governors had not been permitted to succeed themselves because of the fear that long-term officeholders would accumulate too much power. With one party—the Democratic Party—always winning elections, the possibilities for abuse and concentration of power were great. Factions within parties competed with one another, but these factions would come and go. Term limits promised at least a degree of change every few years. The one-term limitation also reflected intragovernmental jealousies. Members of the General Assembly feared a loss of their power if governors could serve as long as eight years without interruption. Even under the current four-year scheme, legislators thought the governor too powerful. Further, the legislature's ranks included many aspirants for the governorship. The one-term limit enhanced their prospects. Other Council of State officials could and usually did seek reelection, often with little opposition. Secretary of State Thad Eure had first been elected in 1936 and would remain in office through 1988, but he was a leading foe of gubernatorial succession and rarely missed an opportunity to warn of the dangers of concentrating too much power in the chief executive's hands.[40]

North Carolina had had one case of gubernatorial succession in the twentieth century, when Luther Hodges assumed the office in November 1954 after the death of William B. Umstead and then ran for reelection, as permitted under the constitution. Hodges believed that serving for six years enhanced his effectiveness both in the state and in dealings with other state governors and the federal government. In 1977, the most prestigious advocates for a succession amendment were the still-living former governors—Democrats Sanford, Moore, and Scott and Republican Holshouser—all of whom issued strong public statements in favor of a constitutional amendment. Lieutenant Governor Green, ever protective of legislative prerogatives and suspicious of Hunt, opposed the amendment. Moreover, Green wanted to run for governor in 1980, and his chances would drop precipitously if Hunt were eligible to run again. Despite Green's vigorous efforts, both legislative houses approved the measure, making it applicable to him and putting a constitutional amendment before the voters in 1977. The outcome reflected Hunt's tremendous skills of persuasion.

The outcome remained in doubt. Senator Ervin emerged as the most prestigious opponent, reflecting his long-held fears of executive power and "machine rule" and his more covert personal reservations about Hunt. Ervin's relationship with the Sanford-Bennett wing of the party had long been strained. He saw Hunt as a Sanford protégé who was pushing the Democratic Party in a more liberal direction.[41] Having lost the skirmish in the legislature, Green and his allies mounted a statewide campaign against the amendment. Anti-Hunt people joined in the effort. The most formidable opponents might have been allies of Senator Helms, most notably the Congressional Club apparatus. They, like Ervin and Green, had both ideological and personal reasons for wanting to stop Hunt. The Congressional Club worked against the amendment but did not seriously commit financial resources to the efforts.

Key Hunt operatives in the counties, the centurions of the Hunt apparatus, worked to get out the vote. Leaders from the African American community, organized labor, women's organizations, and the teachers' lobby flexed their muscles. Hugh Morton, a noted photographer, state chronicler, entrepreneur, and owner of Grandfather Mountain, chaired the Committee to Reject or Re-Elect, a name designed to convince voters that the proposed amendment would give voters more choices in selecting governors since voters would be able to vote a governor up or down at the end of a four-year term. To stress the bipartisan nature of the effort, former Governor Holshouser cochaired the pro-amendment campaign and argued that it might help the Republican Party in the long run.[42]

The amendment passed in the November 1977 referendum, receiving just shy of 53 percent of all votes cast. The amendment could have been written so that it would take effect starting with the governor elected in 1980, which would have removed Hunt from the equation. In that case, however, the amendment almost surely would have been defeated. The Hunt organization's massive effort carried the day. At the victory celebration, jubilant supporters of the governor wore "Hunt Again" buttons. The change strengthened the governor's political position and increased the overall power of an already moderately powerful office. It also had repercussions for politics in general. The governorship would likely be available to fewer people. And the ever-jealous legislature might move to set up rival power centers.

## THE WILMINGTON DILEMMA

Hunt's biggest headache arose from events in 1971, the year of firebombings and shootings in racially tense Wilmington. At that time, Hunt was working relentlessly to be elected lieutenant governor. After the 1972 conviction of the Wilmington Ten, a long series of appeals followed. By the time of Hunt's 1977 inauguration, the whole conflict had achieved legendary status. People on the left from Amnesty International and civil rights organizations saw the trial and subsequent conviction of the Wilmington Ten as a mockery of justice and a throwback to the days when white racists ruled. Many Wilmington whites were firmly convinced of the Wilmington Ten's guilt and believed that they and their sympathizers were revolutionaries, hostile to the American system of government. For both sides, the facts almost seemed secondary to emotions, prejudices, and even deep-seated hatreds.

Elements of the national news media had taken up the cause of the Wilmington Ten. In early 1977, the CBS program *60 Minutes*, then one of the most watched television shows in the United States, raised doubts about the guilty verdict. Morley Safer's analysis stressed that white racists had attacked the Gregory Congregational Church. Safer pointed to the pervasive climate of racism in Wilmington and conflicting testimony in the case. About the same time as the *60 Minutes* report, President Carter had launched a campaign promoting human rights around the world. To their chagrin, Carter and his allies faced allegations that the United States violated human rights and that the most gross violation was the "injustice" done to the Wilmington Ten. And false testimony at the trial had played a key role in their convictions. Unfolding evidence and disclosures did not prove the innocence of the accused, but the American legal system sets a high bar for conviction—a proof of guilt beyond reasonable doubt. People on both sides believed what they wanted to believe. In the eyes of those who cared most about the case, there seemed no room for compromise.

In January 1978, the North Carolina Court of Appeals in Raleigh rejected a petition to order a new trial. Hunt then faced pressure to pardon the Wilmington Ten. Not only the public at large but also close Hunt allies were divided. If he granted the pardons, the national media and human rights crusaders would get off his back. A pardon might even enhance Hunt's national political prospects. Friends, and maybe Hunt himself, dreamed of a Hunt bid for the presidency one day. Yet a full pardon of the Wilmington Ten would have been unpopular with a majority of white North Carolinians, which would have jeopardized Hunt's plans to run for reelection in 1980. Addressing the state over television and radio on January 23, Hunt explained that he had spent many hours reviewing the facts of the case and studying the record of each defendant, speaking personally with several of the accused. Hunt had also met with Ben Chavis's mother, Elizabeth. Hunt spoke with his usual gravitas: "I cannot and I will not pardon the defendants."[43] Hunt insisted that the trial had been fair and that the jury had made the correct decision. He issued no formal pardons, but he did reduce the sentences in many cases to time already served. Hunt added, "These were troubled times in North Carolina. I also considered the defendants' ages—they were young, several of them high school students. Also, this was the first sentence for several of them. I have given long and prayerful consideration to all of these factors."[44] The practical impact was that most of the defendants were released from prison, although Ben Chavis remained in jail. The decision left unsettled basic questions of right and wrong.

Yet it was a deft political move on Hunt's part and might have come close to representing his true beliefs about what should be done in the case. Wilmington Ten defense counsel James Ferguson called Hunt's action "a crass political appeal to the basest instincts of the people of the state."[45] Those favoring harsh "justice" were typically more accepting of Hunt's action, even if they thought Hunt a bit soft. Within a short time, few North Carolinians would have decided to vote for or against Hunt on the basis of his Wilmington Ten decision. In the end Hunt had achieved the practical result he wanted without causing an uproar.

Supporters of the Wilmington Ten shifted their attention to the national level. The defendants' advocates urged President Carter to intervene. Specifically, members of civil rights organizations and the Congressional Black Caucus wanted Carter to press Hunt for a full pardon. Carter refused. As a former governor of a Deep South state, he sympathized with the pressures Hunt faced. Carter did, however, acquiesce in a U.S. Justice Department brief challenging the conviction in federal court. District judge Franklin Dupree denied the motion to declare a mistrial. Attorneys went to the U.S. Fourth Circuit Court of Appeals in Richmond. In the interim, Chavis pursued studies at the Duke Divinity School under a released-time program. Citing Chavis's impeccable academic record at Duke and the desirability of having Chavis spend Christmas at home, Hunt ordered Chavis released on parole in December 1979. A year later, the Federal Court of Appeals overturned the convictions, accepting the argument that defense attorneys had not been informed of conflicting testimony from prosecution witness Allen Hall at the trial.

North Carolina officials were tired of the saga and had no wish to pursue a new trial. The process had been flawed from the beginning.[46] In one of her last acts as governor, Beverly Perdue extended a full pardon to the Wilmington Ten at the end of 2012.

During the course of his administration, specific Hunt actions upset elements of his winning coalition—advocates of racial equality, educators, and liberals. Yet, they, along with others, had backed key Hunt initiatives and crucially the constitutional amendment letting him seek another term in 1980. On the basis of his first term alone, Hunt held a place as one of North Carolina's transformative governors, with a long-lasting impact. Society was more committed to equality in 1979 than in 1970, but the potential for explosive racial outbreaks remained. At the same time, the United States faced a crisis in confidence, with economic stress at home and humiliation overseas.

## CHAPTER EIGHT

# Eyes toward Washington

The achievements of the Hunt administration stood out in a period when the Democratic Party and the country lurched from one crisis to another. Jimmy Carter approached the presidency with the spirit of a pietistic preacher and the mind of an engineer. His self-righteous nature and penchant for efficiency at the expense of the usual political courtesies turned off Democratic figures, including Speaker of the U.S. House Thomas P. "Tip" O'Neill of Massachusetts and the Kennedy family, at a time when Carter needed all the help he could get. Stagflation, an unusual combination of higher unemployment and higher prices, created discontent. Many Americans saw a weak if well-intentioned president. His approval ratings plummeted.[1]

## THE SEEDS OF DISCONTENT

Carter completed negotiations on a treaty to transfer the Panama Canal to Panama at the end of the century, a move aimed at pacifying Latin American nationalist elements. Ratification of the treaty required a two-thirds majority in the Senate, not an easy feat. Carter succeeded, with North Carolina Democrat Robert Morgan providing one of the needed votes. With support from former president Gerald Ford, the treaty drew some Republican votes, which were essential for the necessary two-thirds. Jesse Helms ferociously fought the treaty, which he considered a giveaway and an act of national cowardice. Carter's most tangible defeat came in the aftermath of the November 1979 seizure of the staff at the American embassy in Iran. This time, Carter's negotiating skills did nothing to solve the crisis, the biggest blow to national confidence since the Vietnam War.[2]

The 1978 elections had hinted at Democratic problems to come. Republicans gained seats in both houses of Congress, though Democrats still had a 58–41 edge in the Senate and a 277–158 advantage in the House. Republicans picked up scattered seats in the North Carolina General Assembly, but Democrats held 45 of 50 seats in the Senate and 106 of 120 in the House. Most important, Helms proved that he was no fluke.

The Democratic Party had been bullish on defeating Helms in 1978. Nine candidates entered the primary field for the opportunity. Four were serious contenders: conservative Winston-Salem legislator Lawrence Davis, a man of prominent family connections; moderate Luther Hodges Jr., son of the former governor and a leading Charlotte banker; neopopulist insurance commissioner John Ingram of Cary, a Phi Beta Kappa college graduate, lawyer, and maverick former legislator from usually Republican Randolph County; and liberal state senator McNeill Smith, a well-established Greensboro attorney. In the May primary, Hodges topped Ingram, 260,868–170,715. Hodges had the support of party wheelhorses: backers of his father, old Sanford hands, conservative Democrats, and legislative leaders. Ingram, who had good connections with county-level Democrats, sharpened his rhetoric against the "special interests."

To the surprise of almost everyone, Ingram won the May 30 runoff primary with 244,469 votes to Hodges's 206,223. Pro-Hodges Democrats suspected Republicans of infiltrating the Democratic primary to vote for Ingram on the premise that he would be an easier opponent for Helms. Ingram had ruffled feathers in the legislature and the corporate world and had paid little deference to his political elders. But tampering from the other party was not easy in North Carolina's closed primaries, in which participants had to be formal party registrants.[3] And Republicans did suspect that an Ingram candidacy would split the Democratic Party.

Helms won with 57 percent in the November election, attracting conservative Democrats including former party chair Gene "Magnolia Mouth" Simmons of Tarboro. Helms carried all the state's major urban counties, including Democratic Durham. Ingram took rural Democratic strongholds and the African American vote. Helms campaigned as an economic and anti-abortion conservative, appealing to the state's "values voters." Much as Ingram represented the economic populist strain in society, Helms personified the populism of the Right—social populism. However, his rhetoric was more subdued than in the 1972 race, as he had the upper hand and did not want to frighten potential supporters. This time, he emphasized his opposition to appeasement and international communism. He also wanted to keep the Panama Canal in U.S. hands. With Helms's reelection, the burgeoning conservative movement was poised to provide a counterweight to the Hunt brand of expansive government.

Helms's supporters, led by Tom Ellis and Carter Wrenn, had built the Congressional Club into a formidable fund-raising force. The club was started as a mechanism to pay off Helms's 1972 campaign debt. By 1978, it was one of the most effective fund-raisers in the United States. Its direct-mail money-raising was innovative, with techniques that would be widely copied in the years ahead.[4]

The North Carolina government clashed with the Carter administration on two major issues. Secretary of Health, Education, and Welfare Joseph Califano launched an assault on smoking and the tobacco industry. He advocated more restrictions on the product, and North Carolinians such as agriculture commissioner Jim Graham feared for the state economy. Farmers' biggest concern was the federal tobacco price-support program, which had so far survived with the protection of Congress, the Agriculture Department, and Carter.

The second clash with Washington, also on Califano's watch, came when officials of the department's Office of Civil Rights, with prodding from North Carolina civil rights advocates, threatened to cut off Title VI federal funds from North Carolina's university system, a move that would have devastated the university budget. Califano and the department's civil rights office began to lean hard on the UNC system to reallocate programs to historically black institutions.[5]

A horrific event came in November 1979 in Greensboro. Nelson Johnson, a veteran crusader against poverty and social discrimination, had organized a chapter of the Communist Workers' Party chapter, which decided to stage a symbolic "Death to the Klan" rally and march. Klan members fired on the biracial marchers, killing five. At the climactic moment, no local police were present, but television cameras recorded the event. This was a battle between groups of political extremists, but the Klansmen fired the shots and committed the criminal offense. But none of the Klansmen was convicted of a crime in connection with the incident.[6]

### 1980: THE REPUBLICAN SURGE

Governor Hunt had survived the turmoil with his popularity intact. Yet tensions built between Hunt and former governor Bob Scott. Scott wanted to be president of the state community college system and thought he had Hunt's support.[7] Hunt, however, left the decision to the State Board of Education, chaired by his friend, David Bruton. Bruton backed Larry Blake, a Canadian college officer. The board voted 8–2 for Blake over Scott. Scott felt betrayed, believing that Hunt should have pressured the board. In a 2006 interview, Hunt said, "I thought the board would choose Scott."[8] But many Hunt people, especially former Sanford backers such as Bert Bennett, disliked Scott. Hunt did not want to go to the wall over this issue.

In 1980, Scott challenged Hunt in the primary for governor and accused Hunt of being too stingy on educational spending. Scott stressed his roots as an economic populist committed to lifting the state. However, liberals and minority groups stayed with Hunt, as did many conservative Democrats. Hunt won 524,844–217,289 and carried all one hundred counties. For the time being, he seemed the ultimate consensus politician.

Carter had two strong challengers for the 1980 Democratic presidential nomination, a foreboding signal for an incumbent president. On his left was Massachusetts senator Edward M. "Teddy" Kennedy, who brought his famous name and passionate oratory to the campaign. The other challenger, California governor Edmund "Jerry" Brown Jr. campaigned as an unorthodox liberal, embracing science, technology, and tough choices for the country and what he called "Spaceship Earth." Carter easily won the North Carolina Democratic primary. Kennedy was too liberal for the state, and Brown might as well have been from Spaceship Mars. Kennedy delivered a rousing convention speech, but Carter clinched the nomination.

After defeating Kennedy and Brown, Carter knew that the autumn campaign would be difficult. Yet it seemed possible that Carter might eke out a victory. His Republican opponent, another former California governor, Ronald Reagan, took political positions to the right of anyone who had been elected president since the 1920s. Democrats suspected that the public would not want Reagan to hold the nuclear trigger. Was he another Barry Goldwater? Further complicating the election, Illinois Republican congressman John Anderson ran as an independent. Though he had earlier been a conservative, Anderson had moved leftward and promoted open government and environmentalism. Reagan proved to be the most adept campaigner. As a trained actor with a winning smile and perfectly modulated baritone voice, Reagan connected with the masses better than any presidential candidate since John Kennedy.

The race appeared to be close. Reagan sought moderate support by selecting his leading primary opponent, George H. W. Bush, as his vice presidential running mate, a choice that initially angered Helms and other early Reagan backers. Bush mollified social conservatives when he switched from a pro-choice to a pro-life position on abortion. Most professional polls showed Reagan with a national lead, but the Gallup poll found a race almost even. However, nearly all surveys put North Carolina and a lot of the core South in the Carter camp, hinting that native pride might be trumping other issues.[9]

The concurrent Senate race in North Carolina at first attracted minimal attention outside the state. Robert Morgan was the heavy favorite for a second term over Republican John East. Morgan, popular across factional lines within the state Democratic Party, had a voting record that had been moderate to mildly liberal.[10] He made friends in the Senate, but his office in Washington lacked the levels of polish and service of his earlier operation as attorney general. He often seemed to be caught between the liberal forces of his own party and the powerful conservative currents building both nationally and back home. Morgan had not mounted a strong defensive action with all-out fund-raising and organization building. He was confident of his reelection. Unknown to him at first, a tumor was growing in his ear.

Not the most obvious of senatorial picks, East was still a plausible Republican choice to challenge Morgan. The state's Republican congressmen, Jim Martin and Jim Broyhill, had little incentive to abandon safe seats. Nor were they favorites of the now-dominant Helms wing of the party. Wounds still festered from the Ford-Reagan primary battle of 1976. Former governor Jim Holshouser had name recognition but little taste for a bruising primary battle against the Right for what in any event might be an uphill fight against Morgan.

Looking for a respectable conservative candidate who would not embarrass his wing of the party or the party itself, conservative operative Tom Ellis urged East, a political science professor at East Carolina University, to run and promised abundant resources, both financial and strategic. Ellis sought a candidate from eastern North Carolina, Morgan's home base. A quarter century later, Ellis recalled, "I didn't really know [East] very well, though I knew he had run for Congress and secretary of state."[11] He recognized that East was articulate, and his adopted county of Pitt (Greenville) was almost as much of a base for Morgan as Morgan's home county, Harnett. (Morgan was a graduate of and leading advocate for East Carolina University.) Equally important, Ellis knew that East was a committed conservative, one whose conservatism was more intellectually based than Helms's. East was neither timid nor camera shy. He and his wife, Cissy, were receptive to Ellis's overture. East's seeming boldness came as a surprise to his good friends. His neighbor, longtime Republican activist Wayne Holloman, was "shocked" when East confided, "I'm going to run for the Senate."[12]

Born in Springfield, Illinois, East had attended Earlham College in Indiana, before spending two years in the Marine Corps. In 1955, already married for two years and awaiting discharge, he contracted polio at Camp

Lejeune, on the North Carolina coast. East would not walk again without support devices. By 1959, he had received a law degree from the University of Illinois. He practiced law briefly in Naples, Florida, yet was not happy. The typical courthouse of that day was not friendly to the physically disabled. East went back to school, this time to study political science. After receiving a master's degree and a doctorate from the University of Florida in 1963, East joined the faculty of East Carolina College, where he specialized in political theory. He leveled attacks on what he labeled "the secular new Jerusalem," a government welfare society bereft of traditional moral and religious values. He published in academic journals such as *Modern Age* and popular conservative magazines, notably *Human Events*.[13]

Two years after East's arrival in Greenville, longtime First District Congressman Herbert Bonner retired because of serious illness. Walter Jones Sr. of Farmville, who had represented Pitt County (Greenville) in the state legislature, won the special Democratic primary, then considered tantamount to election, on December 18, 1965. East mounted a spirited challenge to the well-connected Jones. While Jones prevailed with 21,773 votes, East won a surprising 14,308 and, in a first for a Republican, carried two of the district's fifteen counties, Beaufort and Washington.

In 1968, East was the Republican nominee for secretary of state against the venerable Thad Eure, occupant of the position since 1936 and the self-proclaimed "oldest rat in the Democratic barn." East this time campaigned as a member of the Republican team. Eure beat East 792,406–637,095, 55.5 percent to 44.5 percent.

In recognition of his efforts for his party, East was named a Republican national committeeman from North Carolina in 1976 and again in 1980. As a member of the Republican platform committee at the 1976 convention, he gained national publicity for pushing the document to the right on social issues such as abortion. Behind him now stood some of the shrewdest political minds ever assembled in a North Carolina campaign. Led by Tom Ellis and Carter Wrenn, they knew how to mobilize their base as well as stir the sensitivities of the wavering. They were avant-garde in the development of modern campaign techniques.

The East campaign turned its media guns directly on Morgan, finding unflattering pictures and transmitting them to the television screen. In one case, Morgan, a straitlaced individual in private life, had the appearance of a man who had been riding a tractor all night fortified by corn liquor. And, indeed, Morgan was tiring. The tumor in his ear, an acoustical neuroma, sapped his usual energy. The problem was potentially fatal but could be cured by surgery; however, in the face of what had become a surprisingly animated effort from the opposition, Morgan saw more need to worry about political mortality, and his doctor said that the surgery could wait until after the election, when he could also recuperate during the congressional recess.[14]

Jimmy Carter still had a polling edge in North Carolina, even if he was in the fight of his life nationally. The Congressional Club's commercials urged voters to "vote Reagan-East." That seemed a risky strategy. But the club stuck with the line until Election Day.

Governor Hunt, the first beneficiary of the drive he had led to permit gubernatorial succession, maintained a huge advantage over his Republican challenger, I. Beverly Lake Jr., a former Democratic legislator from Raleigh and the son of the two-time gubernatorial candidate and retired North Carolina Supreme Court justice. Lake, whose political career seemed promising, had little to gain from the race except the long-term goodwill of his newly adopted Republican Party. Until recently Lake had been a conservative Democratic legislator from Wake County. For now, the main question was the size of Hunt's margin and whether he could come close to matching his 1976 avalanche.

November 4, 1980, brought its first shock waves just after sunset in the eastern time zone. Radio and television networks did not quite proclaim Reagan the winner, but any listener of mild political smarts got the message with stunning certainty. When the counting was over, Reagan led in the electoral vote, 489–49. His popular vote was a superficially less impressive 50.7 percent of the national total. Carter had received 40.7 percent, while Anderson had garnered 8 percent. Reagan carried North Carolina, and East pulled an upset in the senatorial election. Reagan's 10 percent national lead put him at the exact point which journalists and political scientists have conventionally said is needed to qualify an election as a landslide.

There is another and more conceptually revealing definition of a landslide. V. O. Key Jr., the pioneer in southern political studies and empirical political science, produced a text of American politics used by a generation of college students. In it, he laid out conditions for a true landslide. First, it should be a big popular vote margin, though Key did not define "big." Second, it required the replacement of a president (whether running for reelection or retiring) of one party with a new president of an opposing political party. Third, the presidential returns would reverberate on other levels, most specifically the congressional level. The out party's candidates (the candidates in the party of the newly elected president) would be beneficiaries of the cascade from the top of the ticket and hence a part of the landslide. The out party would take control of Congress or at least gain tremendously. A landslide thus is a party victory, not just a personal victory. A scholar who had an underlying confidence in the institution of democracy and the ultimate wisdom of American voters, Key saw democratic elections as the linchpin of a free society. When an in party incurred the displeasure of the public, elections provided an opportunity to get rid of the old and experiment with the new. Key cited Franklin Roosevelt's 1932 victory over Hoover and the Republicans in the depths of the depression and Dwight Eisenhower's 1952 win over Democrat Adlai Stevenson, who bore the burden of the then unpopular Truman administration, as classic landslides.[15] So a landslide was not quite so much a matter of the size of a presidential victory as it was a popular voice for change, albeit one where a segment of the electorate might resist the flow.

A core principle of a democratic republic is majority rule with some protection for minority rights. The voters may often seesaw from one party to the other and back. However, landslide elections such as those in 1932, 1952, and now 1980 provided the victorious party with some claim to a mandate, a decisive call from the electorate to cast out the old and ring in the new. Adding to his mandate, Reagan surpassed expectations. The media and "informed opinion" celebrate those who perform better than predicted. Reagan had a rare opportunity. He wanted to promote a climate of freedom for private enterprise, a lesser role for government, lower taxes, and a strong military that would impede the communist dragon.

Until the preceding weekend, the election remained close. Following the one debate, where Reagan looked refreshed and lively while Carter seemed the programmed engineer, more voters focused on the idea of a change in national direction. With 53 seats, the GOP won control of the U.S. Senate, an event that had last occurred in 1952. The Republicans also gained in the House elections, going from 158 seats to 190. Reagan hoped that moderate and conservative congressional Democrats from the South would vote for his programs.

Reagan carried North Carolina with 915,016 votes to Carter's 875,635 and Anderson's 52,800. The bigger surprise was East's wafer-thin victory over Morgan in the Senate race, 898,064–887,653. Together, the Libertarian and Socialist Workers Party candidates had 11,953 votes. Based on exit polling, the national television networks had declared Morgan the winner early on election night, but the next morning, East was senator-elect.

East's victory seemed a vindication of the "Vote Reagan-East" campaign. The inclination was to point to the Reagan coattails or to call the East victory a fluke. What happened was more complex. East polled a slightly higher percentage of the state vote than did Reagan. True, Reagan had a three-way race, but Anderson got few votes in North Carolina. In the classic coattails situation, the presidential candidate not only adds strength to others of his party but also runs well ahead of the party ticket. Such was not the case here.

At least three other factors boosted East. First and most important, 1980 saw the Republican Party landslide. Widespread frustration existed among the voters.[16] In a number of other states, Republican congressional candidates ran as well as Reagan. East and two Republican House challengers, Eugene Johnston from Greensboro and William Hendon in the mountains, benefited from the Republican tide. Johnston upset twelve-year veteran Richardson Preyer in the Sixth, while Hendon beat incumbent Lamar Gudger in the often-close Eleventh District. Second, in close races, campaigns matter. East and the strategists from Helms's wing of the Republican Party mounted the superior campaign. East's campaign outspent Morgan's, 55 percent to 45 percent, and made better use of its resources. East himself came across on television as a credible Senate choice, articulate, informed, and wanting to change the course of the country.

Second was American chauvinism. In a conversation shortly after the election, East asserted that the key to his victory was Morgan's vote for the Panama Canal Treaty.[17] In such a close race, there could be many keys to victory, but the Panama Canal "giveaway" resonated in a state with a strong nationalistic and military bent and where national pride and patriotism rivaled and at the same time reinforced chauvinism.

Third, the Morgan campaign was flawed—as it turned out, fatally. He plausibly but wrongly expected to win without difficulty. Consequently, the campaign failed to put the needed stress on fund-raising and organization. When the alarm bell rang in the fall, the hour was late. Morgan's health crisis took a political toll. He tried, but his normal strengths as a campaigner were not there. The Republicans seized on the opening to define Morgan as a wavering senator, not in tune with North Carolinians. Morgan, quite a patriot himself and a veteran of the Korean conflict, was at least for the moment left twisting in the wind.

Both Reagan and East were strong in what was becoming North Carolina's Republican spine, a combination of formerly Democratic-leaning and politically marginal counties stretching from just north and west of Charlotte up through the western piedmont and foothills. This was furniture and textile country. The bulk of the population was working class or marginal middle class and hostile to labor unions.

Despite the stagflation of the Carter era, a lot of people in this region had improved their lot since the Great Depression. Neat split-levels and

1960s ranch-style layouts were as much a feature of the landscape as were the mill houses. So were air conditioners.[18] But this area was an integral part of the Bible Belt, a broad expanse of territory encompassing parts of the Lower Midwest, much of the South, and nearly all of North Carolina.

More than ever, abortion loomed as a national issue. North Carolina had more liberal laws on the issue than many other states. After the U.S. Supreme Court officially legalized most abortions in *Roe v. Wade* (1973), the idea of tampering with human life in such a fundamental way enraged more and more Christians, both Catholic and Protestant.[19] At first, the issue was muted in presidential politics. Jimmy Carter, a moderate on the issue, was also an evangelical Christian.

In the 1980 campaign, Republicans Reagan, East, and others put the "sanctity of human life" high on their political agenda. Reagan was a convert on the issue, having been vaguely pro-choice in earlier life. After his conversion to Republicanism, he saw the issue's power among theologically conservative Christians. It was not as vital to his core message as lower taxes and a bigger military, but Reagan consistently attacked the *Roe v. Wade* decision. East was a more committed abortion opponent. His background was Presbyterian USA and United Methodist, both churches that wavered on the issue, but East had led the successful effort to put a strong anti-abortion plank in the national 1976 Republican platform.

Republicans now had the edge among rank-and-file evangelicals, a change that had political reverberations over much of the American southland as well as ominous implications for the old Roosevelt New Deal Democratic coalition. Reagan and East were the voices of the latest surge in social populism, a doctrine whose might Helms had already demonstrated.[20]

During the fall campaign, East had made appearances at major Republican events. He welcomed newspaper interviews. But more than any major state campaign to date, he relied on television. In a typical setting, he would be sitting at a desk, with books in the background, a posture that obscured the fact that he could not stand or walk unaided.[21] Liberal academics might have played down their profession, but in East's campaign, it was part of the message. East, who had taken a leave of absence from the university for the fall campaign, said that many of his students had encouraged him to run. As a teacher of government, he now took their advice. From his desk, East hammered away on the issues. East cut a good figure on television. He appeared to be strong and virile, his mostly bald head further enhancing the image, and his midwestern accent proved no handicap, since he sounded like many television and radio announcers, though one whose voice was closer to tenor than bass. In both paid advertisements and news interviews, East spoke with authority and erudition, and he had no legislative record to defend.

Morgan never again sought public office. When the tumor was removed, the operation left him without hearing in one ear and some facial paralysis on one side. Otherwise, Morgan's health remained good, and he resumed his law practice and participation in Democratic campaigns and civic activities.[22]

The Republican senatorial campaign was a dress rehearsal for things to come. Moderate Democrats targeted by a well-designed media advertising blitz were sitting ducks. But Democrats failed to grasp the significance of what had happened and considered East a fluke, much like Helms eight years earlier. The campaign themes of Americanism and moralism had widespread appeal.

One Democrat seemed more invincible than ever. In his race against Lake, Hunt garnered 63 percent of the popular vote, a figure more impressive than his 65 percent in 1976 given the context of the 1980 Republican landslide. Hunt's pull probably rescued numerous other Democrats from the jaws of defeat. Democrats lost state legislative seats but retained a 40–10 lead in the Senate and 96–24 lead in the House, stronger positions than they had occupied after the Republicans' 1972 breakthrough. Hunt's position at the top of the ticket probably aided the entire state-level Democratic ticket. Hunt was poised to do what no other North Carolina governor had done—serve a second consecutive four-year term. No North Carolina Democrat of the twentieth century had stood on quite so lofty ground as did Hunt at the end of 1980. Though modest in stature, he was the political bull elephant of a generation, maybe a century.

### REDISTRICTING AND THE RACE EQUATION

The most hotly contested and consequential North Carolina election between 1980 and 1984 was in the reconstituted Second Congressional District. For years, the old Second had been represented by L. H. Fountain of Tarboro, a courtly, conservative Democrat known for his white linen suits. Personally and ideologically, Fountain was closer to Republican Helms than to many of his fellow Democrats. Fountain's home county, Edgecombe, lay on the eastern edge of a district that extended from the coastal plan into the tobacco-growing and culturally conservative Virginia border counties of the northern piedmont. Much to Fountain's dismay, liberal Orange County was added to the district after the 1970 census, but Fountain retained the seat.

Following the 1980 census, the state legislature adopted a redistricting plan that would have protected all eleven incumbent representatives—

seven Democrats and four Republicans. Fountain's Second was gerrymandered to exclude Orange County, creating an odd shape that critics dubbed "Fountain's Fishhook." To help Fountain, Orange, Durham, and Wake Counties were placed together in an urban Fourth District. The National Association for the Advancement of Colored People (NAACP) and North Carolina Republican Party filed a federal lawsuit challenging the plan. The NAACP wanted a district where an African American would stand a chance of winning. The Republican Party believed that putting more racial minorities in one district would make other neighboring districts both more white and more Republican. On December 8, 1981, before the courts had acted on the complaint, the Civil Rights Division of the U.S. Justice Department invalidated the congressional map. Acting under the Voting Rights Act of 1965, the Justice Department ruled that the legislature was motivated by racial considerations when drawing Fountain's district. Durham, a logical geographic fit in the new Second District, had been excluded because of its large and well-organized black community. Rather than resist, the state legislature held a special session in February 1982. The revised Second District linked Durham with nine rural counties already in Fountain's district. The Justice Department approved the plan on March 10. Fountain then announced his retirement.[23]

Close to 30 percent of the new district's population resided in Durham County. Blacks then constituted 35 percent of Durham's voters, with liberal whites a growing force. Two counties in the district, Edgecombe and Warren, had black population majorities and the potential of black voting majorities. Caswell, Halifax, and Vance Counties were close to 50 percent nonwhite.

Henry McKinley "Mickey" Michaux (pronounced mi-Shaw) of Durham announced his candidacy for the seat. An attorney, he had spent a decade in the state legislature and had served as a deputy district attorney and for several months as acting district attorney. He called himself a fiscal conservative, but his views placed him more in the mold of a national Democrat than a conservative state Democrat. Michaux, then fifty-one, was African American and the member of a wealthy and prominent Durham family.[24]

Two whites also vied for the congressional seat. From Nashville, near Rocky Mount, came I. T. "Tim" Valentine. Valentine had been a member of the N.C. House for three terms in the 1950s and state Democratic Party chair from 1966 to 1968. Valentine, an attorney, was linked in the public mind with conservative Democrats. While his instincts were conservative on fiscal issues, he was moderate to liberal on environmental and social policies. Former Speaker of the North Carolina House James Ramsey of Roxboro in Person County also sought the seat. Ramsey, also an attorney, was closely linked with business interests and a political moderate.

Michaux's strategy was to win support from African Americans in all parts of the district and white liberals concentrated mainly in Durham. The campaign stressed voter registration. By this time, North Carolina had adopted a roving system under which people could register to vote at churches and community centers. Michaux would speak during church services and community functions, after which roving registrars would sign up people not already registered. Local black action committees, the AFL-CIO, and the League of Conservation Voters also mounted registration drives. From February 1982 until the June 29 primary, black registration in the district rose from 57,765 to 74,511, a gain of 29 percent. White registration went from 146,980 to 153,744, a 4.6 percent increase. With motivated supporters and an intense get-out-the-vote drive, Michaux hoped to prevail. A key would be Durham County, the one place where some prominent whites openly backed Michaux.[25]

In the first round, Michaux received 47,132 votes (44.5 percent), Valentine 34,708 (32.7 percent), and Ramsey 24,179 (22.9 percent). Ramsey did not endorse either candidate in the runoff. Both Michaux and Valentine redoubled their efforts, knowing that voter turnout among blacks (for Michaux) and whites (for Valentine) was the key to victory. However, both candidates shunned open talk of race in their normal campaign appearances. Valentine forces, however, did attack the unified black vote in Durham. One Valentine ad referencing the term "bloc vote" called it the "block vote," easily misread as "black vote."

The state runoff primary on July 27 featured low-profile judicial races and few local races, leading to a record-low turnout in most of North Carolina. In the Second District, however, the number of votes cast rose from 106,010 in the first primary to 109,914 in July. Valentine defeated Michaux, 58,033–51,056 (53.5 percent to 46.5 percent), a result that surprised Michaux, whose camp had thought that "the white turnout would be much lower."[26] White turnout held steady or slightly increased nearly everywhere in the district. So did the black vote. Outside Durham County, Valentine took roughly 90 percent of the votes cast by whites; in Durham, about two-thirds of white voters opted for Valentine. Throughout the district, 95 percent or more blacks voted for Michaux.[27]

As a result of this campaign, Michaux and other African American activists mounted a drive to change long-standing electoral practices. Talk of ending second primaries or declaring the leading candidate with

40 percent or more the winner after the initial primary picked up steam. Under such a procedure, Michaux would have won the nomination in June. Such a change would not be radical—most states did not hold run-offs after primaries. Critics countered that under the no-runoff rule, a candidate with only 25 percent or 30 percent of the vote might win a party's nomination and weaken the party in the general election.

No change came right away, but over time, a consensus began to build for a 40 percent rule. African Americans started to question the traditional methods of congressional and legislative reapportionment. While blacks had comprised between 22 and 33 percent of the state's population, no black since George White in 1898 had been elected to Congress from the state. Prominent minority politicians, including Michaux, called for the creation of a black-majority congressional district. Minorities believed that the white-dominated Democratic Party took their votes for granted and did not want to share power and prestige.

In the general election, Valentine faced Republican Jack Marin, an ally of Helms's Congressional Club. Marin's campaign questioned Valentine's values and called him a liberal, but the tactic did not work, and Valentine beat Marin, 59,617–34,243, with Michaux getting 15,990 write-in votes, one of the best write-in showings in the history of North Carolina elections. Declaring victory, Valentine delivered a stinging attack on the Congressional Club and what he considered its smear techniques.[28] In Congress, Valentine established a record as a political centrist, more liberal than many of his primary supporters might have preferred.

### TRENDS OF THE EARLY 1980S

Reagan persuaded Congress to adopt much of his program: expanding the military, cutting taxes, and slowing the growth in domestic spending. However, recession had hit much of the country. Major technology centers such as Boston and North Carolina's Research Triangle remained healthy during the recession. But in 1982, North Carolina Democrats picked up seats in Congress and added slightly to their numbers in the legislature. Two Republicans elected to Congress in 1980, Hendon and Johnston, lost their seats, leaving Broyhill and Martin once again the state's sole Republicans in the U.S. House.

In his second term, Hunt focused more on building on the foundation of his first term—the public school initiatives, the North Carolina School of Science and Mathematics, and an aggressive business recruitment program—than on dramatic new initiatives. He visited public schools more than some superintendents and supervisors did.[29]

Over some opposition in the legislature and the Council of State, Hunt won a battle for the establishment of the state-supported North Carolina Microelectronics Center in the Research Triangle. At its groundbreaking in 1982, he said, "We will not just need the three Rs but the three Cs: computers, calculators, and communications. We need to make our children as familiar with the computer terminal as they are with pencil and paper." The state was in "a race for the future."[30] The center opened in 1984. Hunt delivered pep talks throughout the state. He encouraged business leaders worldwide to consider North Carolina for their new operations. The state legislature, once dominated by conservatives, now had a blend of conservatives, moderates, and liberals in leadership positions and blacks and women gradually made their way up the seniority ladder. Liston Ramsey, a retired merchant and old-fashioned economic populist, was elected Speaker of the House in 1981. Jimmy Green, reelected lieutenant governor in 1980, continued his frosty relationship with Hunt. Both Green in the Senate and Ramsey in the House based committee appointments on personal loyalty, not ideology.

Back in the 1950s, conservative Democrats such as Graham Barden and Alton Lennon had outnumbered Harold Cooley and other populists in North Carolina's congressional delegation. By the 1982–84 period, the nine Democrats from North Carolina voted as moderates or liberals. Some, such as Charles Rose Jr. of Fayetteville, came from the Sanford wing of the party. Others, including Walter Jones Sr., moved toward chairing committees and tried to vote with the national party unless its positions were wildly at variance with public opinion back home. More and more, committed conservatives ran as Republicans. Broyhill and Martin were by no means ultraconservatives, but their overall voting records differed little from those of East and Helms. And among U.S. senators, East and Helms were unsurpassed in their conservative zeal. Helms built seniority and clout; East chaired a subcommittee of the Judiciary Committee on separation of powers and achieved national visibility as a critic of abortion. The House remained under Democratic control, but the Republicans used their new majority position in the Senate to promote the Reagan administration's military buildup and tax cuts. Helms, East, and House Democrats worked together on some common goals: the expansion of North Carolina's military installations, protection of the federal tobacco program, and resistance to continued pressures from career bureaucrats in the Department of Health, Education, and Welfare to remove all vestiges of segregation from the state's higher education system.

Conservative Republicans, the state's Democratic leaders, and university administrators feared that idealists in the Justice Department were out to dismantle the system, and UNC president William Friday saw a threat to university autonomy and educational quality.[31] Helms and East pressured top Reagan administration officials, including the secretary of the Department of Health, Education, and Welfare, Terrell Bell, and Attorney General William French Smith to restrain the Office of Civil Rights, which wanted to cut off federal funds from the North Carolina university system if a settlement could not be reached.[32] Tortuous negotiations continued, but with the Office of Civil Rights under political pressure. Eventually, the two parties agreed that the UNC system would set a goal of 10.6 percent black enrollment at historically white universities and 15 percent white enrollment at historically black universities. Civil rights leaders and professionals in the office were angered by the deal and at the political pressure that had led to it. UNC system officials, in contrast, saw the settlement as a reasonable compromise that protected the university's educational integrity and autonomy. Throughout the dispute, the civil rights lawyers, federal bureaucrats, and UNC officials all were firmly convinced of the righteousness of their respective positions. It was a moral crusade.

Hunt, for his part, stood on lofty ground. Polls suggested that he could overwhelmingly defeat Helms in a 1984 Senate contest, a feat that might put the presidency within Hunt's reach.

## CHAPTER NINE

# The New South Meets the New Right

By the mid-1980s, the South had assimilated into the American culture as never before. No longer America's stepchild, the region had come a long way since the 1930s, when Franklin D. Roosevelt labeled it the nation's number 1 economic problem. Whatever ingrained prejudices remained, the legal and political systems embraced the principles of racial equality and gender equality, even though the Equal Rights Amendment had failed to win ratification by enough states to become part of the U.S. Constitution.

White southerners continued their political drift toward the increasingly conservative national Republican Party, espousing the conservative gospel preached by Ronald Reagan.[1] Since 1964, two southern Democrats—Lyndon Johnson and Jimmy Carter—had been elected president, shattering the thesis that a southerner could not win that office. However, the Californian Reagan embodied the spirit of white southerners, especially males, more than did either Johnson or Carter.

## THE GATHERING STORM

Few but the most die-hard Democrats doubted that Reagan would come out on top in 1984. Reagan, who had barely carried North Carolina over Carter four years earlier, now appeared even stronger in North Carolina than in the country as a whole. Reagan tried to make middle-class white Americans feel good about their country. No president had spoken so eloquently and forcefully against communism and its evils. The boom in defense spending brought more money to military-dependent areas such as eastern North Carolina.[2]

Former vice president Walter Mondale moved ahead in the race for the Democratic nomination, turning back challenges from Colorado senator Gary Hart and the Reverend Jesse Jackson, a South Carolina native then living in Chicago. Hart, a new-style liberal who believed in the sanctity of technology and innovation, did well in early primaries but later faltered.

Jackson promoted a "rainbow coalition" of blacks and others who had been shut out in the past. With African American support, he won the South Carolina Democratic primary, but his prospects were considered poor from the beginning. Mondale had support from the party establishment and organized labor. Many top North Carolina Democrats, including senator Robert Morgan, liked him. Mondale took the North Carolina with 342,224 votes; Hart had 289,877, and Jackson 243,945. The summer national convention tapped Mondale, who chose U.S. Representative Geraldine Ferraro of New York as his running mate.

North Carolina Democrats remained hopeful about outgoing Governor Hunt's prospects of defeating Helms in the Senate race. Polls had tightened since 1982, yet Hunt had much going for him.[3] Other governors might have had deeper support, but no twentieth-century leader had maintained such broad goodwill for as long as Hunt. His was surely one of the country's better state-level operations. He had an organization in each county, built on past campaign veterans. The so-called keys were kept abreast of matters related to Hunt interests in the county and were expected to relay pertinent local political information to top Hunt lieutenants in Raleigh. With the governor's encouragement, the organizations sought to bring new people— especially rising young stars—into their camp. Hunt built relationships with business, civic, and religious leaders, many of whom saw themselves as close friends of the governor. He could count on a large and enthusiastic cadre of supporters, some who would dig deeply into their bank accounts for him.

Liberals believed that Helms's 1972 victory had come from a combination of luck, Democratic disunity, hate, racism, and long Nixon coattails. And in 1978 Helms had defeated economic populist Democrat John Ingram, who had incurred the wrath of the party establishment. Many Democrats consequently thought that a well-financed, responsible centrist could beat Helms.

Helms, too, had advantages. More than most politicians, Helms came across as a man of faith at a time when many church people believed that religious values were under assault from a secular society.[4] Second, Helms equated capitalism and Americanism. Helms had built close ties with bankers when he was an executive in their state association in the 1950s. Leading bankers, including mild progressives such as Wachovia's Archie Davis, continued to support Helms. Business in general saw the senator as a loyal ally. Helms's office was one of the most efficient and constituent-friendly in Washington.[5] So while no political centrist, Helms wore powerful armor into the 1984 campaign.

Still, Helms was in trouble. A man of considerable charm and humor in his personal dealings, Helms's national image was that of a gut fighter constantly on the attack. His oral delivery was sometimes snarling. Most blacks and some whites—especially migrants from the North—viewed Helms as a throwback to the old-time southern demagogue. Liberals from Boston to Hollywood, some with fat checkbooks, were eager to defeat a man they saw as a symbol of right-wing extremism, a latter-day witch-hunter in the mold of Wisconsin senator Joe McCarthy in the 1950s.

No one doubted that Helms was a polarizing figure, yet his congressional supporters were dejected when an early internal poll showed Helms in perilous political health, facing a near-death scenario in any matchup against Hunt. Pollster Arthur Finkelstein, who typically did not share specific poll results with Helms, thought that the senator needed a wake-up call. The poll indicated that Helms had an unfavorable rating of close to 40 percent as well as a favorable rating also near 40 percent.[6] In the 1980s, such a rating presaged almost certain defeat for an incumbent politician. To make matters gloomier, the same poll indicated that Hunt's rating was 70 percent favorable and 20 percent unfavorable. As Helms and Hunt were the best-known politicians in the state, the figures were thought unlikely to change drastically. However, high unfavorable scores tended to be more stable than favorable scores. Hearing the bad news, Helms said that he probably would not run again, but Helms's close friend and political ally, Tom Ellis, urged him not to give up, whatever the odds.[7] Helms and the Congressional Club decided to go for another race, one that would have the highest stakes yet.

Ellis, Carter Wrenn, Alex Castelanos, and other strategists knew that their only hope was to drive down Hunt's approval rating.[8] They believed that Hunt's support was broader than it was deep. A major Hunt strength was also a weakness. He was the most skillful of politicians. Few were as good at bringing opposing forces together and smoothing the waters. On controversial matters such as the resolution of the Wilmington Ten dilemma, some voters were bound to be angry at any decision that Hunt might have rendered. But his actions usually satisfied a majority of the population.

In the eyes of the Helms forces, they had an opening through which to nip into Hunt's image—the idea that he was a bit too much of a politician, that he could not quite be trusted. They hoped to portray Hunt as a wishy-washy individual who would mislead the public to protect his personal interests and who would tell the people one thing and do another. Out of their strategy sessions arose the catchy Helms campaign slogan, "Where do you stand, Jim?" Helms's advisers had a gut feeling that much of the public admired Hunt's political talents and competence but did not love him. In contrast, Helms could be portrayed taking a stand, whatever the consequences.

The Helms ads proved to be among the most effective in American campaign history. Before the campaign was over, Hunt had faced far more negative radio and television ads than any other North Carolina candidate to date. This election marked the beginning of a new era in American politics. From the spring of 1983 through the summer of 1984, ads focused on alleged inconsistencies in Hunt's record.[9] The ultimate consensus builder and master of the art of compromise, Hunt proved an easy target.

By Election Day, the race had become the most expensive senatorial contest in American history. In the fall of 1983, Hunt's campaign launched ads, but they lacked the zing of Helms's. Hunt's ads focused on protecting social security and subsidizing school lunches. By May 1984, Helms was even with Hunt or slightly ahead in public and private polls.

Race proved to be another Achilles heel for Hunt. Starting in 1983, anti-Hunt ads used racial symbolism. To knock Hunt out on an accusation of racial liberalism might initially have seemed a stretch. Although he had advocated racial equality since his teen years, Hunt shielded himself from charges that he might be far out in front of public opinion on the issue. When pushing for racial equality, he spoke of the needs of "*all* the people," saying that the needy and the hardworking middle classes, whatever their race, needed the opportunities that government could promote. By the 1980s, this position had become a mainstream idea.

In addition, Hunt spoke of maintaining "law and order" with almost the stridency of leading Republican politicians. Since the mid-1960s, "law and order" had been a coded phrase used by populist-style conservatives to scare whites with the threat of crimes committed by young black men. When Hunt spoke of law and order, he stressed that he meant the protection of all citizens, whatever their color. The public in general applauded his support for the police and his tough stance against criminals.[10]

But in the early 1980s, white racial animosities had been rekindled. By 1983, nineteen states had established holidays honoring Martin Luther King Jr. In August of that year, the U.S. House of Representatives voted to make the third Monday in January a national holiday in the slain civil rights leader's honor. The vote was 338–90, with a majority of white southern Democrats voting for the measure. When the bill reached the Senate floor in October, Helms said he would wage a filibuster against it, attempting to talk it to death. Helms first attacked the bill on the basis of its cost and lost productivity. Then, however, he went on to attack King as failing to share in American values. Helms portrayed King as a hypocrite who used religion for his own political purposes and accused him of "collaboration with communism." Furthermore, Helms alluded to King's alleged extramarital affairs taped by J. Edgar Hoover's Federal Bureau of Investigation.[11]

Former senator Sam Ervin, now a hero to many Democrats and liberals for his role in ousting Nixon, was an ardent foe of the King holiday—so ardent that he called Helms frequently to encourage him and to propose possible strategies in the attempt to block the holiday. Helms appreciated the support but eventually started to duck Ervin's calls. Ervin, like Helms, had resigned himself to racial integration. But along with many old-time segregationists, he shared Helms's disdain for King.[12]

Meanwhile, President Reagan announced that he would sign the King holiday bill if it reached his desk, a significant development, since Reagan was known to be unenthusiastic about the proposed legislation. When asked about the bill, Hunt always expressed his support for it. Privately, he could not have been happy over the timing. Hunt was astute enough to know that Helms's campaign could use the issue to its advantage in the upcoming campaign.

At the last minute, North Carolina senator John East introduced a substitute bill to establish a national civil rights day on James Madison's birthday. Helms introduced another making Thomas Jefferson's birthday a national holiday. Despite such delaying tactics, the King holiday bill passed, 78–12, with King's widow, Coretta Scott King, watching from the gallery. Reagan signed the measure.[13] Helms's opposition helped raise money for his senatorial campaign, and most important, in North Carolina it crystallized racial animosities that had been lurking just below the surface.

Given Helms's philosophy of government, he probably would have opposed creating a new national holiday—one where federal government employees would have the day off—for any purpose. Such a stance might have gone almost unnoticed. But his action on the King holiday was an incendiary act, lighting fires among both supporters and foes of King. Helms was in the national limelight as never before.

Another troublesome development for Hunt was Jackson's presidential candidacy. The media took Jackson more seriously than it had Shirley Chisholm in 1972. Jackson was a powerful orator, the ideal media figure. His candidacy symbolized the coming of age for blacks in American politics. Though he never came close to winning the nomination, Jackson won

South Carolina's 1984 presidential primary and ran third in North Carolina's. As a courtesy, Hunt had received Jackson at the governor's mansion when he visited North Carolina in March 1983. Later, a statewide Helms newspaper ad featured the two together. The tall Jackson towered over Hunt, the imagery suggesting that the preacher dominated the governor. The caption read "Governor James B. Hunt wants the State Board of Elections to boost minority representation in North Carolina. Ask yourself: Is this a proper use of taxpayer funds?"[14]

The Hunt forces fought back. Their most inflammatory ad attacked Helms for his support of right-wing dictatorships in El Salvador and Nicaragua, a position that placed Helms at odds with much of Congress and the Reagan administration. A Hunt ad in the summer of 1984 showed photos of dead victims of the regimes. The message that Helms had some responsibility for the atrocities was not well received in North Carolina.

Six months before the election, Helms had won the campaign ad war. His portrayal of Hunt as a slippery politician and a surrogate of civil rights leaders resonated more loudly with the public than did Hunt's counterattacks. The match of the political giants was essentially even. The outcome would remain in doubt until November.

While Hunt and Helms had been their parties' presumptive Senate nominees since 1982, the Democratic Party moved headlong toward what would be one of its most competitive gubernatorial primaries ever.

### THE BATTLE FOR GOVERNOR: DEMOCRATIC FRATRICIDE

Few Democratic primaries were more heated than the first and second of 1984. Before the year was over, the internecine warfare of the Democratic primary for governor would cast its long shadow over the Helms-Hunt Senate race. After eight years of Hunt, there was a pent-up demand among potential successors, and many were bound to be disappointed. Governor Hunt, who had close ties with several of the candidates, vowed to remain neutral. He also asked his top campaign people to stay out of other campaigns. But he was unable to control his financial supporters. Hunt did not want to taint or damage his own campaign against Helms. Of the ten candidates for governor, six were serious contenders. Of these, three had close political ties to Hunt.

H. Edward (Eddie) Knox, the former mayor of Charlotte, had been a Hunt friend going back to the days when they were allies in student politics at North Carolina State University. Knox had labored in the vineyards for Hunt's gubernatorial campaigns, traveling around to county and regional rallies. Tom Gilmore, who had also been in college with Hunt at North Carolina State, was a farmer of an intellectual bent and a representative from Guilford County in the N.C. House. Like Hunt, Gilmore had been a president of the state Young Democratic Clubs and an activist in the campaigns of progressives Terry Sanford and Richardson Preyer. Lauch Faircloth, a shrewd businessman and landholder, had been a key figure in the campaigns of Kerr Scott, Terry Sanford, Bob Scott, and Hunt. He was Hunt's secretary of commerce and consequently had major responsibilities for promoting industrial development and tourism. Faircloth also had been a member of the State Highway Commission in Hunt's administration and its chair during Bob Scott's tenure.

Knox, Gilmore, and Faircloth knew that Hunt could not afford to become personally involved in the first primary donnybrook, but each man saw himself as politically close to Hunt. Each might have believed that he would get Hunt's vote in the secrecy of the voting booth.[15] And all hoped to get the backing of a significant share of Hunt people.

Of the other three viable candidates, Lieutenant Governor Jimmy Green had been a Hunt antagonist for years. Regarded as the most conservative of the major contenders, Green was foremost a pragmatist and political dealmaker. He had made friends across ideological lines in the legislature as he rose through the ranks to become Speaker of the House. Green seemed as eager as the other contenders to boost teacher salaries and had close ties with retired state employees. Former insurance commissioner John Ingram also was back. His political career had peaked in the 1970s, but Ingram still won admirers for his economic populism and attacks on the "special interests." Few had forgotten Ingram's stunning upset victory over Luther Hodges Jr. in the 1978 senatorial primary.

The sixth heavyweight was Rufus Edmisten, the sartorially fit, handsome, pumpkin-faced attorney general. Edmisten, who had come up politically as an aide to Senator Sam J. Ervin, was never regarded by the old Sanford crowd of progressive Democrats as a political ally. But Edmisten had for years been one of the most loyal attendees at state and county party functions. He and Hunt had been cordial and worked well together. So while Edmisten was no Hunt man in the sense of Faircloth, Gilmore, or Knox, he was not an antagonist in the mold of Green.

Ideologically, Gilmore and Ingram were the most liberal of the 1984 contenders. But while Gilmore had economically populist tendencies, his style was more in the mode of Preyer—earnest, serious, and articulate, and not a good-old-boy style politician. Ingram continued to cite his credentials as a fighter for the average citizen against the corporations.

The centrists in the race were Faircloth, Edmisten, and Knox, with Faircloth the most conservative. He stressed his ties with business and had come from meager circumstances to make millions. But he possessed a populist streak and had been on the liberal bandwagon in nearly every primary. Former governor Sanford raised money for Faircloth's campaign. Knox attracted business support from his home city of Charlotte, many moderate Democrats, and some African Americans.

Knox's folksy style rivaled that of Edmisten. A consensus builder, Knox portrayed himself as the logical heir to Hunt. Despite his past ties to the conservative Senator Ervin, Edmisten could fairly be judged the most liberal of the three centrists. He was a staunch Democratic loyalist, and as attorney general he had, like his predecessor, Robert Morgan, pursued a consumer protection policy. Business interests were wary of Edmisten, however. Unlike Hunt in earlier campaigns, Edmisten had not gone all-out to cultivate corporate North Carolina when he launched his campaign.[16]

A lot of old-time eastern North Carolina courthouse Democrats were in Green's camp, as were people wanting a low-tax, probusiness agenda. But Green could not count on overwhelming support from even the most conservative Democrats. Faircloth and Knox siphoned off business support, while both Edmisten and Faircloth had built ties with Democratic wheelhorses on the county level.

In the first primary, Edmisten finished first with 295,051 votes, followed by Knox with 249,286, Faircloth with 153,310, Gilmore with 82,299, Green with 80,775, and Ingram with 74,248, while four other candidates collected 19,930 votes. Although Edmisten was the front-runner, he took less than one-third of the total vote. Knox did the inevitable and called for a runoff primary, one where personality and personal attacks overshadowed policy and ideology.

On the same day there had been a Republican gubernatorial primary in which retiring Charlotte-area congressman Jim Martin beat Ruby Hooper, 128,714–11,640. From the outset, Martin was perceived as the most formidable Republican candidate for governor to date. As former chair of the Mecklenburg Board of County Commissioners and ten-year congressional veteran, he was on par with top Democrats both in experience and prestige. Yet Martin's chances seemed even at best. Three Democrats—Edmisten, Knox, and Faircloth—had each won more primary votes than the combined total for Martin and Hooper. And the total vote for the ten Democrats was 955,899 to the two Republicans' 140,354. Some of the difference could be accounted for by the tradition that many Republican-leaning voters registered Democratic and participated in that party's primaries to have a voice in electing local officials. In addition, the 1984 Democratic primary was heated, with the outcome in doubt until the end, while the Republican primary was a cut-and-dried affair with no doubt about the result.

Republicans hoped that Ronald Reagan's coattails would help Martin and other Republican candidates, including Helms. Democrats were confident that however well Reagan might do, Hunt's pull in the Senate race would shield their candidates from any Republican onslaught. At worst, they expected Hunt to run about even with Helms. And though Hunt's huge poll advantage had evaporated by the spring of 1984, Democrats still thought that he might win. So while Martin could not be counted out, his prospects seemed dubious.

Not yet figured into the political assessment was the potential explosiveness of the Edmisten-Knox runoff. Both men positioned themselves as moderates with a common touch and empathy for hardworking people. And both were about as folksy as any two runoff contenders have ever been.

Differences on specific political issues always emerge, but there was no ideological clash in the mode of the 1960s races. However, the 1984 race in many respects reflected the 1972 clash between Skipper Bowles and Pat Taylor. As in the 1972 runoff primary, liberals and conservatives, blacks and whites, feminists and male chauvinists could be found in both camps. Like the one in 1972, this primary turned bitterly personal. As in 1972, deep animosities developed among the campaign workers for the two candidates. And each candidate's attitude toward the other became increasingly hostile.[17]

Edmisten defeated Knox, 353,357–326,278, in the runoff. For some time, Knox and his family had been seething over Hunt's aloofness in the gubernatorial campaign. Over the years, Hunt had offered encouraging words to Knox about his promising political prospects. But in politics, a shade of difference exists between encouraging words—words the recipient might take as an implied promise of political support—and an endorsement. Hunt asked his top campaign officials and cabinet members not to get involved in the 1984 governor's race. He encouraged them to put all their marbles in the Senate race. However, some key Hunt backers, among them Marvin Speight of Farmville, publicly worked hard for Edmisten.

After the election, Knox went public, claiming a betrayal by Hunt. His wife and brother then announced their support for Martin.[18] While Knox offered no formal endorsement, his bitterness toward Edmisten and Hunt left little doubt that he would vote for Republicans Martin and Helms. Hunt later described himself as "shocked" by Knox's action.[19]

Going into the fall campaign, Republican Martin stressed issues that had earlier served the Democrats well, such as education, transportation improvements, and promoting a favorable climate for business. Martin opposed abortion but did not make the issue a big campaign theme. He saluted Reagan's tax cuts and argued that selective local tax cuts could help the state economy.

Edmisten stressed education and infrastructure issues and tried to come across as more of an economic populist. But Edmisten carried more baggage, including the drag of the unpopular presidential ticket and the legacy of a Democratic primary where personal attacks had transcended issues. He spent valuable campaign energy wooing former Knox and Green supporters.[20]

### LATE CAMPAIGN FURY

Whatever his political opportunism, Jim Hunt was as morally righteous as anyone involved in modern North Carolina politics, shunning alcohol, tobacco, and all but the mildest profanity. So the accusations by Bob Windsor, the editor of the *Orange County Landmark,* received little credence. Windsor was a Helms supporter and seemed to thrive as much on making waves as on ideology.[21]

On July 5, the *Landmark* published a story referring to rumors that Hunt had a "lover" while a student at North Carolina State, "a pretty young boy."[22] The story also cited reports that Hunt had a call girl on his office staff. The newspaper identified the reports as rumors and presented no evidence, but for a few days, the matter topped all discussions of state politics. Hunt was outraged: "I'm not going to take it. You know, when I got into this campaign I knew it was going to be rough, but I really never had an idea that it was going to get this mean and vicious."[23]

Responding to Hunt's hint that the Republican campaign might have a hand in the charges, Helms issued a statement: "I feel deeply for the governor, and especially for his family because my own family has endured a steady stream of invective directed at me by politicians, editors, and communicators for the past twelve years. . . . Let me say as emphatically and unequivocally as I know how that I believe Governor Hunt to be personally a moral family man. Any suggestion to the contrary is repugnant, unfair, and has no place in a political campaign. . . . I know how they must feel because my own family has, as I say, had to endure bizarre suggestions, widely circulated, that I am somehow linked to the murder of men, women, and children when in fact there is not one shred of evidence to support such a suggestion."[24] Helms's statement was deft, simultaneously disassociating him from Windsor, expressing sympathy for Hunt and his family, and alluding to official Hunt campaign ads linking Helms with murder in Central America. Windsor's insinuations, which he withdrew after Hunt threatened to sue, did not gain wide credence among the general public, but the matter constituted a serious diversion for a Hunt campaign needing to devote all its energies to gearing up for the final stretch.

The television and radio bombardment showed no letup in the fall. Helms and Hunt appeared at their parties' respective rallies, as did gubernatorial nominees Martin and Edmisten. But while accepting all the party support they could get, all four men ran their own campaigns as separate units. Neither Helms nor Hunt had previously been so hard-pressed. But for all the energy and money invested, little movement occurred in public opinion. The outcome might hinge on the magnitude of Reagan's victory in the concurrent presidential race. The Martin-Edmisten race was more genteel than the Edmisten-Knox affair had been. Martin maintained a slight edge throughout the fall.

### THE VERDICT OF '84

The year 1984 marked the high point for the national Republican Party in the second half of the twentieth century. Reagan's 59 percent of the national popular vote did not quite match Nixon's 62 percent in 1972, but the two men recorded nearly identical electoral vote landslides: 525–13 for Reagan over Mondale in 1984 and 520–17 for Nixon over McGovern in 1972. (Reagan lost only Minnesota and the District of Columbia; Nixon had lost only Massachusetts and the District of Columbia.) Reagan had Republican majorities in the U.S. Senate after the elections of 1980, 1982, and 1984. Republicans had controlled neither house of Congress during Nixon's six years in office. Reagan won because of his charisma and a well-defined conservative message: opposition to communism, high taxes, abortion, and expanded government along with support for a strengthened military. Reagan also warmly embraced the values of an earlier and simpler era. Nixon had neither charisma nor a clearly defined message. Reagan had both.

North Carolina gave Reagan 1,346,481 votes and Mondale 824,287, a resounding 62 percent for Reagan. This figure was 9 percentage points below Nixon's state showing in 1972 but still constituted the second-best state showing for a Republican presidential candidate in the twentieth century.

For all the drama of the senatorial race, the final outcome was close to what final polls had suggested—a narrow victory for Helms. Helms's 52 percent showing was a tribute to his political prowess. He had defeated

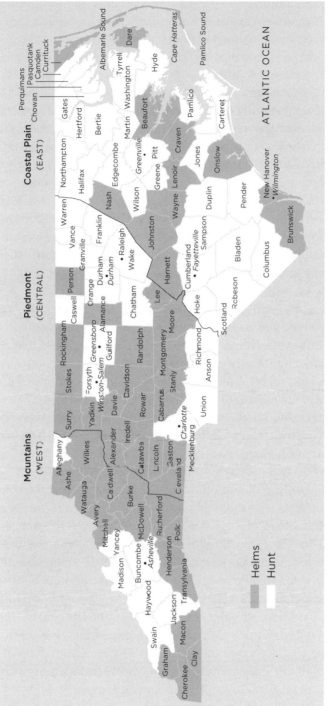

**Map 7. Results of the 1984 senatorial election—Democrat Jim Hunt versus Republican Jesse Helms**

a man in the pantheon of great North Carolina leaders, someone in the league of Charles Aycock and O. Max Gardner, a mover and shaker as well as one of the most talented of politicians. Helms managed the win even though he began the campaign with negative poll ratings at a level usually fatal to incumbent politicians. Against politically wounded Democratic opponents in 1972 and 1978, Helms had had victories of near 55 percent. Measured against more overwhelming opposition in 1984, his victory was impressive, even though he ran far behind Republican presidential candidate Reagan and slightly behind gubernatorial candidate Martin.

Propelled by nearly unanimous black support and backing from many educated white professionals, Hunt carried the counties that were home to the state's five largest cities. Mecklenburg, Guilford, and Forsyth were close—near 51 percent for Hunt. He won Helms's home county of Wake, 75,974–65,062. Indeed, Hunt narrowly carried Helms's home precinct in Raleigh's affluent Hayes-Barton neighborhood. Durham, where blacks and socially liberal whites opposed Helms, cast 64 percent of its votes for Hunt.[25]

Race was the big divide statewide. Hunt could muster only 35 percent of all white voters, and he needed at least 38 percent. Between 95 and 99 percent of blacks voted for Hunt. Hunt received a majority of the white votes in only five counties: the mountain Democratic strongholds of Jackson, Madison, Swain, and Yancey and piedmont Orange, home of the University of North Carolina at Chapel Hill.[26]

Hunt received an anemic 51 percent of the total popular vote in the coastal plain, well below what a Democrat needed to win a statewide election. Though a lifelong resident of the region, Hunt failed to get a majority of white votes in any of its forty-one counties. In his home county, Wilson, he received only about one-third of all white votes. In seven coastal plain counties, Helms won more than 75 percent of all white voters, and Hunt had previously run strongly in those counties. Across the state, Helms did especially well among whites in counties where blacks constituted more than one-third of the population. In such counties, many nominal Democrats voted for Helms. In counties with small numbers of blacks, more white Democrats stuck with Hunt, leading to his greater strength among whites in mountain counties and Dare County on the coast.[27]

Martin defeated Edmisten, 1,208,167–1,011,209, taking more than 54 percent of the vote. He swept the piedmont with almost 58 percent and took two-thirds of the votes in his home county of Mecklenburg, a county that Hunt Democrats won in the N.C. Senate race. Martin won 55.7 percent of the mountain region's vote. Edmisten led in the coastal plain, but his 53.4

percent there was a lackluster showing for a Democrat. The Democrats retained all other major statewide offices, but even well-entrenched incumbents such as the secretary of state could not muster 60 percent. The Democratic advantage in the state congressional delegation dropped from 9-2 to 7-4. Party shifts in the state legislature favored the Republicans but did not alter the fundamental balance: a 44-6 edge for Democrats in the Senate dropped to 38-12; a 102-18 advantage for Democrats in the House dropped to 82-38. As in the past, the legislature's Democrats included a few liberals, many business-friendly moderates, and some conservatives whose basic political sympathies, if not their votes in the privacy of the voting booth, lay with Helms.

The state had experienced a political shake-up but not an earthquake. Helms would begin his thirteenth year in the U.S. Senate. The congressional delegation was back in the same partisan balance that had existed after the elections of 1980, 1972, 1970, and 1968. Republicans had held slightly more seats in the N.C. Senate after the election of 1972 and the same number—twelve—as after the election of 1928. But thirty-eight in the N.C. House of Representatives was their highest number yet in the twentieth century. Governor-elect Martin wanted to bring change in Raleigh, both in policies and in ways of doing things. But in many respects, he was in the mold of progressive Democratic governors of the past.

Both Helms and Martin benefited from the Democratic fissures in the aftermath of the party's bitter gubernatorial primary. Lieutenant Governor Green's wife, Alice, had hosted a reception for Republican Martin at the Greens' home in Bladen County. Green lifted not a finger for Hunt. Unlike other members of his family, Knox did not formally endorse Helms. But throughout the fall, he made known his disdain for Edmisten and bitterness over Hunt's aloof position in the primary. Historically, big southern Republican gains had come when Democrats were split, and 1984 was a classic example of this phenomenon.[28] The Democratic split emanating from the governor's race hurt Hunt almost as much as it did Edmisten. And both were damaged by the weak Democratic presidential ticket.

### THE PASSION PLAY: HUNT VERSUS HELMS

The mainstream media called it a "battle for the soul" of North Carolina, though those who bandied this slogan about were probably Hunt supporters or fiercely anti-Helms. Hunt provided the best chance yet to defeat Helms, a man whom opponents considered a racist, a demagogue, and a witch-hunter—a throwback to the meanest instincts in American society. Years later, Helms strategist Carter Wrenn said that appeals to white prejudices were central to this and all Helms's campaigns.[29] Except for elections where Alabama's George Wallace and Georgia's Lester Maddox were candidates, those involving Helms were among the most racially polarizing of any in the second half of the twentieth century. However, the Helms campaign style was always more refined than those of Wallace and Maddox.

Helms's appeal, while linked to racial anxieties, went further. Ardent Helms supporters were few in the mainstream media and the academic communities. Helms backers usually did not use the slogan "battle for the soul" of North Carolina. Yet many of them saw the campaign precisely as a fight to preserve moral and religious values threatened by communism, atheism, and the onslaught of a secular culture in which courts and bureaucrats had taken prayer out of the public schools. All the while, crime rates had soared. Homosexuality—always present but until the 1970s rarely discussed in refined company—now came into public view. Gay rights movements swept northern and western urban areas and made some headway into the South. The abortion rights and feminist movements rankled social conservatives. Helms proudly portrayed himself as the chief target of gays and radical feminists.

Both Ronald Reagan and John East had benefited from a newly awakened religious conservative movement in 1980. The strongest push to energize and register conservative evangelicals came during Reagan's first term. The movement was national, but its greatest impact was in the states of the old Confederacy. The precise numbers are difficult to verify. One estimate of new evangelical voters went as high as 150,000. This estimate is difficult to confirm, and political crusaders whatever their moral persuasion are prone to exaggerate.[30] What is certain is that conservative white evangelicals had been mobilized to a greater extent than before.

Republican rhetoric about moral values, for all its pull in a Bible Belt state, might not have been enough to defeat the politically towering Jim Hunt in an ordinary year. Not only had he been among the most astute and successful politicians, but he was a regular churchgoer who had established a reputation for moderation and prudence in public policy. He was a can-do politician who portrayed even his boldest actions as efforts to achieve mainstream goals that would help North Carolinians achieve their highest aspirations. Yet in the 1984 campaign, the longest one North Carolina had seen up to that time, Helms had the edge in winning souls.

In this twenty-six-million-dollar campaign—the most expensive senatorial campaign to that date in any state—neither Helms nor Hunt forces could attribute the outcome strictly to the power of money. Both candidates had plenty to spend. Years earlier, Helms's Congressional Club allies and consultants had been ahead of the curve in developing new campaign strategies. They were master fund-raisers. While much of the money came from the usual conservative sources—big oil, national manufacturers' organizations, and conservative patrons from Pittsburgh to Los Angeles—a new emphasis was placed on raising money from small donors. The technique resembled one that had worked for radio and television evangelists. Mail fund-raising appeals went out to prospective contributors: persons who were active in evangelical religious movements, registered Republicans, or those having ties with conservative organizations. Typically, the response rate from early mailings was sparse. But after a series of mailings, fund-raisers had a list of thousands of people who would have sent in at least one contribution, no matter how small. Previous donors were likely prospects for future contributions.

Over a period of time, conservatives developed a huge donor base. Individuals could be counted on to make regular contributions to the cause—helping Ronald Reagan and Jesse Helms oppose the perceived moral threats posed by such liberals as Senator Ted Kennedy of Massachusetts.[31] Years later, liberals including Barack Obama utilized a similar fund-raising technique with great success. But Helms's Congressional Club and its related fund-raising organization, Jefferson Marketing, pioneered the tactic. Hunt also raised money in record amounts through liberal sources in Boston, New York, Hollywood, and North Carolina—much of it from people who thought Helms was a twentieth-century Savonarola. But the Helms campaign did the best job of tapping funds from those wanting to exorcize the demons in American society.

Both Helms and Hunt saturated the airwaves with commercials. Helms's were the more clever and successful—indeed, among the wittiest ever seen in a North Carolina political campaign. And they ran on radio and television in both 1983 and 1984. One featured the voice of a sincere-sounding man with a perfect radio announcer voice in an exchange with an "ordinary citizen" sounding like a country bumpkin on the *Andy Griffith Show*. The ad pointed out that Hunt claimed to be a strong law-and-order man but that when the legislature rejected an anticrime bill, Hunt was, according to the smooth man with the perfectly modulated voice, "on his way to Hollywood." Then the Mayberry-type citizen said, "Was he gonna be in a movie?," to which the announcer responded that Hunt had gone to Hollywood "to raise money to run against Jesse."[32]

This ad conveyed the message that Hunt was a self-promoter, not minding the store at home, and that his absence had contributed to the failure of anticrime legislation, a hot-button issue at the time. Still another ad portrayed Hunt as an advocate of high taxes. It showed a clip of Hunt at a national governors' conference "voting for tax increases"—in fact a hypothetical vote dealing with a resolution to the effect that increased taxes might pave the way for improvement in such public services as education. The narrator intoned, "Jim Hunt raised his hand." As he stressed each word, the television image was manipulated so that Hunt's hand went up in slow motion. Later Helms ads ended with the slogan, "Jim Hunt—a Mondale liberal," tying the governor to the Democratic presidential candidate.[33]

Mondale was an albatross for Hunt throughout the campaign. Had the Democratic nominee been Jimmy Carter—even the wounded Carter of 1980—Hunt might have prevailed. In 1980, Reagan had led Carter by only 39,383 votes in North Carolina. In 1984, Reagan's margin over Mondale was 522,194. In earlier races for lieutenant governor and governor, Hunt had endorsed the national presidential ticket and suffered little damage. This time, however, the opposition nationalized the state contest. Hunt's tepid endorsement of Mondale provided just the ammunition the Helms forces needed.

Hunt political ally Phil Carlton told of his difficulty in trying to persuade white business and professional people in Edgecombe and Nash Counties to support Hunt. Many of them expressed admiration for Hunt as governor and said that if it were another race for governor, they would prefer Hunt to Helms. But in a refrain familiar to many observers of North Carolina politics, they added, "We need somebody in Washington to fight Teddy Kennedy and the liberals. Jesse may be a little extreme, but he'll take a stand."[34] Hunt asserted that he would be a more effective senator than Helms and that he would vote in North Carolina's interest, not Kennedy's or Mondale's. Some voters bought Hunt's argument, but not enough to propel him to the Senate.

The bitterest and most closely contested elections in democratic societies can best be viewed as passion plays. Passion reflects powerful emotions: love, hate, anger, greed, fear, and boundless enthusiasm. In the immediate situation at hand, the candidate or spiritual force that can command the greatest fervor often prevails. The victory may be short-lived, and at times the judgment of history differs from that of the voters or the crusaders. Jesse Helms, when speaking in a jammed-to-capacity Smithfield warehouse or to an auditorium full of evangelical Christians, evoked a response matching that of the best.

He spoke both with sincerity and a hard-to-match zeal as an American patriot. If Helms's words did not roll with the eloquence of a Bryan or

Roosevelt, he—like they—could move his audience from laughter to anger in a flash. Helms stoked their fears. The Mondales, the Jesse Jacksons, and the faceless government bureaucrats, listeners feared, threatened their values and ordered society.

Hunt was a loud talker—often louder than Helms. The Democrat spoke of his aspirations for the state's people and America: an open school door for everyone, jobs, and moral values. By 1984, he could also claim a record of propelling a poor state forward in education as well as industry. People listened. They applauded. A few partisans even shouted. He stoked their hopes. But Hunt was no match for Helms in lighting fires. Hunt preached and cajoled. Helms carried the torch and led the charge. His followers believed in the man and the cause.

### THE MARTIN ASCENDANCY

From the standpoint of programs and day-to-day governance, the governor usually has much greater impact than a senator, however dynamic that senator may be. Martin's race for governor had been overshadowed by the Senate race and enhanced by the preceding Democratic gubernatorial primary. Now he held the top elected office. Martin had political credentials equal to earlier governors, but he was in many respects cut from different cloth. Martin was born in the 1930s in Savannah, Georgia, a city redolent with old-fashioned southern charm and Spanish moss but also down at the heels, not the shining jewel it would become late in the twentieth century. Martin's father was a Presbyterian minister, and like many sons of Presbyterian preachers, he went to Davidson College on the northern, rural edge of North Carolina's most urban county, Mecklenburg.[35] (Former governor Jim Holshouser had finished at Davidson in 1956.)

Martin graduated and married Dottie McAulay in 1959. In lightning time—three years—he earned a doctorate in chemistry from Princeton and returned to Davidson as a chemistry professor. Martin established a reputation as a demanding but popular and able teacher.[36] He doted on classical music and composed some of his own scores. Davidson was part of an informal but elite group of southern private colleges.[37] Martin found the Davidson environment nourishing, but the outside world beckoned. He relished the idea of more civic and political involvement.

At first, Martin was not sure whether he was a Democrat or Republican. He was a progressive with conservative instincts and supported the tenets of capitalism. His decision to become a Republican rested partly on the premise that the long-entrenched Democrats were the party of the status quo in North Carolina. Moreover, the fledgling Republican Party seemed more welcoming to the young and ambitious. Propelled by the city of Charlotte, Mecklenburg County had loosened its ties to the Democrats. From the 1966 election to 1972, Martin was both a professor and Republican county commissioner. From 1969 to 1972, he chaired the Mecklenburg Board of County Commissioners, where he championed land planning and zoning.[38] That position made him, along with the mayor of Charlotte, the highest-ranking official in local government. After twenty years in office, Charles Jonas, long labeled "Mr. Republican" in North Carolina, announced that he would retire from the U.S. House. In 1972, Martin easily won the Republican nomination for the seat over a more conservative candidate, Graem Yates.[39]

Martin faced Democrat Jim Beatty in the November 1972 general election. Beatty, a 1957 graduate of UNC–Chapel Hill, was considered a rising star in state politics. He was the first person ever to run the mile in less than four minutes in indoor competition, shortly after Roger Bannister of Great Britain accomplished the feat outdoors. Beatty had served in the N.C. House, representing Mecklenburg County in the 1967 and 1969 sessions. In 1972, Martin rode the Republican tide to defeat Beatty, 80,356–56,171, in the district that consisted of Mecklenburg, Iredell, and Lincoln Counties. The Nixon landslide over McGovern helped boost his margin, but Martin would likely have won even in a good Democratic year, since he was one of the best-known officials in what had become a Republican-leaning district.[40]

Martin's Washington voting record was consistently conservative, but he shunned "extremism." He and Holshouser were kindred spirits, and both men had frosty relationships with the Helms wing of the Republican Party during the 1970s. Both Martin and Holshouser favored incumbent Gerald Ford over Reagan for the 1976 Republican presidential nomination. Defying tradition, the dominant Helms forces denied both the governor and the congressman positions in the state delegation to the Republican National Convention in Kansas City.[41]

Once inaugurated as governor, Martin faced constraints from the Democratic legislature. Nevertheless, he influenced public policy, successfully pushing for tax reform and reduction in 1985 and a major roads initiative in 1986. Not wanting to raise taxes, he advocated devoting a higher percentage of state revenues to public education. Like his Republican predecessor, Holshouser, Martin proved that the state could operate smoothly with different parties in control of the legislature and the governorship. Divided government was easier in Raleigh than it might have been in some other state capitals or Washington since no fierce ideological divide separated

Martin from the legislature as a whole, and many members of both parties shared Martin's basic philosophy. So did North Carolina's corporate leaders, some of whom held key positions in his administration.[42]

### THE 1986 ELECTIONS: A MILD DEMOCRATIC RESURGENCE

Democrats eyed the 1986 midterm election with cautious optimism. Reagan remained popular among Republican partisans but had fallen into disfavor among independents. He began to run into roadblocks as a White House team run by former treasurer secretary Donald Regan could not hold a candle to the first-term operation headed by James Baker. The perception grew that the administration was out of touch in domestic and foreign affairs. And there was history: the party not occupying the White House has often performed well in congressional elections held during the president's sixth year.

The big national race in North Carolina was for the U.S. Senate. John East had initially hit Washington energetically, his wheelchair zipping around the Senate office building and the Capitol. Because of the Republican takeover of the Senate in 1981, East had opportunities rare for a freshman. Strom Thurmond of South Carolina, the new chair of the Senate Judiciary Committee, appointed East to chair the subcommittee on separation of powers. From that position, East held well-publicized hearings focusing on what he considered the federal courts' pro-abortion position. Presiding over the subcommittee, East came across as the academic he had been for most of his adult life, pedagogical and forceful, with every word perfectly placed. To liberal critics, he seemed almost a clone of Helms. Newspaper cartoons in North Carolina gratuitously portrayed East as being in Helms's breast pocket, a mere handkerchief, so to speak. East was labeled "Helms on Wheels."

But East's conservatism had developed quite apart from Helms's. Although East never had the mass following of Helms, North Carolina's junior senator was revered by Congressional Club conservatives. According to Carter Wrenn, East "was a brilliant man. He was the purest in motive, most intellectual."[43] Tom Ellis, who came to know him well, similarly praised East as the most intellectually gifted of politicians. When Ellis would float an idea to East or Helms for a possible press statement, Helms, though a talented wordsmith, might take days to come up with the statement; East could write a perfect announcement within minutes.[44]

In 1983, however, East's health began to fail. He was suffering from thyroid problems, which doctors initially failed to diagnose and which brought on a host of physical ailments as well as depression. As time went on, short office absences turned into longer ones. In 1985, his problems required an extended hospital stay, and he reluctantly concluded that he could not seek reelection. East returned to his office and the Senate floor, but the old spirit did not return.

Terry Sanford, having retired from the presidency of Duke University and looking for a new challenge, eyed East's Senate seat. Sanford had remained active in national and state politics, yet many thought he could never again be a serious aspirant to state political office. Few governors had been as unpopular at the end of their terms. In 1968, three years after leaving the governorship, Sanford had explored the possibility of a challenge to the incumbent conservative Democratic senator, Sam Ervin. It would have been a bitter race, and Sanford would have had little chance of winning. He saw the futility of a challenge. National-level Democrats recognized Sanford as a man of superior talents, but that recognition did little to help his bids for the Democratic presidential nomination in 1972 and 1976, which ordinary North Carolinians did not embrace.[45]

However, Sanford had spent the past decade building rather than burning bridges. As president of Duke, he won the admiration of conservative trustees. Few college presidents had better links with money managers and foundations. Whatever Sanford might lack in public charisma, his political acumen was, if anything, sharper than in his gubernatorial days.

Sanford began to sound out friends about a possible run for the U.S. Senate in 1986. Sam Poole, who had worked with Sanford in his presidential campaigns, was a key figure in the conversations. In late 1985, Poole accompanied Sanford, Herman Clark, and Paul Vick to the Virgin Islands, where they explored the pros and cons of a race but reached no final decision.[46] A defeat could mark an ignominious end to what had been, despite setbacks, an illustrious career in public service. Sanford believed that he would gain more recognition than the typical freshman senator. Presumably, the Democratic Senate leadership would enjoy showcasing a long-time Helms foe.[47]

Republican congressman James Broyhill had long eyed higher office but was reluctant to abandon a safe House seat that provided seniority and influence in Washington. He saw an opening when East announced plans to step down. Western North Carolina Republicans encouraged Broyhill to take the plunge, partly because they believed that he would be the party's strongest candidate and partly to contain the influence of the Helms organization and Congressional Club in party ranks. The Congressional Club backed Campbell University professor David Funderburk, who had recently been American ambassador to Romania. Ideologically, the politically untested Funderburk was close to East, who had indicated that Funderburk was his favored replacement. With the support of Governor Martin, who had close ties with western Republicans and corporate leaders but also a cordial relationship with a few members of the Helms wing of the party, Broyhill easily beat Funderburk in the Republican primary, 139,579–63,593. Former Ku Klux Klan member Glenn Miller was third with 6,652.

Before a Sanford-Broyhill matchup could become official, Sanford had to go through the formality of a Democratic primary. He won with 409,394 votes, handily outpolling his nine opponents, who totaled just under 280,000 votes. For the first time since 1960, Sanford had won a statewide race. The wide victory margin provided a big boost to his general election campaign.

Lauch Faircloth, a longtime Sanford ally, had initially planned to seek the Democratic nomination and thought that he had a commitment of support from Sanford. Faircloth withdrew after Sanford announced his candidacy but felt that he had been betrayed by an old friend.[48]

By mid-1986, East's health appeared to be improving, and he was showing up regularly in the Senate. He signed papers to go back to his old faculty position in the political science department at East Carolina University. Returning to his Greenville home for the weekend, East outwardly seemed in good spirits. But after visiting with his daughter, Chip, on Saturday night, East went to his garage and started the car, poisoning himself with carbon monoxide. In a note, he expressed frustration toward the doctor at Bethesda Naval Center who had failed early on to discover his thyroid condition.[49]

East's funeral was held at Greenville's Jarvis Memorial United Methodist Church, a large brick edifice with a neo-Gothic interior that was too small to seat all the mourners. Those in attendance included Republican senatorial leaders and conservative evangelist Jerry Falwell. Tom Fetzer, a former member of East's staff and later Raleigh mayor and chair of the state Republican Party, remarked later, "I loved John East. He loved young people. He was warm and had a sense of humor. He was more approachable than Helms."[50]

As early as East's funeral, the media began to speculate about whom Governor Martin would name to finish out the final month's of East's term.[51] Martin selected Broyhill, who was already the Republican nominee for the seat, hoping that incumbency and the privilege of calling himself Senator Broyhill would help his candidacy.

In the fall campaign, Sanford stressed his accomplishments, both military and civilian. Knowing that Democrats were vulnerable to insinuations

of a lack of patriotism, he campaigned in a bomber jacket and lost no opportunity to remind voters of his World War II record as a paratrooper.
Sanford and his supporters also pointed to his 1961–65 gubernatorial term
as one of the most far-reaching and dynamic of any in the state's history.
More than twenty years later, the controversies over the food tax and integration of public facilities had faded into the background. Sanford boasted
that on his watch, the state had made strides in education, economic development, and race relations. He said that the Reagan administration was
out of touch on economic issues. Although Sanford was gentler toward
Broyhill than he had been toward I. Beverly Lake twenty-six years earlier,
he asserted that Broyhill did not relate to ordinary people.[52]

Despite having won admiration as a hard worker during his twenty-four
years in the House of Representatives, Broyhill came across to those who
did not know him—the great majority of state residents—as more aloof
than the homespun Sanford. Broyhill was friendly enough in campaign
mode but looked like a patrician.

The interest group dynamics of 1986 worked to Sanford's advantage. Like
most Democrats, he had the backing of blacks, organized labor, attorneys,
and teachers' groups. Reflecting longtime associations and friendships,
Sanford also had a big slice of the banking and developers' lobbies. Sanford was a progressive in the North Carolina model, the kind of Democrat
who had long been comfortable in corporate boardrooms. Broyhill was the
favorite of the traditional big three industries—furniture, textiles, and
tobacco—as well as of some bankers. He had the organizational muscle
of the Martin administration, a substantial asset. Helms also campaigned
hard for Broyhill, but much of the Helms organization was lukewarm toward
the candidate, not relishing the idea of a traditional western North Carolina Republican holding East's old Senate seat.[53] In Washington, Broyhill
had been a consensus man, albeit one with a conservative voting record.

Sanford, now sixty-nine, campaigned almost as vigorously as he had two
and a half decades earlier. He kept a campaign pledge to visit all one hundred counties. Knowing that Broyhill, a resident of Lenoir in the foothills,
would do well in the mountain region and rural western piedmont, Sanford aimed to building strong majorities in the piedmont cities and in the
historically Democratic but socially conservative coastal plain. The east—
the coastal plain—had been good to Sanford in his 1960 race for governor
against Robert Gavin, but Sanford had been unpopular there at the end
of his term. In 1986, Sanford assiduously courted eastern business, civic,
and farm leaders. In an era of television campaigning, a medium used ex-
tensively by both Sanford and Broyhill, he also worked the east through

old-fashioned store-to-store and gas station–to–gas station campaigns. Whatever he lacked in oratorical skills and television charisma, Sanford was always a master of retail politics—the person-to-person approach. He was naturally folksy, and he knew instinctively what to say and what not to say, whatever the background of those he was courting.[54]

Sanford beat Broyhill, 823,662–767,668, not a landslide but a good showing in the 1980s for a North Carolina Democrat seeking a high-profile national office. Sanford led in the major cities of Durham, Greensboro, and Raleigh as well as in a few mountain counties with potent Democratic organizations. But the forty-one-county coastal plain region gave Sanford his winning margin. He carried every county in the region, including those that had been strongholds for Ronald Reagan, George Wallace, and Jesse Helms. Sanford won the majority of white votes in some eastern counties and more than one-third of the white vote everywhere in the region, a sharp contrast to Hunt's showing there two years earlier.[55] Broyhill led in most mountain counties, the western piedmont, and the central piedmont. He narrowly carried urban Mecklenburg County, the state's largest. He had won the Republican base vote and some white conservative independents and Democrats, but not enough. The candidate of much of corporate North Carolina, Sanford spoke to the needs of the lower-middle and working classes.

It was a sweet victory for Sanford. He benefited from a national Democratic tide. The party recaptured the U.S. Senate, going from 47 to 55 seats, and boosted its hold in the U.S. House of Representatives. In North Carolina's mountain Eleventh Congressional District, Democrat James M. Clarke regained the seat he had lost in the 1984 Republican landslide and returned the Democratic edge among North Carolina congressional representatives to 8–3. (The Eleventh District seat had changed party hands in each election beginning in 1980.) Democrats also made slight gains in the N.C. Senate and House of Representatives. But Sanford's win reflected his own political skills, not just the national Democratic momentum. Aside from Helms and Martin, Broyhill was the state's most prestigious Republican. Despite his lack of passion, he would have defeated a lesser Democrat.

Few figures had better symbolized the bitter political divide than Sanford and Helms. But in keeping with Senate tradition—and probably just a slight chuckle at the irony—Sanford asked his senior colleague Helms to escort him to the front of the Senate at inauguration time.

## THE DECADE ENDS

In the summer of 1988, national Democrats were bullish on their prospects of winning the presidency, maybe with a commanding majority. After eight years as a loyal aide-de-camp to Reagan, Vice President George H. W. Bush was the inevitable Republican nominee, despite a primary-season challenge from Kansas senator Robert Dole. Bush picked Indiana senator Dan Quayle as his vice presidential running mate. Bush's grasp of the details and operations of government far exceeded that of not only Reagan but also the typical nominee of either party. He had been American envoy to China and head of the Central Intelligence Agency. However, he was a mediocre speaker.

The Democrats nominated Massachusetts governor Michael Dukakis, who proudly pointed to his family's Greek background and achievement of the American Dream. His cousin, Olympia, was a famous actress. Dukakis represented a new style of Democrat who believed in the wonders of technology and a new enlightenment. Like Bush, he did not have a dynamic presence. But America seemed ready for a change. Dukakis picked the moderate and business-friendly Senator Lloyd Bentsen of Texas as his running mate. Dukakis led by as much as 17 percent in national polls when the Democratic National Convention concluded in July. He led narrowly in North Carolina.[56]

Bush needed a miracle and a brilliant strategist. And, indeed, he already had a great strategist, South Carolina's Lee Atwater. In some respects, Atwater was a younger version of North Carolina's Tom Ellis, the man who had engineered victories for Helms and East. Like Ellis, Atwater would go for the jugular. At their August convention, the Republicans portrayed Dukakis as out of touch with hardworking, law-abiding, patriotic Americans. At the outset of Bush's acceptance speech, he declared that the campaign was about values. Bush's speech, though far from the most eloquent ever at a convention, was one of the most effective.[57] His poll deficit turned into a lead that he maintained through the November election.

In the speech and afterward, Bush contrasted his support for the death penalty with Dukakis's opposition, a popular position as crime had soared in the 1970s and early 1980s. With the exception of George Wallace's 1968 bid, no modern presidential campaign had been so imbued with the spirit of social populism. On economic issues, however, Bush was a conventional 1980s conservative, promising "no new taxes" and minimal regulation of business.[58]

Bush won forty states, though Dukakis's 46 percent of the popular vote was the best Democratic presidential showing of the 1980s. Bush had 58 percent of the vote in North Carolina, where he won all three geographic regions and all the state's big urban counties except Durham. Dukakis carried some heavily Democratic rural and small-town counties in the coastal plain and eastern piedmont that had large African American or Native American populations or well-oiled Democratic machines. Whites voted overwhelmingly for Bush, while nearly 90 percent of blacks backed Dukakis.

Reflecting his incumbency, popularity, political smarts, and the Republican tide, Martin was reelected for a second term with 56 percent of the popular vote. He, too, carried all three of the state's regions and all of the large cities except Durham. While popular in Democratic circles and an astute politician, his opponent, Bob Jordan, never had a serious chance. A good person-to-person campaigner, Jordan lacked Martin's broader popular appeal. And the major money sources did not want to bet on a losing horse. Off the record, leading Democrats said that Jordan was tone-deaf and lacked a message.[59] But no Democrat, with the possible exception of former governor Hunt, would have been a serious match for Martin in 1988.

The Martin-Jordan race, like all the partisan contests of 1984, split along racial lines, with more than 85 percent of blacks voting for the Democrat and a big majority of whites for the Republican. Race rhetoric—open or more indirect—had not been an element of either campaign, so the media and other analysts focused little on the racial divide. However, intense racial divisions now characterized voting in nearly all high-profile elections.

In a mild upset, Republican Jim Gardner narrowly defeated Democratic state senator Tony Rand of Fayetteville in the race for lieutenant governor. Rand was one of the most powerful and effective of legislators, though one who bruised some egos over the years. Gardner had bruised still more egos. Back in 1968, he had waged a competitive race against Bob Scott. In 1988, the now gray-haired Gardner remained photogenic and an enthusiastic speaker. And in 1988, he was more of a Republican team player. He hoped to move into the governorship four years later.[60]

The Democrats maintained their 7–3 edge in the congressional delegation. Republicans picked up 3 seats in the N.C. Senate yet had only 13 seats, 2 below their level after the 1972 election. The Democratic edge in the N.C. House was 96–24, an advantage greater than the 85–35 ratio after the 1972 election. Incumbent Speaker Liston Ramsey seemed headed for another term, having gotten commitments from nearly all Democrats in the chamber.

However, Democrats of various political stripes resented Ramsey's authoritarian ways and some legislators began to whisper about toppling Ramsey.[61] An almost unthinkable alliance arose joining anti-Ramsey Democrats with Republicans, nearly all of whom resented Ramsey's fierce partisanship. Governor Martin, who saw Ramsey as out to torpedo his programs, became a leading behind-the-scenes advocate of such a coalition. Secret conversations among legislators resulted in a commitment from the House Republicans to back Edgecombe County Democratic representative Joe Mavretic for Speaker. Nineteen Democrats joined forty-five of the forty-six Republicans in electing Mavretic. The dissident Democratic ranks included conservatives, moderates, and liberals.[62] One of the coalition leaders, Roy Cooper of Nash, was later elected attorney general as a Democrat. Another, Walter Jones Jr. of Farmville, the son of a sitting member of Congress, later won election to the U.S. House after switching to the Republican Party. The coalition adopted a power-sharing arrangement, with Republicans having a major voice and vice chairs on every standing committee. Martin's proposals were now assured a fair hearing in the N.C. House.

For years, Democratic legislative leaders had dreamed of stripping the lieutenant governor of the power to appoint committees and committee chairs in the Senate. They had held back because such action could be seen as a slap in the face to a fellow Democrat—and, perhaps more important, a future governor. Party leaders now welcomed the opportunity to go after Gardner. Most Democrats did not like him politically or personally and wanted to lower his chances of becoming governor. The power to appoint committees had been authorized by Senate rules, not the constitution. The Democratic majority changed the rules at the outset of the 1989 session, stripping the lieutenant governor of his appointive powers. Gardner remained the presiding officer and had the right to break tie votes, responsibilities established by the constitution. The other powers of the lieutenant governor went to the president pro tem of the Senate, a position that emerged as one of the most influential in state government. Gardner was left as a figurehead, ironically giving him more time to run for governor.[63]

Secretary of State Thad Eure, an icon of North Carolina politics, retired in 1988 after fifty-two years in the post. Eure was a stereotypical southern Democrat: a conservative who always voted the straight Democratic ticket from the White House to the courthouse. His antics delighted partisan rallies. Eure insisted that his office door remain open at all times, both when alone and with others. Few knew as much about legislative procedures.[64]

The new secretary of state was another colorful if more progressive politician, former attorney general Rufus Edmisten, who had lost the governorship to Martin in 1984. In 1989, therefore, the Democrats were down but not out. Aside from governor and lieutenant governor, they held all of the Council of State positions.

The Republicans anticipated a bright future. Their presidential candidate had won North Carolina and the country for three elections in a row. At the end of the 1980s, the Republicans seemed to have a lock on the Electoral College, an overwhelming advantage going into presidential contests. Consistently Republican states included Illinois, California, all the mountain West, and the South. In North Carolina, Helms appeared to be firmly entrenched as he looked toward running for a fourth term in 1990. Martin could not seek a third consecutive term, but Gardner seemed an even bet to replace him. And the Republicans shared control of the N.C. House of Representatives with Democrats for the first time in the century.

The 1980s had begun and ended on sour notes for the Democrats. More than in earlier decades, North Carolina reflected mainstream America. The way had been paved partly by progressive leaders in the 1960s and 1970s. Along with modernization, political conservatism—support for capitalism and low taxes—had become a dominant trend. Conservatives and Republicans were in a stronger position than they had occupied ten years earlier. To many voters, the Republicans were the party of Americanism—patriotism, traditional social values, and faith in God. Reagan, Bush, and Helms had demonstrated the mass appeal of social populism in North Carolina and beyond. At the end of 1989, as in 1980, conservatives and much of the American public worried about the threats of crime at home and burdensome government regulations. World communism, the bogeyman for so many years, was on the wane. But national security remained a big issue for the nation and military-friendly North Carolina. Conservatism had never seemed so alive and well.

## CHAPTER TEN

# Breaking New Ground

There were few hints of a dramatic political turn. The middle class prospered. Inflation slowed. The urban South led the nation in economic growth. North Carolina's cities and resort areas boomed. Charlotte pursued a major cleanup after a blast from Hurricane Hugo in September 1989, a storm that had continued to wreak havoc when it moved inland from the South Carolina coast. Despite its severity, the damage was a mere hiccup for what had become one of America's most dynamic cities. Most political observers assumed that George H. W. Bush would coast to reelection in the 1992 presidential election and that Jesse Helms would be elected to a fourth term in the Senate in 1990, probably defeating a moderate white Democrat. The conventional wisdom said that the Democrats had a permanent majority in the U.S. House of Representatives. The Republicans appeared to have the long-term advantage in electing presidents, an electoral vote lock based on strength in the South, the Midwest, the West, and parts of the Northeast.[1]

North Carolina had a Republican governor, but Democrats still held the upper hand in the state legislature. Democratic Speaker of the House of Representatives Joe Mavretic temporarily led a coalition of Democrats and Republicans after the 1989 coup, but few observers thought that the Republicans could win a legislative majority on their own. Before the decade was out, old notions about political norms would be challenged as never before.

Underlying economic and social forces reshaped the state, which was on the cusp of moving from majority rural to majority urban. From 1980 to 1990, North Carolina's population had grown from 5,881,776 to 6,628,637—enough that it gained a seat in the U.S. House of Representatives. Metropolitan areas—mainly in the urban crescent close to Interstate 85—and resort communities led the way. The rural nonfarm population grew fast in zones twenty to forty miles from cities. New houses filled old farm fields. Early twentieth-century dwellings met the wrecker's ball or decayed except in a few cities, where the grander ones became valued trophy properties. At mainstream restaurants, blacks and whites often dined together. And no longer did the presence of an interracial couple automatically evoke raised eyebrows or icy stares from the whites in the room.

## THE GANTT CHALLENGE

Harvey Gantt's campaign was the central story of the 1990 election season. Through the 1980s, blacks had little chance to win statewide Democratic primaries. They might lead in the initial primary, only to lose the runoff. In 1990, Gantt, a former mayor of Charlotte, hoped to change this dynamic. He sought the Democratic nomination and the challenge of facing Helms. The leading white progressive Democrats—the Sanford and Hunt crowds—feared that Gantt's race and liberalism made him a sure loser.[2]

Hunt had no appetite for taking on Helms after the 1984 bloodbath. Instead, he eyed a 1992 race for governor, when Jim Martin would be ineligible to run again. Congressional Democrats did not want to vacate their safe seats to pursue a losing cause. William Friday, the retired president of the state university system and host of a popular public television interview program, might have been the Democrats' dream candidate. At seventy, he remained full of energy. He was a keen student of politics who had managed to stay above the partisan fray. Democratic money sources, notably organized labor from outside the state, promised to pour money into a Friday Senate campaign. His polling numbers looked good. Friday was intrigued by the idea until he received a visit from a former UNC student and personal friend who worked for the Raleigh law firm of top Helms strategist Tom Ellis. The young attorney warned Friday that the Congressional Club had a thick file him. Friday believed that the attorney had approached him as a friend and not as an agent of the Helms's forces. He decided not to run, fearing that a bitter race would tarnish his sterling reputation and that of the university.[3] While never politically close, Friday and Helms long maintained a friendly personal relationship.

Harvey Gantt was a World War II baby, born near the front edge of the baby boom on January 14, 1943, in Charleston, South Carolina, where his father worked in the busy shipyard. At the time, South Carolina vied with Mississippi as a symbol of the lost Confederate cause and a defender of white supremacy.

Gantt and his parents believed that he could achieve the American Dream. He was a first-rate student and athlete, quarterbacking his high school football team. He helped integrated Clemson University in 1963, maintaining a poise throughout the process that won praise from an unlikely North Carolina source—conservative television commentator Jesse Helms, then an outspoken critic of the push for desegregation.[4]

Gantt graduated from Clemson in 1965 and joined a leading Charlotte architectural firm. He enrolled in graduate school at the Massachusetts Institute of Technology in Cambridge and earned a master's degree in city planning in 1970. Gantt returned to Charlotte, where he founded an architectural firm and dabbled in politics. In 1979, after serving on the city council, he challenged Jim Hunt's friend and ally, Eddie Knox, for the mayoralty. Knox won that contest, but Gantt ran again and took over as mayor after the 1983 elections. He won another term before losing to Republican Sue Myrick in 1987. He then began to contemplate a race for the U.S. Senate. He was a man of bold ambitions and dreams, undeterred by setbacks.[5]

Democrats in the Hunt-Sanford mold, still fearing that Gantt or any African American would lose in a race against Helms, finally settled on a second-tier candidate, Mike Easley, the Brunswick County district attorney. Easley had developed a reputation as a scrappy prosecutor who relentlessly pursued drug dealers. He was a political moderate; as a rookie, he had less to lose than did more seasoned politicians. The exception to establishment support for Easley was Charlotte, where much of the business and political leadership backed Gantt for the nomination. Gantt espoused economic populist themes and a woman's right to choose on reproductive matters. He tried to project an image of soundness and moderation as opposed to the "extremism" of Helms. Easley's subliminal message was that he could beat Helms, while Gantt could not. Easley boasted of being tough on crime, an issue that the Republicans had dominated in the late 1980s.

In the first primary, Gantt led Easley, 260,179–208,934. The other four candidates together had 223,283 votes, more than half of which were for John Ingram. Easley called for a runoff, and history suggested that he had a good chance of winning. Three of the eliminated candidates were white; the exception was the Reverend Bob Hannon, who had received just 7,982 votes. As a moderate white, Easley might have expected to get most white votes. Yet surveys between the two primaries indicated a lead for Gantt. There was reason to believe that the polls were misleading. A year earlier, preelection polls had shown Douglas Wilder, an African American, with a big lead in the Virginia gubernatorial race, but he barely won the election. In Gantt's case, however, the polls were on target: He defeated Easley in June, 273,567–207,283, marking the first time an African American had won a statewide Democratic primary in North Carolina.

Gantt's victory reflected both his personal appeal and the changing composition of the Democratic primary electorate. Despite an aloof bearing, Gantt had charisma. He lacked a dramatic speaking style but came across as a thoughtful man who could communicate. Unlike some blacks with a dynamic presence, Gantt did not seem to scare off white voters. Both on television and in public addresses, Gantt was more eloquent than Easley. Easley possessed political smarts, but at this stage, his public persona was no match for Gantt's.

Gantt had carried other advantages into the primary. His connections in Charlotte and local pride made the city his base of support. In Mecklenburg County, he took 80 percent of the vote, a powerful showing that helped him take 66 percent of the vote in the populous piedmont region, far more than enough to overcome Easley's 52 percent lead in the coastal plain and 57 percent in the mountains. Coastal plain voters were polarized, with whites voting overwhelmingly for Easley and blacks for Gantt.[6]

The total vote had dropped from 693,496 in May to 480,850 in June. Gantt's vote, however, rose by more than 13,000. Gantt voters were more energized than the supporters of other candidates. The gradual leftward shift in the Democratic primary electorate also aided Gantt. More and more, conservatives were gravitating to the Republican Party. With fewer local races to draw them to the polls—the typical motivator in a runoff primary—conservatives had no powerful incentive to vote. In the racial atmosphere the 1960s, the presence of a serious black candidate would have drawn white voters. Such intense emotions had died down by 1990, at least among registered Democrats. And conservative Democrats could vote for Helms in November. Democratic primaries were no longer as important to the final choice as in earlier days.

The Helms forces relished the opportunity to run against Gantt. As summer turned to fall, however, there was reason to think that they had miscalculated. Early in the summer, some polls had Gantt narrowly ahead, though history suggested that the polls would turn around after the Helms campaign began its attacks. Neither campaign geared up until August. From June 20 to August 25, Helms appeared at only one campaign event in his home state. A long and tortuous congressional session kept him in Washington for much of September. Melvin Watt, Gantt's campaign chair, and other Charlotte-based lieutenants decided to run their own show rather than to go through the Democratic Party, a decision that required planning and preparation time. Not wishing to get in the way, the party apparatus also held back on its efforts. The campaign followed more of a British-model short election season than the late-twentieth-century

American model of a long, drawn-out campaign. When the battle began in earnest, Gantt still led in published opinion polls. At the same point in the 1984 campaign, Hunt had been running slightly behind Helms.[7]

Still, Gantt had handicaps. Few, if any, serious candidates for top office in North Carolina had been as liberal on both economic and social issues. Gantt would have been more ideologically suitable in Massachusetts or Minnesota than in North Carolina. He backed the expansion of the federal government's role in the economy, and while many North Carolina Democratic candidates supported abortion rights, few had been as outspoken as Gantt. Gantt also made known his sympathies for gay rights.[8] He backed affirmative action for racial minorities. Gantt unapologetically spoke against the death penalty.

Gantt's race was paradoxically both an asset and a handicap. On the plus side, liberals could rejoice that an African American—and one who had made history in the civil rights movement—was carrying the banner in the crusade against Jesse Helms. Perhaps no white male could have captured as well the hearts and minds of the Helms haters, both in and out of North Carolina, as Gantt did. Self-proclaimed progressives, especially among college students and the highly educated, also saw Gantt as a breath of fresh air. Gantt drew large crowds.[9]

Yet the color of Gantt's skin remained a handicap when seeking high political office in a southern state, and public opinion polling probably did not reveal the extent of that handicap. While the results of the Democratic primary had suggested that Gantt's image played well among some white voters, Helms's strategists suspected that many white North Carolinians—including a few people who had voted for Hunt in 1984—would vote against Gantt or any other African American. Some would admit it, while others would rationalize a race-based vote on other grounds.

The Helms campaign initially appeared reluctant openly to play the race card. Attacking Gantt because of his race or for his liberal positions on race-related issues such as affirmative action might have been simpler if he had been a white liberal or a white moderate. Undecided voters, notably moderate to conservative white women and young people, might be turned off by overtly racist appeals. Helms strategists sought the right balance.

In mid-August, the Helms's campaign, again directed by the Congressional Club, released a barrage of radio ads aimed at eastern North Carolina audiences. These ads attempted to portray Gantt as someone on the wrong side of the great cultural divide—a North Carolina version of George McGovern, Jesse Jackson, or Michael Dukakis. The ads attacked Gantt for his opposition to capital punishment, his ties to gay and lesbian political groups, and his opposition to Helms's efforts to keep "taxpayers' money [from] going to pornographers."[10]

Helms's campaign later unleashed two ads that were more overtly racial, one designed to turn out voters and the other to sway voters. The first was the "white hands ad," which almost immediately achieved classic status. A pair of white hands crumpled up a job rejection letter as the announcer said, "You needed that job and you were the best qualified. But they had to give it to a minority because of a racial quota."

The ad probably converted few voters from Gantt to Helms, and indications showed that some voters—not just Gantt supporters—were turned off. The ad was pulled after only a few days.[11] But it did stir up interest in the issue of quotas and race. While no polling data prove this with certainty, the "white hands ad" likely drew people to the polls who otherwise would not have voted, and those voters likely supported Helms. Court decisions, most notably the 1978 *Bakke* case, had ruled quotas unconstitutional, but many whites believed that businesses and universities maintained informal quotas under the guise of affirmative action.[12] Throughout his career, Helms positioned himself as the chief warrior in the fight against quotas, real or imagined.

The other ad, while less dramatic, might have been more effective because it cast doubt on Gantt's character yet highlighted affirmative action and Gantt's race. In 1985, Gantt bought and sold part of a Belmont television station, WZY. The ad alleged that he had taken advantage of a minority preference provision in federal law designed to help blacks going into business and then had sold his interest at a handsome profit. A follow-up ad said that Gantt had used his "minority status" to "become a millionaire." While apparently within the letter of the law, the deal had indeed raised eyebrows at the time.[13] Helms hammered on the theme on the last few days of the campaign.

Abortion remained an issue. The Gantt forces, backed by the National Abortion Rights Action League, had attacked Helms's past advocacy of federal constitutional amendments that would have banned all abortions, presumably even in cases of incest or rape. Rather than attempting to defend Helms's position, his campaign portrayed Gantt as an extremist on the issue and a captive of abortion rights groups and charged that Gantt favored late-term abortions for sex selection. Gantt denied the charge, but the Helms's campaign had set a trap that they sprang after Gantt's denial. Helms strategist Earl Ashe had routinely sent out film crews to tape Gantt's press conferences. At one, Gantt had reaffirmed his pro-choice position, adding, that the reason for an abortion "is really left to the woman . . . whether it's sex selection or whatever reason." An ad produced by Ashe showed that footage of Gantt several times, including in slow motion, catching him in what seemed to be a contradiction. Like other Helms ads, this one ended, "Harvey Gantt, extremely liberal with the facts."[14]

Like the ad attacking Gantt's television station deal, this one raised questions about his honesty. The TV license ad had also reminded voters of Gantt's race. The abortion ad conveyed the message that Gantt was a liberal, out of touch with North Carolina's Christian values.

Despite Helms's advantage, Gantt had a lot of money to spend on television and radio. Both candidates attracted donations from all over the country. Overall, Helms outspent Gantt $17.96 million to $7.81 million. As in the more costly 1984 Helms-Hunt Senate race, money was not the decisive factor in the outcome. But years later, classes would still watch the Helms ads as classics. Gantt's were forgotten.

During the campaign's closing days, Helms, finally released from the long captivity of what seemed a never-ending Senate session, returned home to take charge of the campaign. He crisscrossed the state with a vigor almost matching his campaign against Hunt in 1984. But by the time of his homecoming, Helms had already begun to move ahead in the polls. Helms finished the task. Gantt's rise had almost seemed a Cinderella story, but he was an astute and hard-driving politician backed by a smart team. Helms strategist Carter Wrenn later said that the Gantt campaign of 1990 was superior to the campaigns against Helms waged by Nick Galifianakis, John Ingram, and Jim Hunt.[15]

Gantt ran almost as well against Helms in the 1990 general election as Hunt, the most formidable of North Carolina's Democrats, had six years earlier. That a liberal African American could win just over 47 percent of the statewide vote was a tremendous change. Gantt received nearly 36 percent of the votes cast by whites and nearly 99 percent of the votes cast by blacks.[16] Gantt also appeared to have won a majority of the small American Indian vote, significant in lowland Robeson and Hoke and several mountain counties.

The milieu of each election is different. When Hunt ran in 1984, the party's presidential candidate, Walter Mondale, was a drag on other Democrats. In contrast, 1990 had no presidential race, and the country as well as the state were trending toward the Democrats. The party not only gained seats in the U.S. Congress but picked up 7 seats in the N.C. House (and lost only 1 in the N.C. Senate). Most white party leaders worked for Gantt, though many of them would have preferred if Easley or Hunt had been the nominee. Large numbers of Democrats had defected from Ingram when he ran against Helms in 1978. When Hunt ran in 1984, blood overflowed from the bitter gubernatorial primary. By 1990, beating Helms had become a passion among active Democratic Party members.

Lauch Faircloth, one of the few high-profile Democratic defectors, had long been associated with the party's progressive wing. Faircloth had come to like Helms and was still bitter about what he considered a betrayal by Sanford and other establishment Democrats in 1986, when Faircloth had wanted to run for senator but was pushed aside by Sanford. Other prominent former Democrats, especially erstwhile legislators, quietly backed Helms, but most of them had defected from party candidates on earlier occasions. Overall, however, the party leadership was unified.

Helms took all three of the state's major geographic regions, winning nearly 52 percent of the vote in the coastal plain and piedmont and 56 percent in the mountains. However, Gantt ran better not only than Mondale but also than the 1988 Democratic presidential nominee, Michael Dukakis. Statewide, Gantt ran 5 percent better than Dukakis had in 1988: George H. W. Bush had won 54 percent in the coastal plain, 59 percent in the piedmont, and 61 percent in the mountains. Helms was decidedly weaker than Bush had been in the metropolitan counties: Bush did not take a majority of the vote in Durham County (45.8 percent) but easily prevailed in Forsyth (59.2 percent), Guilford (56.7 percent), Mecklenburg (59.6 percent), and Wake (57.1 percent). In 1990, however, Helms came out ahead only in Forsyth County, where he won 51.9 percent of the vote; his second-best showing was in Guilford (47.4 percent). He was routed in Mecklenburg, where he garnered only 41.8 percent and even in his own home county, Wake, where he received only 43.7 percent of the vote. These counties were among the state's most cosmopolitan and had grown substantially since Helms was first elected in 1972. Mecklenburg and Wake now had many white migrants from northern states. The most urban counties could not control statewide election outcomes, but liberals hoped that the urban trend provided a hint about where the state would head in the future.

The key to Gantt's loss, as with Hunt's earlier loss to Helms, was a poor showing among white voters in smaller cities and rural areas. In Gantt's case, the defection of whites in eastern North Carolina and the northeastern piedmont—counties where blacks comprised a large part of the population—was massive. No Democratic candidates except Hubert Humphrey in 1968 and George McGovern in 1972 had run so poorly among whites in these counties. In most of the coastal plain counties, where Democrats were a big majority of the registered voters, Gantt

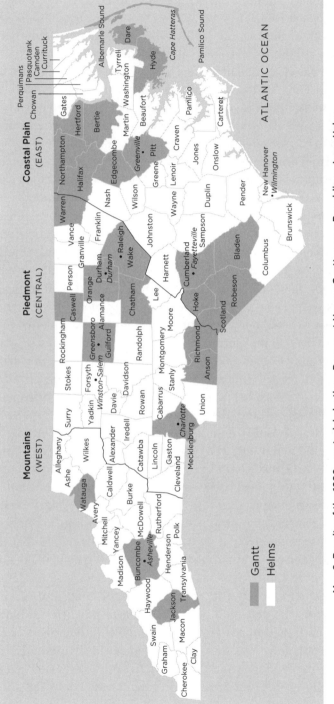

**Map 8. Results of the 1990 senatorial election—Democrat Harvey Gantt versus Republican Jesse Helms**

polled below 25 percent of the white vote. The pattern was the same in all the counties of the rural northeast piedmont near the Virginia border. Because of near unanimous support from blacks, Gantt still carried some of these counties, but he did not receive the margins needed for a state-wide victory.[17]

Gantt's weakness among whites in counties that were more than one-third African American conforms to a thesis outlined by V. O. Key Jr. in his 1949 book, *Southern Politics in State and Nation*. Key said that whites in counties with a large black presence represented a bedrock of opposition to racial equality.[18] By the time Key died in 1963, civil rights for blacks had become the most burning American domestic political issue. Candidates defending racial segregation—George Wallace of Alabama in 1962 and I. Beverly Lake of North Carolina in 1960—had run best among whites in heavily black counties, who most feared any change in the racial status quo.

By 1990, whites, including segregationists of the past, favored (or at least tolerated) desegregated public facilities and voting rights for blacks. However, not all of those white voters were comfortable with the pace of change. Helms's 1990 campaign—or its symbolism—aroused old animosities. Many coastal and northeast piedmont whites were enthusiastic Jessecrats—Democrats who admired Helms's bold attacks on Washington bureaucrats, the late Martin Luther King Jr., and the current gay rights movement. Voting for Helms had become their habit.

Like Hunt six years earlier, Gantt did poorly among whites in the socially conservative small-town industrial belt of the western piedmont, the emerging Republican spine. The "white hands ad" had been aimed at economically insecure white voters who feared losing their industrial jobs. Earlier in the campaign, many of those voters had not seemed energized, but in the end, they voted in large enough numbers to provide Helms a big victory in the textile belt.

Despite Gantt's loss, black political activists hoped to break the color line in other spheres. It was time to draw new congressional districts.

### EARLY 1990S CONGRESSIONAL REDISTRICTING: THE POLITICAL QUAGMIRE

Though U.S. census data are used for many purposes, the constitutional requirement for a census every ten years was initially for the purpose of determining how many members each state would elect to the U.S. House of Representatives. North Carolina had dropped from twelve to eleven seats after the 1960 census, though it remained the tenth-largest state.

From 1980 to 1990, its population grew from 5,881,766 to 6,628,637, enough to regain that seat. The biggest population gains were in areas fanning out from Charlotte and Raleigh. In general, the urban crescent—the area that follows Interstate 85—had grown faster than the state average. Other parts of the state, aside from those on the outer fringes of metropolitan areas, homes of military bases, resort areas, and college towns, had grown modestly or not at all. Even without the additional seat in Congress, the state legislature would have needed to reshape congressional districts to reflect population shifts. While any state welcomes a gain in U.S. House seats, the process of redrawing districts can be a painful one for rural counties that feel more and more overshadowed by the big cities.

In 1991, race emerged as the dominant issue in the redistricting process. Urban black political leaders and many black voters believed that minorities were underrepresented in Congress and the state legislature and that blacks—22 percent of the state's population in 1990—should have the opportunity to win one or ideally two seats in the state's U.S. House delegation. Not since George White left Congress in early 1901 had a black North Carolinian sat in the U.S. House. Mickey Michaux had come close in 1982, only to lose in the Democratic runoff primary.[19] Pressure had subsequently mounted for the creation of a majority-black district. Race, not the rural-urban divide, now dominated the politics of reapportionment.

On the surface, the creation of even one minority district faced obstacles. Each new congressional district would need roughly 552,000 residents. Most of the country's existing majority-black districts had been in large metropolitan areas with concentrated black populations—Chicago, Los Angeles, Philadelphia, and Atlanta. North Carolina lacked a city center of such magnitude. Blacks were concentrated in midsize cities—Charlotte, Durham, Greensboro, Raleigh, Winston-Salem. The counties with the highest percentages of African American residents were located mainly in the central and northern coastal plain or the Virginia border region of the northeast piedmont. But most of them were adjacent to other small counties with white majorities. Even if counties were split between districts, a practice contrary to tradition in North Carolina (but supported by federal courts and the U.S. Justice Department), the creation of a compact majority-black district by combining rural counties seemed impossible.

Another roadblock was formed by the state legislature's principal political goal of protecting sitting members of Congress, especially Democrats. All of the incumbent Democrats had moderate to liberal voting records. If large numbers of blacks were removed from their districts—a necessity in attempting to create a majority- or near-majority-black district—conservative Republicans might defeat Democratic incumbents. Majorities of whites had already voted for Republican Nixon in 1972, Reagan in 1980 and 1984, and Bush in 1988. Democratic representatives in overwhelmingly white districts would face a dilemma: If they adhered to their centrist mildly progressive voting records, they would be out of sync with the views of their more heavily white new constituencies. If they moved to the political right, the Democratic House leadership in Washington and local Democrats would be irritated. Moreover, even sharp moves to the right might not pacify Republican-trending white voters in the districts.[20]

Nor were the sitting white Democrats eager to have districts that were 40 or 45 percent black, a more realistic goal than a true black majority. (Tim Valentine's Second District had been at this level, and Walter Jones Sr.'s First District was close.) Near-majority-black districts could make the incumbent more vulnerable to a challenge from an African American candidate in the Democratic primary, where African Americans would likely cast a higher percentage of the votes than in a general election. The ideal situation from the standpoint of a white Democrat in eastern North Carolina—and elsewhere in the state where possible—was a district of 30–35 percent black and 65–70 percent white, the perfect blend to protect a mildly progressive centrist Democrat on both the left and right flanks.

The rumored retirement of two incumbents provided some flexibility in drawing districts. For several years, First District Representative Jones had considered retiring for health reasons. Second District Representative Valentine was in better health but had contemplated returning to Nash County. But whatever their decisions, the pent-up demand for more minority representation would not die. Pressure for change intensified as civil rights advocates promoting greater black power gained unlikely allies in Washington—the Bush administration Justice Department. The new alliance made political sense. Civil rights organizations such as the National Association for the Advancement of Colored People wanted more minorities in Congress. The Civil Rights Division of the U.S. Justice Department, now Republican-dominated at its top levels, wanted more majority-black districts because concentrating blacks would leave adjoining districts whiter and consequently more Republican, resulting in an overall benefit to the party.

This approach represented a new twist on an old strategy. In the 1880s and 1890s, the conservative white Democrats who dominated the North Carolina legislature had created a district extending from the northeast piedmont to the central coastal plain, where blacks (then Republicans) were a majority of the population—the district known as the Black Second. The legislature sought to make other districts whiter and more Democratic (conservative). The members of the Bush Justice Department, unlike the 1880s North Carolina legislature, accepted the concept of racial equality, and (or perhaps because) they saw it creating an opening for Republican advances. They would find an ally in the Voting Rights Act of 1965.

Congress had overwhelmingly adopted the Voting Rights Act despite the opposition of the entire North Carolina delegation. The measure had been designed to remedy the long-standing problem of the southern states' attempts to bar or to discourage black voter registration. The act had banned literacy tests in six southern states and parts of North Carolina on the grounds that the literacy tests were used to keep blacks from registering regardless of whether they could read and write (a provision Congress later extended to cover the entire United States).

Under Section 5 of the 1965 act, known as the preclearance provision, local and state jurisdictions covered by the act were required to secure the approval of the U.S. attorney general or the U.S. District Court for the District of Columbia before implementing any new voting or election law. Over time, the U.S. Justice Department interpreted the preclearance provision as covering the drawing of electoral district boundaries, including district lines for congressional districts, state legislative districts, and city council wards, and city proposals to annex territory. However, the federal courts rendered conflicting decisions on precisely what constituted discrimination or the "dilution" of minority voting under Section 5.[21]

Congress grappled with the issue in 1982, when it debated the extension of the Voting Rights Act. Congress ultimately extended the act for another twenty-five years. In 1982, Congress dealt with the electoral district issue by amending Section 2 of the Act. Under the new language, state or local jurisdictions were, as a precondition for approval of election changes, required to show that they had not discriminated in the past ten years and that they had made efforts to improve their rates of minority voting. Congress also adopted a "results standard," stating in Section 2 that a violation had occurred when the "totality of circumstances" indicated that the election process was not equally open to all voters regardless of race and that minorities had less opportunity than other voters to participate and to elect representatives of their choice. The Senate Judiciary Committee report listed factors that might suggest a violation of Section 2: a history of polarized voting (most blacks voting for one candidate and most whites for another candidate); the degree to which minorities were denied access to the slating process (the selection of party nominees); a history of racist political campaigns; and a few or no minorities having been elected to office from the area in question.[22]

One U.S. Supreme Court case from several years earlier, although it dealt with seats in the N.C. House and Senate, provided a degree of guidance for congressional redistricting. Plaintiffs in *Thornburg vs. Gingles* (1986) argued that seven North Carolina legislative districts diluted black voter strength and consequently violated Section 2 of the Voting Rights Act. In an opinion invalidating six of the seven districts, the Court outlined three standards for determining whether racial voter dilution had occurred. Two of these standards appeared applicable to congressional redistricting: (1) a racial minority must show that it is politically cohesive and (2) that the majority (whites in this case) vote as a bloc against the minority's preferred candidate.[23]

After months of contentious debate and legal maneuvering that involved the state legislature, state attorney general's office, and U.S. Justice Department, the state legislature adopted a new congressional district map that gave African Americans a good shot at winning in two districts: the irregularly shaped First, which incorporated heavily minority areas across a wide swath of the coastal plain and northeast piedmont, and the Twelfth, which extended from Durham to Gastonia. The Twelfth, one of the most oddly shaped districts in American history, roughly followed Interstate 85 and portions of Interstate 40 with bulges in predominantly black areas along the way.

Robinson Everett, the erudite and politically moderate attorney and Duke law professor who had fought the plan tooth and nail through the federal courts, called it "political pornography."[24] Everett would continue his efforts against racial gerrymandering, but for the moment the proponents of black-majority districts had the upper hand. The new districts were crudely drawn and may have violated the spirit of the U.S. Constitution, but civil rights advocates saw such districts as justified after a century of deliberate and at times brutal suppression of blacks' attempts to exercise their citizenship rights.

In February 1992, the Justice Department formally approved the new plan. Forty-three percent of the state's blacks lived in either the First or the Twelfth District. Blacks seemed certain to win in the Twelfth and to have a good shot at winning the First. State Republicans criticized the new plan, which, despite isolating many blacks into two districts, had tried to protect sitting Democrats as best it could. (Jones had already decided to retire.) State-level Republicans and some Democrats, turned off by what they saw as the raw politics of the plan, later embarked on an extended court battle.

But the new map was ready to go for the upcoming 1992 primaries and general election.[25]

Melvin Watt, Harvey Gantt's campaign manager in 1990 and a Yale-educated lawyer, had connections with both the civil rights movement and the Charlotte power structure. He secured the Twelfth District nomination in 1992, after facing competition from a figure probably better known statewide, Mickey Michaux of Durham, the longtime legislator who had almost won the former Second District seat in 1982. Larry Little, a Black Power and civil rights advocate active in Winston-Salem politics, also ran. Watt, propelled by heavy support from Charlotte, the district's largest city, won with 47 percent of the vote to Michaux's 28 percent and Little's 15 percent. In 1989, North Carolina law had been changed in response to civil rights advocates, including Michaux, and the U.S. Justice Department. If the top finisher in a primary had more than 40 percent of the vote, he or she automatically became the nominee.

The race in the rural First District was a spirited affair. Multiple African American candidates threw their hats into the ring, the best known of whom was Eva Clayton of Warren County. She had been a member of the Warren County Board of Commissioners since 1982 and had served as its chair during much of this period. Clayton's husband was a lawyer in Warrenton. Eva Clayton had worked with Floyd McKissick of the Congress of Racial Equality in an effort to build the new black town of Soul City in Warren County, though that project never reached fruition. Active in local antipoverty efforts, she had served as the assistant secretary of administration for community development in 1977–81 under the Hunt administration.[26]

Her leading opponent in the 1992 Democratic primary was Walter Jones Jr., the son of the retiring member of Congress from the First District (who died in September 1992). The younger Jones was a veteran state legislator from Pitt County and like his father a political moderate. In the first primary, Jones defeated Clayton, taking 38 percent of the vote to her 31 percent. But in the runoff primary, the white Jones faced the same challenge that blacks had faced in earlier elections. Candidates of one race—in this case blacks—united to support the candidate of their race over the candidate of another race. Eva Clayton prevailed in the runoff, 55 percent to 45 percent.

### 1992: A PARTISAN STANDOFF

At the beginning of 1992, George H. W. Bush was the odds-on favorite for reelection, though his standing in the polls had declined from its lofty level in the spring of 1991—the highest that any president had experienced. The Democratic field seemed weak after New York governor Mario Cuomo and other heavyweights decided not to seek the nomination. By late 1991, the forty-five-year-old governor of Arkansas, Bill Clinton, who had held that post for more than a decade, emerged as the Democratic front-runner. He never lost that status despite rumors of adultery, draft evasion during the Vietnam War era, and youthful experimentation with illegal drugs. Clinton was attractive, an able speaker, and a political centrist who blended liberal and conservative ideas. In Arkansas, he had been adept at building biracial coalitions, a necessity for any southern Democratic governor. Clinton knew how to appeal to swing voters across the country and offered the hope that some southern states might come back into the Democratic column. In 1992, North Carolina had moved its presidential primary from March back to May so that it would come at the same time as the state's other primaries and consequently save money. Even before Clinton won the North Carolina Democratic primary, he was the presumptive nominee.[27]

Like most modern political conventions, the 1992 Democratic National Convention was a public relations extravaganza on behalf of the certain nominee—Bill Clinton. Clinton tapped Tennessee senator Al Gore, a 1988 contender for the presidential nomination, as his running mate. Gore, a moderate liberal, had an aloof bearing but possessed a keen intellect. The choice was popular with North Carolina Democrats, who hoped a next-door neighbor would help the party's ticket win the state.

The Republicans nominated Bush for a second term in August. Having made a pledge at the 1988 convention—"Read my lips, no new taxes!"—Bush had alienated many Republicans and conservatives when he later approved new taxes as part of a spending compromise with the congressional Democrats.

The country's mood had turned sour during a mild economic recession in 1992, though the mood might have been bleaker than the actual economic conditions merited. Then came Texan H. Ross Perot, the rich, short, and colorful entrepreneur who seemed frank and unadorned. Perot called for balanced budgets and a renewal of the national spirit. He directed his wrath at Bush, whom he blamed for the national malady. Perot secured a ballot position in every state and made his biggest splash in the late winter, spring, and early summer. Polls showed him competitive in a three-way race. Near convention time, Perot withdrew from the race and gave Clinton a left-handed endorsement, saying the Democrats "had their act together." Perot remained on the ballot and left open the option of resuming an active candidacy. But he had already inflicted heavy damage on

Bush—irreparable damage, as it turned out.[28] Perot resumed his campaign on September 30.

There was little doubt about the identity of Democratic nominees for top North Carolina offices in November. Terry Sanford, who would be seventy-five at the time of the 1992 election, hoped for a second Senate term. Polls suggested that he had a good chance of winning reelection. Sanford was popular among his fellow senators and, despite his liberal record, retained an element of goodwill in North Carolina. Helms remained uncomfortable with his longtime nemesis occupying North Carolina's other Senate seat, but the two old warriors usually were civil to one another.

The Congressional Club sought a candidate to oppose Sanford. When Campbell University president Norman Wiggins declined to run, Congressional Club strategist Tom Ellis made overtures to Lauch Faircloth. Soon thereafter, Ellis asked Faircloth to challenge Sanford.[29] With the promise of Congressional Club backing, Faircloth agreed to run against his former friend. Faircloth defeated Charlotte mayor Sue Myrick in the Republican primary and readied for a campaign targeting Sanford's liberalism.

Jim Hunt announced that he would run for governor. His defeat by Helms eight years earlier had been shattering: If Hunt had won, he might have occupied the same sort of national position as Bill Clinton did in 1992. Twenty-two years after that bruising senatorial election, Hunt still found it a difficult subject to talk about. Asked about the loss in a 2006 interview, he looked pained and responded, "I was devastated. On the Monday morning after the inauguration [of Jim Martin as governor in January 1985], I went to my new law office. The phone did not ring all morning. Now that really hurt." Hunt said that he agonized over his defeat for months, thinking it to have been an unfair outcome. But over a period of time, he became more philosophical, realizing that life had to go on. As a partner in Poyner and Spruill, a Raleigh law firm, he soon was making money, by far the most he had made during his life. But he also remained active in state civic affairs and in national as well as state Democratic activities.[30]

Though he had not yet turned fifty, Hunt had assumed the role of elder statesman, almost as much of a ball of fire as he had been years before. But the change of lifestyle did give him an opportunity to think and reflect as he spent much time on his Rock Ridge farm and commuting from Rock Ridge to Raleigh. Hunt worked hard for the Democratic ticket in 1986, 1988, and 1990 and stayed in close touch with the state's corporate leaders. As a private citizen, Hunt continued his interest in education. He might have achieved more affection and respect during those years than he had gained as governor. Ironically, Hunt's loss to Helms probably widened his long-term impact on North Carolina politics, government, and public policy.

After eight years, Martin was constitutionally ineligible for reelection, and he had already signaled that he was tired of politics.[31] But for the mandated limit, he would have been the Republicans' best bet for victory. Democrats yearned to recapture the governor's office and feared that Republican lieutenant governor Jim Gardner would be hard to beat. Hunt was the only Democrat who would have an edge over Gardner, and by the early 1990s, the former governor was ready to return to office.

Hunt first had to win the Democratic primary, where his strongest challenger was Attorney General Lacy Thornburg, a credible candidate who, like his predecessors Robert Morgan and Rufus Edmisten, had been a people's champion in the office. But Thornburg was no match for Hunt, who took 65 percent of the vote and ninety-six of the state's one hundred counties.

Gardner prepared for battle. For years he had been controversial within his own political party. Gardner was brash and unwilling to step aside for others. His political career, like his business career, had been an up-and-down affair.[32] But more and more, the Republican Party unified around him as Martin's heir apparent. Gardner's election to the lieutenant governorship in 1988 had been a big breakthrough for the party. He was a good fund-raiser. Nevertheless, ill feeling lingered from the mean-spirited 1972 Holshouser-Gardner gubernatorial primary, in which pro-Holshouser establishment Republicans blamed Gardner for the negative tone. Nor had old-time Republicans forgotten Gardner's on-and-off flirtation with the 1968 presidential candidacy of George Wallace when Gardner was the GOP standard-bearer in the gubernatorial race. Despite such breaches of etiquette within the party, Gardner had paid his dues. He had campaigned tirelessly at party rallies, served a term in Congress, and run a competitive race for governor. He had also supported the Martin administration in its battles with a Democratic legislature except when Martin proposed a tax increase. And bucking Martin in that instance enhanced Gardner's claim to be the logical nominee of a generally antitax party.

The Hunt-Gardner matchup was not a genteel affair. The stakes were high for both candidates. For Hunt, this election could provide redemption, and he thought it was an opportunity to complete the tasks he had begun in the 1970s—state economic and educational development. For Gardner, the governorship would be the culmination of a long and uneven political career—the achievement of a goal that had seemed within his grasp back in 1968. Like Hunt, Gardner spoke of the need for economic development and a favorable business climate. But many voters had a better notion of how Hunt would perform as governor. This time, both Hunt and Gardner campaigned for their parties' presidential candidates, Clinton and Bush. A month before the election, Hunt was the favorite to win the governor's race and Sanford the favorite in the U.S. Senate race.

The bombshell of the 1992 senatorial campaign in North Carolina came less than a month before the election. Doctors at the Duke Medical Center advised Senator Sanford that he needed immediate open-heart surgery. It could not wait until after the election. The public was not told the full story, but Sanford had an infected heart valve, and his life was in peril. Among the first to send get-well wishes was his opponent, Faircloth. The dynamics of the contest changed as on-the-fence voters expressed doubt about Sanford's stamina.[33] After mid-October, Faircloth was the slight favorite in the race even though a recuperating Sanford returned to the campaign trail on a limited schedule just before the election.

On November 3, the North Carolina winners were Republicans Bush and Faircloth and Democrat Hunt. The state's delegation to the U.S. House of Representatives, which had grown from eleven to twelve, now would have eight Democrats and four Republicans. As expected, two African Americans—Eva Clayton in the First District and Melvin Watt in the Twelfth—won the two newly drawn black-majority districts. The Democrats gained three seats in the N.C. Senate for a 39–11 majority, while the Republicans gained 3 seats in the N.C. House, leaving the Democrats with a 78–42 advantage. There had been no fundamental shift in the partisan balance. But the election did provide hints about where the state and country might be headed. It was also the first time since the Civil War that a Democrat had won the presidency without North Carolina's electoral votes.

The big story in the national election was Clinton's victory. He won a plurality of the national popular vote—43 percent, compared to 37 percent for Bush and an impressive 19 percent for Perot. Bush's total was the second-lowest percentage garnered by any major-party presidential candidate in the twentieth century. All the polling data suggested that Perot voters would have split evenly between Clinton and Bush if Perot had not reentered, though some of them would have still voted for Perot or not voted at all.

Clinton won an electoral vote landslide over Bush, 370–168. Perot won no state and consequently no electoral votes. Clinton built his victory on his strength in the Northeast, Upper Midwest, and the Far West, with one of his strongest showings coming in California, which had voted Republican in eight of the previous nine presidential elections. In the South, the Clinton-Gore ticket won Arkansas (Clinton's home state), Tennessee (Gore's home state), Louisiana, and Georgia. The only state that the Clinton campaign had targeted for victory but lost was North Carolina.[34] Bush led in the state with 1,134,661 votes (43 percent) followed by Clinton with 1,114,043 (just under 43 percent) and Perot with 357,864 (14 percent). Clinton had a tiny lead in North Carolina's Election Day exit polling. In the twentieth century, North Carolina had been closer only in the election of 1956, when Democrat Adlai Stevenson edged out Republican Dwight Eisenhower. Support for both Bush and Clinton was evenly spread across the state, with Clinton narrowly leading in the coastal plain and Bush narrowly leading in the mountains. Bush's modest 36,000-vote lead in the piedmont provided his victory margin. Clinton, however, won the Durham, Greensboro, and Raleigh areas. He also took the central cities of Charlotte and Winston-Salem but lost their suburban areas and hence the counties of Mecklenburg and Forsyth.

Winning the U.S. Senate race with 50 percent of the votes cast to Sanford's 46 percent (and 4 percent for various minor party candidates), Faircloth did best in historically Republican mountain counties and in the conservative small-town industrial belt of the piedmont. Faircloth swept most midsized cities of the coastal plain. Sanford, however, led narrowly in the coastal plain at large as a consequence of his strength in rural counties, especially those with large black populations. While Faircloth was more outspokenly conservative than in the past, ideology was not the key to the outcome. The party bases stuck with their candidates—Republicans and conservatives for Faircloth, Democrats and liberals for Sanford. Nor was Sanford's liberal voting record crucial in the end. However, Sanford was the only member of the North Carolina congressional delegation to oppose the 1991 resolution that authorized President Bush to send troops to Kuwait and Iraq. The ensuing Persian Gulf War had been quick and popular, but it was likely Sanford's aging heart that took him from the Senate.

Hunt received 1,368,246 votes (52 percent) for governor. Gardner trailed with 1,121,955 votes (43 percent), and Libertarian Scott McLaughlin had 104,983 votes (4 percent). Hunt had a solid victory, even if his support remained below his levels of 1976 and 1980. Hunt led Gardner in all major regions of the state, narrowly in the mountains and solidly in the piedmont and coastal plain. Hunt easily carried every major metropolitan area but lost the midsize towns of the industrial western piedmont—Gastonia, Hickory, Kannapolis, and Salisbury.

Hunt was poised to begin an unprecedented third four-year term as governor and was likely already eyeing a fourth. If the losses of Clinton and

Sanford had little impact on the races of state-level Democrats, Hunt's position at the top of the state ticket surely redounded to the benefit of his party. Hunt had solid Democratic majorities in both houses of the state legislature, and he had campaigned for a lot of these Democrats, both veterans and newcomers. While tensions would always exist between the governor and the legislature, they were now the lowest in recent memory. Former lieutenant governor Jimmy Green, who had been a constant irritant for Hunt in the 1977–85 period, had retired from politics and was bogged down in legal difficulties stemming from his longtime operation of a tobacco warehouse.[35]

Hunt solidified his ties with the business leaders who mattered the most in building the modern North Carolina economy—bankers, utility executives, developers, and computer and software magnates. At this point, Hunt was not a pioneer in the mold of his political heroes Kerr Scott and Terry Sanford, but no governor since O. Max Gardner had been as adept at exercising the levers of power. Hunt saw himself as a governor for the demands and realities of the rapidly approaching new century, not the 1940s or the 1960s.

### EARTHQUAKE ON A BLUE MOON

General elections featuring no race for president, U.S. senator, or governor are called blue moon elections, taken from the expression "once in a blue moon," meaning a rare occurrence. But such elections are hardly as rare as their name implies. North Carolina had had blue moon elections in 1970 and 1982, and another was coming up in 1994. Normally, the blue moons had been the least consequential of elections. The stakes were lower, the campaign was less fervent, and the voter turnout was light. Early in 1994, there was little reason to expect a break from the past pattern.

But as the 1994 elections approached, discontent was in the air. Republicans saw an opportunity to recover from setbacks of the early 1990s. Republican U.S. House of Representatives minority leader Newt Gingrich and his allies drew up a pact they called the Contract with America, pledging that if they won the congressional elections, they would lower taxes and reduce the size of government, completing the campaign begun by Ronald Reagan in the 1980s.[36] Economic conservatives had been displeased with former president George H. W. Bush and his compromises with Democrats, especially the tax increase. They hoped to undo the damage and to stop Clinton in his tracks.

For the most part, social conservatives had stuck with Bush, applauding his stands against abortion and for the death penalty. Many of them loathed Clinton. One of Clinton's early announcements, probably speeded up by inquiries from the media, was a new policy that permitted gays to enlist in the U.S. military. Though Clinton had promised this change during the campaign, the pledge did not gain a lot of attention until the new executive order was announced. The reaction was swift and negative—from segments of the military, conservative talk show hosts, and the religious Right. Congress attempted to undo Clinton's order. Ultimately, a compromise known as "Don't Ask, Don't Tell" enabled gays who kept their sexual preference under wraps to serve in the military.

If Clinton enraged the Right, he disappointed much of the Left. His most publicized campaign pledge was to provide health care insurance for all Americans, a program involving government mandates, insurance company participation, and government subsidies. First Lady Hillary Rodham Clinton chaired the health care task force. When it failed to gain traction, partly as a consequence of political miscalculations by the administration and partly as a consequence of a well-financed opposition campaign, liberals turned sour on Clinton. Disenchanted voters often sit out the next election.

Clinton's popularity eroded in North Carolina after his narrow 1992 loss there—a reflection of outrage over the idea of gays in the military and a general sense of moral decline. And as in the country at large, liberals and Democrats were not energized; however, Governor Hunt and top state Democratic officials remained popular. Their popularity was expected to rub off on the incumbent Democrats, at least those seeking to retain state and local offices. Hunt, however, had no spot on the ballot in this blue moon election. His presence might have provided a shield at least for state-level Democratic candidates.

Just after dark, the tremors began in North Carolina and across much of the country. For the first time since the 1952 election, the Republicans became the majority party in the U.S. House of Representatives, with 230 seats to the Democrats' 204. The Republican Party also won a majority in the U.S. Senate, 53–47. While the Republicans had controlled the Senate for the first six years of the Reagan administration (1981–86), their 1994 senatorial victory was a stunning reversal of the 57–43 Democratic advantage for the first two years of Bill Clinton's term.

The North Carolina House delegation went from eight Democrats and four Republicans to eight Republicans and four Democrats: David Funderburk over Richard Moore in the Second District, Richard Burr over A. P. "Sandy" Sands in the Fifth, Walter B. Jones over Martin Lancaster in the Third, and Fred Heineman over David Price in the Fourth. Republicans Funderburk, Burr, and Jones won with votes to spare. Heineman, whose accent betrayed his New York roots, squeaked by Price 77,773–76,558. Two surviving Democrats, Charlie Rose of the Seventh District and Bill Hefner of the Eighth, won by margins under 5 percent. Meanwhile, Helms had two years left in his Senate term, while Faircloth had four years remaining.[37]

The outcome of the N.C. House of Representatives election marked an equally dramatic turn in state party fortunes. The Republicans won a 68–52 House majority. Even a 61–59 Republican edge would have constituted a major upset and a shift in the balance of legislative power. Suddenly, top Republicans emerged as key House leaders: Harold Brubaker of Randolph County as Speaker, Leo Daughtry of Johnston County as majority leader, and Carolyn Russell of Wayne County as Speaker pro tem. Democrats barely managed to retain a 26–24 majority in the N.C. Senate, a dramatic fall from their 39–11 position going into the race. Had there been a 25–25 tie, Democrats would have maintained de facto control, as the Democratic lieutenant governor Dennis Wicker had the constitutional authority to break ties. For the first time in the century, the Republican Party was entitled to choose a majority of members on all House committees. Not since the Republican-Populist coalition after the 1894 and 1896 elections had the Republicans been in such a strong position at the beginning of a legislative session. The House of Representatives revolt of 1989 and subsequent brief party coalition had been fueled in part by Republican votes, but insurgent Democrats provided much of the impetus.

The state Republicans stressed what they saw as a need for lower taxes to promote the economy. Most of their candidates supported both the public schools and the university system, but they advocated increased efficiency. Like Hunt, Republicans backed accountability in the school system with mandated tests to measure the results. The Republican Party also presented itself as an agent of change—a popular theme for those out of power since the advent of democracy. Over the years, North Carolina Republicans had portrayed the state Democrats as the tired, worn-out party, representing the status quo. Accusations intermittently arose—sometimes veiled, at other times openly expressed—that the Democrats perpetuated a climate of corruption, in which big contracts went to companies in cahoots with the party and bags of money were passed out to influence votes on the county level. These charges often lacked specificity and were whispered rather than leveled directly, but many voters suspected that the Republicans' accusations contained at least an element of truth.[38] Voters might still like Governor Hunt or the legendary Democratic commissioner of agriculture, Jim Graham, but nevertheless favor a shake-up in Raleigh.

For all the local concerns, the big shift in North Carolina also reflected the national climate: distaste—temporary for some voters—for President

Clinton, the mobilization of both religious and antitax conservatives, and the relative apathy of pro-Democratic liberals, including black voters. In 1994, no state broke from its partisan moorings more widely than North Carolina. The state was a leader in the revolt, not simply following the national trend. The Republican Party had achieved major breakthroughs in the elections of 1972, 1980, and 1984, but the magnitude of the victory was at least as great in the blue moon election of 1994.

## 1996: A SENSE OF DÉJÀ VU

Election sequels, like movie sequels, are rarely as gripping as the originals. Nor does great drama typically result when elections feature entrenched incumbents who are prohibitive favorites for reelection. The 1996 race for Jesse Helms's seat for the U.S. Senate would be a sequel with plot lines much like those seen in 1990. The 1996 races for governor of North Carolina and president of the United States featured incumbents—Hunt and Clinton—who had the advantages of organization and political inevitability. Clinton had problems in North Carolina, but polls conducted early in the year put him far in front of possible Republican candidates in the match for the national popular and electoral votes. The political chattering classes spoke of the incumbents' vulnerabilities, but only the boldest and most partisan seriously expected upsets.

Harvey Gantt had for years been building support for another run against Helms. White establishment Democrats, including Terry Sanford and some in the Hunt camp (though not Hunt himself, at least publicly), promoted the candidacy of former pharmaceutical executive Charles Sanders. Sanders was a respectable candidate—a physician, a talented business entrepreneur, and smart enough that he was probably Gantt's intellectual equal. Establishment Democrats believed that Gantt's time had passed and that a fresher—and white—contender would offer better prospects of beating Helms. Sanford-style Democrats and Helms strategists agreed on at least one point: the white moderate would stand a slightly better chance of ousting Helms than the more liberal and politically tarnished Gantt.[39]

But neither the Helms backers nor the white moderate progressive Sanford Democrats could control the primary outcome. By the 1990s, many old-time conservatives had stopped voting in Democratic primaries. In 1990, Gantt had demonstrated his appeal to the blacks and white liberals who now wielded enormous influence in Democratic Party primaries. Gantt supporters could also point to his strong showing against Helms in the 1990 general election. Gantt backers believed that he could fare better against Helms than Sanders by boosting turnout among blacks, the young, and liberals. The primary campaign was a gentle one, with attention focusing on which candidate might do better against Helms rather than on policy differences between Gantt and Sanders.

Gantt prevailed, 308,837–245,297. Gantt led Sanders in fifty-eight counties, including all of the more populous ones except for Buncombe (Asheville) and Onslow (Jacksonville–Camp Lejeune). The stage was set for a rerun of Gantt versus Helms.

Governor Hunt had seemed unscathed by the big Republican gains in the 1994 election. He subsequently outwitted Republican legislators by proposing even bigger tax cuts than they offered. The mid-1990s thus witnessed one of the biggest outbreaks of tax-cutting fever in North Carolina history, certainly a contrast to earlier and later days. Hunt, like Clinton at the same time, pushed for welfare reform to get people off the welfare rolls and into the workforce. The effort had tangible results, both for the welfare system and for Hunt's political image.[40]

In the United States as a whole, the mid- to late 1990s were one of the most prosperous periods ever. While the boom was driven in part by wild speculation in technology software—the "dot com" boom—a lot of new jobs were created by the American and North Carolina economies. This prosperity benefited Hunt, who could argue that his tax-cutting package had helped boost the economy.

Hunt's Republican opponent, Robin Hayes, was an heir of one of North Carolina's legendary industrial families of the old economy—the Cannons of Kannapolis. In the fall 1996 campaign, Hayes stressed his economic conservatism, but he found it difficult to combat Hunt on the big issues of the 1990s: tax cuts and welfare reform. Hayes tried to gain traction by stressing social conservatism—opposition to abortion and support for family values—and drew support from much of the organized, evangelical Christian Right. But for politically moderate evangelicals, Hunt was an attractive alternative to Hayes. As always, the incumbent governor attended church regularly and came across as pious. He blended his religious fervor with his enthusiasm for education and economic development. He was a known quantity and better than ever at making the voters feel good. Hayes later evolved into a skillful campaigner, but in 1996 he was inexperienced and often came across as stiff despite an appealing smile.

### HELMS VERSUS GANTT II

The 1996 Helms-Gantt race lacked the flair and venom of their 1990 matchup. Most campaign watchers expected another Helms victory, despite his fading health and polls showing a close election. Gantt's effort lacked the spark of his 1990 campaign, partly because he was already well known and no longer able to offer a fresh face and new ideas. His reputation had been hurt by bitter attacks from the Helms's forces in the scorched earth 1990 donnybrook.

Despite Helms's fragile health, the challenge of a campaign seemed to provide him with a second wind. Furthermore, the travails of illness and surgery had introduced Helms to a man who became one of his closest friends and a political counselor. Bertram (Bert) Coffer, an anesthesiologist, met Helms during preparations for his surgery in the 1980s. He went to Helms's Hayes-Barton house in Raleigh for a preoperative consultation. Coffer professed amazement at the humility shown by the senator and his wife, Dorothy. Coffer appreciated their warmth and seeming modesty as his own origins had been humble. His family's Lee County homestead had lacked creature comforts such as electricity until 1947, late even by rural North Carolina standards.[41]

After the surgery, Coffer offered to assist Helms in any future political endeavors. The doctor also organized anesthesiologists into a potent political force. When Helms was depressed or "in a funk," as Coffer put it, in a 1996 interview, the family would call in Coffer to help out. The senator had more trust in Coffer than in anyone else outside the immediate Helms family.[42] Coffer acted as treasurer of the Helms's campaign in 1996, but that title understated his role. Without Coffer's friendship and counsel on both personal and political matters, Helms's political career might have ended in 1996.

By 1996, Helms had broken with the Congressional Club over fund-raising techniques and other matters. Helms thought that club leaders were more interested in maintaining their power base than in helping his campaigns. For their part, club leaders believed that Helms neither understood nor appreciated modern campaign techniques. To a point, Helms and the Congressional Club had simply tired of one another. Helms and his Senate office staff knew that they required seasoned hands to run the campaign. For all his people skills and ability to connect, Helms still did not comprehend all of the nuts and bolts of putting together campaigns.[43]

The 1996 campaign had no trouble coming up with a talented team, including some staffers who had ties to the Congressional Club and earlier campaigns. Terry Edmondson, who had risen through the ranks of the Rocky Mount–based Hardee's fast-food chain, acted as campaign chair and a major fund-raiser. Edmondson had impeccable conservative connections, and he knew how to organize. David Tyson, a Congressional Club veteran who had broken with Carter Wrenn, was also a leading strategist in the 1996 campaign. Overall, the campaign lacked the strategic and organizational discipline of earlier ones run by the Congressional Club, but it was nonetheless effective.[44] Helms outspent Gantt, $14.59 million to $8 million.

Starting in late 1995, the campaign tried to soften Helms's image and to stress his record of constituency service. These ads continued into 1996, but as time passed Gantt came under fire both in attack ads and in Helms's speeches. One intriguing line of attack—given Helms's disdain for Bill Clinton—was the campaign's attempt to portray Helms's positions on key issues as closer to Clinton's than to Gantt's. Specifically, campaign ads noted that both Clinton and Helms favored capital punishment, while Gantt opposed it. Another ad said that Clinton and Helms opposed gay marriage and that Gantt did not. Their accusation on the capital punishment issue was true, but the one on gay marriage was dubious. Though Gantt opposed discriminating against homosexuals, he had not specifically endorsed the idea of gay marriage. But the point was made: Gantt was more liberal than Clinton and out of touch with conventional North Carolina values.

The "white hands ad" from 1990 was not resurrected. Helms's strategists did bring back the campaign ad claiming that Gantt had used his minority status to buy a share in a television station "under false pretenses" and then sold it at a huge profit to a white-owned company. The state Republican Party printed leaflets with the pictures of Gantt and the state's two black members of Congress, Eva Clayton and Mel Watt, suggesting that such a triumvirate in Washington would be extremist and dangerous. Helms's forces said the line of attack was fair, as the three were ultraliberal on policy matters. Critics saw it as a revival of a racist campaign technique used in the 1940s, 1950s, and 1960s against whites who were moderate on racial issues.[45]

The Gantt campaign was populist in rhetoric, if not always in spirit. But many working-class whites—people who benefited from programs such as social security and Medicare—generally turned a deaf ear to Gantt's message. They found Helms's social populism more appealing— patriotism, morality, and support for capital punishment. Gantt backed abortion rights, gay rights, and environmentalism. More and more, the old Roosevelt–New Deal Coalition seemed to have collapsed. Blue-collar white southerners—most of whom did not belong to labor unions—had favored Republicans Ronald Reagan in 1984 and George H. W. Bush in 1988. At the same time blacks, both middle class and working class, overwhelmingly supported candidates who were both economically and socially liberal. Many black voters were deeply religious and fundamentalist and opposed abortions and homosexual rights. However, they saw the

Democrats as the good guys on matters of fundamental human rights and equality. The civil rights movement had caused many whites to leave the Democratic Party but had drawn in many blacks. The struggle for equality and recognition was a holy crusade. In the southern United States, the old liberal dream of a coalition of the average people and poor rising up to overthrow the rule of the affluent had long had tough sledding.[46] Whether the old liberalism was even relevant to the South or nation of the late 1990s remained an open question.

## NOT CAUGHT IN A NATIONAL TIDE

With 49.2 percent of the national popular vote, Clinton won a near landslide electoral victory in 1996. Republican Robert Dole received 40.7 percent and independent Ross Perot 8.4 percent. Republicans and media critics such as commentator Rush Limbaugh gleefully pointed to Clinton's failure to win 50 percent, but such a feat is difficult to accomplish when a race features a strong third-party or independent candidate. (Ronald Reagan had won a bare majority, 50.7 percent, in his great victory of 1980.) Clinton's electoral vote lead over Dole was 379–159, with Dole's strength concentrated in the South, the Great Plains, and the northern Rockies. Dole took North Carolina with 1,225,938 votes (48.7 percent), while Clinton and Perot followed with 1,107,848 (44 percent) and 168,059 (6.7 percent), respectively. Despite trailing Dole in the cumulative electoral vote of the eleven states constituting the old Confederacy, Clinton narrowly led Dole in the region's popular vote, carrying Arkansas, Florida, Louisiana, and Tennessee. But North Carolina and Georgia were among the few states in which Clinton had done less well relative to the Republican candidate than he had in 1992. In North Carolina several factors were in play: Clinton's failure to target the state and advertise in 1996, resentment over the administration's antitobacco stand during its first term, and a Bible Belt mentality resenting Clinton's sexual peccadilloes and stands in favor of abortion rights and gay rights. Reflecting a gradual trend toward the Democrats and growing liberalism in a few urban centers, the counties of Mecklenburg (Charlotte) and Guilford (Greensboro) narrowly favored Clinton. These counties had voted Republican in many elections of the preceding three decades. However, Dole carried the broader piedmont region and the mountains. The coastal plain was almost evenly split, with a large black vote for Clinton canceling out a big white majority for Dole.

Helms defeated Gantt, 52.7 percent to 46.9 percent—a gain of a fraction of a percentage point for Helms over his 1990 vote. Some Perot backers and a few Dole backers voted for Gantt, but a few Clinton supporters voted for

Helms—likely economically populist white Democrats unwilling to vote for a black, but neither polling data nor raw election data prove that. Overall, Gantt received 66,627 more votes than did Clinton. As in 1972, 1978, and 1990, Helms led in all of the state's major geographic regions. As in 1990, Helms's leads were narrow in the piedmont and coastal plain, while Gantt led in the major urban areas of Asheville, Charlotte, Durham, Fayetteville, Greensboro, and Raleigh.

Many North Carolinians suspected that the election was Helms's last hurrah.[47] But as chair of the Senate Foreign Relations committee and a member of the majority party with great parliamentary skills, he had never been more influential in Washington. The Clinton administration would have to deal with him on a day-to-day basis. With no Republican governor to stand in his way, Helms was symbolically the leader of the North Carolina party. With physical and mental decline setting in, however, he would become more and more dependent on aides to handle the details.

The Gantt campaign had been competently run. He worked closely with the state Democratic Party organization, hoping to capitalize on the strength of the other leading Democratic candidate, Hunt, whom nearly all politicos thought was bound for a big reelection victory—perhaps as much as 60 percent of the vote. Though the governor had firm control over the Democratic Party machinery, he still had key people for whom he came first and the party second. So while Hunt had good words for Gantt and encouraged the party apparatus to support Gantt's campaign, he still maintained a safe distance. Hunt's top operatives knew their mission was to provide the governor with a huge reelection margin and would not let Gantt get in the way of that objective.

### 1996: A PARTISAN STANDOFF

Aside from the senatorial and the state presidential outcomes, Democrats found much to cheer in the 1996 election. Hunt beat Hayes for governor, 56 percent to 43 percent—not the 60 percent for which Hunt's campaign had hoped but nonetheless a powerful morale boost for the Democratic Party after its 1994 debacle. Partly reflecting Hunt's coattails and partly reflecting a recovery from their 1994 low point, the Democratic majority in the N.C. Senate grew from 26–24 to 29–21. The Republican majority in the N.C. House shrank from 68–52 to a tenuous 61–59. Hunt was now better positioned to exploit divisions simmering in the Republican ranks.

The state's congressional delegation changed from an 8–4 Republican majority to a 6–6 partisan tie. The Democrats won the rematch in the Fourth District—Raleigh, Chapel Hill, and southern Durham—where former representative David Price ousted freshman Fred Heineman, 76,558–72,773. Price, a professor, was a better match stylistically for the district than the rough-hewn Heineman. Price had been caught off-guard in 1994. Yet the 1996 rerun was a hard-fought battle, as a portion of the recent arrivals in Raleigh from the north related to Heineman's plainspoken style and antitax conservatism.

The other party change came in the conservative Second District, where in early 1995, Republican David Funderburk might have looked forward to a long tenure. Despite the district's historically Democratic roots, Funderburk's steadfastly conservative stands on both economic and moral issues were in tune with the voters' tastes. The Second District's boundaries encompassed such towns as Dunn, Rocky Mount, and Smithfield where both mainstream conservatism and fringe groups such as the Ku Klux Klan and the more upscale John Birch Society had thrived since the 1950s.

By the autumn of 1996, Funderburk faced two challenges, one over which he had no control, the other a dispute over who did have control. Longtime state legislator and then superintendent of public instruction Bob Etheridge won the Democratic nomination to oppose Funderburk. Etheridge, a political centrist with progressive tendencies, came across as a plain old country boy, but one who was passionately interested in educational opportunities as well as agriculture. Though more diplomatic and cautious, he possessed some of the populist spirit of the former governor Kerr Scott. Despite the Second's more recent swing to the right, Scott's brand of populism and rural road paving was part of the area's legacy, even decades after Scott's death. In North Carolina, a candidate who can combine the progressive and populist appeals is hard to beat.

Funderburk's integrity had been called into question in the aftermath of an October 21, 1995, incident in which Funderburk's Ford swerved across the center lane. A van driver in the correct lane lost control of his vehicle while trying to avoid Funderburk's car. The van tipped over, injuring its occupants. Funderburk and his wife, Betty, asserted that she had been driving the Ford, while witnesses and the State Highway Patrol officers at the scene said that Funderburk was driving. Regardless of who had the controls, the occupants of the Ford did not stop to check on the injured people in the van. Nor did Funderburk or his wife place a 911 emergency call on his cellular phone. Instead, he called his lawyer.

Funderburk initially was charged with lying to law officers and reckless driving. He and prosecutors struck a bargain in which he agreed to plead no contest to charges of reckless driving in exchange for the dropping of the lying charge. Public opinion held that the congressman was driving and that Betty Funderburk, playing the role of dutiful wife, was taking the blame to save her husband's political career. Having been elected as the candidate of morals and family values in 1994, David Funderburk was now a scarred man.[48] In the November 1996 election, Democrat Etheridge prevailed over Funderburk.

After six years of battle in the 1990s, the major political parties remained closely matched. However, a fundamental change had taken place in national politics. Between 1968 and 1988, the Republicans had won five out of six presidential elections, appearing to have a lock on the electoral college. Democrat Clinton's 1992 victory broke the lock. The electorate was closely divided. But after 1994, Republicans had success in Congress unparalleled since the 1920s.

What kept the Republicans in such a strong position was the transformation of the American South from overwhelmingly Democratic-leaning to Republican-leaning. Liberal Democrats believed the change reflected underlying racism. However, the shift had wide-ranging causes. Political scientists Earl Black and Merle Black have pointed to a variety of factors: the rise of middle-class society, concerns about taxes, religious values, and migration trends.[49]

In North Carolina, the Republicans maintained their edge in statewide contests for national office—president and U.S. Senator. More than in 1990, the Republicans were a force to be reckoned with in legislative politics. In the 1996 election, they maintained their majority in the N.C. House of Representatives, first won in 1994. But Governor Jim Hunt was the political captain, much as he had been in the late 1970s and early 1980s. A frail if reenergized Senator Jesse Helms would not be around forever. Neither political party seemed likely to gain a monopoly on North Carolina politics. A two-party system had arrived. But, as had long been true, the state's agenda was often driven more by people and factions than by parties.

The most intriguing political story in the 1990s involved Harvey Gantt, the man who could not quite win. Gantt's mobilization of black and white voters signaled that change was coming. That an African American could run a competitive U.S. Senate race against any white candidate, hinted that the state was no longer a captive of its history.

## CHAPTER ELEVEN

# Partisan Mix

Despite the Clinton interlude, conservative Republicans had driven much of the national political agenda since 1980. Beginning in 1994, the GOP controlled Congress. And the same year, Republicans had assumed control of the N.C. House of Representatives, long the domain of moderate to conservative Democrats. Republicans zealously pursued a tax-cutting agenda. Yet government continued to grow. From 1992 onward, the Democrats held the governorship. As the twentieth century ended, two figures towered above all others: Republican senator Jesse Helms and Democratic governor Jim Hunt. When Ronald Reagan was elected in 1980, Hunt and Helms had stood on the same lofty pedestals that they occupied two decades later, but they lacked immortality. Helms now had begun to fail both physically and mentally despite being at the zenith of his national power and influence. Hunt remained vigorous, but his long governorship was about to end.

Terry Sanford, who rivaled Helms and Hunt in long-term impact, died on April 18, 1998, at the age of eighty. He had recovered from open-heart surgery years earlier but succumbed to cancer of the esophagus and liver. The funeral at Duke University's neo-Gothic chapel was a huge affair, with luminaries from across the land. Helms was among the mourners, walking with a cane because of recent surgery. Afterward, Sanford was interred in the chapel crypt, close to Duke family members who had built a tobacco industry and had a university named for them.[1]

Sanford had been an innovative university president, a serious thinker, a mediocre U.S. Senator, and one of the greatest governors of the twentieth century. To the end, he was the dreamer who wanted to transform his bold ambitions into reality. Though conservatives derided him as a liberal, he was not a modern liberal who wanted government to expand in all spheres. Nor was he a populist, stirring up the people against big business, though he did work to improve the economic plight of the underdog. Few governors and innovators had worked so closely with corporations and their foundations as Sanford had. He was a progressive. Sanford believed that education and enlightenment were the keys to a better world. He rose above ideological battles.

## 1998 ELECTIONS

There was no national tide benefiting either political party in 1998. The Republicans maintained their 55–45 seat advantage in the U.S. Senate. The Democrats picked up three seats in the U.S. House, but Republicans held a 230–204 edge. Yet the absence of Republican gains meant that the Democrats defied the traditional pattern whereby the party occupying the White House loses seats in the midterm elections. North Carolina experienced a Democratic trend, with Democrats recapturing the N.C. House of Representatives after four years of Republican control. The Democrats built a 66–54 majority, a shift from the Republican advantages of 66–52 after the 1994 elections and 61–59 after the 1996 elections. Democrats strengthened their hold on the N.C. Senate, winning 35 of 50 seats, a big gain from their 26–24 edge after the 1994 elections and 29–21 advantage after the 1996 elections.

The state and national news media were most interested in Democrat John Edwards's victory over incumbent Republican U.S. senator Lauch Faircloth. While Faircloth had both financial and organizational support from the state and national Republican Parties, he lacked the cadre of loyal and enthusiastic supporters that had provided Helms's base in past elections. Much of the religious Right was lukewarm toward Faircloth. He usually voted with them, yet they suspected that he was not enthusiastic about their agenda. Privately, Faircloth had little taste for their deeply held pro-life beliefs. Moreover, from the start the old Congressional Club group and Faircloth had a bumpy relationship. Club members backed Faircloth in 1998, but their hearts were not in the campaign. National conservative activists, including Arthur Finkelstein, who had ties to the Congressional Club, did assist Faircloth.[2]

Business groups, skeptical of Edwards's trial lawyer background and his sugarcoated populism, put their apparatus to work for Faircloth. Faircloth had been a reliable vote for the agenda of the U.S. Chamber of Commerce and the National Association of Manufacturers. As a freshman senator, Faircloth had maintained an efficient constituent service operation and worked closely with Helms to bring federal money to the state. Faircloth and Helms had developed a mutual fondness over recent years. Both senators disliked Bill Clinton and worked to make life difficult for him. At North Carolina functions, Faircloth focused on the evils of the administration. He courted and quietly maintained friendly relations with a lot of his old Democratic buddies, but his attacks on the Clinton administration angered the Democratic base.[3] Edwards had the money to be competitive—his own money, trial lawyers' money, and the generosity of big Democratic contributors from the North and West. Before challenging Faircloth, Edwards had to prevail over a strong and able candidate in the Democratic primary, D. G. Martin. Martin, a lawyer from Charlotte and rising star in state politics, had better connections inside the party and had almost won election to Congress in a Republican-leaning district before moving to Chapel Hill to work with the university system. Edwards initially did not seem the most logical of choices. He was barely known in Democratic circles. A busy man dedicated to his law practice, Edwards had found time to vote in only about half of the recent elections. Sporting a hairstyle vaguely reminiscent of the early Beatles, Edwards now devoted his energy and money to winning the Democratic nomination. Born in South Carolina and raised in the mill town of Robbins, North Carolina, in Moore County, Edwards spoke eloquently of the challenges of a working-class background. His message resonated with members of the working and middle classes as well as with Democrats who saw him as a likely winner. Edwards prevailed over Martin in the Democratic primary, 277,468–149,049.

In the general election campaign, Edwards was as skillful on television as he had been in the courtroom. He had a ready smile and projected well before a camera. His smooth economic populist message resonated with working- and middle-class people. He offered no spellbinding oratory in the manner of Franklin Roosevelt or Charles Aycock but a conversational style more suited to modern television audiences. In a moving story, Edwards sometimes claimed that before his teenage son, Wade, was killed in a car accident, the boy had urged him to run for office.[4]

In the election, Edwards's solid 55 percent in the coastal plain and lead in all the major piedmont cities provided the votes he needed for a victory over Faircloth. While losing Republican-leaning counties, including Moore, Edwards kept Faircloth from running away in these areas. Statewide, Edwards outpolled Faircloth, 51 percent to 47 percent. Edwards's lead was cemented by pro-Democratic groups who voted at higher levels than usual. Voter News Service exit polling indicated that blacks comprised 20 percent of the 1998 electorate, slightly higher than the usual 16–19 percent.

Combining determination and patience, Edwards looked a good bet to rise in national Democratic politics. He was smart, photogenic, and articulate enough to maintain media attention. He seemed a good family man, and the heartrending story of his son's death would have appeal far beyond the North Carolina electorate.

When Edwards went to Washington in January 1999, the Clinton impeachment controversy was boiling. Clinton had lied to a grand jury as the country watched a juicy sex scandal unfold. Although it was almost certain that Clinton would win out in the end (a two-thirds vote in the Senate is required to remove a president from office), the Republican-controlled U.S. House of Representatives voted out articles of impeachment against Clinton. When the time came for senators to speak their piece at the official trial, one of the most effective—and a key player because of his legal background—was John Edwards, who spoke against Clinton's removal with the aplomb of a great lawyer calmly but passionately presenting his final summation to the jury. By this point, even Clinton's bitterest foes were resigned to defeat. He would stay in office. But Edwards had established himself as a man on the rise, a man of good sense and morality.

With the Edwards victory and other gains, 1998 rated as a good year for North Carolina's Democrats. A look at long-term trends provided a more disturbing picture, however. The Democrats had a state party registration edge over the Republicans, 2,394,935–1,540,836—a ratio near 1.5:1. But as recently as 1992, the Democratic advantage had been 2:1. And in 1976, it had been 3:1. Back in the 1960s, Democrats had advantages of more than 4:1.

Still more telling were the results of public opinion surveys in which voters were asked their party preferences. In 1968, when Republicans were making inroads in elections, 60 percent of North Carolinians called themselves Democrats and 21 percent Republicans. In 1998, 32 percent claimed the Democratic label and 36 percent the Republican. The number of self-proclaimed independents had gone from 19 percent to 22 percent.[5] The ranks of registered Democrats included many who were in fact independents and even a few Republican loyalists.

If Democrats were tempted to feel smug about their 35–15 advantage in the N.C. Senate and 66–54 advantage in the N.C. House of Representatives, they might look back to the 1978 elections, when their advantage had been 45–5 in the Senate and 106–14 in the House. Even after the Democratic debacle of 1972, the Democrats held a 35–15 advantage in the Senate—the same as in the "good" year of 1998—and an 85–35 advantage in the House.

The Republican gains over the last twenty years had come as socially or culturally conservative voters had abandoned the Democrats. Moreover, many economic conservatives, favoring low taxes and free markets, joined the Republican ranks. Despite Edwards's triumph, North Carolina, like most of the U.S. South, leaned Republican in national politics. And Democrats had reason to be nervous about state-level races.

### THE HIGHER EDUCATION CRUSADE

The competition between the Democrats and Republicans dominated news coverage in the aftermath of the 1998 elections and Clinton impeachment trial. Conservatives and liberals of various political stripes—religious fundamentalists and economic libertarians, environmentalists and civil libertarians—were spoiling for a fight. But other issues—not always ones splitting along ideological or partisan lines—faced North Carolina voters.

The biggest and most consequential issue in 2000 related to a proposed $3.1 billion bond issue to finance higher education capital improvements for universities and community colleges. Higher education operating expenditures had increased rapidly, yet campus physical facilities were woefully inadequate. Buildings and laboratories had begun to show signs of stress and neglect. Past presidents William Friday and C. D. Spangler Jr. were visionaries, and they had promoted academic programs and a university system more open to the masses. Faculty and staff salaries were a higher priority than capital needs. Administrators had recognized the need for a massive building and repair project but feared that it could not command popular support.

After arriving from California in 1998, the new university system president, Molly Broad, mounted a campaign for the huge capital spending boost. "As an outsider, I was naive enough to think that it might pass," Broad recalled in 2008 after she assumed the presidency of the American Council on Education in Washington, D.C.[6] The community college system president, Martin Lancaster, a former state legislator and former member of Congress, was also a key figure in the crusade. Community college administrators believed that their system had been shortchanged in the allocation of monies, squeezed between the university lobby and the K–12 lobbies. But now the community college and technical school interests found that an alliance with the state universities offered the best chance of generous funding to cope with the current inadequate physical plant and future growth.[7] Coupling passage of bonds for the university campuses and for the community colleges in a single vote by the public served the interests of the entire higher education sector.

The lobbying efforts of state universities and community colleges and allied interest groups paid handsome dividends in November 2000. The bond issue passed overwhelmingly, winning approval from 73 percent of voters overall, including majorities in all one hundred of North Carolina's counties. In eighteen counties, including Durham, Orange, Pitt, and Robeson, all of which had state universities, more than 80 percent of voters backed the bonds. The lowest level of support occurred in conservative, rural, and Republican Stanly County, where it received 60 percent of the vote. But statewide, Republican support was crucial in turning what could have been a horse race into a landslide rarely seen in bond elections.

Broad attributed the bond issue's success partly to enthusiastic support from Senator Helms. Shortly after taking office in 1998, Broad had visited Washington to meet the members of North Carolina's congressional delegation. Helms, who had long felt estranged from the university system despite his friendly relationship with former UNC system president Bill Friday, appreciated the personal visit from Broad.[8] Helms successfully pushed for the North Carolina congressional delegation to back the bond issue unanimously.

A coalition of conservatives, liberals, Republicans, Democrats, business, and labor led the charge. Voters skeptical of the universities could justify a yes vote to help their local community college or technical school, with its emphasis on practical skills. The outcome confirmed the state's long-standing reputation for progressivism on matters relating to higher education and infrastructure. It was also a vote cast in self-interest. Parents wanted to maximize their children's opportunities. Business leaders believed that educational advances would boost the state's long-term economic development and prosperity. Symbolically, the timing was perfect. One hundred years earlier, Charles Aycock had led a public education crusade and established education as a sort of official state philosophy, a quasi religion. Almost forty years earlier, Terry Sanford had renewed the crusade. And now, Governor Jim Hunt, an equally outspoken proponent of education, linked education with both general prosperity and the achievement of the American Dream. At crucial times, North Carolinians have usually come down on the side of public education. In the 2000 election, both progressivism and populism triumphed.[9]

### 2000: THE CAMPAIGN

Republicans had reason to be bullish on their 2000 election prospects. On the presidential level, Texas governor George W. Bush, the son of the former president, built a reputation as a consensus politician. He was a self-proclaimed conservative, but much of his rhetoric seemed moderate and conciliatory. Incumbent president Bill Clinton remained popular despite his scars and prepared to leave office as only the second president since Dwight Eisenhower to have served two full terms. Vice President Al Gore of Tennessee was the Democratic heir apparent. Since the Clinton sex scandals, Gore and Clinton had maintained a frosty if officially correct relationship. Gore lacked Clinton's charisma and seemed a poor match for Bush in likability. So in midsummer, Bush was the front-runner, a position reinforced by the Republican National Convention. Gore staged a rebound at the Democratic National Convention in late August and maintained an edge in national public opinion polls throughout September. He fell behind again in October after the initial presidential debate, during which his sarcastic sighing and breathing were audible even on the radio.

Throughout the campaign, Gore trailed in North Carolina and in most of the South. There would be no friends and neighbors vote in this election. He seemed to be a drag on the state Democratic ticket. Republicans cloaked themselves in the mantle of Bush.

The North Carolina Democrats' goal was to win the governorship and other state executive offices and to retain an edge in both houses of the state legislature. In the fall of 2000, the U.S. Census Bureau worked away on its tabulation of state population. The 2001 legislature would bear responsibility for drawing new legislative district lines as well as congressional district lines. The Democrats hoped to draw lines in such a way as to eradicate the losses they had suffered back in the 1994 elections. Republicans also saw the 2000 election as crucial. Building on Bush's strength, they wanted to win the governorship and to retake the N.C. House of Representatives. Both goals seemed at least an even bet.[10]

The outcome of the governor's race remained in serious doubt. Democratic attorney general Mike Easley squared off against Richard Vinroot, the Republican mayor of Charlotte. Vinroot hoped to do well in the urban piedmont and mountains. A native of Rocky Mount and resident of Southport, near Wilmington, Easley aimed for a big lead in eastern North Carolina. In the Republican primary, many easterners had backed Leo Daughtry of Johnston County, while others had supported Chuck Neely of Raleigh. Scars remained, and Easley hoped to benefit. The graying Vinroot, a former basketball player aging well, cut an impressive figure. His voice carried across any room, and he looked robust on television. Easley could not win the race on oratorical skills or former athletic prowess. But he had an appealing trait. He knew how to connect with ordinary voters, including white males, who often shunned Democratic candidates. He had a plain, unassuming style and a fondness for stock car racing. Easley had already demonstrated his political prowess by defeating two-term lieutenant governor Dennis Wicker for the 2000 Democratic gubernatorial nomination. And a key Easley campaigner in 2000 was Harvey Gantt, the man who had defeated Easley for the Democratic senatorial nomination in 1990. Easley had campaigned vigorously for Gantt in the 1990 general election against Jesse Helms. Now Gantt showed his gratitude.

Both Easley and Vinroot were disciples of the North Carolina mantra: improved educational opportunities, good roads, and economic development. In keeping with Republican philosophy, Vinroot stressed what he saw as the need for a business-friendly tax structure and the lowest tax rates possible. Easley was cautious on tax matters, fearing that a revenue crisis was brewing, in part because of the 1995 competition between Hunt and legislative Republicans to cut taxes. As mayor of Charlotte, Vinroot had advocated the privatization of public services where feasible, arguing, like many other conservatives, that this approach would save money, increase efficiency, and cut the size of government. Partly as a consequence of his activist role as attorney general, Easley took a more expansive view of government, whether in the realm of expanding school programs, protecting consumers against big business, or fighting crime. He stressed his record as a hard-line prosecutor and unyielding supporter for the death penalty.[11]

All the while, Senate President Marc Basnight and Speaker of the House Jim Black spearheaded efforts to raise enough money to maintain Democratic supremacy in the legislature. With the Basnight organizational effort and money apparatus in place, the Democrats appeared certain to keep control of the Senate, although the situation in the House looked shakier. The soft-spoken Black was one of the most effective campaign fundraisers the state had known, but Republicans appeared to be on the upswing. More than enough Democratic representatives were in jeopardy to give the Republicans a good shot at capturing control. If they could win one chamber of the legislature, the Republicans would be in strong position in the upcoming battles over reapportionment. The Democrats had for decades drawn district lines with an eye toward keeping control, and the Republicans hoped to use their leverage in the House of Representatives to counter that long-term advantage. But first they had to overcome the state Democrats in organizational and financial prowess.

## 2000: DIVIDED OUTCOME

Like the presidential election of 1876, the 2000 election was the stuff of legend. Reflecting the candidates' personalities—Republicans George W. Bush and Dick Cheney facing off against Democrats Al Gore and Joe Lieberman—the campaign itself was on the dull side, any excitement engendered by its closeness in its waning days. But election night was a thriller. Not until a December Supreme Court decision stopped a Florida recount did the public know for certain that Bush would be the next president. With Florida's electoral votes, he had 271, one more than he needed for victory. Yet, Gore led in the national popular vote, 51,003,894–50,459,211. Leftist independent Ralph Nader, who was not on the ballot in North Carolina, received 2,834,410 popular votes but no electoral votes.

Bush won a landslide in North Carolina, garnering 1,631,163 votes to Gore's 1,257,692, with scattered votes for the Libertarian and the socially conservative Reform Party candidate, Patrick Buchanan. Bush led comfortably in the coastal plain, piedmont, and mountain regions. Gore won the heavily academic and liberal Durham–Chapel Hill area and rural counties where minorities comprised 45 percent or more of the voters—the northeast coastal plain, sections of the northeast piedmont along the Virginia border, and a few counties along the South Carolina state line. Bush scored big in predominantly white precincts, whether they were working class, high income, rural, or suburban.

North Carolina's voting patterns largely mirrored those of the South as a whole. Excluding the southern states, Gore would have won with ease. Aside from narrow losses in Florida and his home state of Tennessee, Gore probably ran as poorly in the South as a liberal northern Democrat would have. In North Carolina, Gore had still another minus. Never had a presidential candidate taken such a strong stance against tobacco. Going back to a speech at the 1996 Democratic National Convention, Gore had declared war on nicotine. By 2000, tobacco's days as North Carolina's king were gone, but smokers as well as abstainers who had family roots in tobacco remained a political force. Pro-tobacco attitudes were most prevalent in the rural and small-town eastern half of the state, where Democrats needed a big vote. Gore's fate was sealed in North Carolina long before the campaign drums began to roll.

Democrats fared better in the state races than either party had expected. Their victories were all the more impressive since Jim Hunt was not on the ballot to lead the charge. Nevertheless, he led the charge. Hunt worked tirelessly for the Democratic victory, and his efforts might have been crucial in the tightly fought contest for control of the N.C. House of Representatives. But the man at the top of the Democratic ticket, Mike Easley, had much to do with shielding the Democrats from the lava flowing down from the presidential race. Easley was no party man in the classic sense. He had always maintained an independent streak. However, Easley had one tremendous asset. He was the perfect counterpoint to Gore. If Gore's demeanor was pompous, Easley was almost the stereotypical good old boy. Furthermore, his halting rhetoric concealed a political shrewdness. His cultural values approximated those of many North Carolina males. But in a break from North Carolina's history, Easley was not a Baptist, Methodist, or Presbyterian; he was a Catholic, an affiliation that until recent years would have barred him from the governorship, first by law and later by local prejudice. But the religion issue never arose. Easley disdained the press, especially the big urban newspapers, but despite or maybe because of his lack of polish, he seemed at home with ordinary people in a way that no recent North Carolina governor could match.

Easley defeated Vinroot, 1,530,324–1,360,960, taking nearly 60 percent of the coastal plain vote and just over 51 percent in the populous piedmont, enough to overcome Vinroot's 52 percent to 47 percent lead in the mountain region.[12] In his home county of Mecklenburg, Vinroot had a lackluster 133,728–126,480 advantage, reflecting a gradual shift toward the Democrats in formerly Republican-leaning Charlotte, a trend propelled by growing numbers of African Americans, newcomers, and people associated with academia. In addition, factionalism was boiling over in the Mecklenburg Republican ranks.

Across the state, Vinroot suffered from divisiveness stemming from the earlier Republican primary. Many Leo Daughtry and Chuck Neely primary backers remained bitter about the hard-fought intraparty squabble. Some of these voters thought Vinroot too much of a moderate, while others simply disliked him. This dissent among Daughtry's numerous supporters in eastern North Carolina, combined with Easley's eastern roots, helped build Easley's lead in the coastal plain. His margin there turned what would have been a close race into a comfortable victory.

Basnight's organization showed its muscle in the state senatorial races, enabling the Democrats to hold onto their 35–15 lead in that body. The Democratic candidates had outspent their opponents by more than 4:1— nearly $7 million to the Republicans' $1.6 million. The House outcome was the cliff-hanger. When all the votes were counted, the Democrats held a 62–58 advantage. Democratic House candidates outspent Republicans approximately $7.1 million to $4.4 million. Totaling all votes cast in Senate and House races, the numbers looked better for the Republicans. Democratic Senate candidates combined to win 1.68 million votes, while Republicans won 1.64 million, a difference notably less stark than the huge Democratic edge in seats won. In House elections, the Republicans garnered 1.79 million votes and the Democrats had 1.71 million. The Democrats again fared better in seats won than in votes won.

These results affirmed Democratic skills both in the art of redistricting and in raising money. Democrats' control of legislative majorities during the 1991 reapportionment battles had enabled them to draw the legislative maps, and, in keeping with long-standing American political traditions, they drew those lines to their party's advantage. Second, Basnight, Black, and Hunt led the Democrats in building a huge advantage in organization and finances.[13] The party had as diverse a cadre of backers as any state Democratic or Republican Party. Support came not only from the usual Democratic sources (educators, lawyers, labor unions, and environmental groups) but also from big business (bankers, accounting firms, architects, builders, land developers, software executives).[14] Republicans, too, had their money sources, raising funds from bankers, utility executives, and builders. But overall, the Democrats had the edge. It was not unusual for business executives to support Bush for president and Hunt or Easley for governor and then contribute handsomely to Democratic campaign coffers for General Assembly races.[15]

As governor, Easley pushed hard for infrastructure improvements and business development. But his greatest passion was pre-K–12 public education. Even in lean budget times, he and the legislature increased funding for preschool programs. Public schoolteachers won substantial pay increases when other state employees did not. Easley was less vocal in his support for public universities, but President Molly Broad considered him a shrewd and effective ally, and the state's community colleges continued to grow.[16]

### 2001–2002: THE FRUITS OF GROWTH AND THE POLITICS OF TRAGEDY

When the figures for the 2000 census came trickling in, North Carolina's growth rate for the preceding decade was 21.4 percent, one of the highest outside the American Southwest and far surpassing estimates. The prognosticators had failed to measure the magnitude of the Hispanic migration into an area where whites and African Americans had long predominated. Casual observers had noticed a large Spanish-speaking influx around 1995, as had Census Bureau samples. But the numbers were still larger than anticipated. Yet more significant was the big migration into states such as North Carolina and Georgia from the Midwest, Northeast, western states, and other southern states. This movement had contributed to North Carolina's growth since the 1970s but reached new heights in the 1990s. Most of these migrants were white, but blacks also arrived in increasing numbers, and Asians continued to move into the cities and military-base towns.

Unlike the majority of Hispanics, many of the newcomers who arrived from other states were citizens and already eligible to vote in U.S. elections.

As in the past, the population growth occurred unevenly. Most counties in the coastal plain and mountain regions grew more slowly than did the state as a whole. So did a few piedmont counties—mostly places with economies based on textiles, tobacco, or old manufacturing plants. Charlotte, Durham, and other big cities saw the largest influxes of African American migrants. Among military-base counties, the population of Cumberland (Fayetteville, Fort Bragg) grew by only 10.3 percent, while Onslow (Jacksonville, Camp Lejeune) saw an increase of a measly 0.3 percent.[17]

The high-growth counties fell into three categories: city, suburban, and resort. Wake County (Raleigh) grew at a 48.3 percent rate. Neighboring Johnston County, straddling the coastal plain and piedmont, had a 50 percent increase as it transformed from an agricultural and manufacturing area to suburbs housing the population overflow from Wake County. Union County, east of Charlotte, experienced a similar transition and grew by 47 percent. The population also grew tremendously in rural places that were now becoming resort meccas—specifically, Brunswick and Pender Counties, near Wilmington, and Currituck and Dare Counties on the northeast coast.[18]

The growth gave North Carolina a thirteenth seat in the U.S. House of Representatives in 2001. The extra seat might ease the pain of redistricting just a bit, but the state's diversity assured a battle. State legislative seats offered the potential of a still bigger fight.

In 2001, however, the usual political agendas were blown to bits by terrorist groups. The attacks in New York and Washington, D.C., stunned and horrified much of the world. A decisive George W. Bush at first seemed up to the challenge, and a patriotic fervor swept the country. U.S. armed forces attacked Afghanistan and later Iraq, and the protracted war on terror began. Attitudes toward the Bush administration, the military conflicts, and national directions eventually split the country and North Carolina in ways not seen since the Vietnam War and civil rights movement. For a while, however, any political advantage from the tragedy and expanding wars boosted the Bush presidency. Many voters from Virginia and North Carolina to the Gulf of Mexico thought that opposition to Bush policies was unpatriotic and disloyal to American soldiers abroad. The clouds of war cast a shadow on North Carolina's politics.

## CAMPAIGN 2002: THE RETURN OF THE NATIVES

In August 2001, Jesse Helms announced that he would not seek reelection the following year. The race to replace him was wide open, and despite

Edwards's 1998 victory in the election for North Carolina's other Senate seat, Republicans had recent history on their side.

Among those interested in replacing Helms was Elizabeth Hanford Dole, who received encouragement from many North Carolina Republicans. Originally from Salisbury, in the western piedmont, Elizabeth Hanford had graduated Phi Beta Kappa from Duke in 1958, a time when the school had considerably higher admissions standards for women than for men. She received a law degree from Harvard in 1965, and then went to Washington, D.C., where she worked in the Johnson and Nixon administrations. In 1975, she married Senator Bob Dole of Kansas. Elizabeth Dole subsequently served as secretary of transportation under Reagan, secretary of labor under George H. W. Bush, and president of the American Red Cross. She sought the Republican presidential nomination in 2000 but dropped out early in the race. In the first years of the new millennium, Dole was the best-known female politician in America other than Hillary Rodham Clinton. Dole had aged well and still spoke with a charming, almost syrupy southern dialect, a sort of steel magnolia.

Dole made the rounds, meeting leading North Carolinians in and out of the Republican Party. She was a quick study and learned the ins and outs of her native state, though she had not lived there for most of her adult life. She approached key figures and said with a glowing smile and firm handshake, "It warms my heart to meet you" before launching into a discussion of that person's great contributions to the state. Frequent and often well-publicized visits over the years to her mother in Salisbury made Dole seem a genuine North Carolinian, although her professional and social lives had been centered in Washington. To run for the Senate, she moved her residence back to Salisbury. Probably no other candidate would have had as much popular appeal and fund raising success in North Carolina as Dole did. Others, most notably former Senator Lauch Faircloth, eyed the seat, but with cooperative Republicans clearing her path, Dole faced only token primary opposition. She would be a tough candidate for the Democrats to beat.

Of the nine candidates who sought the Democratic nomination, the media took three seriously. Dan Blue, an African American from Raleigh, had been Speaker of the N.C. House in 1993–94. His public demeanor was low key. The color of his skin might still be a handicap, but it was no longer a two-strike burden. Secretary of State Elaine Marshall, who had defeated legendary stock car racer Richard Petty in 1996, had a long record of civic and party service and immense energy. But both Blue and Marshall lacked the kind of money needed to run a twenty-first-century senatorial campaign.

Erskine Bowles emerged as the unofficial candidate of the Democratic establishment. He had the pedigree, the connections, the experience—and the money. Bowles had served as the treasurer for the innovative but ultimately losing campaign for governor run by his father, Skipper, in 1972. Bowles moved comfortably in the world of high finance and built experience in his adopted homes of New York and Charlotte. Bowles also served as President Bill Clinton's assistant chief of staff from 1994 to 1995 and chief of staff from 1996 to 1998. During the aftermath of the Monica Lewinsky scandal, Bowles felt betrayed by Clinton, who had withheld the truth from his aide. Yet, Bowles was a model presidential assistant, on a level with Ronald Reagan's James Baker in the 1980s. Bowles built a reputation as a straight shooter and for returning phone calls.[19] Skipper Bowles had grown up with Helms in Monroe, and the two men remained friends. Erskine Bowles would likely not have run if Helms had still been in the picture.

With impeccable connections in Washington, in Charlotte, and on Wall Street, Bowles could raise the money for a modern senatorial campaign. In addition, he was wealthy enough to throw his own money into the effort. Bowles seemed businesslike, solid, and friendly and inspired confidence. He lacked the ebullient personality and upbeat spirit of his father, but Democrats hoped that the younger Bowles was more suited to the times. He took the lead for the nomination and never lost it, receiving 277,329 votes to Blue's 184,216 and Marshall's 97,392. Other candidates had a combined vote of 80,088. Bowles barely topped 40 percent, so he did not face a runoff. But in any runoff, he would have been the favorite.

Bowles faced a tall order in the general election. Both Bowles and Dole came across positively in their campaign commercials. The televised debates were combative, though not mean. Dole supported the Bush foreign policy and war effort while saying that she would be an independent senator. Befitting the political situation at the time, Bowles took a cautious position on the security and foreign policy crises, supporting the fight against terrorism without giving Bush a blank check. While paying at least lip service to the issues of concern to evangelical Protestants and socially conservative Catholics, Dole did not hammer away on these themes. Bowles knew he could not carry the majority of the white evangelical Christian vote, but he hoped to cut into it and run well among mainstream Protestant groups.[20]

Dole defeated Bowles, 1,248,664–1,047,983, collecting 52 percent of the coastal plain's vote, 55 percent in the piedmont, and 56 percent in the mountains. Dole narrowly carried the county where Bowles grew up, Guilford, and the county he now called home, Mecklenburg. Despite her 54.4

percent statewide victory, Dole trailed badly in the academic centers of Durham and Chapel Hill and in most counties where minorities—blacks or Native Americans—comprised more than 40 percent of the population.

The contest was partly a referendum on the current president, as midterm elections tend to be. Bush's approval scores had declined from their peak levels of September and October 2001, but he remained popular with a large segment of American voters and still larger segments of North Carolina voters. In 2002, Republicans defied tradition and gained seats in the U.S. Congress. Dole's strength reflected the national trend. No Democrat, with the possible exception of Jim Hunt, could have beaten her.

### CAMPAIGN 2002: DEMOCRATIC DIKE HOLDS BACK REPUBLICAN TIDE

The 2000 census had given North Carolina a new seat in the U.S. House of Representatives, and that seat went to the Democrats in 2002 thanks to artful district drawing by the 2001–2 session of the legislature. State senator Brad Miller, a Raleigh Democrat, chaired the redistricting committee that mapped a Democratic-leaning seat extending from Raleigh to Greensboro by way of marginal to Democratic rural areas in between. At the time, observers called it the "Brad Miller seat," and sure enough, Miller became its first occupant. All of the state's incumbents were reelected, so with the new seat, the Republican edge in the state's U.S. House delegation dropped to 7–6.

The Democratic Party lost seats in both chambers of the state legislature in 2002. Their 35–15 advantage in the Senate dropped to 28–22, the second-smallest margin since 1900. And the Republicans retook their slim 61–59 margin in the House, a feat they had achieved only twice in more than a hundred years. It appeared to be a great moment for the GOP, but Democrats suddenly seemed poised to overturn the result, but not through another election. Instead, Democratic Speaker of the House Black and other party leaders looked toward a deal with one or more of the Republicans.

The stakes were high—so high that the Democratic leadership was ready for a protracted battle, one that would be resolved by neither bullets nor ballots. Could some Republican House member be persuaded to become a Democrat? More precisely, would a Republican defect if offered the proper inducements? On rare occasions, politicians may change parties for ideological reasons—Ronald Reagan, for example. They come to see their political philosophy evolving more toward the other party. In other instances, legislators feel slighted by their own party, by the denial of a position as committee chair or some other perk. And in a few cases, politicians switch for political expediency. Their district seems to be shifting from supporting one party to the other. To survive, the legislator goes with the flow and announces a sort of born-again conversion.

Before the new legislature was sworn in early in 2003, Republican representative Michael Decker of Kernersville announced that he would be switching to the Democratic Party. Decker had always been reliably conservative on both economic and social issues. Moreover, his district, a mix of suburban and semirural areas near Winston-Salem, was one of the state's most Republican. His announcement placed him at the center of the state's political universe.[21]

Several years later, a hard-charging state prosecution team revealed the riddle of Michael Decker's change of heart: he had received fifty thousand dollars from Black, along with the promise of a state government job for Decker's son. The State Bureau of Investigation provided evidence that Black had passed the money to Decker, partly cash and partly laundered checks, in the men's room of an International House of Pancakes. In 2007, Decker admitted to taking the bribes and consequently received a four-year prison sentence. Black never entered a formal guilty plea but instead entered an "Alford plea," meaning that he did not admit guilt but acknowledged that a jury would probably find him guilty.[22] Further scandals relating to Black loomed on the horizon.

Unaware of the skullduggery, political observers in early 2003 marveled at Jim Black's persuasive skills, but work remained to be done. Decker's switch meant an evenly divided House of Representatives and the possibility of a protracted deadlock between the parties. After extended negotiations, Black and other Democratic leaders reached a deal with dissident Republicans: Black and moderate Republican Richard Morgan of Moore County would serve as co-Speakers of the House, with Black presiding one day and Morgan the next. In reality, Black remained top dog. But Morgan, too, had a lot of clout, partly because he wielded the gavel and powers of the House half the time and partly because he and Black had a good working relationship. Democrats accepted the "coalition" as the best result they could have achieved under the circumstances. Most Republicans felt robbed and were furious, though a few—those who were in Morgan's good graces and who had not been happy with past Republican caucus leadership—benefited.[23]

## THE 2004 ELECTIONS

The 2004 elections provided North Carolinians with a full plate. There were contests for the presidency, the governorship, and the U.S. Senate seat being vacated by John Edwards, who was seeking the Democratic presidential nomination. His effort began as a bold but long-shot bid. He achieved immense national exposure and, at least among economic-populist-style Democrats, enough goodwill that eventual Democratic presidential nominee John Kerry tapped Edwards as his vice presidential running mate. The pair made a joint appearance in Raleigh and for a few weeks following the Democratic National Convention, the Kerry-Edwards team appeared to have a chance to carry North Carolina.[24]

Soon after the Republican National Convention, however, the Democrats' hopes of winning North Carolina or any southern state outside Florida vanished. The Kerry-Edwards ticket took cautiously moderate to liberal positions on most issues, including the war in Iraq, but the Bush effort, guided by guru Karl Rove, portrayed the Democrats as out of touch with mainstream American values and hinted that Kerry and Edwards were elitist snobs. The Republicans reminded voters of Kerry's opposition to the Vietnam War after serving with distinction in Vietnam. Experience in the courtroom had given Edwards a common touch, but the ticket would rise or fall on voters' perceptions of Kerry. As the campaign progressed, Edwards employed his charm and soft oratory in competitive states such as Ohio.

Overall, the Democratic duo conducted a credible campaign, and they would have claimed the presidency if they had pulled out a victory in Ohio. Bush and Cheney received 62,040,610 votes while Kerry and Edwards received 59,028,444. Ralph Nader (not on the North Carolina ballot in either 2000 or 2004) garnered 411,306 votes, only one-seventh as many as he got in 2000. Bush-Cheney took 286 electoral votes, 16 more than they needed for victory, while Kerry-Edwards had 251 votes in the electoral college. Nationwide, 60.7 percent of eligible voters turned out, the highest figure since 1968. The Republicans routed the Democrats in North Carolina, 1,961,166–1,525,849, taking 56.4 percent of the votes in the coastal plain, 55.4 percent in the piedmont, and 59.9 percent in the mountains. The Democratic ticket led in the usual strongholds: counties where African Americans or Native Americans comprised a large portion of the population plus Chapel Hill and Durham, which were more Democratic than in any presidential election since the Franklin Roosevelt era. Kerry also took Guilford (Greensboro) and Mecklenburg (Charlotte) Counties, another signal that once Republican-leaning metropolitan areas were trending Democratic, a pattern that also appeared in other parts of the country. But Bush carried many rural and once-Democratic counties across the state. He also swept the rapidly growing counties that were moving from rural and small-town to suburban: Johnston, southeast of Raleigh, and Union, east of Charlotte. Republican base counties of the western piedmont and mountains also delivered for the ticket.

The Democratic Party had seen Erskine Bowles as its best bet for the Senate seat being vacated by Edwards. He had the recognition and the proven ability to raise money. Bowles had two handicaps: the Democratic presidential ticket's weakness and his Republican opponent, Richard Burr, a rising star in the GOP. According to his Wake Forest college roommate Tom Fetzer, Burr had shown little interest in politics as a student.[25] Burr later said that Fetzer's political enthusiasm had in fact been contagious. After college, Burr went into business but kept an eye on government affairs, abruptly deciding to run for Congress in 1994 after listening to a National Public Radio report on governmental waste.[26] Burr won the Fifth District seat that covered much of northwestern North Carolina and Winston-Salem. Burr had face-to-face appeal rivaling John Edwards's as well as a mastery of how population trends and technology were reshaping politics. He built alliances among Republicans and friendships across party lines.

Both Burr and Bowles fought hard, Burr running as a national Republican and Bowles running as an independent Democrat. In hindsight, the outcome was predictable: Burr won, 1,791,450–1,632,527. His coalition was similar to Bush's. A majority of voters in this red state wanted a conservative senator sympathetic to the Bush agenda.

Bowles, however, remained at the center of state affairs. Following Molly Broad's resignation in 2005, the UNC Board of Governors tapped him for the presidency of the state university system. He had bipartisan support, and he stressed both publicly and privately that he was "getting out of politics." In fact, however, he was moving into one of the most political and significant roles a North Carolinian could have. His background would serve him well.

In the governor's race, Democratic incumbent Easley easily prevailed over his young and energetic Republican opponent, Patrick Ballantine of Wilmington. Ballantine was an attractive enough candidate, and despite his relative youth, he had been the Republican leader in the N.C. Senate. Easley had a tremendous financial advantage. The campaign centered on education—Easley's turf. The Republicans tried to make hay on Democratic political corruption, a more legitimate issue than much of the public realized at the time, but the accusations fell on deaf ears. Within the GOP ranks, moderates and conservatives still fought one another, and Ballantine did not fit readily into either category. Ballantine had hoped to capitalize on his eastern North Carolina roots. However, Easley was from Southport, just down the road from Wilmington.

Easley won nearly 59 percent of the votes in his home coastal plain region and more than 56 percent in the piedmont. He also led narrowly in the Republican-leaning mountain region. What stood out across the state was the gap between the Easley vote and that of the Kerry-Edwards presidential ticket. While most pronounced in eastern North Carolina, the gap was present all across the state. From the mountains to the sea, there were counties where Easley won landslide victories and the Kerry-Edwards ticket lost. The spread was most pronounced in rural and small-town counties. Easley's victory was in large part a personal one rather than a party victory. Yet his strength helped Democratic state legislative candidates.

Thanks to skillful reapportionment after the 2000 census and the organizational and money-raising prowess of Senate President Marc Basnight and Speaker of the House Jim Black, the Democrats kept their hold on the state legislature, taking a 29–21 advantage in the Senate and a 63–57 edge in the House. The Democrats had polled fewer total votes in House races across the state than had the Republicans. Indeed, Democrats had last won a majority of the total votes in House races in 1992. Their election successes reflected skillful reapportionment of districts after the censuses.

Easley's second term was much like his first, featuring a zeal for public education and a frosty relationship with the press. Some observers thought the governor to be lazy, partly because of his erratic hours and frequent visits to his Southport home. Appearances might have been deceiving. According to Franklin Freeman, a key staffer for both Easley and Hunt, Easley worked almost as hard as did Hunt, whom Freeman considered perhaps the hardest worker he had ever known. Easley's schedule was the most unconventional of any governor. He often retired for the evening at 10:30 or 11:00. He would then arise around 2.00 in the morning and work for two to three hours. People checking their phone messages the next day might find a 3:00 A.M. call from the governor making a request or asking for information. Easley usually returned to bed until around 8:00 in the morning.[27]

Easley's wife, Mary, possessed political smarts and served as his confidante and adviser. Overall, she presented a good front for the administration. She had previously been a law professor at her husband's alma mater, North Carolina Central University, and near the end of his second term, she was hired for an administrative and outreach position at North Carolina State University.

### THE 2006 DEMOCRATIC RESURGENCE

Two-term presidents often face the voters' sting in the sixth year of their administrations. In November 2006, it was George W. Bush's turn. Democrats picked up five seats in the U.S. Senate, and with the support of two Democratic-leaning independents, the party captured control of the chamber. Defying most professional analysts' predictions, the Democratic Party won a 233–202 majority in the U.S. House of Representatives, ending a twelve-year Republican reign there.

The Democratic advance penetrated North Carolina. This was a blue moon election with no presidential or senatorial contests but two heated races for Congress. After a series of tight contests in the mountainous Eleventh District, Democratic leaders saw an opportunity to pick off incumbent Republican Charles Taylor. The Democrats tapped Heath Shuler, a former football star at the University of Tennessee who was telegenic, a family man, and politically ambitious. He campaigned as a moderate who understood his district's cultural values and was anti–gun control, pro-life, and religious. Though now having cast his lot with the Democrats, Shuler might have been a Republican in another time and place. Former Helms staff members recalled that Shuler used to drop by the conservative senator's office, and they had the impression that he admired the man and at least some of his political stands.[28]

Taylor had not been in big trouble, but there were whispers of scandal, most often from Democrats. He had been in Congress since 1989 and had been a big Republican political figure for longer. Maybe voters were ready for a fresh face. Shuler, with his good looks and hard-to-pin-down ideology, was just what the Democratic doctor ordered. The national party fundraising committees poured money into his campaign, and the state party made the Eleventh District its top priority. Shuler won, 124,972–107,342.

Not wanting to waste precious funds on "hopeless" causes, the national Democratic Party did not get involved in schoolteacher Larry Kissell's challenge to Robin Hayes in the Eighth District, although the challenger did have help from labor unions and the state Democratic Party. The district's party registration statistics had long looked favorable for the Democrats, and the district was full of Democratic-leaning economic populists as well as Republican-leaning social populists. Hayes had been an astute representative, paying close attention to constituent problems. On a few domestic issues—for example, his support for federally subsidized rail passenger service and federal money likely to help his district—Hayes parted company with the Bush administration. Moreover, if his campaign ran short of funds, he could tap his personal fortune as a member of the textile-manufacturing Cannon family. Nevertheless, the decision not to help Kissell constituted the biggest miscalculation by either national political party: Hayes squeaked out such a narrow victory, 60,926–60,597, that more advertising, phone banks, and ground organizing would likely have put Kissell over the top. Democrats had learned a lesson they would remember two years hence. But Hayes and the Republicans would be on guard.

Democrats gained 2 seats in the N.C. Senate, giving them a 31–19 edge, and 5 in the N.C. House, which now stood at 68 Democrats and 52 Republicans. Democrats were at their strongest level since they had been routed in 1994. Senate President Pro Tem Marc Basnight was one of the most influential—perhaps *the* most influential—public officials in the state.[29]

### THE ROAD TO LEWISBURG

Political corruption has been a fact of politics for a very long time. But in the early 2000s, a number of big North Carolina actors were being charged, convicted, and sent to prison. Among the most prominent were agriculture commissioner Meg Scott Phillips (granddaughter of Governor Kerr Scott and daughter of Governor Bob Scott). Next came Frank Ballance, who had replaced Eva Clayton as representative from the First Congressional District. But the biggest and most consequential scandal again involved Speaker of the House Jim Black.

In addition to the fallout from the 2002–3 Decker affair, Black faced other charges. He had been an avid supporter of Governor Easley's push for a state lottery, a popular way of raising money for education and other state services. As vocal an education backer as former governors Charles Aycock, Terry Sanford, and Jim Hunt, Easley had campaigned for the lottery both as candidate and as governor. Despite widespread support for such an "easy" way of getting money, Easley, Black, and other supporters knew it would be a difficult legislative sale. Protestant Christian clergy, both evangelical and liberal, looked askance at lotteries, which they saw as gambling, sinful, and/or bad public policy that encouraged needy families to waste money in hopes of striking it rich. Against the odds, however, the legislature had approved a lottery, with Lieutenant Governor Beverly Perdue casting the tie-breaking vote in the Senate. In the process, Black had used his position to gain lottery contracts for a private company, Scientific Games. He worked to get a key ally on the state lottery commission. The whole matter was a shady story of influence peddling and political corruption to benefit public officials and a private company.[30]

Another breach was the most self-serving of all. Black took a twenty-nine-thousand-dollar bribe from two chiropractors in exchange for promoting a bill to reduce patient insurance copayments for chiropractic treatments—a federal offense to which he pled guilty in 2007. Black, like many other illustrious American personalities who ran afoul of the law, found himself in the federal prison at Lewisburg, Pennsylvania.

Without breaking the law, Black, an eye doctor, had pushed through legislation requiring eye exams for public schoolchildren, an act of mercy for tomorrow's generation that also benefited the eye care providers' balance sheets. Late in his career, he was a manifestation of Lord Acton's warning that power corrupts. His actions, both legal and illegal, contributed to an enormous rise in cynicism as North Carolinians realized that widespread corruption existed in a state long thought to be relatively free of that blight.

For all the frenzy over the betrayal of the public trust by Jim Black and other officeholders, however, North Carolina and America of 2007 were more open and democratic places than in the past. And the exposure of Black and corrupt officials was made possible by a vigilant news media.

### THE DEATH AND SHADOW OF HELMS

Jesse Helms died on July 4, 2008. Over the years, Helms's detractors had labeled him a demagogue. Former Helms strategist Carter Wrenn, who had fallen out with Helms by 2007, said it for the record.[31] Some who called Helms a demagogue likened him to the most sinister of the genre: Theodore "The Man" Bilbo of Mississippi, Eugene Talmadge of Georgia, and Ellison D. "Cotton Ed" Smith of South Carolina, early and mid-twentieth-century politicians who stirred racial hatred. Critics also linked Helms to more recent firebrand politicians such as Strom Thurmond of South Carolina and George Wallace of Alabama.

A common dictionary definition of "demagogue" is a leader who uses impassioned appeals to people's emotions and prejudices to achieve and maintain power. The definition leaves a lot of room for the imagination. Longtime political columnist and wordsmith William Safire said that a demagogue is "one who appeals to greed, fear, and hatred; a spellbinding orator, careless with the facts and a danger to rational decision."[32]

Yet one person's demagogue is another's hero. Scholars believe that word was explained first by Euripides in ancient Athens. To the Greeks, a demagogue was "a man of loose tongue, intemperate, trusting to the tumult, leading the populace to mischief with empty words."[33] In the classic sense, the demagogue is a public figure who says one thing and often does another. The ego and ambition of the messenger take precedence over the implementation of the message. The American South from the 1880s to the 1960s was full of demagogues. For example, Georgia's Gene Talmadge traveled the roads attacking big corporations while taking their money under the table. The southern demagogue was typically loud, flashy, and crude. Even when well-to-do, they pretended to be commoners. Demagogues are most apt to pop up when society has frustrations. The South from the 1870s to the 1970s was the most psychologically troubled of any part of the country.[34]

Jesse Helms was a master at tapping people's frustrations, from the television studio to the tobacco warehouse to the halls of Congress—frustrations about race, communism, atheism, and basic morality. On segregation and federal civil rights legislation, the early Helms was on the wrong side of history and the American Dream. But he shared this position with an enormous number of white southerners, including politicians such as North Carolina's erudite Senator Sam Ervin.[35] Whether such views were simply backward or downright malevolent could be argued endlessly.

Helms never backtracked on his abiding advocacy of capitalism, opposition to communism, and support for Judeo-Christian principles of morality, at least as he saw them. Like most politicians, he was ambitious and could be cunning and even petty toward those who crossed him. But more than most, if his sense of right and wrong collided with his political well-being (and it seldom did), he stuck with his principles, no matter whom he angered by doing so. In public policy debates, he never sought to be Mr. Congeniality.

Yet on a personal level, with a few well-publicized exceptions, he was one of the most cordial and civil members of Congress. He built a friendship of sorts with the liberal Paul Wellstone of Minnesota, who had said before going to the Senate that he despised the idea of serving with Helms. Both at home and in Washington, Helms treated those of lower stations in life with the utmost consideration, and he preferred not to advertise his acts of charity and kindness.[36] All the while, Helms was one of the plainest and most unassuming members of Congress, a man of simple tastes in food, music, and entertainment.

Social critic Eric Hoffer and historian T. Harry Williams have articulated a rival concept of the mass leader. The term "mass leader" better fits Helms than does the term "demagogue." Mass leaders share certain traits with demagogues. They are skillful politicians who appeal to people's emotions. According to Williams, the mass leader sets a popular movement into motion.[37] And in Hoffer's words, the mass leader "articulates and justifies the resentment dammed in the souls of the frustrated" and moves "to harness man's hungers and fears to weld a following and make it zealous unto death in the service of a holy cause."[38] In Hoffer and Williams's view, a mass leader must possess "audacity, an iron will, faith in himself, his cause and his destiny" and a "sense of communion with his followers."[39] Mass leaders can be good or bad or leave a mixed legacy.

Notable mass leaders have included Franklin Roosevelt, Adolf Hitler, Queen Elizabeth I, Mahatma Gandhi, Joseph Stalin, Martin Luther King Jr., and, in his latter days, Abraham Lincoln. That list could also be expanded to include Huey Long of Louisiana, Billy Graham, Daniel Webster, John C. Calhoun, and Jesse Helms. The typical demagogue fans the flames and makes mischief but has little long-term impact. The mass leader makes a difference. He or she alters the course of history for good or evil or both.[40]

North Carolina's inflamed racial atmosphere of the 1960s and early 1970s was a big factor propelling Helms into the Senate. Moreover, race, in conjunction with other forces, helped him win reelection in at least three other elections—1984, 1990, and 1996. And Helms fought a rearguard action on racial issues, from trying to block the establishment of the Martin Luther King Jr. holiday to the renewal of civil rights legislation. That he believed in what he was doing did not put him on the side of the angels.

Yet Helms stood as an iconic figure of the late twentieth century for his accomplishments. He and his political apparatus rescued Ronald Reagan's 1976 campaign for the Republican presidential nomination, partly by helping him win pivotal North Carolina and partly through national efforts on his behalf in the later primaries and subsequent general election. Although Reagan lost that nomination to incumbent president Gerald Ford, Helms and the party's right wing won on big platform issues, and they kept Reagan politically alive. Helms's forces also helped Reagan win the GOP nomination in 1980.

That nomination sealed the conservative command over the Republican Party. When Reagan showed signs of deviating from the right (wing) path, Helms tried to pull him back on the premise that "Reagan should be Reagan," not a moderate in the Ford mold. In the 1980s, the GOP found its ideological identity, always prodded by Helms. Its mantra: a free market economy with minimal government regulation, states' rights, a slowdown in "social engineering" to achieve the perfect society, and a leap in military expenditures with the goal of halting the advance of communism. In later years, Helms advocated human rights for people in Tibet, long oppressed by the Chinese.

Helms's loudest hue and cry was on religious issues with moral overtones: opposition to abortion, pornography, and gay rights; support for religious education, "family values," and prayer in public settings. Over

the decades, American and Western culture had become more accepting of sexual differences and explicit sexual behavior in the movies and
on television. Consensual sexual intercourse between unmarried adults
also became more common, even among some religious activists. Helms
decried the trend, but the permissive tide continued, sometimes propelled by Republican-leaning media groups such as Rupert Murdoch's Fox
conglomerate.

Helms and allies Jerry Falwell and Pat Robertson had an impact on the
abortion debate. The country as a whole remained closely split on the pro-
choice/pro-life debate. But in 2000 more than in 1973 or the pre–*Roe v.
Wade* 1960s, the anti-abortion coalition kept the pro-choice advocates on
the defensive. Indeed, in the late 1950s and 1960s, Helms's North Carolina
had among the nation's most liberal laws on abortion, with public funds
supporting needy women who wanted abortions. Thanks to Helms and
a mobilized coalition of leading Catholic clergy and evangelical Protestants, the climate became more restrictive. Nonetheless, on most issues
of concern to religious conservatives, the journey down the road to permissiveness and secularism at most slowed down; it was not reversed.
Federal court rulings, liberals, civil libertarians, and Democrats in the U.S.
Congress and state legislatures formed the human barrier that stopped
or slowed the anti-abortion march. But as a political movement that prevailed in elections, the Right had a big impact: the elections of Reagan and
two Bushes. Religious conservatives were motivated as they had not been
since the 1920s.

Many mass leaders—and demagogues—are bored by details. Helms
was a first-rate administrator and a master of detail. Everyone who
worked for Helms knew that he insisted on accountability and efficiency.
And only a few twentieth-century senators mastered the details of the
chamber's arcane procedural rules and traditions as well as Helms.
He had two tutors: Senators James Allen of Alabama and Robert Byrd
of West Virginia. Allen was an ultraconservative Democrat who reveled
in tying up the Senate on procedural points. Byrd combined economic
and cultural populist strains. In the 1960s and 1970s, he took umbrage
at protesters in the streets, whether they were Black Power advocates or
long-haired student radicals. He saw Helms as a gut fighter and an ally.[41]
Allen and Byrd found Helms to be a quick study. With mastery of the
Senate rules comes power, and Helms soon had gained grudging respect
from other senators. After the Republicans won control of the Senate and
Helms had built seniority, he became chair of the Agriculture Committee and then the Foreign Relations Committee. At that point, neither the

Washington bureaucracy nor overseas governments could ignore Jesse Helms.

Other controversial senators, notably Huey Long in the 1930s and Joe McCarthy in the 1950s, flouted Senate rules and traditions. Helms embraced them and consequently became a force to be reckoned with. To the end, Helms saw himself as a crusader for Americanism, patriotism, and religious values, defending good against evil. Said one longtime associate who asked not to be named, "Jesse had balls." To his fiercest critics, Helms was evil, even satanic. He was a political giant, much too big and complex for a simple epitaph.

### THE INIMITABLE CRAFTSMAN

Jim Hunt was sui generis, one of a kind, unlike any other post–Civil War governor either in personality or in political philosophy. He managed simultaneously to be effusive and polished and to convey a sense of gravitas. As Hunt got older, he seemed as energetic as ever. And he remained a man on a mission. Hunt pushed the state toward new frontiers. Hunt was the diplomat who never lost sight of his goals.

In early 2006, Hunt had major colon surgery, and doctors ordered him to take it easy for a few weeks. Still in the recovery stage, he desperately wanted to attend a fund-raiser for Democratic legislative candidates at which major business and political figures would be present. Hunt got clearance to go on the condition that he stay for only a short while. Of course, he stayed much longer, and when his longtime friend, Burley Mitchell, approached Hunt's wife, Carolyn, about getting him to leave, Carolyn said, "Jim has a couple more people he wants to talk to." Mitchell responded, "Yes, and on his way to the cemetery, he'll still have a couple of people he wants to talk to."[42] Hunt soon regained his usual robustness and resumed his heavy schedule. From his modest office at Womble, Carlyle, Sandridge, and Rice, a Raleigh law firm, Hunt continued to broker deals and to promote North Carolina. He remained a major behind-the-scenes figure in Democratic politics.

Hunt's personal tastes always remained simple. As governor and as private citizen, he spent as much time as possible on his Wilson farm. He was as comfortable on a tractor as in the corporate boardroom. Like his archrival, Helms, Hunt was not one to flaunt his position or to show off material possessions.

Losing the U.S. Senate race to Helms in 1984 paved the way for Hunt to make a stronger mark on North Carolina than would have been the case if he had gone on to Washington. His second eight years as governor were more cautious and conservative than his first eight years. But both times, Hunt was the model progressive, promoting all levels of education; infrastructure improvements; wider economic opportunities for people of varied genders, races, and backgrounds; and economic expansion. Some liberals of the economic populist bent thought that he was too cozy with the bankers and industrialists. Hunt demurred: "The liberals just don't get it."[43] Hunt believed that progress and human betterment demanded a partnership of public officials and politicians with business leaders and educators.

Starting with Hunt in 1992, the Democratic Party won five North Carolina governors' races in a row, a record of success for the party unsurpassed anywhere else in that period. During the same period, Republican presidential candidates won North Carolina four of five times. Hunt claimed a lot of the credit for the Democrats having performed so well in state elections.[44] He was right. Despite differences with Hunt on specific policy issues, core groups such as liberal ideologues, minorities, educators, trial lawyers, and organized labor stuck with the party. Also supporting the party with their checkbooks were leading bankers, builders, entrepreneurs, software executives, and manufacturers.

In earlier days, southern bankers and industrialists had often dictated policy to their state Democratic Parties. However, many of those business leaders gravitated to the Republican Party beginning in the 1950s. North Carolina was no exception to the trend until Hunt convinced many modern business executives that the new North Carolina Democratic Party was not their enemy. As governor, he worked for business-friendly tax policies, sometimes to the dismay of liberal reformers. But he also appealed to business leaders' sense of civic and state pride. These efforts resulted in the development and expansion of charitable efforts in a state that had long possessed a philanthropic spirit. And business leaders saw how government programs for education and sometimes for the environment could benefit them. Major Republicans—Jim Holshouser and Jim Martin—shared much of the same philosophy. They, like Hunt, were what Paul Luebke, a liberal sociologist, writer, and 2009 chair of the Finance Committee in the N.C. House, called "modernizers."[45] Under Hunt's tutelage, progressivism thrived as never before. Before large groups, he artfully blended business-friendly rhetoric with economic populist ideals. The stated goal: the betterment of the human race.

Hunt, like Helms, was a devout churchgoer, and he believed that his policy goals—better education and ending racism—reflected his abiding religious faith.[46] Hunt, like Helms, was a righteous warrior. But the two political giants saw the world through contrasting prisms. Helms was the fearless defender of causes that he cherished. Hunt was a builder, a master craftsman. While Helms's time had come and gone, Hunt stood ready to help those who might carry on his mission in the 2008 campaigns. As a private citizen, he remained North Carolina's First Democrat and a leading figure in the party establishment. Together, Helms and Hunt personified much about North Carolina politics not only at the turn of the century but also for the entire last third of the twentieth century.

## CHAPTER TWELVE

# Seismic Shifts

Not since the 1894–1900 period had North Carolina been so politically volatile as it was from 2008 through 2012. First, the Democrats made strides not imagined a few years earlier. North Carolina emerged as a major swing state in presidential politics. Soon thereafter, Republicans achieved hitherto unseen levels of support on the legislative level. However, North Carolina also seemed less like a typical southern state in its political behavior, and Democrats chose Charlotte as the site for their 2012 national convention.

## 2008: THE OUTLOOK

The lack of incumbents eligible to run was a defining feature of 2008. No sitting president or vice president would be on the ballot. Governor Mike Easley was ineligible to run after two consecutive terms. Of North Carolina's three top-tier races—president, governor, and U.S. Senate—only the race for senator featured an incumbent, and Elizabeth Dole appeared likely to win a second term. Despite the party's setbacks two years earlier, North Carolina remained a Republican-leaning state in presidential and senatorial races. The state seemed comfortable with Dole's issue positions. On a very few issues, her voting record had been less conservative than the voting records of Senators Jesse Helms and Richard Burr. She projected a moderate image to white women, a key voting bloc.

Too, there was the "waitress thesis," outlined best by veteran *Raleigh News and Observer* reporter Rob Christensen. Dole was one of the most famous women in America. Wherever she went, the public, including restaurant waitresses, rushed up for her autograph. The autograph seekers included people who showed no interest in the typical politician, female or male. The senator was a celebrity.[1] She had long appeared in magazine surveys of "most admired women." Although she would be seventy-two by the time of the election, she remained articulate and good-looking, and she had lost none of her public charm.

Seeing her strength, leading Democrats either were afraid to challenge her or lacked the fire in the belly for an all-out fight. Jim Hunt was close to the same age as Dole. Though he was as jaunty and active as ever despite his recent colon surgery, Hunt had no taste for what would have been a bruising and difficult race for the U.S. Senate. Easley might have run a competitive race, but Dole would have been the favorite among oddsmakers. Other credible Democrats included state senator Kay Hagan of Greensboro, but most hesitated to risk their reputations and money.

Dole had another advantage. Whatever the outcome of the national presidential race, North Carolina appeared likely to be in the Republican presidential column for the eighth time in a row. A Republican victory in the presidential race would, it was believed, help Dole and other incumbent Republicans.

Yet Dole was more vulnerable than she seemed. She had not tended to the political details back in North Carolina. Republican fund-raisers and contributors felt ignored. One of the best of them was Raleigh's Bert Coffer, the anesthesiologist who had developed a close friendship with Jesse Helms. Coffer had turned the anesthesiologists into a potent political force and had links to physicians in other specialties and businesspeople. Coffer was distraught about what he considered the tone-deafness of Senator Dole and her staff. In an October 2006 interview he said that Republican contributors were furious, and he anticipated having difficulty raising money for her reelection campaign. Other Republican activists, most not wishing to be quoted by name, expressed similar misgivings.[2]

Dole also faced problems with the wider public. Jesse Helms was a hard act to follow. Helms's staff had been among the best in Washington—accessible, effective, polite, and responsive, even when they were unable to satisfy callers. Dole had been a cabinet member, and a forcefully effective one, heading both the Transportation and Labor Departments, but the transition from the executive branch to Congress is not easy. Accessibility, or at the least the perception of accessibility, is vital. And Dole's time was precious. She chaired the Republican senatorial campaign committee in 2006. In this capacity, she spent a lot of time raising money for other Republican senators seeking reelection. This limited the amount of time she could devote to her constituents in North Carolina.[3] It was a testimony to Dole's good name, ability, and charm that she remained favored to win reelection despite dissension building both in and out of the Republican Party.

Pundits expected North Carolina to play a minimal role in the presidential race. Its primary would not come until May, late in the process, when nominations would likely be sewn up.

Early in 2008, North Carolina's John Edwards remained a contender with organizations in key caucus and primary states such as Iowa and New Hampshire. But if his bid were doing well, a primary win in his home state would be mere icing on the cake, and if he was doing poorly nationally, North Carolina's vote would come too late to do him any good. Edwards positioned himself on the left end of the political spectrum. More than anyone else in the race, he posed as the economic liberal. His speeches had lost none of their flair. Edwards's compassionate-sounding rhetoric equaled his 2004 standard, but the tone was angrier. Some observers had viewed Edwards as the moderate four years earlier. By 2008, only his southern origins and dialect provided hints of moderation. Nonetheless, a flock of moderate North Carolina Democrats—primarily attorneys and party activists—backed Edwards, believing that he was the one Democrat with a shot to take the state in November.

He had competition from New Mexico governor Bill Richardson, who had served as secretary of commerce in Bill Clinton's administration and had wide support among fellow Hispanics. Another contender, Senator Joe Biden of Delaware, had a voting record similar to Edwards's but was more of a Washington team player. As fellow members of the Foreign Relations Committee, Biden and Jesse Helms had developed a mutual trust and friendship. In contrast, Helms had detested Edwards.

By January, Edwards's star had begun to dim, partly because two celebrities dominated the battle: Hillary Rodham Clinton and Barack Obama. In addition, however, Edwards, the self-proclaimed man of the people, began to commit political blunders with increasing frequency. He built a megamansion outside Chapel Hill. His behavior seemed to show a touch of narcissism.

Hillary Clinton projected as the hard-nosed political realist with a pragmatic bent. But for conservatives, perhaps no one since Bobby Kennedy in the 1960s had been such a lightning rod. Like Elizabeth Dole, Clinton made lists of most admired women in America. But unlike Dole, Clinton was also among the most hated. Detractors saw her as a leftist feminist, hostile to traditional American values.

With Obama came risks. He was black and ostensibly liberal and would be a poison pill to white conservatives in North Carolina. Moreover, Obama's political career was based in Chicago, which defenders saw as the most American of cities but critics perceived as a cesspool of political corruption. Moreover, as a child, Obama had lived in Indonesia, and rumormongers whispered darkly that he was a Muslim. Later revelations of his membership in the Reverend Jeremiah Wright's "radical" Chicago Protestant Christian Church added still more heat to the boiling cauldron. Yes, Obama was a passionate speaker, but so were Jesse Jackson and Malcolm X, and neither of them had connected with white listeners. Obama did.[4]

An Obama candidacy might unleash new political forces. Win or lose, he had the potential to attract record numbers of African Americans, other minorities, and young whites to the polls. The country was changing. Since the 1960s, immigrants had been flooding into New York, Chicago, Florida, and California. Liberal whites, Asians, and African Americans had moved into the South, including North Carolina. It was a new country and a new state—maybe. The Obama candidacy was intriguing.

## THE PRIMARIES

Among the states likely to give Obama a boost early in the nomination battle were South Carolina, Alabama, and Georgia—all states where blacks were a big share of the Democratic primary electorate, but states that neither Obama nor any other Democrat could hope to carry in the November general election. And indeed, South Carolina's late-winter Democratic primary lifted Obama to front-runner status in the quest for the Democratic nomination.[5]

Edwards's star continued to fade, Biden and Richardson never gained traction, and the Democratic race narrowed to Clinton and Obama. Obama moved into a solid lead after February victories in the "Chesapeake primaries," Virginia and Maryland, and effectively clinched the nomination with wins in Indiana and North Carolina in May. Obama had seen the North Carolina primary as crucial. He set up one of the largest and most energized operations ever seen there in a primary, using both paid workers and volunteers. Their slogan afterward was "On to November." Whatever the long odds in the state, the Obama campaign decided that it would keep the North Carolina organization in place, a position supported by the newly reenergized state Democratic Party under the leadership of Jerry Meek.

By early March, John McCain had locked up the Republican nomination, though he would not be formally crowned until the early September convention. In 2007 and early 2008, national and state conservative talk radio hosts such as Rush Limbaugh had criticized McCain with a vengeance previously reserved for Bill and Hillary Clinton. But McCain withstood the assault. After his nomination became inevitable, conservative guns turned back toward Hillary Clinton and then toward Obama. Nevertheless, enthusiasm for McCain seemed lacking among committed issue voters who felt he had been too cozy with Democrats. However, McCain took an appropriately conservative pro-life position and generally wanted to hold the line on taxes. McCain won North Carolina's Republican primary, but nearly all media attention that day focused on the Clinton-Obama race and the Democratic primaries for state office. McCain hoped to win North Carolina with ease in November.[6]

In 1972 and 1984, Democratic gubernatorial primaries had torn the party to bits. For a time, party activists feared a similar scenario in 2008. Lieutenant Governor Beverly Perdue and state treasurer Richard Moore had similar ideological bearings. Both had been in the legislature before winning election to their current posts. Both had prestigious academic credentials—Perdue, a doctorate in education administration from the University of Florida, Moore a degree from the London School of Economics and a law degree from Wake Forest. Moore was secretary of public safety and crime control in the latter part of the Hunt administration. Fears that he would politicize the treasurer's post had not materialized. Though her image was less polished than Moore's, Perdue was just as hardworking and hard-driving. They nitpicked away at each other's résumés and honesty, with Perdue prevailing in the primary.

The Republican gubernatorial primary featured three strong candidates: state senator Fred Smith from Johnston County, Salisbury attorney and antitax advocate Bill Graham, and Charlotte mayor Pat McCrory. McCrory, who called himself a conservative, fit into the North Carolina progressive tradition. Like the other candidates, he backed public schools, though he favored competition from charter schools (independent public schools) and a strong network of private schools. He had led the campaign for and implemented a new mass transit rail system for Charlotte. McCrory won the primary.

State senator Kay Hagan of Greensboro, party leaders' choice to challenge Dole, easily won the Democratic primary, but nearly everyone saw Hagan's bid as an uphill climb.

### THE ROAD TO NOVEMBER

With the Clintons no longer contesting the nomination, the Democratic National Convention was an Obama love feast. He tapped Joe Biden as his running mate. Despite his liberal voting record, Biden was popular among North Carolina party leaders and had been a sought-after speaker at party affairs.

After the Republican convention, McCain gained in national polls and in state polls across the country, moving slightly ahead in North Carolina. But McCain had already made one potentially fatal miscalculation and would soon make another. At the convention, he had tapped Alaska governor Sarah Palin as his running mate in a bid to energize the party's conservative base, stir up excitement, and win wavering female voters. After McCain's announcement, the media's knives turned on Palin, who had neither the seasoning nor the temperament to stand up to the assault.

The second McCain miscalculation came in response to the gathering economic storm. In the aftermath of the Wall Street financial meltdown and the collapse of the Lehman Brothers investment bank, McCain announced the "suspension" of his campaign. Saying that the world situation was too grave for politics as usual, McCain called for the cancellation of the first presidential debate, scheduled for September 26 in Oxford, Mississippi. Obama said he would be at the debate, with or without McCain. Not until the morning of September 26 did McCain announce that he would attend. The occasion was full of symbolism for Obama, as the battle over James Meredith's admission to the University of Mississippi in Oxford had occurred forty-six years earlier, almost to the day. While both candidates turned in credible performances, Obama had the edge. McCain's campaign suspension, if strategic, had been a failure. It suggested erraticism. In "Red North Carolina," the polls were tight for the rest of the campaign, and the final surveys were split. Most showed a tie or slight Obama edge, although McCain led in a Mason-Dixon poll.[7]

By September, the Dole-Hagan U.S. Senate race also had tightened. In August, the Democratic Senatorial Campaign Committee released what might have been the most devastating television commercial of 2008 in any state. Two men, who might have passed for Dole's father and uncle, sat in front-porch rocking chairs discussing whether Dole was 92 or 93, giving the impression that they were talking about her age. The ad then shifted smoothly to other themes, pointing out that one organization had rated Dole 93rd out of 100 senators in effectiveness and that she had voted with President George Bush, by then unpopular even in North Carolina, 92 percent of the time. In one swoop, the ad tried to make three points: Dole was ineffective, a Bush clone, and no spring chicken.[8]

The ad was misleading, but even more misleading was a spot launched by the desperate Dole campaign in the last week of the campaign. The ad reported Hagan's presence at a Boston fund-raiser sponsored by Wendy Kaminer and Woody Kaplan, who the ad said had ties to the Godless Americans Political Action Committee. Kaminer and Kaplan were members of the Secular Coalition of America, a group that wants to keep religion out of American public life, but they denied that the fund-raiser was linked with the Godless Americans PAC. The ad ended with a voice that sounded like Hagan's—but was not actually hers—shouting, "There is no God!"[9]

Whatever Kaminer's and Kaplan's beliefs, Hagan was a longtime Presbyterian and had been a Sunday school teacher. She filed a defamation suit. The Dole campaign said that the real issue was Hagan's "judgment" in attending such an event. Unlike the rocking chair ad, this one missed its target. Dole had campaigned as a conventional Republican—pro–Iraq War, anticrime, and skeptical of high taxes. Hagan was critical of Bush but attempted to project a moderate image and an abiding faith in public education. She seemed the embodiment of a North Carolina progressive.

Perdue and McCrory were the most evenly matched of any candidates for governor since 1972. Both had stamina. Perdue was a moderate liberal who had worked closely with Hunt, Easley, and Democratic legislative leaders. She had built ties with Democratic interest groups, especially educators. As lieutenant governor, Perdue's most controversial action had been breaking the Senate's tie vote in favor of the state lottery.

As the Democratic nominee for governor, Perdue stressed the longtime party themes of education and transportation. She criticized McCrory for backing school vouchers—taxpayer support for students attending private schools. She charged that McCrory would divert transportation funds to Charlotte at the expense of rural areas and small towns.[10]

McCrory campaigned on some of the standard Republican themes: lowering income and business taxes to stimulate economic growth, efficiency and accountability in government. He also promised to clean house in Raleigh and break the cycle of Democratic corruption. As much as possible, he shunned hot-button social issues such as abortion. McCrory, like Perdue, favored an expansion of mass transit, both rail and bus, and it had been one of his signature issues during his seven terms as mayor of Charlotte.[11]

Perdue had a money edge in the campaign; McCrory presented the more polished performance in the five debates. Most of the state's major newspapers endorsed McCrory. The liberal and usually Democratic *Raleigh News and Observer* editorial endorsement said that "McCrory comes across as intelligent, ambitious, well-spoken. . . . Bev Perdue is a good candidate, but McCrory suits the moment. He's loaded with energy and fresh ideas."[12] The *News and Observer* and the major daily newspapers in Charlotte, Durham, and Greensboro had the same picks for the three top tier races: Obama for president, Hagan for senator, and McCrory for governor. On the eve of the election, the governor's race appeared to be a nail-biter.

## DEMOCRATS' TRIUMPH

Before the media declared a winner, at 11:00 eastern time on the evening of November 4, 2008, the presidential outcome was clear. Obama had an electoral vote landslide and a popular vote majority. He was the president-elect. However, McCain clung to a lead in North Carolina until after midnight. By 1:00 on the morning of November 5, Obama moved ahead when new returns rolled in from Buncombe County (Asheville). At dawn, he was a few thousand votes ahead, but the race remained too close to call. Finally, on November 6, the Associated Press and other news outlets declared Obama the North Carolina winner. The official tally released in December confirmed Obama's state victory: 2,142,651–2,128,474. The fact that a Barack Hussein Obama, a liberal African American from Chicago, had carried North Carolina, no matter by how small a margin, suggested a political seismic shift. Obama's 49.7 percent in North Carolina was just short of a clear majority. But other successful presidential candidates in the state—Richard Nixon in 1968 and Ronald Reagan in 1980—had won plurality victories rather than majority victories. In the preceding fifty years, the only Democratic presidential nominees with North Carolina percentages exceeding Obama's were John Kennedy in 1960, Lyndon Johnson in 1964, and Jimmy Carter in 1976.

Hagan won a near-landslide victory (2,249,311–1,887,510) over Dole, an outcome few observers had foreseen until a few weeks earlier. And Perdue had a modest win (2,121,320–1,980,761) over McCrory despite a campaign that had been ridiculed as ineffective. Libertarian Mike Munger, a Duke political science professor added spice and vigor to the gubernatorial campaign and received more than 100,000 votes. North Carolina's historic election of its first female governor was overshadowed by the country's election of its first African American president. And the heated senatorial campaign between two women, one an incumbent, also diminished the salience of the gender factor in the governor's race.

In addition, Democrat Janet Cowell won the position of state treasurer, which Richard Moore was vacating because of his earlier run for the Democratic gubernatorial nomination. In an upset, Democrat Beth Wood defeated incumbent Republican Les Merritt in the state auditor's race. Merritt had been an activist, vigilant in conducting investigations, especially when he suspected Democrats of malfeasance. Few expected his defeat. Whereas the Council of State and the governorship and lieutenant governorship had long been the exclusive province of middle-aged or older men, six of the ten statewide elected officials were women: the governor, the secretary of state, the superintendent of public instruction, the labor commissioner, the treasurer, and the auditor.

Democrats kept control of the state legislature with a 30–20 margin in the Senate and a 68–52 edge in the House. Of the one hundred boards of county commissioners (the county legislative bodies), sixty-four were now controlled by the Democratic Party. As recently as the 2004 elections, Republicans had won forty-four of those boards.[13]

The icing on the cake for Democrats was Larry Kissell's victory over veteran Republican Robin Hayes in the Eighth Congressional District. National Democrats, state Democrats, and interest groups had thrown all the resources they could muster into the rematch of the 2006 race, and this time Kissell emerged with the win. It was a Democratic night, solidifying their hold on the state.

### OBAMA VICTORY: THE NEW MATHEMATICS

The composition of Obama's victory in North Carolina was unprecedented. Obama won big margins in the five counties with the state's largest cities: Mecklenburg (Charlotte), Wake (Raleigh), Guilford (Greensboro), Durham (Durham), and Forsyth (Winston-Salem). Any one of these counties could claim to have provided Obama's 14,177-vote margin in the state.

| | *Obama* | *McCain* | *Obama popular vote margin* |
|---|---|---|---|
| Durham | 103,456 | 32,353 | 71,103 |
| Forsyth | 91,085 | 73,674 | 17,411 |
| Guilford | 142,101 | 97,718 | 44,383 |
| Mecklenburg | 253,958 | 153,848 | 100,110 |
| Wake | 250,891 | 187,001 | 63,890 |
| Totals | 841,491 | 544,594 | 296,897 |

Three other urban/suburban North Carolina counties also provided Obama with majorities exceeding his state lead: Buncombe (Asheville), Cumberland (Fayetteville, Fort Bragg), and Orange (Chapel Hill). Together, these counties gave Obama a 63,000-vote lead. Without the eight big-margin counties, a 14,000-vote Obama edge would have been a 348,000-vote McCain win, a better performance for Obama in 2008 than for Kerry in 2004 and Gore in 2000, but far short of victory. Never in a

North Carolina general election for president or any other office had the urban counties teamed up in this way to produce a winner.

In the country as a whole as well as across the South from Virginia to Texas, urban areas had experienced a Democratic tidal wave. Even in the five Deep South states that McCain won (Alabama, Georgia, Louisiana, Mississippi, and South Carolina), places such as Charleston County, South Carolina, and Jefferson County (Birmingham), Alabama, went for Obama. They and many other southern cities had gone Republican in most presidential elections from 1952 through 2004. Likewise, three of the largest North Carolina cities—Charlotte, Greensboro, and Winston-Salem—had supported Republican Dwight Eisenhower in 1952 and 1956 and had often backed Republican presidential candidates thereafter. Raleigh/Wake County had first moved into the Republican presidential column in 1968, when Nixon won there. But from 1968 through 2004, Wake County went for only one Democratic presidential candidate, Bill Clinton in 1992, and then just by a whisker. Among the urban counties, only Durham had a strong history of backing Democratic presidential candidates. Except for Al Smith in 1928 and George McGovern in 1972, Durham had been Democratic for the preceding century. In 2008, however, the metropolitan centers had finally made a real difference in the election's outcome.

A powerful showing among minority voters helped Obama in all the state's cities, but he scored impressively in many predominantly white precincts heavily populated by academics, architects, attorneys, managers, medical doctors, and migrants from other parts of the United States. This phenomenon was most pronounced in the Research Triangle (Chapel Hill–Durham–Raleigh) but existed in every major piedmont city and Asheville. Exit polling indicated that Obama had won 35 percent of North Carolina's white vote, a big jump from John Kerry's 27 percent in 2004.[14] While losing a majority of North Carolina counties outside the urban clusters, Obama's percentage showing in most counties was better than that of any Democratic contender since Clinton. And except in a few rural mountain counties that were heavily white, Obama won a higher percentage of the votes than had Kerry in 2004. The result was a precedent-shattering if razor-thin Obama victory. Obama narrowly lost the coastal plain, the first time in more than a hundred years that a Democrat running for any office had won the state while losing the coastal plain.

Independent exit polling indicated that Obama had won 95 percent of the black vote, 10 percentage points higher than Kerry received in 2004. The increase in minority voter turnout would not in itself have turned North Carolina from red to blue if Obama had not won a vital slice of white voters,

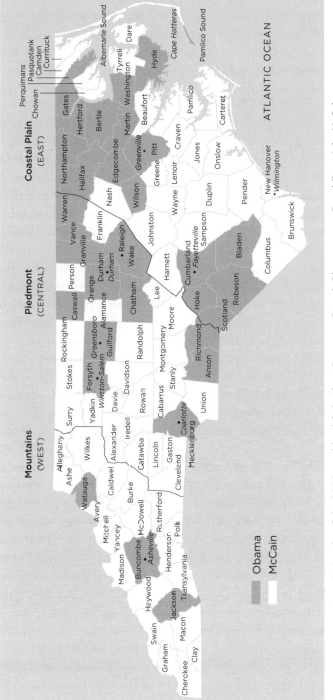

Map 9. Results of the 2008 presidential election—Democrat Barack Obama versus Republican John McCain

but success in mobilizing African Americans kept him in the game. Losing Democrats in the past—Jim Hunt in the 1984 Senate race against Jesse Helms and Harvey Gantt in 1990 and 1996 Senate races against Helms—won around the same percent of the white vote. But in 2008, winning an almost identical percentage of white voters, Obama claimed the state.

### WHY OBAMA WON: THE MAN AND THE TIMES

So why did Obama win, and what did his victory say about the transition in North Carolina and more broadly in American politics? Across the country, including the Sunbelt states, the economy had begun to stumble into the scariest of post–World War II recessions. North Carolina's unemployment rate exceeded the national average and would soon equal that of such trouble spots as Ohio and Alabama. On top of the rise in unemployment was a credit squeeze. Middle-class families lost their homes to foreclosure. And the banking sector faced its most serious crisis in decades. Charlotte, which liked to boast of its world-class financial status, feared retrenchment and major job losses. The severity of the crisis did not become apparent until mid-autumn. Bad economic times often herald the defeat of the party currently holding the presidency, but in the United States, voters' final decisions boil down to their comfort levels with the candidates.

Candidate appeal—speaking skills, personality, personal attractiveness, and charisma—always exerts a pull. Obama might well have been cast as a presidential candidate in a Hollywood movie. He spoke with a quiet eloquence. But unlike so many captivating African American orators—Shirley Chisholm, Jesse Jackson, Malcolm X—Obama did not turn off white moderates. His message of hope resonated. Obama portrayed himself as the embodiment of the American Dream. If he could aspire to be president, hope was alive and transcended barriers of race and humble origins.

Obama had a good solid build yet was not physically overpowering in a way that separated him from the general public. Few recent politicians so skillfully combined passion and personal magnetism. Unlike some others in that select group—Bobby Kennedy in the 1960s most immediately comes to mind—Obama had not yet inspired an irrational fear and hatred among those of opposing political persuasions, who were aiming their spears at Hillary Clinton in 2007 and early 2008.

The electorate perceives both winners and losers in ways that neither can ultimately control. John McCain's résumé would have been the envy of any politician: Annapolis graduate, playboy turned war hero, prisoner of war in the Hanoi Hilton, scourge of his captors, patriot, member of Congress, U.S. senator, close friendships across ideological and partisan boundaries, expertise on foreign policy. He was less dynamic than Obama but a decent enough speaker. He would be seventy-two at the time of in-auguration, but Ronald Reagan had pushed up the acceptable age limit. But his erratic performance as a candidate and his wavering policy positions turned off some voters. Obama adroitly pounced on McCain without seeming mean and deflected the more controversial aspects of his own past liberal positions. More and more, Obama seemed to embody the times, while McCain was of another era. No two candidates in the 2008 arena could have so perfectly symbolized the generational divide. And perhaps no other Democratic candidate could have pulled North Carolina from the red column to the blue. The young and the minority voters had turned out at levels not seen before. The message of change resonated.

So Obama had the advantage on the economy and candidate attrac-tiveness: personality, speaking skills, aura, and symbolism. But in all but the most lopsided races, campaigns matter. Both sides spent vast sums in getting out their supporters and cutting down the competition. Campaigns are the essence of democracy, and democracy can be mean, vicious, and divisive.

### WHY OBAMA WON: THE CAMPAIGN

Old-style political campaigns stress organization to get out the vote. American presidential candidates were taking this approach in the 1840s. But modern campaigns, at least for the big prizes, spend enormous sums on communications and advertising: computer files, direct mail, phone banks, radio, and television outreach. Since Skipper Bowles's 1972 guber-natorial campaign and Jesse Helms's campaign for senator in the same year, North Carolina had been a trendsetter in this new approach to politics, which threatened to obliterate the old. The goal is not only to turn out the vote for your own candidate but to rip the opposition apart in ways that will demoralize the candidate and his supporters and depress their voter base. And with voters not affiliated with either party a growing force, the new media campaigns try to draw in people who have loose political moorings. Like all recent campaigns. McCain's and Obama's devoted immense re-sources to communications and advertising. Moreover, Obama's enhance-ment of techniques that had been used in 2000 and 2004 was a centerpiece of his campaign.[15]

Jerry Meek, the chair of the North Carolina Democratic Party, also understood how technology could revolutionize campaigns. The Inter-net provided voters in remote places or those who lacked the flexibility to participate in the normal political channels the opportunity for direct involvement in politics. The electronic revolution, which hitherto had seemed to dehumanize campaigns, suddenly made them more personal, at least for the computer-savvy. Moreover, members of this group were disproportionately young and in early middle age, and many of them had not previously been in the loop. As in the spring primaries, Obama used the Internet not only for fund-raising but also to give people a sense of belonging or connection to the campaign. His organization bonded the old-style campaign, stressing organization and personal contact, with the new-style campaign, attempting to sway large categories of voters.[16]

The Obama campaign reinvigorated the old politics even as it used the new. Building on its effort in the May primary, the Obama organization in North Carolina grew into the largest the state had ever seen in a presidential campaign. At its peak, shortly before the November election, the Obama organization claimed at least four hundred paid staff members and an uncountable but tremendous number of volunteers, some of whom helped in the campaign offices, while others were a presence only on the Internet. McCain, in contrast, had only thirty-five paid staff members in North Carolina, not a small number by traditional standards for a presidential campaign. But a 10:1 staff disadvantage in a state McCain had to win to have a shot at the presidency was simply untenable.[17]

McCain did have built-in organizational strengths. The North Carolina Republican Party, like many of its counterparts across the nation, ran a sophisticated operation that used phone banks as well as direct mail. Individual counties had Republican offices. And many—though not all, as is sometimes supposed—white evangelical Protestant Christian churches passed out "voter guides" that stopped just short of formal endorsements of McCain and other Republican candidates. The guides highlighted McCain's opposition to abortion and Obama's pro-choice position. Pastors spoke of the sanctity of traditional marriage between a man and woman and the looming threat of gay marriage, a possibility they feared would become reality in an Obama administration.[18] Obama had said that he strongly supported traditional marriage but also had expressed generalized support and sympathy for gay rights without specifically endorsing gay marriage.

The Democrats, too, had support organizations designed to counteract the Republicans. Organized labor had been a weak force in North Carolina, benefiting Democrats there primarily through national unions' financial resources. In this race however, labor unions—both national and their North Carolina affiliates—provided campaign workers who enhanced the Democrats' organizational prowess. In addition, the North Carolina

Association of Educators, which had characteristics of both a professional association and labor union, had long been one of the state's most effective lobbies. The association's human resources and organizational talents, in cooperation with those of other groups, probably contributed to Obama's narrow victory. Attorneys, and not just trial lawyers, backed Obama in large numbers with their cash and yard signs. Environmental groups, feeling jilted by past Republican presidents, also aided Obama.

Some African American churches, like some white churches, shun partisan political activity. Others, including many that are Protestant Christian and evangelical, had a long history of support for politically liberal candidates, both black and white, believed to embrace the core teachings of Jesus and a social gospel that stressed racial equality. Their preachers and pastors and congregants might take conservative positions on a range of social issues, including abortion, but their political views were typically Democratic. Under North Carolina's voter registration laws, officially certified registrars could be present and sign up people to vote after a worship service. Based on long tradition, some ministers used their pulpits to urge parishioners to vote as part of their Christian duty. So one aspect of the church mission was to get members to the polls. In 2008, for the first time, many counties opened early voting sites on Sunday. Prayer and civic duty became closely linked.[19]

Using public data from elections boards and commercial data, the Democratic campaign went after both sporadic and occasional voters and newly registered voters, the latter of whom were disproportionately young and black. Taking advantage of liberalized early voting policies and "one-stop" registration and voting at designated sites, the Democrats and allied groups urged their partisans and others inclined toward Obama to vote early.[20]

Around 2.6 million people had voted before Election Day, with another 1.6 million voting on November 4 itself. McCain had a big lead among Election Day voters, but it was not quite large enough to overcome Obama's advantage in early voting. Had there been no early voting, the Obama supporters would have still turned out in tremendous numbers on Election Day, but they would not have been able to overcome McCain's advantages among habitual voters, who are the most likely to go to the polls, rain or shine.[21] However, the Obama for America team and Democrats had outorganized and outfoxed the Republicans in the crucial weeks before Election Day. New laws passed by the Democratic-controlled legislature had made this achievement possible.

Under one-stop voting policies adopted by the state legislature and implemented by the Board of Elections, new registrants could vote on the same day they registered, except on Election Day itself. Consequently, huge numbers of people registered and voted at the same time. In 2008, there were 974,850 new registrants, 750,101 of whom voted in the fall election. Veteran state elections executive director Gary Bartlett called the turnout "amazing." New registrants usually vote at low rates, sometimes below 50 percent. But newly registered voters are much more likely to vote if they can do so immediately after registering. Bartlett believed that the new policy was crucial to Obama's North Carolina victory.[22]

The process of organizing, energizing, and getting people to the polls is sometimes called the ground war of politics. In closely contested North Carolina, the Democrats and their ideological, professional, and spiritual allies won the ground war of 2008. But for all the Democratic prowess in the art and science of conducting an effective ground war, it is an axiom of modern politics that the battle over the airwaves—television and to a lesser degree other media—determines election outcomes. Both amateur and professional political observers declare that the candidate who spends the most money on television will win the election, and that statement usually holds true. However, it may do so in part because the likely winner is apt to raise more money among both committed supporters and people who want to get something out of the incoming administration. Television continued to play a central role in 2008, but the electronic campaign crossed new frontiers.

Obama had the advantage in television spending in North Carolina, though McCain's television campaign surpassed its Democratic and Republican predecessors. Obama for America spent almost $9.5 million on campaign ads in the state, and groups allied with the Democrats together spent almost $1.1 million more on Obama's behalf. The Republican National Committee and its affiliated McCain campaign arm spent nearly $5.23 million on the presidential campaign in North Carolina. The McCain for President organization (the equivalent of Obama for America) spent just over $1.2 million. So while the official Obama campaign organization vastly outspent McCain, the Republican party made up much of the deficit. (The Democratic National Committee provided Obama with a paltry $1,213.) Part of the spending gap reflected the Democrats' early start. Obama for America had aggressively run TV ads at a time when Republicans assumed that McCain could take North Carolina with minimal effort. In later stages, both campaigns bought just about all available time slots. For the whole campaign, Obama outspent McCain nearly 7:1 on radio, $280,000–$39,000.[23]

The impact of other technologies cannot be measured in monetary terms, but their effect was immense and played to Obama's strengths.

E-mail had been part of the ground war effort but was also used for mass messages sent to all fifty states. Obama could deliver his messages directly to mass numbers of voters without the intervening filter of news reporting services. As Bill Clinton had used fax messages as part of a rapid response to attacks in 1992, the Obama team used e-mail in 2008.

Obama also used text messaging, the preferred communication method among young people by 2008. Concurrently, Obama utilized computer-based social networking sites such as My Space, Facebook, and Twitter, the new rage at election time. The Obama campaign established pages on all the major websites, and users became his virtual friends. Indeed, Obama had announced Biden's selection as his running mate via a text message to all his "friends."[24]

Obama's personal website was organized around volunteer groups, enabling the campaign to collect user information such as e-mail addresses and phone numbers. The campaign also used the web to promote real-life campaign events and to portray Obama in the most favorable light. Most important, these other sites and e-mail together gave voters of many ages but especially those between eighteen and thirty a sense of belonging not seen before in a political campaign.

Like most contemporary political candidates as well as his party, McCain maintained an active web presence. However, it paled in comparison to Obama's. In the end, Obama won the votes of 74 percent of North Carolina's most technologically savvy voters—those aged between eighteen and thirty.[25] The new electronic media blurred the distinction between the ground war (human-based organizing to get out the vote) and the air war (mobilization and persuasion through television and radio). Obama realized early on the potential of this third wave of campaigning.

Like the 1960 presidential campaign race between Kennedy and Nixon, the 2008 election revolutionized American campaign techniques. In so doing, it had transformed what had been a reliably red presidential state—North Carolina—into a horse race.

## THE ASCENT OF TWO DEMOCRATIC WOMEN: THE RACES FOR SENATOR AND GOVERNOR

Despite Democratic panic over the "Godless America" television commercial, most analysts believed that Hagan was poised to defeat Dole. Yet Hagan's 9 percent victory surpassed most expectations. Dole eked out a 2,300-vote edge in the Republican-leaning mountain region, while Hagan received 93,000 more votes in the coastal plain. Her margin in the populous piedmont was 272,000. Like Obama, Hagan rolled up huge leads in the piedmont cities, and except in Charlotte, Chapel Hill, and Durham, she ran even better than Obama did.

In the exit polls, Hagan had a 53 percent to 41 percent lead among women, while Dole led among men, 50 percent to 47 percent. Among white men, Dole had a more solid lead. Hagan had the support of 71 percent of voters between ages eighteen and twenty-one and 72 percent of first-time voters, figures that echoed Obama's support levels and benefited from his get-out-the-vote drive. And Hagan received 96 percent of the black vote. Dole was not without pockets of strength, but they were already deeply embedded in the Republican Party: among self-identified white evangelical Christians, for example, Dole led Hagan 67 percent to 31 percent.[26]

Suburban areas varied enormously in their voting. Hagan ran powerfully in the suburbs of Chapel Hill, Durham, and on the west side of Raleigh. She ran poorly, as do most Democrats, in the semisuburban counties to the north and east of Charlotte. Yet even there, Hagan had done better than past Democratic contenders. Rural areas divided along racial and cultural lines. Rural blacks voted as heavily for Hagan as did urban blacks, and she was strong among Native Americans. Traditionally Democratic rural bastions usually voted for Hagan, while Republican areas voted for Dole. In short, race, culture, and party history outweighed the happenstance of a rural dwelling. However, precinct-level data suggest that Hagan outperformed Obama among white voters in rural and historically Democratic parts of the coastal plain and in mountain counties.[27]

While a Hagan victory had been expected from October on, public opinion polling and anecdotal evidence suggested a governor's race as tight as the state presidential race. Both Perdue and McCrory conducted credible campaigns and had smart advisers. And few could question the paper credentials of either. From the beginning, McCrory had the edge on image. He was steady and rarely committed a blunder. Perdue continued to be plagued by her seeming nervousness and country accent. But well before Obama, Perdue was declared the winner by the Associated Press and election night projections. The vote was close yet clear, 2,121,320–1,980,769, a difference of 3 percent. Perdue narrowly lost both the piedmont and mountain regions but won big in eastern North Carolina, her home region, 637,004–466,043. She also had scored well in the piedmont's major cities, and she narrowly and surprisingly carried McCrory's home base of Mecklenburg County (Charlotte), where Obama had run better than any Democratic presidential candidate since Franklin Roosevelt.[28]

There was the widespread perception that Perdue won on Obama's coattails, and she was helped by Obama in ways that she would not have

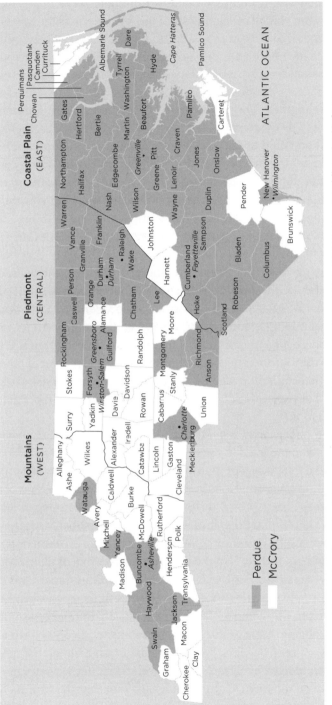

Map 10. Results of the 2008 gubernatorial election—Democrat Beverly Perdue versus Republican Pat McCrory

been helped by any other Democratic nominee. Yet hers was no coattails victory in the classic sense. Perdue's 140,551-vote margin was almost ten times higher than Obama's 14,187, though far below Hagan's 361,801. The governor's race had a life of its own, and large numbers of voters made their decisions for governor independently of those for president.

Nevertheless, Perdue benefited from the Obama campaigns to get voters to the polls. Despite McCrory's moderate stance on many issues, blacks voted as overwhelmingly for Perdue—95 percent—as for Obama. If blacks had voted at their 2004 level (85 percent Democratic), McCrory would likely have achieved a narrow victory.[29] Unlike some past Democratic gubernatorial candidates, Perdue had not shunned her party's presidential nominee, a prudent strategy in this election. Conversely, McCrory was hurt by the state of the national Republican Party. Although he poured out a good dose of appropriately conservative rhetoric, McCrory was more a pragmatic than an ideological conservative, a stance that helped him among swing voters but did little to energize the Republican base.

On balance, the presidential contest helped North Carolina Democrats, and it was crucial in the governor's race. Perdue built a winning coalition resembling that of Obama and Hagan: minority voters, city dwellers, young people, liberals, and a healthy slice of moderates. Her victory reflected the Democratic victory. But in a close election, personal qualities and determination also count. However much sophisticates derided her television appearances, Bev Perdue had few peers in persistence and determination.

Perdue had proved herself a tough-minded politician, willing to do what it took to move up in the ranks of the good-old-boy network. Women had come a long way. For many years, North Carolina lagged on women's issues: inhumane conditions in early textile mills, the rejection of the Nineteenth Amendment providing for universal female suffrage in 1920, hostility toward the Equal Rights Amendment in the 1970s. Margaret Harper's unsuccessful runs for nomination for lieutenant governor in 1968 and 1972 had broken ground. So had the repeated reelections of Elaine Marshall as secretary of state and Cherie Berry as labor commissioner. And the state's most prominent female officeholder, Elizabeth Dole, had lost her bid for reelection but was being replaced by Kay Hagan. But the governorship was the symbolic pinnacle of the state's hierarchy, and voters have long been reluctant to break barriers. While Perdue's crash through the glass ceiling was overshadowed by Barack Obama's election, her victory was almost as significant on the North Carolina stage. In 2008, North Carolina had voted for an African American for president and a woman for governor. And Mike

Easley, a Catholic, was completing two terms as the governor. This was not 1900 or 1950.

The challenges of governing remained daunting, of course. According to former New York governor Mario Cuomo, "You campaign in poetry. You govern in prose."[30] Obama, the most poetic of campaigners, immediately faced the most vexing of post-1930s economic crises and the challenges of guiding a governing coalition. However, the Democratic-controlled Congress in Washington adopted much of his program, including the most comprehensive and controversial health insurance plan since the Lyndon Johnson era.

Obama had more options than did Perdue and her fellow governors. Most states, including North Carolina, have constitutionally imposed borrowing constraints. Though North Carolina's economic crisis was less severe than that of some states, conditions were still in a bad way. Perdue had not been accused of campaigning in poetry, but she was surpassed by few in determination. Her campaign platform was ambitious, following the model of earlier progressive governors. While she hoped that better times lay ahead, Perdue's agenda in 2009 turned out to be one of trying to balance painful spending cuts with intrusive tax increases to support essential programs.[31]

The North Carolina legislature was also in the throes of change. As always, it bore responsibility for approving painful remedies for state problems. The legislature was under a court order to equalize public schools across the state, and it faced harsh economic realities. It had seen worse challenges in the Great Depression of the 1930s, but not in the ensuing eighty years. In the Senate chamber, Lieutenant Governor Walter Dalton, who was a veteran legislator, President Pro Tem Marc Basnight, and Democratic leader Tony Rand provided political savvy.[32] The Republican minority guaranteed spirited debate and thorough vetting of the issues. Across the rotunda, in the House of Representatives, a new team was in charge, in part because of former Speaker Jim Black's fall from power. Experienced representatives calmed the waters, but they were situated ideologically to the left of typical southern legislative leaders.

While both moderate and liberal Democrats wielded influence in the 2009 session of the N.C. House, the leadership included faces that would have been unlikely in the 1970s or 1980s. Joe Hackney, a liberal and pragmatic representative from Orange County, was the House Speaker. Durham's Mickey Michaux, who had run a historic but losing campaign for

*Seismic Shifts* / 307

Congress in 1982, chaired the powerful Appropriations Committee. Also precedent-shattering was Paul Luebke's ascent to being in charge of the House Finance Committee. Luebke, a veteran representative from Durham and New York native, had never kept his ideology a secret. He had been one of the most liberal members of the legislature. Moreover, he was a sociology professor who for years commuted from his Durham home to his teaching post at UNC-Greensboro. He was widely published and began to specialize in the political sociology of North Carolina, producing a groundbreaking 1990 book on North Carolina politics.[33]

The chairs of the appropriations and finance committees have long had among the most influential and time-demanding jobs in state government and have typically been available only to political friends of the Speaker of the House who have close ties to the state's political and business establishments. The chairs of both committees are hounded by a range of interests seeking government assistance or special breaks. In a good year, the Senate and House appropriations committees may recommend government largesse and break new ground with grants for innovative programs. The House Finance Committee, which has immense clout in the chamber as a whole, may write legislation redistributing the tax burden and providing relief to some interests.

In a time of economic growth and an abundant tax harvest, both Michaux and Luebke might have used their posts to expand social programs in a wide range of spheres, including education and social services. Luebke might also have promoted "equity" in the broader society, maybe even nudging North Carolina toward his principles of neopopulism. Instead, he, like Michaux, was caught in the maelstrom of the meanest economic crisis and revenue shortfall since World War II, facing questions about where to cut and whose taxes to raise. As always, the governor led the way, but final decisions rested with the N.C. House and Senate. In the end, major programs survived intact. However, freezes occurred in many areas, and educators and other state employees did not receive salary increases.[34]

At the same time, federal and state investigators were looking into the administration of former governor Mike Easley, who faced accusations that his campaign had failed to report private airplane flights and in-kind contributions from private sources (typically support or subsidies other than direct financial contributions). Easley ultimately paid a one thousand dollar fine to settle the state charges, and the federal charges were not pursued, although one of his top aides, Ruffin Poole, went to prison for tax evasion.[35] Federal prosecutors also looked into accusations that Easley's wife, Mary, had improperly secured a job at North Carolina State University. Although no indictment was forthcoming, she was fired by the university.[36]

### THE SEESAW TIPS

The central political event of the 2009–11 period was the general election of 2010. Midterm elections often produce setbacks for incumbent political parties on both the state and national levels, but few have been as pronounced as that of 2010.[37] Months before November, the North Carolina trend had been clear. While Obama's approval rating had held up surprisingly well considering the continued recession, the Democratic Congress, the Democratic legislature, and Governor Perdue saw their ratings sink into the cellar. And more Democrats—most notably former senator John Edwards—than Republicans had been embroiled in deep scandal. Republicans were energized, and many Democrats were disheartened.

From the beginning, incumbent Republican Richard Burr was favored to win a second term in the U.S. Senate, although his seat had seemed jinxed as it had changed hands in every election since 1974. He had significant advantages: strong constituency service, a keen grasp of North Carolina politics and demographic trends, an engaging personality, and, perhaps most important, the prospects of a good Republican year.

The Democrats lacked a well-financed candidate. Veteran party activist and secretary of state Elaine Marshall sought and won the Democratic nomination after a bruising primary battle against Cal Cunningham, a hard-driving and photogenic young attorney from Lexington. Neither Marshall nor Cunningham had the money for an expensive campaign, but the rhetoric turned personal. Cunningham's campaign produced a series of slick brochures that featured hardly recognizable unflattering photos of Marshall and questioned her ties to lobbyists. The candidates' positions were strikingly similar on major issues, and after the primary, Cunningham and Marshall held an upbeat joint press conference. Nevertheless, scars remained.

In a good Democratic year, Marshall might have been competitive with her Republican opponent. In 2010, however, the odds were stacked heavily against her. During the autumn campaign, both Burr and Marshall adhered closely to their respective parties' positions on most issues. Burr won by nearly 10 percent in the coastal plain and piedmont and 20 percent in the mountains on his way to a statewide victory in which he received 1,458,046 votes to 1,145,074 for Marshall and 55,6897 for Libertarian Michael Beitler. The Democrats continued to show strength in the cities. Marshall carried Asheville, Charlotte, and Durham and led in the cities of Greensboro and

Raleigh but narrowly lost their counties, Guilford and Wake, respectively.[38] Outside the cities, university communities, and Black Belt counties, Burr ran strongly nearly everywhere.

The state congressional delegation went from eight Democrats and five Republicans in the aftermath of the 2008 election to seven Democrats and six Republicans after the 2010 election, with the only party shift occurring in the Second District, where Renee Elmers defeated incumbent Bob Etheridge in a district that had narrowly gone for Obama in 2008. Etheridge had lost his cool when responding to a provocative campaign incident.[39] The Democrats' ability to prevent further GOP gains reflected their crafting of congressional districts after the 2000 census.

The state legislative races provided the major shake-up of the 2010 season in North Carolina. The Senate went from a 30–20 Democratic advantage to a 31–19 Republican edge. The House went from 68 Democrats and 52 Republicans to 67 Republicans and 52 Democrats. If all Senate Republicans voted together, they would have more than the 60 percent needed to override a veto from the governor or to amend the state constitution. House Republicans lacked a veto-proof supermajority by four votes but hoped to gain several Democratic backers on key legislation. The timing of the legislative victory augured well for the Republicans, since it would enable them to control the redistricting after the 2010 census. The governor cannot veto reapportionment matters; only the courts could block any plan approved by the Republican General Assembly.

Two experienced GOP lawmakers captured the top leadership posts. Phil Berger of Rockingham County in the north-central piedmont was elected Senate majority leader, while Thom Tillis from the Charlotte suburbs became Speaker of the House. Berger, Tillis, and their fellow Republicans wanted less government involvement in the economic sphere and restraint on taxes and spending. The new leadership supported a strong government presence in education but also wanted an increase in the number of charter schools, which are supported by public funds but operate free of government constraints in many areas. On this matter, if no other, North Carolina Republicans had the Obama administration as an ally.[40]

Even in the best of economic times, the new Republican majority would have likely promoted a sweeping reexamination of state programs. To some government itself *was* the problem. Going back to Goldwater and Reagan, national GOP leaders believed that the regulation of business and the imposition of higher taxes impeded economic growth.

Yet many of the new state legislators as well as veteran ones were products of the state's public schools and universities and remained boosters of their favorite institutions. Very few actually wanted to massacre public education, however fearful Democrats might be about Republican intentions.

The overall economic picture and state fiscal situation remained dire assuring that cuts and freezes would remain in place. This along with the ideological proclivities of the Republican majority suggested that now cuts were on the horizon.

Nevertheless, a few programs did see spending increases. For example, more than a thousand new teaching positions were funded in the first through the third grades to reduce the class-size funding ratio from 1:18 to 1:17. New funds were provided for the operation of recently opened or renovated college buildings and for the opening of a new dental school at East Carolina University.

But there was a towering list of cuts, quite unlike anything seen since the Great Depression of the 1930s. The pressure for the spending cuts came in part from the Republicans' refusal to extend a sales tax increase that was scheduled to expire on June 30, 2011, and the resulting revenue shortfall. Except for money to support enrollment increases, the universities saw cuts nearly everywhere, often in the 15 percent range.[41] For the moment, the universities and community colleges remained intact and their operations and overall outreach remained at higher levels than existed in the 1990s. Creative administrations found ways to shift funds and achieve greater efficiencies.

The fundamental missions of the public schools also remained intact, but teaching and aide positions were cut, while funds for guidance counselors and social workers were reduced. As in the universities, the budget cuts were painful but not yet devastating, though their full effects might not yet have been felt. State funding for instructional supplies was slashed by 46 percent, and the number of support staffers was reduced.

Republican control of the legislature made a big difference on social issues, most prominently abortion and gay rights. Two U.S. Supreme Court decisions, *Roe v. Wade* (1973) and *Planned Parenthood v. Casey* (1992), limited the options for restricting abortions.[42] However, the 2011 legislature passed a law intended to discourage abortions. In keeping with the Court's decision in *Casey*, the measure required a twenty-four-hour waiting period for women seeking abortions as well as ultrasound scans of the fetus, to be described to the patient by medical personnel, and parental consent for minors.

Republican representative Paul Stam of Apex, in Wake County, successfully pushed a constitutional amendment banning gay marriage. Amendment 1 resembled other measures adopted around the country. North Carolina's Defense of Marriage Act provided that marriage between one man and one woman would be the only domestic or legal union valid or recognized in the state. The bill passed by a 75–42 vote in the House and a 30–16 vote in the Senate but would not go into effect unless a majority of the electorate approved it in a referendum. Amendment 1 appeared on the ballot in May 2012, along with the state Democratic and Republican primary election.

The amendment passed overwhelmingly, with 2,157,980 voters supporting it and 840,802 opposed. In sixteen counties, Amendment 1 received more than 80 percent support. Most of these counties were rural and in the mountains or southeast coastal plain, with populations that were overwhelmingly white and Republican-leaning. However, two of the coastal plain counties that supported the amendment so strongly, Bladen and Columbus, had large minority populations. Bladen had gone for Obama in 2008. Only eight counties voted no, led by Orange (Chapel Hill), where 79 percent of voters opposed the measure. Five of these counties were heavily urban or, like Orange, university-influenced: Durham, Wake, Mecklenburg, Buncombe, and Watauga. Another county that voted no, Chatham, was formerly rural but has experienced a population influx from neighboring Orange, Durham, and Wake. Dare (Manteo and Cape Hatteras) also voted no: It has grown rapidly as people have moved to the coast. All the no counties except Dare had gone for Obama in the 2008 election.

Large majorities of both blacks and whites supported the amendment. Whether the pro-gay-rights stands of Obama and the national Democratic Party would result in a voter backlash remained to be seen. However, indications in the summer of 2012 were that only minimal damage would result among African American voters.[43]

In June 2011, John Edwards had been indicted on charges of using nearly one million dollars in undercover payments from political backers to hide his pregnant mistress, Rielle Hunter, during the 2008 presidential campaign. A companion charge alleged that Edwards had falsified his legally mandated campaign financial reports to conceal those payments from government or public scrutiny. The trial was originally scheduled to begin in October 2011 but was then delayed to 2012 because Edwards's attorneys needed more time to interview witnesses.[44]

Edwards maintained an upbeat facade throughout the ordeal, flashing a big smile both for a mug shot and when heading out of a preliminary court hearing in Greensboro. It was an ironic fate for one of North Carolina's most renowned late-twentieth-century trial lawyers and a man who nearly rose to the vice presidency. On May 31, 2012, after nine days of deliberation, a jury announced that it was hopelessly deadlocked on five of the six charges against Edwards. He was acquitted on the charge that he accepted illegal campaign contributions of $375,000 from Rachel "Bunny" Mellon in 2008.

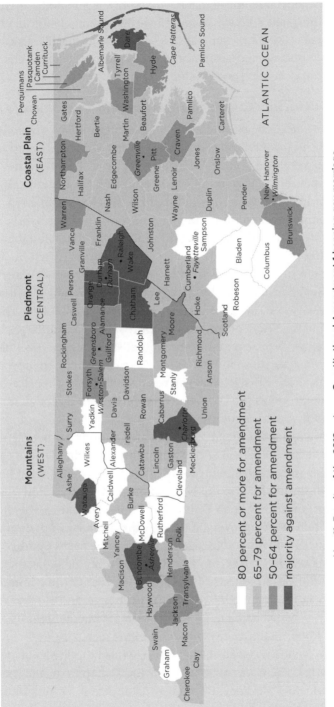

Map 11. Results of the 2012 vote on Constitutional Amendment 1 banning gay marriage

The prosecution announced that it would not call for another trial.[45] But for his entry into politics, Edwards would have been remembered most for his elegantly persuasive courtroom skills. Now it appeared that his legacy would be a notorious political and sexual scandal. Despite his rhetorical championing of the working class and poor, his impact on public policy had been minimal.

## THE RUN-UP TO THE 2012 GENERAL ELECTION

As the 2012 election season began, all indicators from conventional wisdom to the many public opinion surveys suggested that Governor Perdue was in deep political trouble. Well before party primary time, her 2008 opponent, McCrory, appeared to have cemented the Republican nomination. Having come close to winning the governorship in 2008, McCrory had no name-recognition problem. Perdue was further handicapped by scandals involving officials in her administration that tainted her despite the absence of any indication that she was personally corrupt. Moreover, the fallout from the Edwards scandal hurt the Democratic Party.[46]

With Republicans controlling both houses of the state legislature starting in January 2011, much of Perdue's program was doomed. The level of hostility increased as election season approached. On January 6, 2012, Perdue made the surprise announcement that she would not seek reelection, professing a desire to spend the remaining year of her term advocating for education, an issue that had been a major theme during her stint in office.[47]

Her departure left the Democrats scrambling for a candidate. The timing meant that almost any Democrat would start out behind McCrory in both name recognition and money. Three prominent people with long political résumés emerged as major candidates. Walter Dalton came closest to being the establishment candidate. He had represented Rutherford County, in the foothills, in the N.C. Senate from 1997 until he was elected lieutenant governor in 2008. Dalton had been a legislative wheelhorse and was generally noncontroversial. His leading primary opponent was Harnett County's Bob Etheridge, who had lost some of his political luster as well as his seat in Congress in 2010. The third candidate was state representative Bill Faison from Orange County's Cedar Grove community. His district included Chapel Hill, rural parts of Orange, and much of rural Caswell County, which had a large African American population. Faison was the most liberal of the three candidates in the race.

In May, Dalton received 428,475 votes, while Etheridge had 354,953 and Faison 52,179. There was no runoff, leaving Dalton to turn to the arduous task of defeating McCrory. Like recent Democratic victors, Dalton made public education his trademark issue.

McCrory, who led in the public opinion surveys throughout the campaign, stressed transportation improvements and education reform, including teacher accountability and expansion of charter schools. McCrory called for holding the line on state tax increases and reduction of income and corporate taxes. On education and tax issues, his positions resembled those of the Republican leadership in the General Assembly. McCrory generally took conservative positions on abortion and gay marriage, but he did not stress the social issues in his campaign rhetoric.[48]

The race to succeed Dalton as lieutenant governor was tightly contested. Republican Dan Forrest was a party activist but had held no public offices. He headed an architectural firm and boasted of his business experience, which contrasted with the usual political background of candidates for office. He campaigned as a conservative. The progressive Democratic nominee, Linda Coleman, had been a high school teacher, a Wake County commissioner, a member of the N.C. House (2004–8), and director of the Office of State Personnel in the Perdue administration. Forrest was white; Coleman was African American.[49]

The five Democratic and two Republican incumbent members of the Council of State appeared to have the inside track to reelection. But with the lower visibility of these races, it seemed plausible that a Republican landslide in the gubernatorial race might help other party candidates. North Carolina's election procedures required voters to cast a separate ballot for president, but they could vote a straight ticket for all other offices, with the governor's race at the top of the ballot.

### OBAMA VERSUS ROMNEY

From beginning to end, most of the media called North Carolina a swing state in the presidential election. The selection of Charlotte to host the Democratic National Convention had indicated the state's importance to the Obama campaign. In the first half of 2012, national and North Carolina pollsters suggested that Obama had a lead in the state. But if the national election tightened or moved in Republican Mitt Romney's favor, recent political history indicated that North Carolina would likely shift to the Republican column.[50] Even when winning the state in 2008, Obama was three points behind his national level.

In August, Romney and the GOP vice presidential nominee, Paul Ryan of Wisconsin, had come out of their Tampa convention with little or no poll bounce. While Romney had easily won the GOP nomination, he had stirred little enthusiasm. The pro-small-government, antitax Tea Party movement was unhappy with the choice, and even more mainstream conservatives were not enthusiastic about Romney. His rhetoric was conservative, but his past politics had been centrist. In September, the Obama-Biden ticket emerged from the Charlotte convention with a bounce in nearly all public opinion surveys, perhaps propelled in part by a rousing speech delivered by former president Bill Clinton. For several weeks, Obama seemed to occupy a commanding position in the national race; a narrow victory in North Carolina also seemed possible.

Following Obama's anemic showing in the first debate and Romney's better-than-expected performance, the tide seemed to turn. For the final month of the campaign, the outcome appeared in serious doubt. Though North Carolina was still called a swing state, most analysts, including the *New York Times*'s Nate Silver, publisher of the 538 blog and generally bullish on Obama's chances of winning the national election, predicted a Romney victory in North Carolina. Still, most polls showed the state close.

Moreover, both campaigns poured vast financial resources and personnel into the state and advertised heavily right up to Election Day. The Obama field operation was even larger than in 2008, while Romney's advertising and field office operations far surpassed those of McCain. The Obama campaign also made extensive use of social media, especially Facebook. Nevertheless, North Carolina seemed to be a second-level target state for both campaigns as they poured greater resources into Florida, Ohio, and Virginia. After the early September convention, Obama did not return to North Carolina, though his wife, Michelle, and other luminaries made frequent appearances. Romney visited North Carolina infrequently but spent significant time in the other three up-for-grabs states, even though Virginia had fewer electoral votes. Yet if North Carolina was a second-tier state in the election, radio and television viewers were hardly aware of it as the advertising barrage continued unabated.

As election time approached, major national polling firms Gallup and Rasmussen indicated slight but consistent leads for Romney in the national race. Most other polling organizations put Obama slightly ahead, with good chances to take all the swing states except for Florida and North Carolina. At the very end of the campaign, North Carolina tightened. North Carolina–based PPI, a Democratic polling firm noted for good predictions, had Obama ahead in one statewide survey. Party luminaries such as Bill Clinton and Jim Hunt plugged the ticket.[51]

Campaign rhetoric from both the Obama and Romney campaigns treated North Carolina very much like the swing states in the Midwest and West. The economy was the big issue. Republicans stressed that North Carolina had one of the country's highest unemployment rates, an ironic situation in light of its reputation as a boom state. (The unemployment rate in part reflected the state's past dependence on furniture, textiles, and tobacco.) The Democratic campaign argued that Republican tax and spending policies would seriously wound North Carolina and the country and wreck the Medicare system. In economic matters, both parties were long on rhetoric and short on specifics.

Despite a Republican platform that stressed social conservatism, Romney toward the end soft-pedaled issues such as abortion and gay rights. However, Protestant fundamentalists and evangelicals conducted a major crusade for the Republican. Shortly before Election Day, the aged and frail Baptist evangelist Billy Graham posed for a picture with Romney, seemingly signaling that conservative Christians should vote for Romney whatever qualms they might have about his Mormon faith.[52]

## THE OUTCOME

In America and in North Carolina, the 2012 county-level presidential scorecard bore a remarkable resemblance to that of 2008, though most locales showed a slight drop-off in Obama's percentage. Only two states shifted columns in the presidential race, with both Indiana and North Carolina going from Obama's camp to the Republican candidate. Romney took North Carolina with 2,275,853 votes (50.6 percent) to Obama's 2,178,288 (48.4 percent), with 44,798 votes (1 percent) going to Libertarian Gary Johnson. North Carolina's 2.2 percent shift away from Obama was slightly less than the national average of 3.0 percent, but because his margin of victory had been so thin in 2008, the drop was enough to give Romney the state.

As in 2008, Obama ran powerfully in big-city counties nationwide and in much of the South. The five counties that encompass the cities of Charlotte, Durham, Greensboro, Raleigh, and Winston-Salem provided Obama with a combined advantage of 283,729 votes (58.7 percent for Obama to 40.3 percent for Romney). In the same five counties, Obama's lead in 2008 had been 296,817. Between 2008 and 2012, Obama's percentage of the total vote rose slightly in Durham, stayed about the same in Guilford (Greensboro–High Point) and Mecklenburg (Charlotte), and dropped slightly in Forsyth (Winston-Salem) and Wake (Raleigh-Cary). In 2012, Obama's percentages of the vote ranged from 75.9 in Durham to 53.2 in Forsyth. As in 2008, three other urban counties gave substantial victories to Obama: Buncombe (Asheville, 55.5 percent); Cumberland (Fayetteville, 59.5 percent); and Orange (Chapel Hill, 70.4 percent). Even with the strong support in the big cities and Orange County, however, Obama won barely over 50 percent of the piedmont vote. Romney led in the coastal plain with 51.1 percent and in the mountains with nearly 58 percent.

Across much of the country, there was a slippage in the white vote for Obama, a deficit made up for in part by his strength among blacks and other minorities. Obama's share of the white vote in North Carolina dropped from 35 percent in 2008 to 30 percent in 2012. Nationally, the white vote for Obama ranged from 64 percent in Vermont to 10 percent in Mississippi. It was 20 percent in South Carolina and 34 percent in Virginia, with Obama winning statewide in the latter.[53]

Within North Carolina, Obama won respectable percentages of the white vote in major urban and university counties, often in excess of 40 percent. But only in Durham and Orange did he win an outright majority of the white vote. In Raleigh, however, he carried many predominantly white and well-to-do voting precincts.[54]

In the gubernatorial race, McCrory defeated Dalton, 2,447,988–1,931,750 (54.7 percent to 43.2 percent), carrying all three geographic regions: 53.2 percent in the coastal plain, 54.3 percent in the piedmont, and 61.3 percent in the mountains. Dalton had a cumulative lead over McCrory in the five biggest urban counties, but that lead was built entirely on his wins in Durham and Guilford Counties. McCrory carried Forsyth, Wake, and his home county of Mecklenburg, where he won by fewer than 3,000 votes. There was much ticket splitting in Mecklenburg, which Obama carried by 100,000 votes. Dalton led in counties where blacks constituted more than 45 percent of the population; in the liberal urban counties of Buncombe, Cumberland, and Orange; and in scattered academic centers.

The Republican Party gained tremendously as a result of its control over the legislative and congressional district reapportionment process in 2011. Winning 53 percent of the votes cast in N.C. Senate races, the GOP won 32 of the 50 seats. With 51 percent of the votes cast in N.C. House races, the Republicans won 77 of the 120 seats. The most dramatic change came in the state's U.S. House of Representatives delegation, which switched from seven to six in the Democrats' favor to nine to four in the Republicans' favor even though the total Democratic vote in all of the state's congressional districts rose slightly from 2,143,118 in 2008 to 2,219,165 in 2012. Three of the four reelected Democrats—G. K. Butterfield in the First District, David Price in the Fourth, and Mel Watt in the Twelfth—won by huge margins. The fourth Democrat, Mike McIntyre, took the Seventh District by fewer than 1,000 votes after a recount.[55] The four winning Democrats combined received more votes than did the nine winning Republicans.

In the lieutenant governor's race, Forrest, the Republican, narrowly outpolled Coleman, who declined to ask for a recount. In the seven Council of State races, all incumbents were reelected: Democrats Elaine Marshall

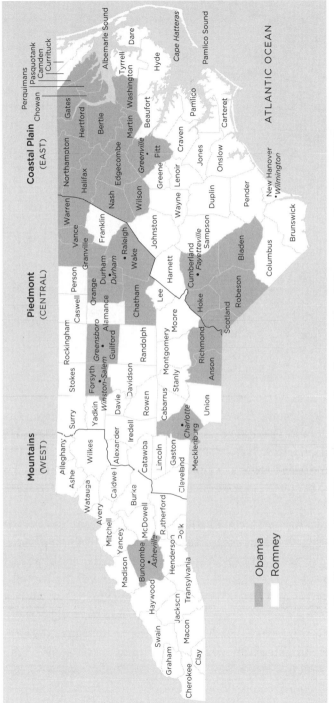

Map 12. Results of the 2012 presidential election—Democrat Barack Obama versus Republican Mitt Romney

Governor Pat McCrory on the porch of the governor's mansion in Raleigh, North Carolina, January 2013. Courtesy of the Office of Governor Pat McCrory.

as secretary of state, Roy Cooper as attorney general, Wayne Goodwin as commissioner of insurance, June Atkinson as superintendent of public instruction, Janet Cowell as state treasurer, and Beth Wood as auditor and Republicans Steve Troxler as commissioner of agriculture and Cherie Berry as commissioner of labor. There had been no party sweep or strong coattail effect.

Not since Reconstruction had Republicans had such a firm grip on state politics—simultaneous control of the governorship and the lieutenant governorship plus veto-proof control of both houses of the state legislature.[56] Yet in presidential politics the state offered hope to the Democrats. After losing North Carolina in the nine of ten presidential contests from 1968 through 2004, the Democrats had won the state electoral vote in 2008 and narrowly lost it in 2012. Like Virginia to the north, North Carolina seemed to be loosening its southern roots. Its largest urban areas were behaving more like metropolitan centers in the Northeast and West. In the state as a whole, party competition had not been so fierce since the 1894–1900 period.

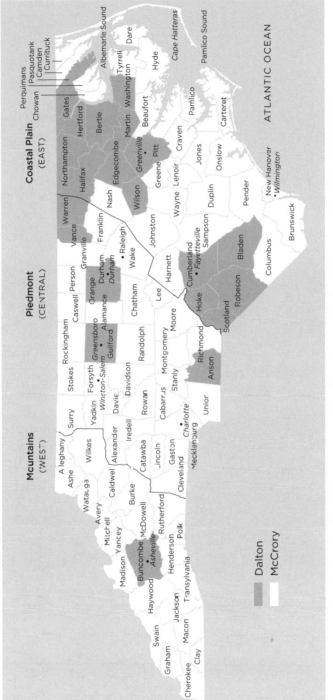

Map 13. Results of the 2012 gubernatorial election—Democrat Walter Dalton versus Republican Pat McCrory

EPILOGUE

# The Perilous Climb

The opportunities and pitfalls of democracy are central to the story of North Carolina politics and of American politics in general. Since the first half of the twentieth century, North Carolina has taken dramatic strides forward. But with political freedom and party competition may come greater risk of paralysis in government.[1] Conflict has been a constant in the American political realm and if anything has intensified in the early twenty-first century. Four themes stand out in the evolution of democracy in North Carolina: racial transition, the rise and consequences of two-party politics and the related ideological battles, the central role of elections, and how individuals—especially those who assumed leadership roles—made a difference. As a southern state, North Carolina's political and social systems long stood on a foundation of white supremacy. Schoolchildren learned that the Declaration of Independence proclaims that "all Men are created equal, that they are endowed by their Creator with certain unalienable rights, that among these are Life, Liberty, and the Pursuit of Happiness." This American ideal is based in part on opposition to oppression, whether that oppression is imposed by sources from within or without. The rhetoric was lofty, but the reality was that by common agreement among many whites, these words did not apply to blacks before the Civil War. Afterward, they did—at least in the official words of the Thirteenth, Fourteenth, and Fifteenth Amendments to the Constitution. For women, full political rights did not come until still later.

Much of the white South fought tooth and nail to preserve the racial caste system until blacks took to the streets and demanded change. National leaders found southern segregation an embarrassment in international relations. By the early 1960s, the civil rights revolution was gripping the land. Within the South, especially North Carolina, a few elected officials began to support more racial equality, some overtly and others covertly.

The Civil Rights Act of 1964 ended legal segregation in public places. The Voting Rights Act of 1965 eliminated political stratagems that southern states had adopted to block African Americans from voting. Race remained a powerful undercurrent in politics. Yet over the decades, attitudes gradually began to soften. As late as the 1990s, a majority of my students of all races said that we would not in our lifetimes see an African American as president of the United States. Even those who believed that a black might one day win the presidency were not so bold as to predict that he or she would in the process gain North Carolina's electoral votes.

Racial cleavages will, in all probability, persist for decades to come. Moreover, many churches, fraternal organizations, and clubs are likely to remain mostly black, white, Asian, Hispanic, or otherwise nondiverse. Be that as it may, the transition from a caste system built on white supremacy to one that embraces racial equality has unquestionably been one of the greatest events in the history of North Carolina and the American South. The pressures for change reflected both moral and political forces within North Carolina and the country at large.

In his 1949 classic, *Southern Politics in State and Nation*, V. O. Key Jr. argued that two-party systems provided more responsible government than systems dominated by one party.[2] He cited several reasons. First, the presence of two identifiable parties—Democratic and Republican, liberal or conservative—enables ordinary voters to distinguish the ins from the outs. If things go wrong—corruption, incompetence, failure—the presence of a two-party system makes it easier to punish or throw out the incumbents and replace them with another party.

Second, at least to a point, organized political parties stand for a coherent set of principles. Under the old southern one-party systems, people of many persuasions camped inside the Democratic Party. It was difficult to know what, if anything, the party as a whole stood for. Key argued that "one-party systems" were really no-party systems, though he acknowledged that the North Carolina Democratic Party contained competing factions that vaguely resembled parties.

Third, Key believed that one-party systems benefit the society's haves rather than its have-nots. The rich and well-educated understood the system's byzantine nature and consequently could penetrate the halls of power through contacts and money. Others lacked the ability or means to do so. If Key, a man of liberal instincts, were alive today, he would be pleased in many respects with the more inclusive body politic. But he would likely be surprised at the way in which the new party system developed.

Since Key's time, all the southern states have moved toward varying degrees of Republican dominance. The emergence of a strong Republican Party in the region resulted from several factors: conservatism on social issues (including race), resistance to government spending and associated taxes, promilitary attitudes, and support for free enterprise. Between 2000 and 2012, North Carolina was about as evenly matched as a state could be. Its partisan politics from 2008 to 2012 were also the most volatile since 1894–1900. The legislature elected in 2008 was Democratic, liberal, and perhaps the most racially diverse ever. In an ironic twist of fate, the fiscal situation resulting from the Great Recession torpedoed initiatives that the legislature and governor might have liked. However, the Democrats were in a position to defend liberal positions on such issues as abortion. Two years later, the tide turned, with Republicans decisively winning control of both houses of the legislature. They further solidified that control in November 2012.

A new political philosophy prevailed. Leading conservative think tanks, such as the Civitas Institute and the John Locke Foundation, had long argued that much smaller government would be better for the state and society. And they contended that lower taxes would prompt the private sector to create more jobs. Now, the state's leading patron of this philosophy, Art Pope, served as McCrory's chief budget architect.

From a long-term standpoint, this period may be most remembered for the extent of the polarization and downright hostility between the two political parties. Most of the remaining Democrats are liberal in political philosophy. Republican legislators are overwhelmingly conservative on both economic and social issues, less prone to compromise than earlier Republican governors Jim Holshouser and Jim Martin. Governor Beverly Perdue struggled to defend Democratic social and spending priorities when she was in office; the recession and partisan wrangling had created the perfect storm.

At least for now, two-party politics do not appear to be more responsive politics, partly as a consequence of the deep divisions in society at large. Many people favor extensive government programs. Others do not, especially when such initiatives require a lot of money. The state and the country are split on abortion. Some consider it murder, others consider it a humanitarian act under some circumstances, still others a routine medical procedure. Compromise satisfies no one. There seems a certain soundness to the earlier argument that two-party competition enhances democracy.

But that thesis must await further testing, at least in North Carolina. One thing is certain, however: The old one-party system is dead.

Elections are critical to a free society. Most often, North Carolinians have selected "progressives" for governor. Nearly all winners have stressed education. Some elections have made a real difference for society and public policy, and a few have been major turning points or watersheds: the Democratic primary victories of Kerr Scott in 1948, Terry Sanford in 1960, and Jim Hunt in 1976. Both the Scott and Sanford victories solidified the progressive strain and broadened democracy, with Sanford doing so with the help of his many allies among the state's business leaders. Hunt's 1976 victory began the closest thing to a political dynasty in the 1948–2012 period, incorporating Democratic politicians, business officials, educators, and civic leaders. This coalition backed innovative educational programs and economic expansion. Hunt was the professional promoter for the state and a model for governors of other states. Holshouser's 1972 win was a borderline watershed, largely because it signified the state's climb toward a two-party system. Because Holshouser's issue positions resembled those of moderate Democrats, his administration kept the state on generally the same course.

In contests for the U.S. Senate, North Carolina has more often opted for conservatives. Only two senatorial contests since 1948 have been watersheds—one for its legacy, the other for its long-term impact on state and national politics. Willis Smith's victory over Frank Porter Graham in the 1950 Democratic primary reaffirmed the potency of white supremacy in the South of that time. More significantly, many of North Carolina's political figures, both progressives and conservatives, began their political careers working for either Graham or Smith. Among them were Terry Sanford and Jesse Helms.

The other watershed was Helms's 1972 general election victory over Democrat Nick Galifianakis. Helms's campaign was probably the most sophisticated to date in North Carolina and set the stage for future campaigns across the country. The election also marked Helms's emergence as a major state and national figure. He would do much to shape the course of the Republican Party. Specifically, Helms pressed the state Republican Party to take more conservative positions. And, along with Ronald Reagan, he pushed the national Republican Party to the right.

The 1984 Helms-Hunt contest was not a watershed, although it might have been the most exciting election of the twentieth century. It affirmed the status quo and conceivably kept Hunt from becoming president. However, the outcome opened the way for Hunt to become a still more important figure in North Carolina when he returned to the governorship for eight years in the 1990s. Whether history will judge the 2010 legislative elections to have been a watershed remains an open question, better analyzed further down the road.

On a national level and especially in the South, the presidential race of 1968 was a milestone. Many hitherto loyal Democrats broke ranks with the party to vote for George Wallace. By 1972, they were ready to vote for Republican Nixon over left-wing Democrat McGovern. Except for the Carter aberration in 1976, North Carolina whites would continue to support GOP presidential nominees for decades.

By the spring of 2013, new realities had emerged in state-level politics. Fundamental policy changes had taken place. Through the twentieth century and into the early twenty-first, both conservative and more liberal administrations had persuaded state legislatures to expand government programs and to cough up the money to pay for them. But now a different outlook prevailed. The reversal was most apparent in the N.C. Senate, where opposition to taxation, environmental regulation, and Democratic social welfare programs were holy causes. Only in fighting crime and enhancing moral standards did the Senate majority favor expanded government roles.

The N.C. House of Representatives followed a similar course, although some of its members appeared to have a pragmatic streak while remaining very much in the mainstream of modern Republicanism. Republicans wanting to reduce the size of state government had long felt isolated from the corridors of power. Now they were political insiders. Governor Pat McCrory's record suggested that he did not always share the conservative disdain for big government, but he went along with the Republican legislative majority on many issues. Furthermore, the tight budget situation dictated cuts in government spending.

Many Republican candidates in 2010 and 2012 had advocated sweeping tax code changes, the most revolutionary of which was a proposal to end the state income tax. That proposal would likely have resulted in huge spending cuts, increased sales taxes, and more user fees such as highway tolls. McCrory cautioned that tax reform would not be easy.[3] In the end, the legislature mapped out a plan for reducing personal income and corporation taxes. McCrory signed the measure. Republicans overwhelmingly believed that reducing and eventually eliminating those taxes would boost the state's economy by increasing both inside and outside business investment and thus create more jobs.

Republicans pointed to North Carolina's low ranking on many economic indices—such as the high unemployment rate and below average family incomes—as proof of the failure of Democratic policies, which had discouraged business investment and growth. Democrats, the NAACP, and liberal church groups cried foul and argued that tax code changes and a resulting cutback in programs would harm the poor and reduce the state's quality of life. Week after week, they staged "Moral Monday" demonstrations at the State Legislative Building in Raleigh and, later, in other cities.

From a partisan standpoint, the most long-lasting result of the 2010 election was that it gave Republicans control over the legislative reapportionment process. Barring court intervention or a political earthquake, their skillful crafting of new districts made it likely that the GOP would control the legislature and consequently have immense influence over public policy for at least a decade.

Watershed election or not, the 2010 contest, reinforced by the 2012 outcome, was one of the big stories in post–World War II North Carolina politics. Paradoxically, the massive Republican advantages had come as the Democrats were showing strength in presidential politics as a consequence of gains in the rapidly growing metropolitan areas.

Individuals make a difference. Certain presidents—Franklin Roosevelt, John Kennedy, Lyndon Johnson, and Ronald Reagan—have had a tremendous impact on the nation and on North Carolina. Along with their programs, ideas, and rhetoric, each left a powerful political legacy. Within the state, Governors Kerr Scott, Terry Sanford, and Jim Hunt and Senator Jesse Helms left deep political imprints. Still others did much to shape the state in policy areas: Luther Hodges on industrial development, Jim Holshouser on the environment, and Jim Martin on transportation. The most effective state-level politicians—Hunt and O. Max Gardner—advocated the umbrella thesis of politics. These leaders were master coalition builders. In their absence, the course of the state might have differed starkly.[4]

According to Gary Pearce, a longtime North Carolina political activist and analyst, "All politicians have two impulses: (1) to help people and (2) to help themselves."[5] The two are often confused. Most politicians are afraid to challenge society's prejudices. Moreover, many lack the vision and the drive to push in bold new directions that challenge old ways of doing things. Nevertheless, a few break out of the box. They are for the ages.

By its nature, democracy invites conflict. People who care about their futures and society's well-being will argue and sometimes engage in civil disobedience. People who believe that the world can be a better place will always lead crusades, and many others will feel threatened by change. Tragedies have occurred throughout the world, and great economic inequalities remain. These economic inequalities are pervasive in North

Carolina even in the aftermath of bold steps forward. North Carolina underwent a series of people-driven revolutions.

Against the backdrop of the past political battles, is there room for optimism? To answer that question, it is useful to compare the present with 1948, 1900, or 1776. Democracy is alive as never before, yet in many respects it is defined by its imperfections. In a system that strives to be free, the seeds of destruction lurk just beneath the surface. The American Dream will remain an ever-elusive goal.

# Comments on Methodology and General Approach

This book is research-based and at the same time reflects personal observations and impressions of the writer. Such personal observations can provide readers with valuable insights, and sometimes there are no reasonable substitutes. For that I offer no apology. Indeed, such an approach was essential to explaining both fairly and honestly the changing times. Scholars should never hold back the truth as they see it.

Yet this book relies heavily on data available to both scholars and the simply curious. Much of the focus is on election data, both state and national. Unless otherwise noted, all North Carolina election figures—state, county, and city—were gathered directly from the State Board of Elections or from official sources, usually the *North Carolina Manual*, published by the Secretary of State's Office throughout the twentieth century and into the twenty-first. Precinct data were collected from individual county boards of elections.

Observations about "predominantly black" or "predominantly white" voting precincts are based on the official breakdowns by race for the relevant precincts. For some early primaries and general elections (primarily pre-1965), these data are not available. However, local newspapers often identified precincts by racial makeup. For example, in Durham the so-called predominantly black precincts were Burton, Hillside, Whitted, and Pearsontown. When white segregationists sought political office, these precincts would vote by greater than 99 percent against the candidate. Beginning in the 1940s, all of North Carolina's major cities had comparable precincts.

Political scientist Donald Strong, *Urban Republicanism in the South* (University: Bureau of Public Administration, University of Alabama, 1960), and journalist Samuel Lubell, *The Future of American Politics* (New York: Harper, 1952) and *The Revolt of the Moderates* (New York: Harper, 1956), also divided southern urban precincts into categories of race and social class. Their categories were based on the observations of local journalists, politicians, and professors. Professors Numan V. Bartley and Hugh D. Graham also utilized this type of precinct analysis in *Southern Politics and the Second Reconstruction* (Baltimore: Johns Hopkins University Press, 1975). Among other cities around the South, they examined precinct returns from Charlotte, Greensboro, and Winston-Salem.

While my analysis relies strongly on raw election returns, I did closely follow polls, especially after 1980. In earlier periods, state-level polls were scarce, sometimes unreliable, and often not made available to the general public, academics, or journalists. The polls that did exist were often commissioned by candidates or parties. Among the most helpful over the past thirty years has been the November exit polls sponsored by the news outlets. These surveys of actual voters offer powerful information for explaining the vote and providing a good breakdown based on race and other socioeconomic factors. The North Carolina–based Elon University poll has specialized in the coverage of recent North Carolina elections.

I conducted forty-five formal interviews specifically for this study; they lasted from one to three hours. In addition, I had conducted forty-seven for earlier but related studies of race and North Carolina politics. I sought individuals who had played central roles in modern campaigns. The list included former governors James Holshouser, Bob Scott, and Jim Hunt. Unfortunately, former Senator Jesse Helms, a key figure in the North Carolina story had fallen into serious mental and physical decline by the time this study was under way. However, I did interview key figures from the Helms campaign, including top strategists Tom Ellis and Carter Wrenn. I also visited the Jesse Helms Center in Monroe, where I interviewed director John Dodd and other key associates. A few persons were interviewed because of their in-depth background knowledge and behind-the-scenes activities. Most notable in this category was former University of North Carolina president William Friday.

I attempted to build a relaxed conversational style into all the interviews, much in the manner of V. O. Key Jr. and his associates. Unlike them, I did take notes on significant points during the interview. But like Key and associates, I wrote a very extensive summary immediately after the interviews. There were numerous requests for confidentiality, but I do not believe that they interfered with my telling of the big story. In addition to the formal interviews, I had mini-interviews, brief contacts, and telephone conversations with other persons who were helpful in answering specific questions.

I have been personally acquainted with many North Carolina movers and shakers of both political parties. Many of them had passed away by the time my book was under way; a few were ill or reclusive. But I had already had extensive conversations with a number of these individuals, and when doing so is helpful in telling the story, I weave their reflections into the text.

# Notes

## PROLOGUE

1. For discussions of North Carolina's political evolution, see Alexander Heard, *A Two-Party South?* (Chapel Hill: University of North Carolina Press, 1952); Burton J. Hendrick, *The Life and Letters of Walter H. Page* (Garden City, N.Y.: Doubleday, Page, 1922), 64–101; Christopher A. Cooper and H. Gibbs Knotts, "Traditionalism and Progressivism in North Carolina," in *The New Politics of North Carolina*, ed. Christopher A. Cooper and H. Gibbs Knotts (Chapel Hill: University of North Carolina Press, 2008), 1–10. For a discussion of the contradictory nature of North Carolina politics, see Rob Christensen, *The Paradox of Tar Heel Politics*, 2nd ed. (Chapel Hill: University of North Carolina Press, 2010).

2. See Alexander Lamis, "North Carolina: The Clash of Polar Forces—Hunt vs. Helms," in *The Two-Party South* (New York: Oxford University Press, 1988), 131–34; Paul Luebke, *Tar Heel Politics* (Chapel Hill: University of North Carolina Press, 1990). For a comprehensive and insightful running portrait of North Carolina politics from the 1980s to the 2000s, see the publications of the University of North Carolina's Howard W. Odum Institute for Social Sciences (http://www.irss.unc.edu/odum/home2.jsp). Under the titles *Inside Politics* and later *DataNet*, the institute delved into state politics in a language that could be appreciated by both statisticians and laypersons. These publications were spearheaded by Thad L. Beyle, with Peter Harkins and Ferrell Guillory also playing major roles.

3. V. O. Key Jr., *Southern Politics in State and Nation* (New York: Knopf, 1949), 205–6.

4. For a similar viewpoint, see Michael Barone, *Our Country: The Shaping of America from Roosevelt to Reagan* (New York: Free Press, 1990), xiii, xiv.

5. William A. Link, *North Carolina: Change and Tradition in a Southern State* (Wheeling, Ill.: Harlan Davidson, 2009); Milton Ready, *The Tar Heel State: A History of North Carolina* (Columbia: University of South Carolina Press, 2005). For thorough studies that take the traditional approach, see Hugh Talmage Lefler and Albert Ray Newsome, *North Carolina: The History of a Southern State* (Chapel Hill: University of North Carolina Press, 1954); William S. Powell, *North Carolina through Four Centuries* (Chapel Hill: University of North Carolina Press, 1989).

6. See esp. David S. Cecelski and Timothy B. Tyson, eds., *Democracy Betrayed: The Wilmington Race Riot of 1898 and Its Legacy* (Chapel Hill: University of North Carolina Press, 1998), 254. See also Glenda Elizabeth Gilmore, *Gender and Jim Crow: Women and the Politics of White Supremacy in North Carolina, 1896–1920* (Chapel Hill: University of North Carolina Press, 1996).

7. Luebke, *Tar Heel Politics*.

8. Christensen, *Paradox of Tar Heel Politics*.

9. Cooper and Knotts, *New Politics*.

10. Author's review of National Weather Service data.

11. *Look Homeward Angel* was published on October 18, 1929, and created such an uproar in Asheville that Wolfe did not visit again until 1937. See Ted Mitchell, "Thomas Wolfe," in *The North Carolina Century: Tar Heels Who Made a Difference, 1900–2000*, ed. Howard E. Covington Jr. and Marion A. Ellis (Charlotte: Levine Museum of the New South; Chapel Hill: University of North Carolina Press, 2002), 110–13.

12. In the early 2000s, Charlotte claimed the title of America's second-largest financial center, trailing only New York in number of bank headquarters. But many other activities contribute to making a city a financial center, including stock and commodities markets, total bank deposits, and brokerage houses. By that standard, Chicago might well be the second largest in the country. Local boosterism aside, Charlotte had claim to being one of the four or five major U.S. financial centers.

13. There is debate over whether the Deep South/Peripheral South distinction remains valid. By many economic and political standards, Alabama, Mississippi, and Louisiana are still states apart from the nation and from much of the rest of the South. To a lesser extent, so are South Carolina and Georgia, although migration from other parts of the country and world are reshaping those two states as well as North Carolina and Virginia.

14. Key, *Southern Politics*, 5–10, 215–18. While conservative on racial issues, North Carolina's Black Belt counties at times supported economically liberal candidates in primaries.

15. Robert W. Winston, "Aycock: His People's Genius," Founders' Day Address, University of North Carolina, October 12, 1933, *University of North Carolina Alumni Review*, November 1933, S4.

16. R. D. W. Connor and Clarence Poe, "Universal Education: The Unfinished Speech," *The Life and Speeches of Charles Brantley Aycock* (Garden City, N.Y.: Doubleday, Page, 1912), 324. At the time of his death, Aycock was challenging Furnifold Simmons for the 1912 Democratic senatorial nomination.

17. Timothy Tyson, "Wars for Democracy," in *Democracy Betrayed*, ed. Cecelski and Tyson, 254.

18. Having looked at the records and newspaper materials on the primary debate, I am persuaded that the direct primary was adopted to provide for some reflection of the popular will when choosing officials. But this was in the backdrop of the virtual elimination of black political participation. The primary was a step toward democracy for white men.

19. Lefler and Newsome, *North Carolina*, 574–75.

20. Clouds will always hang over the 1920 election result. Fraud was rampant in mountain counties and present elsewhere. In addition, Gardner's support for women's suffrage may have cost him the election after opponents tied it to support for black suffrage. Gardner's biographer, Joseph L. Morrison, thought the suffrage debate influenced the outcome. That is possible, but the proof is not solid. See Joseph L. Morrison, *Governor O. Max Gardner: A Power in North Carolina and New Deal Washington* (Chapel Hill: University of North Carolina Press, 1971), 30–35.

21. Daniels, who had led the fight for black exclusion in 1898, now spearheaded a fight for the expansion of democracy to include women. After 1900, he repeatedly stood on the left end of the political spectrum.

22. Powell, *North Carolina*, 470–72. For a comprehensive view of the road program, see Walter R. Turner, *Paving Tobacco Road: A Century of Progress by the North Carolina Department of Transportation* (Raleigh: North Carolina Department of Cultural Resources,

Office of Archives and History; Spencer: North Carolina Transportation Museum Foundation, 2003). Chapter 2, "An Impressive Beginning, 1921–1929," discusses both the political and technical sides of the highway program.

23. Lydia Charles Hoffman, "Cameron Morrison," in *North Carolina Century*, ed. Covington and Ellis, 497.

24. Simmons never formally endorsed Hoover but did say that he would not support Smith and launched frequent attacks on Smith's Catholicism and policies. He was in effect openly backing Hoover.

25. Christensen, *Paradox of Tar Heel Politics*, 66; Lefler and Newsome, *North Carolina*, 607; Morrison, *Governor O. Max Gardner*, 117. For discussion of infighting over university consolidation, see Morrison, *Governor O. Max Gardner*, 95–98, 115–16, 160–63, 212–15.

26. Graham was indeed a social liberal. However, textile executives, many of whom had graduated from North Carolina State College, suspected that Graham sought to strengthen the university in Chapel Hill at the expense of North Carolina State. Yet Graham backed the maintenance of an engineering school at North Carolina State and the closure of the one in Chapel Hill.

27. The Gardner method of operation was looser than Simmons's had been, and Gardner's ideological positions were not always predictable. He was close both to Franklin D. Roosevelt and leading conservative Democrats. Overall, Gardner was the personification of the progressive business-style politician described by Key in *Southern Politics*, chapter 10.

28. Morrison, *Governor O. Max Gardner*, 89–92.

29. Lefler and Newsome, *North Carolina*, 613.

30. Key, *Southern Politics*, esp. 211–15, 228.

31. See Douglas Carl Abrams, *Conservative Constraints: North Carolina and the New Deal* (Jackson: University Press of Mississippi, 1992); Elmer L. Puryear, *Democratic Party Dissention in North Carolina, 1928–1936* (Chapel Hill: University of North Carolina Press, 1962); Ready, *Tar Heel State*, 336–39.

32. Tyson, "Wars for Democracy," 266–67.

33. African Americans had maintained communal links through civic and fraternal organizations in the 1900–1930 period. And lawyers working for the National Association for the Advancement of Colored People had pursued legal challenges to segregation while opposing voter exclusion. Especially in Durham, some black businesspeople moved toward middle-class status, and a few achieved economic prosperity. Money opened doors. As blacks began to vote, white officials quietly tried to make political deals or to reach understandings.

34. *Smith v. Allwright*, 321 U.S. 649 (1944).

35. If one simply looks at percentage growth and teachers' salaries, some of the most dramatic strides occurred during Cherry's administration. The governor and legislature were moving to make up for the World War II salary freezes and the absence of gains during the Great Depression.

CHAPTER 1

1. For a painstaking and entertaining story of Bob Reynolds, see Julian Pleasants, *Buncombe Bob: The Life and Times of Robert Rice Reynolds* (Chapel Hill: University of North Carolina Press, 2000).

2. John William Coon, "Kerr Scott, the 'Go Forward' Governor: His Origins, His Program, and the North Carolina General Assembly" (master's thesis, University of North Carolina at Chapel Hill, 1968), 16, 21–22.

3. Johnson was a proud man, confident of his skills. In his interview with me, Lauch Faircloth described Johnson as one of the most pompous individuals that he had ever known in state politics (Lauch Faircloth, interview by author, July 15, 2006). But with the blessings of establishment Democrats, Johnson seemed headed for the governorship.

4. Joseph L. Morrison, *Governor O. Max Gardner: A Power in North Carolina and New Deal Washington* (Chapel Hill: University of North Carolina Press, 1971), 278–80.

5. Coon, "Kerr Scott," 17.

6. *Raleigh News and Observer*, February 7, 1948.

7. Coon, "Kerr Scott," 22.

8. Ibid., 23.

9. Primary election returns from *North Carolina Manual* (http://www.secretary.state .nc.us/pubsweb/manual.aspx). See also V. O. Key Jr., *Southern Politics in State and Nation* (New York: Knopf, 1949), 215–18.

10. Scott's success was evidence that the organization's grip was loosening. Earlier on, a stodgy, organization-backed candidate would have won. Indeed, Ehringhaus, elected in 1932, was just such a candidate.

11. Robert W. Scott, interview by author, October 16, 2006.

12. Faircloth, interview.

13. Ironically, many elements of the organization Scott was denouncing had backed Scott when he successfully challenged incumbent agriculture commissioner William Graham, who disliked Gardner, in 1936.

14. This election arguably represented the beginning of the end of the dominance of the progressive plutocracy described by Key. The party never had quite the same organizational character after 1948 even though business-friendly Democratic governors continued to win elections for many years.

15. Robert W. Scott, interview.

16. Ibid.

17. David McCullough, *Truman* (New York: Simon and Schuster, 1992), 638–40. On June 22, 1911, Truman had written in a letter that one man is as good as another "so long as he's honest and decent and not a nigger or a Chinaman" (McCullough, *Truman*, 86, 639).

18. Ibid., 779.

19. Kari Frederickson, *The Dixiecrat Revolt and the End of the Solid South, 1932–1968* (Chapel Hill: University of North Carolina Press, 2001), 131.

20. Ibid.; author's analysis of election statistics.

21. *Charlotte Observer*, January 6, 1949; Coon, "Kerr Scott," 59.

22. Frank Guy Braley, "The North Carolina Governor: Gubernatorial Perceptions of the Governor's Legislative Role" (master's thesis, East Carolina University, 1981), 113.

23. It is, of course, not unusual for officials to reverse campaign pledges, but given Scott's previous fierce criticism of the bond issue, this change was particularly dramatic. But Scott's reversal was a fortunate event for the state.

24. Coon, "Kerr Scott," 60–65.

25. The statewide and county voting figures are from the official returns provided by the North Carolina Board of Elections (www.ncsbe.gov). The results were also

published in the *North Carolina Manual*, produced by the secretary of state's office after each election.

26. See Walter R. Turner, *Paving Tobacco Road: A Century of Progress by the North Carolina Department of Transportation* (Raleigh: North Carolina Department of Cultural Resources, Office of Archives and History; Spencer: North Carolina Transportation Museum Foundation, 2003), 51–73.

27. Julian M. Pleasants and August M. Burns III, *Frank Porter Graham and the 1950 Senate Race in North Carolina* (Chapel Hill: University of North Carolina Press, 1990), 12–13.

28. Ibid., 6, 11, 59. In addition to having been a state legislator and Scott's 1948 campaign manager, Waynick had perhaps been North Carolina's most prominent New Deal program director and the state's chief link with Washington in the 1930s. See Michelle Jan Keller Pontinen, "Capus Miller Waynick: New Deal Administrator and Politician" (master's thesis, East Carolina University, 1987).

29. Pleasants and Burns, *Frank Porter Graham*, 47, 79. In addition, J. Spencer Love, the board chairman of Burlington Industries, endorsed Graham early on.

30. Ibid., 73–74.

31. The Grahams' penchant for entertaining probably gained him a lot of support that would otherwise have gone to Smith. Many University of North Carolina alumni considered themselves good friends of the Grahams.

32. William Friday, interview by author, December 7, 2006.

33. Pleasants and Burns, *Frank Porter Graham*, 22, 111–15, 124–27, 255, 259–65.

34. Ibid., 24–27.

35. Tom Ellis, interview by author, October 20, 2006.

36. Ibid.; Pleasants and Burns, *Frank Porter Graham*, 89, 235.

37. Pleasants and Burns, *Frank Porter Graham*, 71–72. Helms often told the story of the Scott-Graham otter.

38. Ibid., 70–71, 77–78.

39. By more recent standards, Daniels was breaching journalistic ethics. Current editors and publishers may be just as partisan as he was, but they generally shun formal political posts.

40. Pleasants and Burns, *Frank Porter Graham*, 199.

41. Ibid., 199–200, 208–9, 224.

42. Ibid., 170–78, 216–28. See also Jack Bass and Walter De Vries, *The Transformation of Southern Politics: Social Change and Political Consequence since 1945* (New York: Basic Books, 1976), 219–21.

43. Pleasants and Burns, *Frank Porter Graham*, 222, 178. Many observers, especially those who are both academic and liberal, blame Adams for the ads, though he has consistently denied involvement. Whatever his role, Adams surely was not the sole party to the attacks as is sometimes suggested. Pleasants and Burns's discussion of this matter is the best.

44. Author's review of pamphlets and Adams's subsequent writing style in the *Dunn Daily Record*.

45. Ellis, interview.

46. *Sweatt v. Painter*, 339 U.S. 637 (1930); *McLaurin v. Oklahoma*, 339 U.S. 629.

47. Pleasants and Burns, *Frank Porter Graham*, 37–39, 208.

48. Ibid., 113; June 1950 article, author's family clipping file.

49. Robert Morgan, interview by author, August 14, 2006.

50. I. Beverly Lake to Frank Graham, July 9, 1950, Frank Porter Graham Papers #1819, Southern Historical Collection, Wilson Library, University of North Carolina at Chapel Hill.

51. Pleasants and Burns, *Frank Porter Graham*, 273.

CHAPTER 2

1. A few hints of change in the racial order could be glimpsed as plaintiffs won cases challenging segregation on the fringes—railroad dining cars and selected graduate school programs. But the fundamental order remained unaltered.

2. Tobacco was the sacred product in the state, pervading rural, small-town, and city economies. Durham and Winston-Salem had huge warehouses where farmers sold their tobacco as well as cigarette manufacturing plants.

3. W. E. Debnam, *Weep No More, My Lady* (Raleigh: Graphic, 1950).

4. Ibid., 9.

5. *Henderson v. United States*, 339 U.S. 816 (1950). Sometimes blacks were curtained off (shielded from sight of other passengers inside the dining car). In other cases, blacks had no eating facilities.

6. *McLaurin v. Oklahoma*, 339 U.S. 629. North Carolina was reexamining its graduate school policy on race as the case wound through the courts.

7. *Sweatt v. Painter*, 339 U.S. 637 (1930). While the Court carefully refrained from overturning the concept of separate but equal, even then the court—liberal members and likely its conservatives—saw the three 1950 cases as bridges paving the route to the end of legal segregation.

8. By extending this ruling, the Court conceivably could have in effect ended legal segregation under most circumstances. Whether this approach would have led to a more peaceful transition than did the 1954 *Brown* ruling is a matter of conjecture.

9. Harry S. Ashmore, *The Negro and the Schools* (Chapel Hill: University of North Carolina Press, 1954), 158–59.

10. Ibid., 160.

11. Frank Guy Braley, "The North Carolina Governor: Gubernatorial Perceptions of the Governor's Legislative Role" (master's thesis, East Carolina University, 1981), 15.

12. Walter R. Turner, *Paving Tobacco Road: A Century of Progress by the North Carolina Department of Transportation* (Raleigh: North Carolina Department of Cultural Resources, Office of Archives and History; Spencer: North Carolina Transportation Museum Foundation, 2003), 55. In addition to Scott's determination to see roads built and the bond issue money now available, the governor had control over the Highway Department and consequently a big say in what specific roads would be paved. The governor appointed highway commissioners who exercised authority over roads within particular districts.

13. Umstead was much better connected than Olive in political circles. Some defections also resulted because he was regarded as the more likely winner than Olive.

14. Candidates in North Carolina at the time were expected to have paid their dues. Successful prima donnas such as Senator Bob Reynolds (1933–45) were unusual. But the Hodges candidacy and election marked the beginning of a new era in the state as well as in national politics.

15. While state-level Republicans garnered more votes than in previous elections, particularly noteworthy about the 1950s was the huge gap between the vote-getting capacity of the popular Republican presidential candidate and that of state-level Republicans. Such a gap existed at no other time.

16. For an excellent analysis of South-wide precinct returns by class and race, see Numan V. Bartley and Hugh D. Graham, *Southern Politics and the Second Reconstruction* (Baltimore: Johns Hopkins University Press, 1975). See also Donald Strong, *Urban Republicanism in the South* (University: Bureau of Public Administration, University of Alabama, 1960); Samuel Lubell, *The Revolt of the Moderates* (New York: Harper, 1956). As data by race were frequently not available from elections boards in the 1950s, I studied the precincts that Lubell cited as predominantly black in the *Revolt of the Moderates*. In the cases of upper-class or silk-stocking precincts, I looked at the precincts cited by Lubell and Strong. Durham, North Carolina, my hometown, was not included in either book. However, I examined African American voting results from 1952 and 1956 for the Burton School, Whitted School, Hillside High School, and Pearsontown precincts, which the *Durham Morning Herald* and the *Durham Sun* called "predominantly black."

17. Edward L. Rankin Jr., "William Bradley Umstead," in *Public Addresses, Letters, and Papers of William Bradley Umstead, Governor of North Carolina, 1953–1954*, ed. David Leroy Corbitt (Raleigh: Council of State, State of North Carolina, 1957), vii.

18. Braley, "North Carolina Governor," 115.

19. Despite the wide ideological gap between many state Democrats and the national party, the party hierarchy saw publicly abandoning ship to be an unpardonable sin. This feeling was as strong among conservative Democrats as liberal Democrats.

20. *Brown v. Board of Education of Topeka*, 347 U.S. 343 (1954); Richard Kluger, *Simple Justice: The History of Brown v. Board of Education and Black America's Struggle for Equality* (New York: Knopf, 1975). For a short but riveting account of the lead-up to Brown, see Juan Williams, *Eyes on the Prize: America's Civil Rights Years, 1954–1965* (New York: Viking, 1987), 2–35. See also Ashmore, *Negro and the Schools*, 95

21. This attitude reflects in part the state spirit and special North Carolina pride. It was also a way of avoiding a stand that could get an officeholder or politicians in trouble.

22. Rankin, "William Bradley Umstead," xlx–xxl. For a perceptive reflection on the reaction to *Brown* and the importance of the decision, see William Cobb, *The Brown Decision, Jim Crow, and Southern Identity* (Athens: University of Georgia Press, 2005).

23. Woodrow Jones, "Reference to Court Decision Received Big Hand: 3000 at Convention," *Raleigh News and Observer*, May 11, 1954.

24. Most other senatorial appointments by governors in the 1940s and 1950s were equally surprising. Rankin believed that Ervin had the inside track all along (Edward L. Rankin, interview by James Lineberry Jenkins, August 20, 1987, C-0044, in Southern Oral History Program, Collection #4007, Southern Historical Collection, Wilson Library, University of North Carolina at Chapel Hill). Rob Christensen also makes note of this incident in *The Paradox of Tar Heel Politics*, 2nd ed. (Chapel Hill: University of North Carolina Press, 2010), 168–69. He, too, thinks that Ervin would likely have been picked even without Carlyle's speech.

25. For an in-depth and balanced analysis of Ervin's career, including his views on race, see Karl E. Campbell, *Senator Sam Ervin, Last of the Founding Fathers* (Chapel Hill: University of North Carolina Press, 2007).

26. Corbitt, *Public Addresses*, 201. While most white North Carolinians opposed the ruling, a few school officials, notably in Greensboro, were ready to implement it. But they were told not to act until the state had worked out a policy.

27. Mark Newman, "The Baptist State Convention of North Carolina and Desegregation, 1945-1980," *North Carolina Historical Review* 75, no. 1 (January 1998): 1-28.

28. Robert W. Scott, interview by author, October 16, 2006.

29. There are some indications that the racial pamphlets might have backfired on the Lennon campaign.

30. *Durham Sun*, June 2, 1954.

31. This account of Umstead's death comes from newspaper clippings (*Durham Herald*, *Durham Sun*, and *Raleigh News and Observer*) in my father's scrapbook and the accounts of friends and relatives who attended the funeral. Some comments are based on conversations with Governor Umstead's daughter, Merle Umstead Richey. His wife and daughter, Merle, a seventh-grader, were at the bedside. The funeral, one of the largest in North Carolina history, was at Umstead's church, the neo-Gothic Trinity Methodist in Durham. Outside, the street was thronged with mourners.

32. Initially, the plan was not to issue the usual edited book of governor's papers as Umstead's tenure had been so short. However, Ed Rankin took the initiative in preparing the volume. (Comment to author from Merle Umstead Richey.)

33. For a good perspective on Hodges's mind and operating style, see Luther H. Hodges, *Businessman in the Statehouse: Six Years as Governor of North Carolina* (Chapel Hill: University of North Carolina Press, 1962). Hodges's book is a cut above the usual political autobiography.

34. Ibid., 79-106. Hodges provides a rationalization for the state's position. See also Ransome Ellis Holcombe, "A Desegregation Study of Public Schools in North Carolina" (Ph.D. diss., East Tennessee State University, 1985), 50-98; William Bagwell, *School Desegregation in the Carolinas: Two Case Studies* (Columbia: University of South Carolina Press, 1972), 1-125.

35. Holcombe, "Desegregation Study," 62-68.

36. In effect, African Americans were excluded from all the political discussions. A small segment of whites were receptive to school integration, but the moderate and militant segregationists excluded other voices.

37. A product of compromise like *Brown I*, *Brown II* (349 U.S. 294 [1955]) likely slowed the integration process substantially. It was an invitation for legal stratagems to avoid integration. But white moderates (including court members) feared that a stronger ruling would lead angry segregationist whites to take to the streets.

38. Frye Gaillard, *The Dream Long Deferred: The Landmark Struggle for Desegregation in Charlotte, North Carolina* (Chapel Hill: University of North Carolina Press, 1988), 31-32.

39. For discussion of this speech, see Holcombe, "Desegregation Study." For the text of the speech, see "Address on Statewide Radio-Television Network, August 8, 1955," in *Messages, Addresses, and Public Papers of Luther Hartwell Hodges, Governor of North Carolina, 1954-1961*, ed. James W. Patton (Raleigh: Council of State, State of North Carolina, 1960-63), 199-202.

40. Among those who later justified active support for the Pearsall Plan as a holding action was Terry Sanford, the 1961-65 governor who would be seen as a pioneer in race relations. See Howard E. Covington Jr. and Marion A. Ellis, *Terry Sanford: Politics, Progress, and Outrageous Ambitions* (Durham: Duke University Press, 1999), 168-76.

41. Campbell, *Senator Sam Ervin*, 102–7. See also Newman, "Baptist State Convention," 13–14.

42. John Lang, observation to author, December 1973.

43. Cooley's address was on radio station WPTF in Raleigh. Cooley's economic populism probably persuaded some voters to stay with him even though they might have opposed his position on the manifesto. In the absence of reliable opinion polling, it seems likely that his position as chair of the House Agriculture Committee kept Cooley in Washington.

44. Covington and Ellis, *Terry Sanford*, 160–65.

45. Ibid., 182–84. Jordan, typical of textile executives, was a fierce opponent of labor unions. Scott had gladly accepted union support, though he could only go so far in backing their agenda.

46. Many older blacks were still Republicans in the 1950s. This observation is also based on Strong, *Urban Republicanism*.

47. *Browder v. Gayle*, 352 U.S. 903 (1956).

48. Covington and Ellis, *Terry Sanford*, 185–86. For a long-range perspective on desegregation in Charlotte, see Gaillard, *Dream Long Deferred*; Bagwell, *School Desegregation*, 79–125.

49. Gaillard, *Dream Long Deferred*, 4–17.

50. See Edward L. Rankin Jr., "Luther H. Hodges," in *The North Carolina Century: Tar Heels Who Made a Difference, 1900–2000*, ed. Howard E. Covington Jr. and Marion A. Ellis (Charlotte: Levine Museum of the New South; Chapel Hill: University of North Carolina Press, 2002), 490–94. See also Hodges, *Businessman in the Statehouse*.

51. John Fischer, "Editor's Easy Chair," *Harper's*, September 1961.

52. See Christensen, *Paradox of Tar Heel Politics*, 161–62. In addition, I have seen the article, pictures, and captions as my family subscribed to *Life* at that time.

53. V. O. Key Jr., *Southern Politics in State and Nation* (New York: Knopf, 1949), 211–15.

54. See John W. Cell, *The Highest Stage of White Supremacy: The Origins of Segregation in South Africa and the American South* (Cambridge: Cambridge University Press, 1982).

CHAPTER 3

1. See Taylor Branch, *Parting the Waters: America in the King Years, 1954–63* (New York: Simon and Schuster, 1988), 271–73. For a comprehensive account, see William Chafe, *Civilities and Civil Rights: Greensboro, North Carolina, and the Black Struggle for Freedom* (New York: Oxford University Press, 1980); Juan Williams, *Eyes on the Prize: America's Civil Rights Years, 1954–1965* (New York: Viking, 1987), 125–35.

2. John Drescher, *Triumph of Good Will: How Terry Sanford Beat a Champion of Segregation and Reshaped the South* (Jackson: University Press of Mississippi, 2000), xv–xxi.

3. For background on Sanford's rise and connection with the Scott wing of the Democratic Party, see Howard E. Covington Jr. and Marion A. Ellis, *Terry Sanford: Politics, Progress, and Outrageous Ambitions* (Durham: Duke University Press, 1999), 110–43.

4. Ibid., 168–76. Sanford used the term "safety valve" twice in meetings with me and others in 1968 and 1970.

5. Drescher, *Triumph of Good Will*, 65–71.

6. Ibid., 63–65.

7. Hodges never endorsed Seawell, but the incumbent governor harbored ill feelings toward Sanford, Lake, and Larkins. He had named Seawell as attorney general when a vacancy occurred between elections.

8. Tom Ellis, interview by author, October 20, 2006.

9. Julian M. Pleasants and Augustus M. Burns III, *Frank Porter Graham and the 1950 Senate Race in North Carolina* (Chapel Hill: University of North Carolina Press, 1990), 223–24.

10. Morgan had made a tentative promise to support Sanford but made it clear that friendship would obligate him to back Lake if he ran, a possibility that was initially considered unlikely. But Morgan's actions suggest that he encouraged Lake to run once his former professor showed a serious interest.

11. Drescher, *Triumph of Good Will*, 93–94.

12. Ibid.

13. Recording in possession of author.

14. Covington and Ellis, *Terry Sanford*, 205–6; Drescher, *Triumph of Good Will*, 93–94.

15. Lake news conference, May 30, 1960, WPTF (radio), Raleigh, N.C.; "School Integration, Spending Labeled Campaign Issues," *Greensboro Daily News*, May 30, 1960; Drescher, *Triumph of Good Will*, 164.

16. Lake news conference, May 30, 1960.

17. Sanford broadcast, May 31, 1960, WPTF (radio), Raleigh, N.C.; "Terry Sanford's Statement," *Charlotte Observer*, June 1, 1960.

18. Sanford broadcast, May 31, 1960.

19. Ibid.

20. Drescher, *Triumph of Good Will*, 169.

21. My analysis of precinct figures offered no proof of the claim that Lake had won the black vote in Iredell County.

22. John Larkins, *Politics, Bar, and Bench: A Memoir of U.S. District Judge John Davis Larkins, Jr.*, ed. Donald Lennon and Fred Ragan (n.p.: Historical Society of Eastern North Carolina, 1980), 69.

23. According to Sanford biographers Covington and Ellis, *Terry Sanford*, 169, Cannon handed Sanford an envelope with a campaign contribution: a rumpled one-dollar bill. But just having Cannon listed as a supporter sent a message to business that Sanford was safe and was not a radical.

24. J[onathan]. D[aniels]., editorial, *Raleigh News and Observer*, June 28, 1960.

25. Sanford's oral response using the word "damn," which was widely circulated in the media, probably further imperiled his political position.

26. Preston W. Edsall and J. Oliver Williams, "North Carolina: Bipartisan Paradox," in *The Changing Politics of the South*, ed. William C. Havard (Baton Rouge: Louisiana State University Press, 1972), 384.

27. Drescher, *Triumph of Good Will*, 236.

28. Sanford's relationship with Ervin remained tense for the remainder of their lives. He would later maintain at least a surface friendship with Jordan and Hodges (Drescher, *Triumph of Good Will*, 228–29).

29. Somewhere around 70 percent had been the norm for Democratic gubernatorial candidates from the 1920s through the 1950s. The exception was in 1928, when Catholic Al Smith was the Democratic presidential candidate. Democratic gubernatorial candidate O. Max Gardner, who supported Smith, won with just over 53 percent.

30. Theodore White, *The Making of the President, 1960* (New York: Atheneum, 1961).

31. Viola Henderson, comment heard by author.

32. In this extremely tight election, personality probably determined the outcome. White, *Making of the President*, was the first to write about this phenomenon in detail. The personality factor is a major theme in his book.

33. I believe that among North Carolina farmers, agricultural subsidies eclipsed foreign policy and race as major concerns.

34. Terry Sanford, Inaugural Address, January 1961, in *Messages, Addresses, and Public Papers of Terry Sanford, Governor of North Carolina, 1961-65*, ed. Memory F. Mitchell (Raleigh: Council of State, State of North Carolina, 1966), 3-5.

35. William Friday, interview by author, January 4, 2007.

36. Willis Whichard, interview by author, July 21, 2006.

37. For a comprehensive discussion of Sanford's strategy in making appointments, see Covington and Ellis, *Terry Sanford*, chapter 11, esp. 243, 272.

38. Ibid., 244, 262, 265.

39. Ibid., 248-49.

40. In 1959, thirty-one states levied personal income taxes. North Carolina's rate ranged from 3 percent to 7 percent, with the top rate reserved for people with taxable incomes above ten thousand dollars a year. North Carolina's rates were about the same as New York's.

41. See Covington and Ellis, *Terry Sanford*, 254-55. Sanford's biographers provide the best account of the political rationale for the sales tax proposal.

42. To a point, Sanford's gregarious nature compensated for his boldness. Governor Scott had been hostile toward legislators. Umstead often worked through aides. Hodges was proud and aloof. Sanford was not above flattery, and he could get down on the level of legislators. He enjoyed a good joke.

43. I believe that the idea that the food tax would catch everyone, though rarely put forth publicly, was crucial to the measure's passage. Partly racist, it sold the proposal to white voters and legislators alike, especially in eastern North Carolina. Furthermore, the fact that big business considered it the least objectionable of taxes sealed its passage.

44. *Durham Sun*, June 15, 1961.

45. After the food tax went into effect, store clerks ringing up a bill were fond of saying "a dollar for the charge and three cents for Terry," even when the items being purchased had been subject to the 3 percent tax long before Sanford's package was adopted.

46. Covington and Ellis, *Terry Sanford*, 290-91. The decision to name a woman caused a stir among male mossbacks in Raleigh. When Sanford told retiring Chief Justice Wallace Winbourne that Sharp would be joining the court, he responded, "But Governor, this is a man's court." For a full account of events leading up to the Sharp appointment, see Anna R. Hayes, *Without Precedent: The Life of Susie Marshall Sharp* (Chapel Hill: University of North Carolina Press, 2008), 209-37.

47. Terry Sanford, *But What about the People?* (New York: Harper and Row, 1966), 7.

48. Covington and Ellis, *Terry Sanford*, 320-32.

49. For an extended account of the payoffs and challenges of the North Carolina Fund and related projects, see George Esser with Rob Bickley, *My Years at the North Carolina Fund: An Oral History* (Durham: Esser; Charleston, S.C.: Booksurge, 2007).

50. Sanford was a pioneer in forging public-private partnerships, but he probably could not have even dreamed about the concept's tremendous success in the Research Triangle Park.

51. In the rural Black Belt counties, dramatic growth in African American voting would not occur until after the passage of the Voting Rights Act of 1965.

52. Sanford, "Inaugural Address," 8.

53. Covington and Ellis, *Terry Sanford*, 250–51. Bill Campbell, the young African American who integrated the Murphy School, was elected mayor of Atlanta in 1993.

54. The statement's wording was clever, almost suggesting there had never been segregation in the parks.

55. Often portrayed as defenders of the status quo, the business titans were often ahead of the general public on racial issues. This was especially true of development-oriented leaders such as bankers who believed that a protracted racial struggle would hurt the business climate.

56. Otis Kapsalis statement, July 1963. Statement made to author's family in presence of author. Kapsalis also said he was acting in "the interest of the community."

57. Though associated with the 1950s effort to maintain segregation, Pearsall was by the early 1960s clearly part of the Democratic Party's progressive wing. Had Pearsall decided to run for governor in 1964, Sanford would likely have backed him.

58. Terry Sanford, "Observation for a Second Century," January 18, 1963, in *Messages, Addresses, and Public Papers*, ed. Mitchell, 574.

CHAPTER 4

1. See Robert Caro, *The Passage of Power* (New York: Knopf, 2012), 307–88.

2. Terry Sanford, *Messages, Addresses, and Public Papers of Terry Sanford, Governor of North Carolina, 1961–65*, ed. Memory F. Mitchell (Raleigh: Council of State, State of North Carolina, 1966), 608.

3. If the Gallup opinion poll trial heats are to be believed, Kennedy could have won reelection without any southern state, and such a feat might have been necessary. In late 1963, hardly anyone thought that Goldwater could beat Kennedy in the national contest.

4. Tying passage to Kennedy's martyrdom was a more effective tactic than arguing for the civil rights bill on its merits.

5. Johnson, the most effective advocate for liberal legislation since Roosevelt, often seemed most comfortable with more conservative politicians in Texas and Washington, whom he understood better than he did the reform liberals.

6. Sanford had exhausted much of his political capital early on as he promoted new legislative programs. During the 1961 session, 75 percent of Sanford's proposals were adopted. These figures are based on the ratio of formal recommendations made to the legislature by the governor to the total number of recommendations passed by the legislature during the two-year period (Frank Guy Braley, "The North Carolina Governor: Gubernatorial Perceptions of the Governor's Legislative Role" [master's thesis, East Carolina University, 1981], 113).

7. Numan V. Bartley and Hugh D. Graham, *Southern Politics and the Second Reconstruction* (Baltimore: Johns Hopkins University Press, 1975), 76. For a less academic-oriented but quite colorful discussion of alliances in the race, see James R. Spence, *The Making of the Governor: The Moore-Preyer-Lake Primaries of 1964* (Winston-Salem: Blair, 1968).

8. William Friday, interview by author, December 7, 2006.

9. Preyer announced his opposition to the proposed Civil Rights Act, probably because he thought that supporting would be political suicide. His support for more

educational expenditures without higher taxes was a safe position and almost identical to Moore's.

10. Bob Scott, who was present at the meeting, had offered an amusing account of this episode in a December 1989 conversation. He mentioned it again in our 2006 interview (Robert W. Scott, interview by author, October 16, 2006). Scott won election as lieutenant governor in 1964.

11. Howard E. Covington Jr. and Marion A. Ellis, *Terry Sanford: Politics, Progress, and Outrageous Ambitions* (Durham: Duke University Press, 1999), 353.

12. "Moore Holds Strong Hand in Runoff," *Raleigh News and Observer*, June 1, 1964. The white working class and much of the middle class saw Moore as a kindred spirit. Even if race had not been an issue, the gentlemanly but aristocratic-seeming Preyer would likely have had problems with working-class voters. Nearly everyone I interviewed from that era—and others in conversations—spoke of Moore's sincerity and down-home demeanor. But more important still, Moore was well positioned to gain nearly all the Lake vote.

13. It was inevitable that the bloc vote issue would arise in any primary runoff if one candidate had won most of the black vote in the first primary.

14. Phil Carlton, interview by author, April 18, 2007.

15. Ibid.

16. Robert Morgan, interview by author, August 14, 2006

17. Ibid.

18. Ibid.

19. Arguably, the teachers' professional association was attracted to Preyer largely on the basis of his connection to the Sanford wing of the party. However, their backing reached a high pitch. I heard Ferrell and associates say that they considered Moore's similarly generous school spending proposals to be "insincere."

20. Looking back, Moore's differences with Sanford and Preyer seem to have related to style and tone, not policies. Paradoxically and to his benefit, Moore was the "anti-Sanford candidate" even though his specific program proposals were arguably as progressive as Preyer's.

21. Scott repeated this theme to me, although he admired Sanford's political qualities and accomplishments (Robert W. Scott, interview). He did not care for Bennett, a leading adviser to Sanford, Preyer, and later Jim Hunt.

22. For an excellent account of Ervin's role (and of Ervin the man and the politician), see Karl E. Campbell, *Senator Sam Ervin, Last of the Founding Fathers* (Chapel Hill: University of North Carolina Press, 2007); for Ervin's opposition to mid-1960s civil rights legislation, see the wonderfully named chapter "Claghorn's Hammurabi," 131–60.

23. The election outcome suggests that the strategy worked: Johnson carried all the Outer South and border states, all of them but Florida by comfortable margins. But many other issues and perceptions were involved, most important the one that Goldwater was an extremist.

24. In 1964 and long afterward, most North Carolinians who voted Democratic for president were straight-party-ticket voters, so Gavin's strategy was a tall order. But my precinct analysis and conversations with the voters in the 1964 election suggest that a few voters did go for Democrat Johnson and Republican Gavin, but there were too few of those voters for Gavin to win.

25. The 1964 election was a milestone in African American voting. Though a majority of blacks had been voting Democratic since 1936, many had stuck with the GOP. After 1964,

Democratic candidates usually won at least 80 percent of the black vote. Most blacks and whites from 1964 viewed the Democrats as more friendly to minority rights.

26. Following the pattern set by Eisenhower and Nixon, Goldwater won a majority of the urban white vote in North Carolina; Johnson did well among rural whites. But among eastern North Carolina whites, the Democrats experienced some slippage, but it was much less there than in similar areas across the South.

27. The climax of the early 1965 protests had come in February and March. The protest had originally been directed at officials in Selma, Alabama, who were determined to prevent any blacks from voting against Sheriff Clark, who symbolized the resistance to change much as King symbolized the fight for change. The movement for reform climaxed with a protest march from Selma to Montgomery. At that point, Governor Wallace assumed a leadership role in the anti-voting-rights fight. As in the past, when violence erupted, the president was moved to act. In 1963, it had been Kennedy reacting to violence in Birmingham. This time, it was Johnson reacting to violence in Selma and Montgomery. See David J. Garrow, *Bearing the Cross: Martin Luther King, Jr., and the Southern Christian Leadership Conference* (New York: Morrow, 1986), 357–430; Taylor Branch, *Pillar of Fire: America in the King Years, 1963–65* (New York: Simon and Schuster, 1998), 591–600.

28. See Mary Jo Jackson Bratton, *East Carolina University: The Formative Years, 1907–1982* (Greenville: East Carolina University Alumni Association, 1986), 371–401; William A. Link, *William Friday: Power, Purpose, and American Higher Education* (Chapel Hill: University of North Carolina Press, 1995), 159–69; Friday, interview; Morgan, interview.

29. Bratton, *East Carolina University*, 371–73.

30. While East Carolina University leaders saw Friday as a major impediment to their goals, his position was more complex. He had doubts about campuses at Charlotte, Asheville, and Wilmington becoming universities, a status that he believed would violate the spirit of the Carlyle report. See Link, *William Friday*, 168–72.

31. William D. Mills, interview by author, August 2, 2006.

32. The words "visionary" and "intellectual" are often associated in the popular mind. But among politicians, effective visionaries are often not intellectuals in any classic sense.

33. *Baker v. Carr*, 369 U.S. 186 (1962).

34. While the population of the coastal plain and mountains was decreasing relative to the rest of the state, each region would constitute a powerful bloc even after reapportionment.

35. Friday had some misgivings about the change to the Charlotte institution, thinking it might inflame the situation. Appalachian State and East Carolina had long been four-year colleges, while Charlotte and Wilmington were just now making the transition. Friday thought the rush a bit unseemly. He also told me in our 2006 interview that he thought that Appalachian, East Carolina, and Charlotte would have grown rapidly in student population and programs whatever decisions had been made in the mid- and late 1960s. He believed that population trends and national trends in higher education had made this inevitable.

36. Bratton, *East Carolina University*, 390, 394–98.

37. Ibid., 397–99.

38. Whether Moore had by then accepted the inevitability of university expansion or was simply trying to protect the interests of the consolidated university is not clear. By 1967, however, the tide for East Carolina likely could not have been stopped.

39. Link, *William Friday*, 168–69.

40. Ibid., 112–20.

41. Ibid., 135–41.

42. Ransome Ellis Holcombe, "A Desegregation Study of Public Schools in North Carolina" (Ph.D. diss., East Tennessee State University, 1985), 115–16.

43. Ibid., 129.

44. Speeches heard by author in October 1966.

45. On secret organizations such as the Klan, reliable statistical data are almost impossible to gather. In this case, anecdotal evidence is probably more reliable than Federal Bureau of Investigation data.

46. Ned Cline, "J. Robert Jones," in *The North Carolina Century: Tar Heels Who Made a Difference, 1900–2000*, ed. Howard E. Covington Jr. and Marion A. Ellis (Charlotte: Levine Museum of the New South; Chapel Hill: University of North Carolina Press, 2002), 573–75. See also *An Unlikely Friendship*, a documentary produced by Diane Bloom that highlights the evolving friendship between Durham Klan leader C. P. Ellis and civil rights activist Ann Atwater.

47. Daniel Killian Moore, *Messages, Addresses, and Public Papers of Governor Daniel Killian Moore, Governor of North Carolina, 1965–1969*, ed. Memory F. Mitchell (Raleigh: State Department of Archives and History for the Council of State, 1971), 634.

48. Data compiled from North Carolina Education Association and North Carolina Association of Educators.

49. The big salary increases of the Moore era in part reflected national economic prosperity and in part resulted from the Sanford tax increases.

50. Moore was in many respects the classic North Carolina progressive conservative. Part of the increase in education financing during his time reflected the number of baby boomers flooding into the system.

51. Friday, interview.

52. Morgan, interview; Robert W. Scott, interview. Others also repeatedly made the same point.

53. Cline, "J. Robert Jones," 573–75.

54. Gunnar Myrdal, *An American Dilemma: The Negro Problem and Modern Democracy* (New York: Harper, 1944).


CHAPTER 5

1. While the Vietnam conflict had seen American involvement from the early 1960s, it did not truly enter the national consciousness until Lyndon Johnson expanded the effort and increased draft calls in the 1965–66 period.

2. See Theodore White, *The Making of the President, 1968* (New York: Atheneum, 1969), 3–30.

3. Lewis Chester, Godfrey Hodgson, and Bruce Page, *An American Melodrama: The Presidential Campaign of 1968* (New York: Viking, 1969), 11–18.

4. Wayne Grimsley, *James B. Hunt: A North Carolina Progressive* (Jefferson, N.C.: McFarland, 2003), 60–62.

5. Displeased with all the candidates, the North Carolina delegation initially pushed outgoing governor Dan Moore as a favorite-son candidate for president.

6. Robert W. Scott, interview by author, October 16, 2006.

7. Ibid.

8. Comment by Terry Sanford to author, April 1968.

9. Robert W. Scott, interview.

10. Wade Bruton, the incumbent, projected a tired and worn-out image to the general public. Liberals viewed Bruton's office as ultraconservative. Conservatives still saw Morgan as a kindred spirit. His relative youth appealed to people of various ideological persuasions.

11. Chester, Hodgson, and Page, *American Melodrama*, 561–75.

12. David M. Kovenock and James W. Prothro, *Comparative State Elections Project, 1968* (Chapel Hill: University of North Carolina, Institute for Research in Social Science, 1970), http://www.icpsr.umich.edu/icpsrweb/ICPSR/studies/7508.

13. Dan T. Carter, *The Politics of Rage: George Wallace, the Origins of the New Conservatism, and the Transformation of American Politics* (New York: Simon and Schuster, 1995).

14. For perspectives on this period, see Kevin P. Phillips, *The Emerging Republican Majority* (Garden City, N.Y.: Anchor, 1970); Thomas Byrne Edsall with Mary D. Edsall, *Chain Reaction: The Impact of Race, Rights, and Taxes on American Politics* (New York: Norton, 1991), esp. chapter 4, 78–79. For a broader perspective in historical context, see Earl Black and Merle Black, *Politics and Society in the South* (Cambridge: Harvard University Press, 1987), esp. chapters 11 and 12.

15. Today, it is often said that Gardner endorsed Wallace, although he did not formally endorse either Nixon or Wallace. Nevertheless, Republicans saw Gardner's neutrality as a slap at Nixon and de facto support for Wallace.

16. For the riot unit's occupation of part of the campus, see William A. Link, *William Friday: Power, Purpose, and American Higher Education* (Chapel Hill: University of North Carolina Press, 1995), 141–53. Scott considered the Chapel Hill administration and to a degree Friday to be weak-kneed on the whole matter. Friday was upset by Scott's intervention in what he considered a balanced university policy. And Sitterson found the whole experience deeply humiliating.

17. Ibid., 155–56.

18. Scott had a problem with intellectual types—professors, city journalists, and like-minded people. In response, many of them viewed Scott as brash and as somewhat lacking in intellectual ability. Paradoxically, I have rarely been around a politician who seemed more open, candid, and witty in expressing and justifying his actions.

19. Robert W. Scott, interview.

20. Frank Guy Braley, "The North Carolina Governor: Gubernatorial Perceptions of the Governor's Legislative Role" (master's thesis, East Carolina University, 1981), 113–16.

21. Ralph Scott was more open-minded and liberal than the typical legislator. Yet he understood power in the General Assembly and had cordial relationships with other bull elephants. His influence contributed to his nephew's success.

22. State government reorganization alone would have established Scott as an important governor. Bureaucrats and their interest group allies frequently resisted the process.

23. Hugh Talmage Lefler and Albert Ray Newsome, *North Carolina: The History of a Southern State* (Chapel Hill: University of North Carolina Press, 1954), 704; Robert W. Scott, interview.

24. Robert W. Scott, interview.

25. Lefler and Newsome, *North Carolina*, 177–81.

26. Robert W. Scott, interview.

27. Most written accounts of the time suggest that classes went on as usual, with students completing required work. But I was on the campus at the time, and I know that a large number of classes did not follow the official policy. Individual instructors ultimately decided what to do.

28. For years afterward, major state histories made little or no reference to the 1971 events at Oxford.

29. For the most detailed discussion of Oxford events, see Timothy B. Tyson, *Blood Done Sign My Name: A True Story* (New York: Crown, 2004).

30. The events in Oxford probably did not become a major national news story because they were overshadowed by the Kent State shootings.

31. The major employers who left Wilmington included the headquarters of a major railroad after the merger of the Wilmington-based Atlantic Coast Line and Seaboard Railroad. The city was probably the most racially polarized in North Carolina.

32. See William S. Powell, *North Carolina through Four Centuries* (Chapel Hill: University of North Carolina Press, 1989), 527.

33. See Grimsley, *James B. Hunt*, 136–48, 151–53.

34. Ibid., 139–42, 150–53.

35. E. Osborne Ayscue Jr., "James B. McMillan," in *The North Carolina Century: Tar Heels Who Made a Difference, 1900–2000*, ed. Howard E. Covington Jr. and Marion A. Ellis (Charlotte: Levine Museum of the New South; Chapel Hill: University of North Carolina Press, 2002), 286–89; Jack Claiborne, *The Charlotte Observer: Its Time and Place, 1869–1986* (Chapel Hill: University of North Carolina Press, 1986), 287–88, 290.

36. *Swann v. Charlotte-Mecklenburg Board of Education*, 402 U.S. 1 (1971).

37. The controversy over neighborhood schools continued off and on for decades. In 2010, Wake County (Raleigh-Cary) had a hotly contested board of education election that turned on the issue of economic diversity. A pro-neighborhood school slate won a majority of seats.

38. Howard E. Covington Jr. and Marion A. Ellis, *Terry Sanford: Politics, Progress, and Outrageous Ambitions* (Durham: Duke University Press, 1999), 367–69.

39. Ibid.

CHAPTER 6

1. Jordan's instincts were conservative, befitting a textile executive. And business interests were happy with his record. But scoring by the liberal Americans for Democratic Action and conservative Americans for Constitutional Action and American Conservative Union typically placed Jordan in 40–60 percent range during his later years in the Senate. For an overall perspective and context, see Ben F. Bulla, *Textiles and Politics: The Life of B. Everett Jordan: From Saxapahaw to the United States Senate* (Durham: Carolina Academic, 1992).

2. Galifianakis had a much more liberal image than Jordan, but their voting records matched about as closely as any two members of Congress from North Carolina. At home in Durham, liberals were angry at Galifianakis, while many conservatives and unreconstructed segregationists saw him as a man of the Left.

3. Nick Galifianakis, interview by author, December 12, 2008. Nick Galifianakis is the uncle of actor Zach Galifianakis.

4. See Pat Taylor, *Fourth Down and Goal to Go*, ed. Edward L. Rankin Jr. (Raleigh: Ivy House, 2005), which is semiautobiographical. It includes good stories, witticisms, and a splendid interview with 1960 and 1964 gubernatorial candidate I. Beverly Lake. However, the information on Taylor's 1972 campaign is sparse. I was acquainted with Taylor in the 1970s and judged him to be ambitious but less consumed than most who rise to the top.

5. Taylor's brother, Frank, developed muscular dystrophy at the age of four. The Taylors were told of a twelve-year-old African American, Arthur "Pete" Pittman, who had been abandoned by his parents and needed a home. They took Arthur into the household to care for Frank. Arthur later adopted Taylor as his last name. According to Pat Taylor, Pete "lived with us as a loving and beloved member of our family. We would all hang our stockings together at Christmas time. . . . Pete was fully our brother" (Taylor, *Fourth Down*, 1–2).

6. Taylor initially urged "moderation" on race issues. By the mid-1960s, he openly, if softly, urged racial equality.

7. Robert Morgan, interview by author, August 14, 2006; Burley Mitchell, interview by author, July 26, 2006.

8. Darlene McGill-Holmes, "Reginald A. Hawkins," in *The North Carolina Century: Tar Heels Who Made a Difference, 1900–2000*, ed. Howard E. Covington Jr. and Marion A. Ellis (Charlotte: Levine Museum of the New South; Chapel Hill: University of North Carolina Press, 2002), 399.

9. Steven Niven, "Wilbur Hobby," in ibid., 571.

10. Howell had mounted the most overtly liberal challenge yet to Virginia conservatives and the remnants of the conservative Byrd organization. He was a classic economic populist. Unlike Hobby, who was attempting to mimic Howell's campaign, the Virginian was a serious force in politics, even though he lost his bids for the governorship in 1969, 1973, and 1977.

11. See Howard E. Covington Jr. and Marion A. Ellis, *Terry Sanford: Politics, Progress, and Outrageous Ambitions* (Durham: Duke University Press, 1999), 199–200; Alex Coffin, "Hargrove 'Skipper' Bowles Jr.," in *North Carolina Century*, ed. Covington and Ellis, 464–66.

12. Bowles's 1972 campaign was pacesetting for North Carolina and to some degree American state politics in general. De Vries combined the principles of empirical political science with an excellent intuition about people. De Vries had developed the theory of split-ticket voting, which differentiated voters who looked at each race in a given campaign year from less sophisticated independents who might vote on emotion for the straight Democratic ticket in one election and the straight Republican ticket in the next cycle.

13. To this point, statewide Democratic candidates in North Carolina had been able to give short shrift to supporters of other candidates in the primaries. So Bowles was following past practice.

14. Jim Holshouser, interview by author, February 10, 2006.

15. Ibid.

16. Gardner was a historically significant figure in that he, more than state Republicans of the past, attempted to draw a sharp ideological distinction between the political parties, with Republicans the voice of an aggressive conservatism. Decades later, his approach had become the GOP standard.

17. Tom Ellis, interview by author, October 20, 2006.

18. Harper, a forceful advocate of gender equality, accepted these personal putdowns with public restraint and a private resentment that she did not reveal until years later.

19. Grimsley, *James B. Hunt*, 54–57.

20. Ellis, interview.

21. Holshouser, interview.

22. Galifianakis, interview.

23. Holshouser, interview.

24. Especially helpful in assessing Helms were my interviews with Burley Mitchell (July 26, 2006), Bert Coffer (October 20, 2006), Tom Ellis (October 20, 2006), William Friday (January 4, 2007), Carter Wrenn (March 5, 2007), Bill Cobey (June 1, 2007), John Dodd (October 24, 2008), Mike Dunne (November 24, 2008), and Jimmy Broughton (June 2, 2008) as well as numerous conversations with former Helms staffers, especially Jonathan Brooks and Mary Lynn Qurnell. Journalist-author Rob Christensen (*The Paradox of Tar Heel Politics*, 2nd ed. [Chapel Hill: University of North Carolina Press, 2010]) and historian-biographer William A. Link (*Righteous Warrior: Jesse Helms and the Rise of Modern Conservatism* [New York: St. Martin's, 2008]) have also provided penetrating analyses of Helms the man and the politician.

25. Dodd, interview; Ellis, interview; William A. Link, *William Friday: Power, Purpose, and American Higher Education* (Chapel Hill: University of North Carolina Press, 1995), 56–57, 63–64, 68; David Middleburg, "Jesse Helms," in *North Carolina Century*, 400–401. Also instructive are Helms's comments on his relationship with Fletcher in Helms's memoir, *Here's Where I Stand: A Memoir* (New York: Random House, 2005), esp. 28–30, 33, 44–45, 54. In contrast, as a young member of the 1947–48 Alabama Legislature, Wallace promoted programs for the poor. See Stephen Lesher, *George Wallace: American Populist* (Reading, Mass.: Addison-Wesley, 1994), 69–72, 81–83. For background and perspective, see Earl Black, "The Militant Segregationist Vote in the Post-Brown South: A Comparative Analysis," *Social Science Quarterly* 54, no. 1 (1973): 66–84.

26. See Link, *William Friday*, 83–98, 132.

27. Ibid., 99  122, 132.

28. Even as laws and court rulings attempted to achieve equality, anger seemed to run at a high pitch. The foundations of white supremacy were collapsing. But Helms articulated the pent-up anger. Link's book, *Righteous Warrior*, praises some aspects of Helms's career, but captures the spirit of anger throughout.

29. This was the most dramatic shift in North Carolina. Yet it was also part of a long-term secular trend. To understand the trend in a national and southern context, see Walter Dean Burnham, "Critical Realignment: Dead or Alive," in *The End of Realignment?: Interpreting American Electoral Eras*, ed. Byron E. Shafer (Madison: University of Wisconsin Press, 1991), 101–35. See also Thomas F. Eamon, "The Militant Republican Right in North Carolina Elections," in *The Disappearing South?: Studies in Regional Change and Continuity*, ed. Robert P. Steed, Laurence W. Moreland, and Tod A. Baker (Tuscaloosa: University of Alabama Press, 1990), 156–73.

30. The dissonance between the highest-level offices and the other offices stands out as a prominent feature of this election. In one form or another, this dissonance persisted for the remainder of the century.

CHAPTER 7

1. Karl E. Campbell, *Senator Sam Ervin, Last of the Founding Fathers* (Chapel Hill: University of North Carolina Press, 2007), 250–96.

2. Phillips, who later emerged as an exponent of economic populism, was a leading conservative or social populist strategist in the late 1960s. In Kevin P. Phillips, *The Emerging Republican Majority* (Garden City, N.Y.: Anchor, 1970), he outlined the feasibility of the political strategy that would be used successfully by Richard Nixon and later Ronald Reagan.

3. Jim Holshouser, interview by author, February 10, 2006.

4. Hodges, Moore, and Terry Sanford were consistently outspoken in their opposition to all attempts to tamper with any governor's power. Later, Governors Jim Martin and Jim Hunt followed the same line.

5. Holshouser said that his personal relationship with Helms was always correct, even cordial. But the bickering between Helms loyalists and the traditional party leadership was a dominant political current of the 1970s and left an imprint for several decades thereafter (Holshouser, interview).

6. Burley Mitchell, interview by author, July 26, 2006; Robert Morgan, interview by author, August 14, 2006.

7. Holshouser, interview.

8. Ibid.; Jim Hunt, interview by author, November 13, 2006; Willis Whichard, interview by author, July 21, 2006.

9. See Mary Jo Jackson Bratton, *East Carolina University: The Formative Years, 1907–1982* (Greenville: East Carolina University Alumni Association, 1986), 415–20; William A. Link, *William Friday: Power, Purpose, and American Higher Education* (Chapel Hill: University of North Carolina Press, 1995), 224–46; William Friday, interview by author, January 4, 2007; Hunt, interview; Janice Faulkner, interview by author, May 6, 2009.

10. Friday, interview; John Sanders, interview by author, October 21, 2005.

11. Bratton, *East Carolina University*, 411–21.

12. See Campbell, *Senator Sam Ervin*, 179–80, 225–26.

13. Jack Bass and Walter De Vries, *The Transformation of Southern Politics: Social Change and Political Consequence since 1945* (New York: Basic Books, 1976), 218–47.

14. Sam Poole, interview by author, July 18, 2006; Howard E. Covington Jr. and Marion A. Ellis, *Terry Sanford: Politics, Progress, and Outrageous Ambitions* (Durham: Duke University Press, 1999), 411–16.

15. Tom Ellis, interview by author, October 20, 2006; Carter Wrenn, interview by author, March 9, 2007.

16. The television and newspaper images of Carter entering and leaving the small Baptist church in Plains, Georgia, might have contributed more to his national victory and acceptance in the South than did any substantive issue. Carter projected as a man of honesty and piety against the background of what the public saw as a scandal-ridden Washington.

17. Such a spectacle would have been unimaginable fifteen years earlier. One of the most dramatic moments in a twentieth-century political party convention was this scene of reconciliation. Almost always, the greatest dramas had centered on fiery speeches, suspenseful roll-call votes, or walkouts.

18. Carter's postconvention leads suggested a victory almost of the magnitude of Roosevelt over Landon in 1936 or Johnson over Goldwater in 1964. By Election Day, he had a razor-thin lead.

19. Green was one of the sharpest political operatives in modern North Carolina legislative politics, a role he later played as lieutenant governor. When he made a personal commitment, he usually kept his word. But he was a master of nuances and could be a double-dealer at times.

20. Remark from Hunt aide Thomas Taft to author in 1976.

21. Winning North Carolina Democrats across the ideological spectrum had, with rare exceptions, such as Robert Rice Reynolds running for senator in 1932 and 1938 and Kerr Scott running for governor in 1948, assiduously courted the business leadership. No candidate had outpaced Hunt in this endeavor. Early on, business leaders had feared that Hunt might be too liberal, but seeing a likely winner and a possible ally, they flocked to his campaign.

22. Wayne Grimsley, *James B. Hunt: A North Carolina Progressive* (Jefferson, N.C.: Mc-Farland, 2003), presents a highly competent account of this period. Grimsley, the son of Hunt's key adviser, Joe Grimsley, was hardly a detached observer, but he had great access and in my opinion writes fairly.

23. Ibid.

24. Ellis, interview; Wrenn, interview.

25. See Gwen Covington, "Howard N. Lee," in *The North Carolina Century: Tar Heels Who Made a Difference, 1900–2000*, ed. Howard E. Covington Jr. and Marion A. Ellis (Charlotte: Levine Museum of the New South; Chapel Hill: University of North Carolina Press, 2002), 413–16.

26. For Lee's account of the election, see Howard N. Lee, *The Courage to Lead: One Man's Journey in Public Service* (Chapel Hill: Cotton Patch, 2008), 20–26. See also Gwen Covington, "Howard N. Lee."

27. Conversation with Howard Lee in the spring of 1976.

28. Poll evidence is scant on the matter of Wallace people voting for Lee. But a few of my family's friends and neighbors who had backed Wallace for president and I. Beverly Lake for governor quickly volunteered that Lee was their top pick in the field.

29. "Small segment" of the population or "special interests" were now the terms white candidates making racial appeals used to refer to black voters. More overt racial language was now out of style.

30. Although the country had gone through the turbulent 1960s, language of an explicit sexual nature remained taboo, at least in the realm of public discourse.

31. Tom Fetzer, interview by author, April 23, 2007.

32. Mitchell, interview.

33. Bass and Devries, *Transformation of Southern Politics*, 222–25.

34. Gary Pearce, interview by author, September 7, 2008.

35. Hunt thrived as a cheerleader and a morale builder. He was uncomfortable firing people and disliked acrimonious debate inside the administration. This conclusion is based on my interviews with Hunt associates such as Pearce and Franklin Freeman and informal conversations with other Hunt associates.

36. Author's conversations with Jane Patterson in the 1970s. Patterson was also one of the most effective crusaders for women's rights in the 1960s and 1970s.

37. All governors wanted loyalists inside the bureaucracy, partly to promote their programs and partly to reward political supporters. But in recent decades, no administration had maintained quite as high a level of monitoring as the Hunt administration.

38. Minority leaders have often wavered on testing as well as broad initiatives such as George W. Bush's No Child Left Behind program. Reform advocates from Hunt to Bush have often linked testing programs to increased emphasis on better programs and funding for disadvantaged schools, with the stated aim of improving school performance.

39. The North Carolina School of Science and Mathematics arguably provided a model for later innovative educational programs such as magnet schools and charter schools.

40. Eure was stubborn and one of the most partisan of Democrats, though he was much more conservative than all the Democratic presidents and the later Democratic governors. He was a leading authority on the state constitution and legislative rules. And he was the most colorful of politicians.

41. Rufus Edmisten, interview by author, July 30, 2008; author's conversations over the years with Ervin associates, Hunt associates, and Sanford associates.

42. Holshouser's support for succession reflected both his belief in a strong executive and his long record as a classic North Carolina progressive.

43. James B. Hunt, *Addresses and Public Papers of James Baxter Hunt, Jr., Governor of North Carolina*, vol. 1: *1977–1981*, ed. Memory F. Mitchell (Raleigh: Division of Archives and History, Dept. of Cultural Resources, 1982–2010), 219.

44. Ibid., 219; for Hunt's entire statement, see 216–21.

45. Ferguson quoted in *Raleigh News and Observer* and other media, January 24, 1978.

46. Neither the court's decision nor later developments really resolved the question of the guilt or total innocence of the Wilmington Ten. And politically, guilt or innocence did not matter. The saga was the outgrowth of a polarized society where racial animosity and ideological perspectives often outweighed all other concerns. But the shadow of racism surely influenced Wilmington and North Carolina society at the time.

CHAPTER 8

1. Michael Barone, *Our Country: The Shaping of America from Roosevelt to Reagan* (New York: Free Press, 1990), 592–93.

2. Ibid., 585–88.

3. The main possibility for outside invasion of the Democratic primary came from the large number of Republican sympathizers still registered as Democrats, either by tradition or so they could vote in what was often the "real election" for county-level offices.

4. See William A. Link, *Righteous Warrior: Jesse Helms and the Rise of Modern Conservatism* (New York: St. Martin's, 2008), 144–47.

5. See William A. Link, *William Friday: Power, Purpose, and American Higher Education* (Chapel Hill: University of North Carolina Press, 1995), 284–86, 303–37.

6. This incident was reminiscent of earlier disputes between management and fledgling labor unions in North Carolina. But in the Greensboro incident, Governor Hunt and most state officials were hostile to the violent troublemakers, the Klan. But they also did not want to be associated with procommunist elements.

7. Bob Scott, interview by author, September 16, 2006. See also Wayne Grimsley, *James B. Hunt: A North Carolina Progressive* (Jefferson, N.C.: McFarland, 2003), 206–9.

8. Jim Hunt, interview by author, November 13, 2006.

9. Barone, *Our Country*, 594–95.

10. Morgan was sometimes labeled a "conservative" senator, but an examination of his voting record places him on the moderately liberal side of the political spectrum.

11. Tom Ellis, interview by author, October 20, 2006.

12. Observation of Wayne Holloman to author.

13. At the beginning of my teaching career, I knew East well. Our offices were close, and we talked frequently about government and politics.

14. Robert Morgan, interview by author, August 14, 2006.

15. V. O. Key Jr., *Politics, Parties, and Pressure Groups*, 5th ed. (New York: Crowell, 1964), 568–72.

16. Barone, *Our Country*, 596.

17. East observation to author, November 1980.

18. Not coincidentally, this industrial area was a center of strength for Helms. For a discussion of this area's influence in the 1984 Helms-Hunt contest, see Paul Luebke, *Tar Heel Politics* (Chapel Hill: University of North Carolina Press, 1990), 151–52.

19. *Roe v. Wade*, 410 U.S. 113 (1973).

20. *Roe v. Wade* did more to stir up a political movement on the right than did any other twentieth-century court decision. In its absence, the alliance between evangelical churches and politicians such as Reagan and Helms might have had greater difficulty gaining traction. See Michael Perman, *Pursuit of Unity: A Political History of the American South* (Chapel Hill: University of North Carolina Press, 2009), 348.

21. Although East had candidly answered questions about his disability in media interviews, many voters did not become aware of it until after he was elected. Most of those with whom I spoke told me that the knowledge would have made no difference in their vote.

22. Morgan, interview.

23. See Thomas F. Eamon, "From Pool Hall to Parish House in North Carolina," in *Strategies for Mobilizing Black Voters: Four Case Studies*, ed. James E. Cavanagh (Washington, D.C.: Joint Center for Political Studies, 1987), 101–36.

24. H. M. "Mickey" Michaux, interview by author, November 13, 2009. (I conducted three interviews with Michaux in prior years.)

25. Eamon, "From Pool Hall to Parish House," 101–7.

26. Michaux, interview.

27. Data from Durham County Board of Elections (http://dconc.gov/index.aspx?page=95&redirect=1).

28. Although many Helms supporters had backed Valentine in the primary, Valentine was a critic of the right wing of the Republican Party from November 1982 until the end of his political career.

29. If Aycock and Sanford had been the great education governors, Hunt was arguably the greatest innovator. And unlike Sanford, Hunt's boldness enhanced his political career.

30. Hunt used the expression "race for the future" over and over as he tied together basic education and new technology. The idea was a factor in the strong support Hunt received from modernizer elements of the business community such as bankers, developers, and software executives.

31. William Friday, interview by author, January 4, 2007.

32. See Link, *William Friday*, 356–63.


CHAPTER 9

1. During the 1984 campaign, public opinion polls began to show for the first time that more southern whites identified as Republicans than Democrats. For the most thorough discussion of this trend, see Everett Carll Ladd, *The Election of 1984* (New York: Norton, 1985). For a broader perspective on this period, see Harold W. Stanley, "Southern Partisan Changes: Dealignment, Realignment, or Both?," *Journal of Politics* 50, no. 1 (February

1988): 64–88. See also Earl Black and Merle Black, *The Rise of Southern Republicans* (Cambridge: Harvard University Press, 2002), 205–37.

2. A cornerstone of the Reagan administration was the largest peacetime military buildup in American history. The impact was especially dramatic in eastern North Carolina. Rural counties, including some poor ones, benefited from military bases twenty to forty miles away, helping to offset declines in agriculture.

3. Hunt had led by as much as thirty points a couple of years before the 1984 election. This lead might in part have reflected an upsurge for the Democrats nationally during the 1982 recession. But at the time Hunt, the consensus builder, simply had broader appeal than Helms, who projected himself to many as an ideological bulldozer.

4. Reagan was not a regular at Sunday morning church services either before or during his presidency. Helms was a regular attendee who also got involved in congregational politics.

5. Helms, like South Carolina's Strom Thurmond, was legendary for constituent service.

6. Tom Ellis, interview by author, October 20, 2006; Carter Wrenn, interview by author, March 9, 2007. See William A. Link, *Righteous Warrior: Jesse Helms and the Rise of Modern Conservatism* (New York: St. Martin's, 2008), 272–75.

7. Ellis, interview; Link, *Righteous Warrior*, 272.

8. Ellis, interview; Wrenn, interview. For an excellent account of the Helms campaign's development, themes, and strategy, see Link, *Righteous Warrior*, 272–81, 284–91.

9. Although Helms's liberal critics blamed Hunt's downfall on a Helms campaign tinged with racism, Helms's success in painting Hunt as too political was an important factor in the contest.

10. Hunt had been part of a new breed of southern politician, along with Reuben Askew in Florida and Jimmy Carter in Georgia. All realized that in light of high crime rates from the late 1960s to the 1980s, Democrats needed to make "law and order" a big issue if they were to win. This strategy had previously worked for Hunt, but the Helms forces now saw a crack in the door.

11. This anti-King campaign theme resurrected the longtime white southern practice of relating black men's sexual desires as a threat to the "purity" of white southern womanhood. The sexual theme had long permeated southern politics.

12. For a perspective on Ervin's racial attitudes, see Karl E. Campbell, *Senator Sam Ervin, Last of the Founding Fathers* (Chapel Hill: University of North Carolina Press, 2007), 133–60, 231.

13. See Link, *Righteous Warrior*, 125, 132–60.

14. The imagery was more important than the message in the ad where Jackson towered over Hunt.

15. Hunt, like so many good politicians, knew how to choose his words carefully. Speaking to a candidate for office, he offered encouragement, empathy, and praise while stopping short of saying he would vote for the candidate.

16. After its re-creation by Morgan (1969–74) and the establishment of a strong consumer affairs office, the state's justice department inevitably ruffled the feathers of many business interests. As an activist attorney general, Edmisten, like Morgan, ran an office with a social populist flavor. Yet he needed business support in the general election.

17. The crowded field, six strong Democratic contenders, might have contributed to the animosity of the campaign. During the runoff campaign, a mad scramble took place to attract supporters of those who had been eliminated.

18. While Knox made no formal endorsement in the Senate race that day, his anger in the news conference seemed more directed at Hunt than at Edmisten.

19. Jim Hunt, interview by author, November 13, 2006.

20. Rufus Edmisten, interview by author, July 30, 2008.

21. Windsor, a voice of the Right, felt estranged from the political order in his home community. I have been unable to find a reason for his deep personal animosity toward Hunt.

22. "Jim Hunt Is Sissy, Prissy, Girlish, and Effeminate," *Orange County Landmark*, July 5, 1984.

23. Daniel C. Hoover and A. L. May, "'I'm Not Going to Take It,' Hunt Says of Article," *Raleigh News and Observer*, July 7, 1984.

24. "Statement from Helms on Article," *Raleigh News and Observer*, July 7, 1984.

25. Precinct election returns from Durham, Forsyth, Guilford, and Mecklenburg Counties. By 1984, racial breakdowns were available for every precinct.

26. Thomas F. Eamon and David Elliott, "Modernization versus Traditionalism in North Carolina Senate Races: Hidden Hope for the Democrats," *Social Science Quarterly* 75, no. 2 (June 1994): 358–62.

27. Ibid., 360.

28. Republicans had also made gains in the aftermath of heated primaries for governor and U.S. senator in 1972.

29. Wrenn, interview.

30. Link, *Righteous Warrior*, 301–2; William D. Snider, *Helms and Hunt: The North Carolina Senate Race, 1984* (Chapel Hill: University of North Carolina Press, 1985), 193. Such estimates are difficult to verify, and political crusaders of every moral persuasion are prone to exaggerate their prowess. In addition, it is difficult to determine how many of the new registrants turned out to vote and to know with certainty how they voted.

31. In political fund-raising circles, the past contributors to a party or ideological cause are known as the "house list." House lists have a much higher return rate than do prospect lists (mailings to prospective contributors based on magazine subscriptions or organizational affiliations). For a discussion of Helms's fund-raising and the role of the Congressional Club, see Link, *Righteous Warrior*, 194–95, 274.

32. This commercial was one of the most effective in painting Hunt as a hyperpolitician, more interested in himself than the body politic. Secondarily, the ad suggested that Hunt was weak-kneed on the crime issue, one of the most potent in the 1980s.

33. Hunt provided a rational explanation for his actions at the governors' conference, but complex explanations are a difficult sale in the heat of a campaign.

34. Phil Carlton, interview by author, April 18, 2007.

35. Despite the numerical superiority of Baptists and Methodists, Presbyterians had a history of rising to political and civic leadership in North Carolina.

36. Comments by Davidson students and faculty members on the Martin era there.

37. Davidson at the time was probably at least the equal of Duke as an enclave of elitist private higher education. For perspective on Martin, see Michael Hill, ed., *The Governors of North Carolina* (Raleigh: Office of Archives and History, North Carolina Department of Cultural Resources, 2007), 100–102.

38. Overall, Martin's record on the board of county commissioners placed him squarely in the progressive camp, not an unusual position for an urban piedmont Republican at the time.

39. Martin prevailed in the primary largely because he was, aside from Jonas, the best-known Republican in the Charlotte area, where his views matched almost perfectly with those of middle-class citizens.

40. Jonas had held the district's seat since 1952. In light of the debacle caused by the post-1960-census attempt at gerrymandering, the 1971 legislature did not try to massacre the district's boundaries for partisan advantage, but it was still considered an area where a strong Charlotte Democrat might win.

41. Rob Christensen, *The Paradox of Tar Heel Politics: The Personalities, Elections, and Events That Shaped Modern America* (Chapel Hill: University of North Carolina Press, 2008), 230.

42. Probably no modern North Carolina administration, including that of Luther Hodges, had greater rapport with corporate leaders than did Martin's. Banking officials, including Charlotte's Cliff Cameron, played central roles in the administration.

43. Wrenn, interview.

44. Ellis, interview.

45. In 1972 and 1976, many North Carolinians harbored bitter memories of Sanford's activism and "liberalism" as governor, a rare incident in history where "food tax" and "liberal" were synonyms. More broadly, many whites still resented Sanford's pioneering acts in race relations. Without a solid home base, he could scarcely have hoped to obtain the Democratic nomination.

46. Sam Poole, interview by author, July 18, 2006.

47. Ibid.; Howard E. Covington Jr. and Marion A. Ellis, *Terry Sanford: Politics, Progress, and Outrageous Ambitions* (Durham: Duke University Press, 1999), 440–43.

48. By the time I interviewed Faircloth in June 2005, his bitterness toward Sanford had died down. Faircloth had gotten revenge by defeating Sanford in 1992, and Sanford had died seven years prior to the interview. In the interview, Faircloth declined opportunities to criticize Sanford and indeed seemed to take pride in his earlier associations with Sanford. For background, see Covington and Ellis, *Terry Sanford*, 441.

49. I learned of the details of East's death at midday on Sunday, when *Raleigh News and Observer* political reporter Todd Cohen called me asking for a statement. Many students had already registered for the classes East was to teach at ECU in the fall, and he had signed and mailed his contract to return to teaching. University administrators received it on the Monday after his death (author's conversations with Maurice Simon, Cynthia Manning Smith, and Tinsley E. Yarbrough).

50. Tom Fetzer, interview by author, April 23, 2007.

51. Ibid.

52. Although Broyhill was an able member of Congress, he was almost a sitting duck for this charge. He was rich. And after six years of a conservative administration in Washington, many voters, even in the southern states, thought the administration had lost its common touch. The climate was ripe for a neopopulist message and resentment of the rich, and Sanford offered that message.

53. Broyhill had often clashed with Congressional Club leaders such as Ellis, a history reflected in their support for Funderburk in the primary. Club operatives had never forgiven Broyhill for his support for Ford over Reagan in the contest for the 1976 Republican presidential nomination.

54. By 1986, Sanford was one of the most seasoned of American politicians. He had seen triumph, adulation, and defeat. This background, combined with luck in timing, sealed his victory.

55. Eamon and Elliott, "Modernization versus Traditionalism."

56. Dukakis's "competitive" poll showing in late summer North Carolina surveys probably was nothing more than a reflection of his strong national position at the time. During the mid- and late 1980s, North Carolina was mildly more Republican than the country as a whole. But a national Democratic lead of 8 percent or more would have surely translated into a close North Carolina contest.

57. There have been times in American history when cultural conservatism—social populism—was more pervasive than in 1988. But never have culturally conservative themes been more shrewdly promoted in a national presidential campaign.

58. For an excellent perspective on the political climate of the time, see Thomas Byrne Edsall and Mary D. Edsall, *Chain Reaction: The Impact of Race, Rights, and Taxes on American Politics* (New York: Norton, 1991), esp. chaps. 6–12.

59. Author's conversations with Democratic strategists not wishing to be identified on the record. This was, however, an opinion shared by observers across the political spectrum.

60. For all their talents, some politicians simply rub a lot of people the wrong way. Gardner's inability to capture the top prize—the governorship—in 1968 and again in 1992 reflected animosities he had aroused both within the GOP and across the board. And in 1992, his defeat also reflected the misfortune of running against Hunt.

61. Few people inside or outside the legislature took the scheme seriously. As a result, Ramsey and his establishment allies were caught off-guard, perhaps a crucial factor in the coup's success.

62. More Democrats would probably have joined the revolt but for fears of incurring Ramsey's wrath. Like the more conservative Jimmy Green, the more economically populist Ramsey had a reputation for burying his enemies.

63. Stripping the lieutenant governor of his appointive powers was one of the leading institutional reforms in the post–World War II state senate. It strengthened the body's independence and made the position of Senate president pro tem one of the most powerful positions in state government.

64. For many years, Eure taught a training session for state legislators that stressed the principles of parliamentary procedures from Thomas Jefferson's time to the present.


CHAPTER 10

1. The electoral lock concept was widely accepted in the late 1980s and early 1990s. In *The Vital South: How Presidents Are Elected* (Cambridge: Harvard University Press, 1992), Earl Black and Merle Black argue that the Republicans had the upper hand in national politics largely as a result of the South's transition from a Democratic to a Republican region in presidential politics.

2. At this stage, the fears harbored by white moderates that a black could not win a high-profile statewide race seem to have been based on "realistic politics," not the moderates' racial prejudices.

3. William Friday, interview by author, January 4, 2007.

4. Marion A. Ellis, "Harvey Gantt," in *The North Carolina Century: Tar Heels Who Made a Difference, 1900–2000*, ed. Howard E. Covington Jr. and Marion A. Ellis (Charlotte: Levine Museum of the New South; Chapel Hill: University of North Carolina Press, 2002), 294.

5. Ibid.

6. The geographic pattern of Gantt's 1990 primary win over Easley bears remarkable similarities to Barack Obama's general election win over John McCain in 2008. Gantt ran powerfully in metropolitan areas and in counties that were 40 percent or more black.

7. For perspective on early polls, see Jim Morrill, "Gantt and Helms Both Like Poll," *Charlotte Observer*, June 16, 1990.

8. Gantt's position on gay rights issues was a milestone in state politics. He was the first serious statewide candidate for top office to embrace equality and access for homosexuals.

9. In this respect as well, Gantt in 1990 seemed a precursor of Obama in 2008. Despite lacking Obama's charisma, Gantt possessed a magnetism rare in North Carolina politics.

10. See William A. Link, *Righteous Warrior: Jesse Helms and the Rise of Modern Conservatism* (New York: St. Martin's, 2008), 369–71, 374.

11. While the "white hands ad" does not quite have the notoriety of the "mushroom cloud ad" produced by the Lyndon Johnson campaign against Barry Goldwater in 1964, it should make any list of the five most powerful political TV ads.

12. *University of California Regents v. Bakke*, 438 U.S. 265 (1978). In *Grutter v. Bollinger* (539 U.S. 306 [2003]), the Supreme Court narrowly upheld more generalized racial and admissions goals that included no specific point system or quota.

13. Link, *Righteous Warrior*, 377.

14. Ibid., 371.

15. Carter Wrenn, interview by author, March 9, 2007. Wrenn told Helms biographer William Link that he and all the Helms campaign leaders had at the time wanted Gantt to get the nomination because they believed he would be the weakest candidate (Link, *Righteous Warrior*, 366). But Wrenn's remarks to me suggest that the Helms forces had underestimated Gantt.

16. 1990 Exit Poll for North Carolina, Voter News Service.

17. See Thomas F. Eamon and David Elliott, "Modernization versus Traditionalism in North Carolina Elections," *Social Science Quarterly* 75, no. 2 (June 1994): 358–62.

18. V. O. Key Jr., *Southern Politics in State and Nation* (New York: Knopf, 1949), 5–11.

19. See Thomas F. Eamon, "From Pool Hall to Parish House in North Carolina," in *Strategies for Mobilizing Black Voters: Four Case Studies*, ed. Thomas E. Cavanagh (Washington, D.C.: Joint Center for Political Studies, 1987), 101–36.

20. White Democrats had to play a balancing act even in their current districts. But some, such as Walter Jones and Charlie Rose, had gained influential committee posts as a result of seniority, enabling them to do a lot for their districts.

21. Earl Black and Merle Black, *The Rise of Southern Republicans* (Cambridge: Harvard University Press, 2002), 332–38.

22. Under the Department of Justice party guidelines, nearly all southern congressional and legislative districts would have been found wanting, often in violation of one, two, or three of the guidelines.

23. *Thornburg v. Gingles*, 478 U.S. 30 (1986).

24. For the most thorough coverage of the North Carolina redistricting dispute and its origins, see Tinsley E. Yarbrough, *Race and Redistricting: The Shaw-Cromartie Cases* (Lawrence: University Press of Kansas, 2002) , especially chap. 2 (titled "Political Pornography"), 21–51. In oral arguments concerning *Shaw v. Reno* at the U.S. Supreme Court on April 20, 1993, Everett alluded to the term. Ibid., 63.

25. Ibid., 20.

26. Charles Clay, "Eva Clayton," in *North Carolina Century*, ed. Covington and Ellis, 468–70.

27. The scheduling of the North Carolina presidential primary was a matter of cost, convenience, and practicality versus national influence. The more practical considerations have usually outweighed the possibility of national influence.

28. There is a widespread myth that Perot's general election candidacy cost Bush the election. In fact, all polls in the fall of 1992 showed Clinton prevailing in a two-way race. If, however, Perot had not conducted a slash-and-burn campaign against Bush in the spring and summer of 1992, Bush might have won. Perot permanently turned some voters against Bush.

29. Tom Ellis, interview by author, October 20, 2006.

30. Jim Hunt, interview by author, November 13, 2006.

31. In February 1990, a *Raleigh News and Observer* article suggested that Martin's taxpayer-funded research office had gathered information on political opponents. Martin, then suffering from a respiratory ailment, left his sickbed to hold a news conference. He denounced the *News and Observer* and Democratic critics. Martin said he would leave politics when his second term expired. He kept his word.

32. See Rob Christensen, *The Paradox of Tar Heel Politics: The Personalities, Elections, and Events That Shaped Modern America* (Chapel Hill: University of North Carolina Press, 2008), 256–57.

33. Sanford's heart surgery was the defining event of the senatorial contest. Sanford's record in Washington was unexciting, but he also had not aroused major animosities.

34. Afterward, Clinton strategists wished that they had targeted Florida instead of North Carolina. That would be their strategy in 1996.

35. Green was eventually indicted and convicted on corruption charges, though he never went to prison. Future governor Mike Easley was the prosecutor in the case.

36. Black and Black, *Rise of Southern Republicans*, 338.

37. The national GOP tide was the driving force. But voters detected a whiff of corruption and blamed the Democrats for it. Angry citizens seemed more motivated to turn out than did others, as is often the case in midterm elections.

38. I have heard many accusations of corruption and fraud, but firm proof and indictments and convictions have been rare.

39. Gantt had no record of serious political corruption, but the 1990 campaign had been bruising. He was no longer an untarnished fresh face.

40. Hunt had survived the setbacks of 1994 remarkably unscathed. But his postelection rhetoric could have come from a Republican playbook. The Hunt-led tax cuts of 1995 damaged the state's finances in the next few years.

41. Bert Coffer, interview by author, October 20, 1996.

42. Ibid.

43. Helms lieutenants and advisers often spoke of the senator's lack of attention to the fine points of campaigning. Yet he was one of the best at staying on message (Link, *Righteous Warrior*, 388–93; Wrenn, interview).

44. While the 1996 voting pattern resembled that of 1990, the campaign was less suspenseful. There was never a point when Gantt seemed an even bet to win despite Helms's increasingly obvious frailty.

45. Although the Congressional Club was not running the 1996 campaign, the leaflets might well have come from an earlier campaign playbook. Overall, the 1996 Helms

campaign had a softer tone—both overt and covert—on racial themes than did the campaigns of 1972, 1984, and 1990. But the leaflets were a throwback to earlier Helms campaigns and even to the 1950 Willis Smith–Frank Porter Graham campaign.

46. Ironically, Helms had greater success than Gantt in making a populist appeal, another example of social populism triumphing over economic populism.

47. For a discussion of Helms's physical and mental decline, see Link, *Righteous Warrior*, 385–87, 419–20, 477–80.

48. The Funderburk incident was yet another illustration that in politics, smart people do incredibly stupid things. The clumsy response to the incident rivaled the driving itself as an act of poor judgment.

49. Earl Black and Merle Black first outlined these points in *Politics and Society in the South* (Cambridge: Harvard University Press, 1987). Events of the next two decades further enhanced the strength of their arguments. While Clinton made inroads in the 1990s, the basic points outlined in Black and Black's book dominated southern politics throughout the twentieth century.

## CHAPTER 11

1. Howard E. Covington Jr. and Marion A. Ellis, *Terry Sanford: Politics, Progress, and Outrageous Ambitions* (Durham: Duke University Press, 1999), 507–9.

2. While portions of the public might have been turned by off by Faircloth's anti-Clinton crusades, more ideologically driven and partisan Republicans saw such crusades as his redeeming feature. So whatever their reservations, political action groups of the Right felt an obligation to back Faircloth.

3. Faircloth associates told me that he typically based his support or opposition to other political figures not so much on their issue positions or party as on whether he liked them or not. In the June 2005 interview with me, Faircloth was outspoken in both his praise and his contempt for various politicians, past and present. Those he liked and disliked covered a broad ideological spectrum.

4. Rob Christensen, *The Paradox of Tar Heel Politics: The Personalities, Elections, and Events That Shaped Modern America* (Chapel Hill: University of North Carolina Press, 2008), 399.

5. David M. Kovenock and James W. Prothro, *Comparative State Elections Project, 1968* (Chapel Hill: University of North Carolina, Institute for Research in Social Science, 1970), http://www.icpsr.umich.edu/icpsrweb/ICPSR/studies/7508. My analysis of polls over the decade suggests that a significant change in the partisan affiliation of southern whites took place around 1984, when Ronald Reagan sought reelection. From that point on, there were generally as many or more Republican identifiers in southern states as Democratic identifiers, even though formal party registration (in those states that required it) continued to show a big edge for the Democrats. The advantage reflected in part voters' desire to vote in the still-important Democratic primaries and in part habit and inertia. Party identification as measured by public polls painted a more realistic picture of party strength than did formal registration figures.

While Republicans had a slight advantage in public opinion polls, the Democrats had the edge among those who turned out to vote in the Edwards-Faircloth race: 41 percent self-proclaimed Democrats, 30 percent Republicans, and 20 percent independents. Also, the Voter News Service exit poll, with 1,610 respondents, indicated that Edwards led 59 percent to 35 percent among those who made their voting decisions in the last three days before the election. See Thad Beyle and Ferrel Guillory, "The 1998 Senate Race: Party Money Plus Organization Lead to Democratic Triumph," *North Carolina DataNet* 22 (October 1999), http://southnow.org/files/2011/10/ncdn22.pdf.

6. Molly Broad, interview by author, May 13, 2008.

7. Infighting has often occurred among the universities themselves and between the universities and community colleges. But the 2000 bond package offered something for everyone, thereby contributing to its momentum.

8. Broad, interview; Jimmy Broughton, interview by author, June 4, 2008; author's conversations with Mary Lynn Qurnell.

9. Hunt and Republicans tried to outdo one another on proposals for reduced taxes after the Republican legislative victories of 1994. During and after that process, the legislature adopted major tax reductions, actions that brought condemnations from the liberal press and educators. And, indeed, education budgets came under pressure. The crisis was less severe than in the 2008–13 period only because the mid- and late 1990s were among the most prosperous times in American history.

10. The ability of the majority political party to draw congressional and state legislative districts is critical, especially in states where the parties are highly competitive. The redistricting actions of the legislature every ten years may have a profound long-term legacy.

11. Easley's seeming lack of polish and sophistication led critics to underestimate his political acumen and talents. But it was in fact one of the secrets to his success. He also knew how to connect on television.

12. The coastal plain again carried the day in a North Carolina election. Conventional wisdom long held that the political gravity was shifting to the populous piedmont region. But from the 1950s through the late 1990s, candidates who posted big winning margins in the coastal plain often overcame candidates who led by smaller margins in the piedmont and mountain regions.

13. Though on balance more liberal than the Republicans, the Democrats were the establishment party in the North Carolina legislature. Interest groups were more concerned with access to power and favors than with ideology or political philosophy.

14. For a long time, the migration to North Carolina of engineers and managers from the North had generally benefited the Republicans. Starting in the late twentieth century, however, new arrivals from the North and West were often more socially liberal than their predecessors. Furthermore, more blacks and other minorities were moving into North Carolina.

15. Like others interested in influencing or gaining from the political process, business leaders had a pragmatic streak. It was in their interest to support Republicans in Washington and Democrats in Raleigh.

16. Broad, interview.

17. Resident armed forces personnel are counted as part of a county's census population. In earlier censuses, the military base counties had been among the most rapidly growing in the state, but size of the military dropped after the end of the Cold War, and there had been transfers away from the bases during the 1990s.

18. In this respect, North Carolina's trends resembled those seen in the country as a whole. But the state's trends were an exaggerated version of the national ones, reflecting its economic boom and popularity among retirees.

19. This is my conclusion based on discussions with associates of both Bowles and Helms.

20. The mainstream or mainline Protestant denominations have moved leftward in recent decades. The trend is most notable in their national leadership and headquarters offices but has also appeared among rank-and-file clergy and to a degree the broader church memberships.

21. The Decker episode and other scandals challenged the state's reputation for clean government, although politicians and reporters had long told stories of clandestine shenanigans.

22. Black came across in person as unthreatening, yet he was a master at rewarding his friends and cutting deals. His unassuming manner was arguably a key to his success.

23. On balance, Morgan and those who followed him were less conservative than many legislative Republicans, but this division related more to personality and power than to ideology.

24. The bullish expectations for the Kerry-Edwards ticket reflected more the initial excitement of local Democrats than it did reality. But a few snap polls just after the Democratic convention showed a close race.

25. Tom Fetzer, interview by author, April 23, 2007.

26. Richard Burr, interview by author, February 19, 2009.

27. Franklin Freeman, interview by author, June 11, 2009. Easley went his own way, snubbing the Democratic Party machinery and many organized interests. Easley and Basnight often had a contentious relationship. But like Hunt, Easley knew how to connect with business leaders, especially those with fat wallets.

28. Broughton, interview; observation of Mary Lynn Qurnell.

29. In a sense, the 2006 midterm elections were like 1994 in reverse. I attribute part of this phenomenon to national trends, but Basnight's prowess was also a factor, especially in the state-level races.

30. See Christensen, *Paradox of Tar Heel Politics*, 279–80, 310. In addition, Christensen's columns in the *Raleigh News and Observer* provided some of the best stories of the scandals and their consequences for the state's image.

31. Carter Wrenn, interview by author, March 9, 2007.

32. William Safire, *Safire's Political Dictionary*, 3rd ed. (New York: Random House, 1978), 163.

33. T. Harry Williams, *Huey Long* (1969; New York: Vintage, 1981), 411. More refined politicians who couched their arguments in references to the U.S. Constitution and tradition might have been as sinister as those labeled demagogues. Whatever their social backgrounds, the typical demagogues spoke in a lower-class vernacular and were especially disdained in the halls of academe and big-city pressrooms.

34. Ibid., 409–12.

35. Though Ervin thought Helms to be extreme and incendiary at points, their fundamental social attitudes were similar. For discussion and evaluation of Ervin's positions on racial segregation, see Karl E. Campbell, *Senator Sam Ervin, Last of the Founding Fathers* (Chapel Hill: University of North Carolina Press, 2007), 132–83.

36. Helms's confidantes and staff members told me that he bristled at suggestions that his personal acts of kindness and charity be advertised in campaigns.

37. Williams, *Huey Long*, 414.

38. Eric Hoffer, *The True Believer: Thoughts on the Nature of Mass Movements* (1951; New York: Harper Perennial Modern Classics, 2002), 111–14, 147–48.

39. Williams, *Huey Long*, 415.

40. Ibid., 415–16.

41. Ironically, Byrd became a hero of political liberals when he attacked George W. Bush for concentrating too much power in the executive branch in the early and mid-2000s. But in the 1970s, Byrd was no less strident than Helms in his attacks on anti-Vietnam War protesters and the counterculture.

42. Burley Mitchell, interview by author, July 26, 2006.

43. Jim Hunt, interview by author, November 13, 2006.

44. Ibid.

45. Paul Luebke, *Tar Heel Politics* (Chapel Hill: University of North Carolina Press, 1990).

46. Hunt, interview.

CHAPTER 12

1. Rob Christensen, *The Paradox of Tar Heel Politics: The Personalities, Elections, and Events That Shaped Modern America* (Chapel Hill: University of North Carolina Press, 2008), 288–89. Especially when speaking before women, Dole told of the abuse she had taken in law school and early in her career.

2. Bert Coffer, interview by author, October 20, 2006.

3. People of all political stripes trying to get through to Dole constantly complained about her inaccessibility. Senator Burr told me there had been a rock-star mentality in Dole's office. She and her staff thought she was famous enough not to be brought down by mediocre constituency service (Richard Burr, interview by author, February 19, 2009). Dole turned down an opportunity to discuss these points and others with me after her election defeat on grounds that she was too busy taking care of her husband, Bob.

4. Senator Harry Reid of Nevada, the Democratic majority leader, was widely condemned for his statement, not revealed until after the campaign, that Obama's relatively light skin and lack of a "Negro dialect" would greatly boost his chances of getting white votes and winning the election. Reid was undiplomatic but on the mark. Obama modified his speaking style depending on whether he was speaking to a mostly white or predominantly black audience. See H. Samy Alim and Geneva Smitherman, *Articulate while Black: Barack Obama, Language, and Race in the U.S.* (New York: Oxford University Press, 2012).

5. The South Carolina primary did not quite mortally wound Hillary Clinton's campaign. But black leaders in South Carolina and around the country saw a not-so-veiled "racism" in her tactics that would at least temporarily strain the bond between Bill and Hillary Clinton and the African American community.

6. No Democratic presidential contender had won North Carolina since the aberrant 1976 Jimmy Carter–Gerald Ford election, so detached observers had little reason to believe that any Democrat could take the state.

7. Comments on state polls are based on the play-by-play reports from the websites Pollster.com and RealClearPolitics.com.

8. To this point, Dole's age and experience had contributed to her political standing, but this ad turned them into liabilities.

9. The ending was a strategic blunder. A shrill voice saying "There is no God," even if the voice is supposedly that of the ad's target, is likely to backfire. Wit is a much more effective weapon.

10. Reflecting what politicians and strategists think is an anti-city-slicker bias in the state's electorate, nearly all statewide candidates from Charlotte have faced accusations that they would favor their relatively wealthy city at the expense of other parts of the state.

11. In supporting rail transit, McCrory was taking a position approved by many members of his party. However, Republican think tanks have criticized federal grants to pay for rail-based transit.

12. *Raleigh News and Observer*, October 26, 2008.

13. North Carolina Association of County Commissioners data reports. My thanks to Steve Modlin for steering me to resources and sharing his wealth of knowledge.

14. Obama's figure was similar to the 35 or 36 percent received by Jim Hunt when he lost to Jesse Helms in 1984. The greatly increased black turnout made the difference for Obama.

15. Much of the "new" technology had been around for a decade or longer. But the vast commercial appeal of Blackberries, iPods, and a new generation of cell phones helped make Obama's campaign a success.

16. For an excellent discussion relating technological advances directly to the North Carolina campaign of 2008, see Eric S. Heberlig, Peter Francia, and Steven H. Greene, "The Conditional Party Teams of the 2008 North Carolina Federal Elections," in *The Change Election: Money, Mobilization, and Persuasion in the 2008 Federal Elections*, ed. David B. Megleby (Philadelphia: Temple University Press, 2011), 108–39.

17. Ibid., 116–17.

18. At the time, Obama had said that he strongly supported traditional marriage but also had expressed generalized support and sympathy for gay rights. In May 2012, however, he changed his position and announced his support for marriage equality.

19. It is unfortunate that the historical role of predominantly black churches has been overlooked in recent years. They have long worked to mobilize voters, at times even more overtly than predominantly white fundamentalist churches. Many African American churches are conservative on social issues such as abortion and gay marriage but are liberal on issues of minority rights and basic human equality.

20. Gary Bartlett, interview by author, July 13, 2009.

21. J. Michael Bitzer, "From Republican Red to Democratic Blue in the Tar Heel State: North Carolina's Urban, Suburban, and Rural Patterns in the 2008 Election" (paper presented at the Citadel Symposium on Southern Politics, Charleston, S.C., March 4, 2010), 15–17.

22. Bartlett, interview.

23. Official North Carolina Campaign Finance Reports for 2008 Election, http://www.ncsbe.gov/content.aspx?id=22.

24. Announcing his choice by text message was probably as much a play to be seen as modern as it was a method of getting the word out. Also, supporters could view the announcement as a "personal" message from Obama.

25. This figure was remarkable, almost stunning. My research suggests that it was unprecedented. The youth vote rarely differs so strongly from that of voters in general and was crucial in turning the state from red to blue in 2008 and possibly to purple for the long term.

26. Voter News Survey exit poll report, November 2008.

27. Conclusions relating to county-level and precinct data are based on official North Carolina Board of Elections figures (http://www.ncsbe.gov/).

28. Election statistics collected from North Carolina Board of Elections returns and *North Carolina Manual* (http://www.secretary.state.nc.us/pubsweb/manual.aspx).

29. Calculations from North Carolina Board of Election statistics and polling data.

30. *New Republic*, April 4, 1985.

31. Other governors and state legislatures faced the same dilemma as Perdue. But prudent leadership and the balanced budget requirement kept North Carolina from falling off a financial cliff.

32. The senate leaders of the early 2000s in many respects personified the North Carolina progressive tradition described by V. O. Key Jr. more than fifty years earlier. See Key, *Southern Politics in State and Nation* (New York: Knopf, 1949), 205-28. They were devoted to education and infrastructure improvements. In addition, they were closely tied to corporate North Carolina and attracted business money to the Democratic war chest.

33. Paul Luebke, *Tar Heel Politics* (Chapel Hill: University of North Carolina Press, 1990).

34. Had economic times been good—on the level of the 1990s—the 2009 legislative session might well have been one of the most expansionist in state history, on a level with 1947 or 1961.

35. Other charges against Easley were also not pursued, including the failure to report a $137,000 discount on a coastal lot in Carteret County and the acceptance of a free golf club membership worth around $50,000.

36. Jay Price and J. Andrew Curliss, "N.C. State Fires Mary Easley," McClatchy News Service, June 8, 2009, http://www.mcclatchydc.com/2009/06/08/v-print/69687/nc-state-fires-mary-easley-as.html. Chancellor James Oblinger of North Carolina State also lost his job because of the scandal.

37. See Larry J. Sabato, "Pendulum Swing," in *Pendulum Swing*, ed. Larry J. Sabato (Boston: Longman, 2011), 3 43. See also Alan I. Abramowitz, "Right Turn: The 2010 Midterm Elections," in *Pendulum Swing*, ed. Sabato, 45-60.

30. City voting is determined by calculating the raw vote for precincts within the city limits.

39. In June 2010, while walking down a Washington, D.C., street, Etheridge was approached by two young men, one of whom had a microphone. Claiming to be working on a student project, one of the men asked Etheridge if he supported "the Obama agenda." Etheridge repeatedly responded, "Who are you?" A scuffle ensued, and Etheridge grabbed one man by the neck. The video—potentially edited to show Etheridge in the worst possible light—was posted to YouTube. Whatever the exact circumstances that led to the incident, there can be no doubt that the congressman lost his temper and made physical contact with the "student."

40. Teacher organizations and unions have been skeptical of the charter school concept, but it has been supported by many conservative think tanks, including North Carolina's John Locke Foundation. Obama and other more liberal politicians often believe that charter schools offer added opportunities in poor and heavily minority areas.

41. "Highlights of 2011-2012 State Budget Passed by Legislature Saturday," *Durham Herald Sun*, June 5, 2012.

42. *Roe v. Wade*, 410 U.S. 113 (1973); *Planned Parenthood v. Casey*, 505 U.S. 833 (1992). In *Casey*, the Supreme Court had upheld three restrictions on abortion: a twenty-four-hour waiting period, parental consent for minors, and counseling a woman on alternatives to abortion.

43. All counties with over 40 percent African American populations supported Amendment 1 in May and Obama in November. No survey research data are available on the county level, but county- and precinct-level data suggest that large numbers of African Americans voted both for the amendment and for Obama.

44. Anne Blythe, "U.S. Said to Be Unlikely to Seek a New Trial," *Raleigh News and Observer*, June 1, 2012.

45. Rob Christensen, "The Parable of John Edwards: Ego Can Boost Too High, Too Fast," *Raleigh News and Observer*, June 1, 2012. The paper devoted two full pages to a review of the Edwards case.

46. A Civitas poll released on July 19, 2011, indicated that McCrory led Perdue, 55 percent to 35 percent. A January 2012 poll conducted by Public Policy Polling found her approval rating to be just below 40 percent. At the same time, Obama had a public opinion rating near 50 percent in North Carolina. Most major polls found similar results.

47. Gary D. Robertson, "Bev Perdue Retiring: North Carolina Governor Reportedly Won't Seek Re-Election," January 26, 2013, http://www.huffingtonpost.com/2012/01/26/bev-perdue-retiring-north-carolina-governor_n_1233586.html.

48. Any generalization on what a candidate has stressed is subject to debate. But my reading of McCrory's speeches and newspaper accounts indicates that education, taxes, economic growth, and transportation appeared to be his major themes.

49. This race, which was more low-key and civil than the gubernatorial contest, remained close to the end. Its relative civility might have reflected both the candidates' personalities and the scarcity of money for big-time advertising.

50. While Obama remained competitive with or slightly ahead of potential Republican candidates in the polls, his overall approval ratings in North Carolina and in the country as a whole suggested that he could be in deep trouble.

51. This was one of the strongest surrogate campaigns ever. There could have been no more prominent stand-ins for the president than Michelle Obama, Bill Clinton, and Jim Hunt. And Republicans from vice presidential nominee Paul Ryan on down consistently visited the state. Yet the Democrats consistently (and, it turned out, correctly) viewed their prospects to be better in neighboring Virginia. Republicans (also correctly) believed not only that they had to win North Carolina but also that Virginia, Ohio, and Florida were essential to put them over the top. On balance, the surrogate strategy, along with heavy advertising, was a wise choice for both parties.

52. Whatever their contrasting theological foundations, the Mormons and Protestant fundamentalists shared similar views on abortion and gay marriage. And majorities or pluralities in both faiths had been backing Republican presidential candidates since 1980, so the alliance made political sense. There is no direct polling evidence that Graham's blessing made a difference for the Romney campaign, but I believe that the symbolism was important.

53. Multiple polling firms and analysts estimated or calculated the white vote for Obama state by state. But the figures are close in all—sometimes identical. I have used the calculations of the Kos Croissant Report, issued on November 10, 2012.

54. Author's Data File, December 2012. I have made an extensive study of North Carolina county and precinct voting covering the period from 1960 to 2012. These data include the racial composition of each precinct.

55. Official returns from the North Carolina Board of Elections.

56. When Republicans won control of the state house in the 1990s, Democrats still controlled the governorship and state senate. In the 1896 election, Republican Dan Russell had won the governorship. In 1894 and 1896, the Democrats were relegated to minority status in the state legislature when the Republican-Populist Fusionists had the majority in both houses, but the Republicans could not have achieved control on their own.

## EPILOGUE

1. This was a fear that George Washington expressed in his farewell address of September 19, 1796.

2. V. O. Key Jr., *Southern Politics in State and Nation* (New York: Knopf, 1949), 298–311.

3. Laura Oleniacz, "McCrory: Tax Reform 'Won't Be Easy,'" *Durham Herald-Sun*, January 3, 2013.

4. Those leaders judged most significant typically have brought about great change. This might hint of a liberal bias in judging effective leaders. Governors such as Sanford and Hunt appear on most lists of great leaders. Yet no one can deny that the conservative Helms had a tremendous impact on North Carolina politics.

5. Gary Pearce, interview by author, September 19, 2008.

# Index

U.S. Senate, U.S. House of Representatives, Democratic Party, and Republican Party have subheadings that refer almost exclusively to politicians, elections, and districts in North Carolina.

Abortion, 209, 252, 300, 317, 325; 1990 U.S. Senate elections and, 233-34; East and, 189, 193, 198, 219; Helms and, 185, 282, 283; Ronald Reagan and, 187, 193, 357 (n. 20); Republican Party and, 189, 193; restrictions on, 311, 370 (n. 42); *Roe v. Wade* and, 193, 311, 357 (n. 20); as social conservative issue, 187, 193, 214, 248

Abortion rights, 214, 230, 232, 254, 255

Adams, Hoover, 28, 29, 118, 339 (n. 43)

Affirmative action, 232, 233

AFL-CIO, 140, 196

African Americans, 117, 185, 222, 225, 261, 268, 273, 304; 1950 U.S. Senate elections and, 29, 94; 1952 presidential election and, 38-39, 76; 1960 gubernatorial Democratic primaries and, 59, 65-66, 68, 344 (n. 21); 1960 presidential election and, 76, 101; 1964 Democratic gubernatorial primaries and, 94, 96, 347 (n. 13); 1964 presidential election and, 99, 101, 347-48 (n. 25); 1972 elections and, 141, 149; 1976 gubernatorial Democratic primaries and, 169, 172, 355 (n. 29); 1976 lieutenant governorship and, 170-72; 1984 presidential candidates and, 201, 204-5; 1984 U.S. Senate elections and, 212, 359 (n. 25); 1990 U.S. Senate elections and, 229-37, 361 (n. 2); 1996 U.S. Senate elections and, 251-52, 254-55; 2004 presidential election and, 296, 306; 2008 presidential election and, 290, 294, 296, 298, 301, 306, 367 (n. 5); 2012 lieutenant governorship and, 315; 2012 presidential election and, 312, 318, 370 (n. 43); Amendment 1 (Defense of Marriage Act) referendum and, 312, 370

(n. 43); American Dream and, 56-57; black churches and, 196, 301, 368 (n. 19); *Brown v. Board of Education* and, 43, 45, 46, 342 (n. 36); as businessmen, 13, 86, 337 (n. 33); congressional redistricting, early 1990s and, 238-42; Democratic Party and, 38-39, 99, 101, 171-72, 251, 255, 347-48 (n. 25); employment opportunities and, 87, 89, 175-76; geographical locations of, 4, 6, 18; Ku Klux Klan and, 111, 131, 132, 351 (nn. 28, 30); migrants to North Carolina and, 175-76, 270; poverty and race and, 114; primaries and, 9, 13, 336 (n. 18); public office and, 36, 118, 124, 138, 140, 145, 171, 176, 195-97, 198; as Republican voters, 51, 343 (n. 46), 347-48 (n. 25); run-off primary abolition with 40 percent rule and, 196-97, 242; segregation and, 13, 36, 43, 47-49, 57, 65, 109, 331; U.S. House of Representatives and, 246; voter participation and, 1, 13-14, 19, 84-85, 102, 123, 337 (n. 33), 346 (n. 51); voting rights and, 1, 7, 8, 9, 13, 14, 112, 324, 336 (nn. 20-21), 346 (n. 51), 348 (n. 27). *See also* "Black Belt counties"; Civil rights; Civil rights demonstrations; Civil rights movement; Desegregation; Race; Racial equality; Racial unrest; Segregation

Agnew, Spiro, 119, 146

Agriculture, 4, 6; 1960 presidential election and, 75, 345 (n. 33). *See also* Tobacco

Akins, Waverly, 170, 172

Alabama, 6, 15, 38, 78, 214, 283, 336 (n. 13); 1968 presidential election and, 99; 2008 presidential Democratic primaries and, 290; civil rights demonstrations and, 87,

102, 348 (n. 27); Montgomery bus boycott, 51–52, 56. *See also* Wallace, George

Alamance County, 50, 80, 125

Albright, R. Mayne, 16, 17–18, 19, 20

Alexander, Hugh Q., 82

Alleghany County, 30

Allen, Gordon, 158, 167

Allen, James, 283

American Council on Education, 263

American Dream, 56–57, 172, 224, 229, 264, 281, 298, 329

American Party, 121, 122, 123

Anderson, John, 187, 190, 192

Andrews, Ike, 129

Anson County, 7, 24, 82, 111, 139

Antipoverty programs, 114

Appalachia, 114

Appalachian State College (Boone), 102, 106, 107, 348 (n. 35)

Arkansas, 6, 53, 243, 247, 255

Ashe, Earl, 233–34

Asheville, 4, 16, 21, 33, 66, 296, 336 (n. 11)

Asheville-Biltmore College, 107

Asian Americans, 7, 84, 136, 269

Atkinson, June, 320

Atlantic coastal plain: 1948 gubernatorial campaign and, 20; 1950 U.S. Senate elections and, 30; 1952 presidential election and, 38, 123; 1956 presidential election and, 123; 1960 gubernatorial Democratic run-off primary and, 66, 67, 73; 1960 gubernatorial election and, 76, 222; 1960 presidential election and, 73–75, 100, 123, 174; 1964 elections and, 94, 97, 100; 1968 presidential election and, 121–23; 1972 gubernatorial election and, 152; 1972 presidential election and, 149, 174; 1972 U.S. Senate elections and, 151, 153; 1976 presidential election and, 174; 1984 gubernatorial election and, 212–13; 1984 U.S. Senate elections and, 211, 212; 1986 U.S. Senate elections and, 222, 223; 1988 presidential election and, 224–25, 235; 1990 U.S. Senate elections and, 231, 235–37, 256; 1992 elections and, 247; 1996 presidential election and, 255; 1996 U.S. Senate elections and, 256; 1998 U.S. Senate elections and, 261; 2000 gubernatorial election and, 268, 365 (n. 12); 2000 presidential election

and, 267; 2002 U.S. Senate elections and, 272; 2004 gubernatorial election and, 277; 2004 presidential election and, 275; 2008 gubernatorial election and, 304, 305; 2008 presidential election and, 296, 297; 2008 U.S. Senate elections and, 303; 2010 U.S. Senate elections and, 309; 2012 gubernatorial election and, 321; 2012 presidential election and, 317, 319; amendment for private schools to avoid integration and, 49; Amendment 1 (Defense of Marriage Act) referendum and, 313; Coastal area land management act (CAMA) and, 160; geography of, 4–6; political affiliation and, 4, 6; population, 1960s, 106, 348 (n. 34)

Attorney generals, 9, 163, 344 (n. 7); Wade Bruton, 80, 119, 350 (n. 10); consumer protection and, 119, 127, 139, 207, 358 (n. 16); Mike Easley, 265–66; Rufus Edmisten, 163, 206, 207, 226, 245, 358 (n. 16); Robert Morgan, 119, 127, 139, 159, 160, 163, 188, 207, 245, 358 (n. 16)

Atwater, Lee, 224

Avery County, 143

Aycock, Charles, 25, 212, 357 (n. 29); death of, 8, 336 (n. 16); as governor, 7, 8, 14; as progressive, 3, 125; public education and, 7–8, 177, 264, 279

Bailey, Allen, 96

Bailey, Clarence, 61

Bailey, Jack, 61

Bailey, Josiah W., 11, 20, 25

Baker, James, 219, 272

*Baker v. Carr*, 106

Ballance, Frank, 279

Ballantine, Patrick, 276

Ballentine, L. Y. "Stag," 26

Bannister, Roger, 218

Baptists, 42–43, 49, 73, 166, 354 (n. 16)

Barden, Graham, 198

Barker, J. Andrew, 170

Barnes, John, 18

Barnett, Ross, 78

Bartlett, Gary, 302

Bartley, Numan V., 332

Basnight, Marc, 266, 268, 269, 277, 279, 307, 366 (nn. 27, 29)

Bass, Jack, 162

Beatty, Jim, 218
Beaufort County, 189
Beitler, Michael, 309
Bell, Terrell, 199
Bennett, Bert, 95, 98, 147–48, 167, 180, 187, 347 (n. 21)
Benson, Ezra Taft, 75
Bentsen, Lloyd, 224
Berger, Phil, 310
Berry, Cherie, 306, 320
Bertie County, 22
Better Roads and Schools group, 24
Bible Belt, 192–93, 214, 255, 357 (n. 18)
Biblical Recorder, 42
Bickett, Thomas, 9
Biden, Joe, 289, 290, 291–92, 303, 316
Bilbo, Theodore "The Man," 15, 280
Birmingham, Ala., 87, 348 (n. 27)
Black, Earl, 258
Black, Jim, 266, 269, 273, 274, 277, 279–80, 307, 366 (nn. 21–22)
Black, Merle, 258
"Black Belt counties," 139; 1948 presidential election and, 22; 1964 Democratic gubernatorial primaries and, 94; 1968 presidential election and, 123; 1972 gubernatorial election and, 153; 1990 U.S. Senate elections and, 235, 237; 2000 presidential election and, 267; 2004 presidential election and, 275; 2010 U.S. Senate elections and, 310; 2012 gubernatorial election and, 318; politics and, 7, 336 (n. 14), 346 (n. 51); whites and, 7, 55, 56, 79, 237. See also African Americans; Rural population
Black Power, 242
Black Student Movement (BSM), 125
Bladen County, 171, 312
Blake, Larry, 186
Blue, Clifton, 98
Blue, Dan, 271, 272
Blue moon elections, 248, 278
Bluford, F. D., 45
Bonds, 10, 18, 82, 263–64; for roads and schools, 23–25, 338 (n. 23), 340 (n. 12)
Bonner, Herbert, 189
Boone, 4, 102, 106, 107, 143, 348 (n. 35)
Bowles, Erskine, 272, 276
Bowles, Hargrove "Skipper," 85, 159; 1972 gubernatorial Democratic primaries and,

140–42, 150, 208; 1972 gubernatorial election and, 148, 149, 150, 152, 153, 168, 272, 299, 352 (nn. 12–13); 1976 gubernatorial Democratic primaries and, 167, 168
Boyd, Olla Ray, 28
Bradshaw, Tom, 177
Branch, Joe, 96
"Branch head boys," 21, 37, 98
Bremer, Arthur, 165
Bridges, Henry, 80
Briggs v. Elliott, 47
Britt, David, 108
Britt Commission, 108–9
Broad, Molly, 263, 264, 269, 276
Broughton, J. Melville, 20, 25, 26, 28, 31, 92, 118
Broughton, J. Melville, Jr., 31, 118, 119
Browder v. Gale, 51
Brown, Edmund "Jerry," Jr., 166, 187
Brown v. Board of Education of Topeka, 47, 49, 51, 55, 103, 340 (n. 8), 342 (n. 37); 1950 U.S. Senate race and, 43; 1954 U.S. Senate race and, 342 (n. 29); North Carolina response to, 39–40, 41, 42–43, 45–46, 60, 61, 341 (n. 21), 342 (n. 26)
Brown v. Board of Education of Topeka II, 46, 47, 55, 61, 342 (n. 37)
Broyhill, James, 82, 163, 165, 175, 188, 197; 1986 U.S. Senate elections and, 220, 221, 222, 223, 360 (nn. 52–53); as congressman, 198; as senator, 221, 222
Brubaker, Harold, 250
Brunswick County, 24, 73, 230, 270
Bruton, David, 186
Bruton, Wade, 80, 119, 350 (n. 10)
Bryan, William Jennings, 9, 12
Bryant, Victor, 104, 108, 128
Buchanan, Patrick, 267
Buncombe County, 170, 252, 294, 295, 317, 318
Burney, John, 65
Burns, Augustus, 25, 31
Burr, Richard, 249, 276, 287, 309–10, 367 (n. 3)
Bush, George H. W., 187, 227, 264; 1988 presidential election and, 224–25, 235, 239, 254, 283; 1992 presidential election and, 228, 242–44, 246–47, 363 (n. 28); as president, 240, 243, 248, 271
Bush, George W.: 2000 presidential election and, 264, 265, 266–67, 269, 283; 2004 presidential election and, 275–76, 283;

2006 elections and, 277–78; as president, 270, 272, 273, 278, 292, 293, 355 (n. 38), 367 (n. 41)

Business community, 14, 16, 140, 185, 285, 358 (n. 16); 1930s and, 11, 12; 1950s and, 38, 43, 51; 1950 U.S. Senate race and, 26, 27, 339 (n. 29); 1952 gubernatorial election and, 36, 37; 1960 gubernatorial Democratic primaries and, 60, 63, 68, 344 (n. 23); 1964 Democratic gubernatorial primaries and, 92, 93, 95; 1976 gubernatorial Democratic primaries and, 168, 169, 355 (n. 21); 1980s and, 207, 216, 222; 1998 U.S. Senate elections and, 260–61; 2000 elections and, 269, 365 (n. 15); African Americans and, 13, 86, 337 (n. 33); desegregation and, 86–87, 346 (nn. 55–56); Helms and, 154, 201–2; higher education and, 264; Hodges and, 53–55, 343 (n. 52), 360 (n. 42); James Baxter Hunt Jr. and, 198, 248, 285, 366 (n. 27); Martin as governor and, 219, 360 (n. 42); Moore as governor and, 97, 113; sales tax on food and, 82, 345 (n. 43); Terry Sanford and, 59, 344 (n. 23); segregation and, 55–56

Busing, 133, 178

Butterfield, G. K., 318

*But What about the People?* (Sanford), 83

Byrd, Robert, 283, 352 (n. 10), 367 (n. 41)

Cabarrus County, 27, 144

Caldwell, John, 169

Caldwell County, 170

Calhoun, John C., 282

Califano, Joseph, 186

California, 166, 246–47

Camden County, 168

Cameron, Cliff, 360 (n. 42)

Campaign advertisements: 1950 U.S. Senate race and, 28, 29, 339 (n. 43); 1964 Democratic gubernatorial primaries and, 95; 1968 elections and, 121; 1972 gubernatorial Democratic primaries and, 141, 299; 1972 U.S. Senate elections and, 153, 299; 1976 lieutenant governorship Democratic primaries and, 172; 1976 presidential Democratic primaries and, 166; 1980 elections and, 189, 190, 193–94; 1982 U.S. House elections and, 196; 1984 U.S. Senate elections and, 203, 205, 210, 215–16, 358 (n. 14),

359 (n. 32); 1990 U.S. Senate elections and, 232–34, 237, 362 (n. 11); 1996 U.S. Senate elections and, 254, 363–64 (n. 45); 2008 presidential election and, 299, 302; 2008 U.S. Senate elections and, 292–93, 303, 367 (n. 8), 368 (n. 9); 2012 presidential election and, 316, 370 (n. 51)

Campaign expenditure: 1972 U.S. Senate elections and, 148; 1980 U.S. Senate elections and, 192; 1984 U.S. Senate elections and, 203, 214–15, 234; 1990 U.S. Senate elections and, 234; 1996 U.S. Senate elections and, 254; 2000 state elections, 268; 2002 U.S. Senate elections and, 272; 2004 gubernatorial election and, 276; 2006 elections and, 278; 2008 gubernatorial election and, 293; 2008 presidential election and, 299, 302; 2010 U.S. Senate Democratic primaries and, 309; 2012 presidential election and, 316

Campaign fundraising, 192; 2002 U.S. Senate elections and, 271, 272; 2008 presidential election and, 300; Congressional Club and, 186, 253; conservatism and, 215, 359 (n. 31); Democratic Party and, 266, 269, 278; Republican Party and, 269, 288

Campbell University, 220, 244

Camp Lejeune, 13, 188–89

Cannon, Charles, 11, 16, 27, 68, 344 (n. 23)

Canton, 92

Capital Broadcasting Company, 144

Capital punishment, 168, 224, 232, 233, 248, 254, 266

Carlton, Phil, 95, 216

Carlyle, Frank Ertel, 50

Carlyle, Irving, 41, 103, 341 (n. 24)

Carlyle Commission, 103, 348 (n. 30)

Carpenter, L. L., 42

Carson, William, 163

Carter, Dan T., 123

Carter, Jimmy, 193; 1976 presidential Democratic primaries and, 165–66; 1976 presidential election and, 172–74, 294, 327, 354 (nn. 16, 18), 355 (n. 30), 367 (n. 6); 1980 presidential election and, 190, 191, 200, 216; human rights and, 181, 182; as president, 184, 186

Carteret County, 73, 108

Cary, 6, 7

Castelanos, Alex, 202

Caswell County, 195, 314

Catawba College, 124

Catholic Church, 10, 68, 71, 72, 268, 283, 307, 337 (n. 24), 344 (n. 29)

CBS, 181

Cecelski, David, 3

Cell, John W., 55

Chambers, Julius, 133

Chapel Hill, 6, 54, 116, 123, 141, 149, 261, 267, 273, 275; black mayor and, 145, 171

Charleston, 131, 229

Charlotte, 32, 38, 96, 205, 207, 228, 261; 1948 elections and, 20, 22; 1950 U.S. Senate elections and, 27; 1990 U.S. Senate Democratic primaries and, 230, 231; 1992 presidential election and, 247; 2000 gubernatorial election and, 268; 2008 gubernatorial election and, 293, 304, 368 (n. 10); 2008 presidential election and, 304; African American leadership and, 229, 242; Democratic National Convention of 2012 and, 287, 315, 316; desegregation of public schools and, 52–53, 109, 133; as financial center, 6, 272, 336 (n. 12); growth, 1940s–1950s, 33; growth, 1960s, 134; higher education wars and, 106, 348 (n. 35); mass transit and, 291, 293, 368 (n. 11); Republican Party and, 51, 218, 265, 266, 360 (n. 39). *See also* Urban population centers

Charter schools, 291, 310, 315, 369 (n. 40)

Chatham, Richard T., 49

Chatham County, 129, 312

Chavis, Ben, 132, 182

Chavis, Elizabeth, 182

Cheney, Dick, 266, 275

Cherry, Gregg, 14, 20, 23, 25, 337 (n. 35)

Chicago, 117, 120, 290, 294

Chiropractors, 279–80

Chisholm, Shirley, 138, 204

Christensen, Rob, 3, 287

Christian Action League, 170

Church of the Black Madonna, 132

Cigarette manufacturing, 32–33, 126, 340 (n. 2)

Civil rights, 84, 176, 195, 237; 1948 Democratic Convention and, 21; 1956 presidential election and, 51; 1960 presidential election campaign and, 69, 70, 71; 1964 presidential election and, 102; 1966 U.S.

House elections and, 110; 1968 presidential election and, 121; African American representation in Congress and, 239–40; John F. Kennedy and, 87, 90–91, 102, 348 (n. 27); white backlash, 112

Civil Rights Act, 91–92, 93, 98, 112, 324, 346 (n. 4), 346–47 (n. 9); Title VI, 109, 186

Civil rights demonstrations, 98; Birmingham, Ala., 87, 348 (n. 27); Little Rock school crisis, 53, 64, 65; Montgomery bus boycott, 51–52, 56, 62; in North Carolina, 58, 61, 73, 75, 88, 94; Selma, Ala., 102, 348 (n. 27); sit-in movement, 62, 85, 86; white backlash, 62, 63, 88

Civil rights movement, 7, 232, 323; 1960 presidential election and, 76; 1976 Democratic National Convention and, 166; deaths in, 98; desegregation and, 46, 48; higher education and, 199, 292; white backlash, 153, 255; white segregationists and, 55, 60, 155; Wilmington Ten and, 181–83, 356 (n. 46)

Clark, David, 27, 29

Clark, Herman, 220

Clark, Jim, 102, 348 (n. 27)

Clarke, James M., 223

Clay County, 49

Clayton, Eva, 242, 246, 254, 279

Clemson University, 230

Clinton, Bill, 254, 291, 364 (n. 49); 1992 Democratic primaries and, 243; 1992 presidential election and, 244, 246–47, 258, 296, 303, 363 (nn. 28, 34); 1996 presidential election and, 251, 254, 255, 256, 363 (n. 34); 2012 presidential election and, 316, 370 (n. 51); impeachment, 262, 263; as president, 248–49, 250–51, 252, 261, 264–65, 272, 289, 364 (n. 2)

Clinton, Hillary Rodham, 249, 271, 289, 291, 298, 367 (n. 5)

Coastal area land management act (CAMA), 160

Coble, Jacob, 154

Cochrane, William McWhorter, 137

Coffer, Bertram (Bert), 253, 288

Coleman, Linda, 315, 318

Columbus County, 177, 312

Commission on Interracial Cooperation, 87

Committee on Education, 45

Committee to Re-Elect the President

(CREEP), 157

Committee to Reject or Re-Elect, 180

Communism, 27, 31, 37, 38, 200, 282

Communist Workers' Party, 186

Community colleges, 82, 103, 141, 186–87, 263, 269, 311, 365 (n. 7)

Community Schools Act, 178

Congressional Club, 180, 219, 360 (n. 53); 1980 elections and, 190; 1984 U.S. Senate elections and, 202, 215; 1986 U.S. Senate elections and, 220; 1990 U.S. Senate elections and, 229, 232; 1992 U.S. Senate elections and, 244; 1998 U.S. Senate elections and, 260; break with Helms and, 253, 254, 363–64 (n. 45); fundraising and, 186, 253; Helms and, 164, 186, 197, 215, 232

Congress of Racial Equality, 86, 242

Connor, Eugene "Bull," 87

Conservatism, 44, 61, 63, 68, 80; 1988 presidential election and, 224, 361 (n. 57); 2008 presidential election and, 291; against Clinton, 248–49; John East and, 188, 198, 214, 219, 221; fundraising and, 215, 359 (n. 31); Helms and, 153–54, 155–56, 161, 163, 185, 188, 198, 213, 214, 219, 282–83, 367 (n. 41); Lyndon Johnson and, 91, 346 (n. 5); Ronald Reagan and, 200, 214, 215; religious, 214, 215, 227, 249, 251, 260, 282–83; Republican Party and, 2, 37, 145, 149–50, 157, 163, 164, 188, 198, 200, 231, 325, 352 (n. 16); television use in campaigns and, 65; William B. Umstead and, 39, 42

Consumer protection, 119, 127, 139, 207, 358 (n. 16)

Contract with America, 248

Cooley, Harold, 49–50, 75, 99, 110, 119, 143, 198, 343 (n. 43)

Cooper, Roy, 226, 320

Copeland, William, 79, 81

Corruption: Jim Black and, 279–80, 307, 366 (nn. 21–22); Chicago and, 290; Democratic Party and, 250, 274, 276, 293, 295, 314, 363 (nn. 37–39), 366 (n. 30); Mike Easley and, 308–9, 369 (nn. 35–36)

Council, Herman, 13, 52

Council of State, 119, 121, 139, 163, 179, 226; 2008 elections and, 295; 2012 elections and, 315, 318, 320

Covington, Howard E., Jr., 50, 135

Cowell, Janet, 294, 320

Craven, J. Braxton, 45

Cumberland County, 270, 295, 317, 318

Cunningham, Cal, 309

Cuomo, Mario, 243, 307

Currituck County, 270

Daley, Richard J., 120, 146, 166

Dalton, Walter, 314, 315, 318, 321

Daniels, Jonathan, 25, 28, 35, 68, 85, 339 (n. 39)

Daniels, Josephus, 8, 9, 10, 11, 12, 27, 28, 336 (n. 21)

Dare County, 73, 212, 270, 312

Daughtry, Leo, 250, 265, 268

Davidson College, 143, 217, 359 (n. 37)

Davie County, 143

Davis, Archie, 54, 128, 201

Davis, Lawrence, 185

Deane, Charles B., 49

Death penalty. *See* Capital punishment

Debnam, W. E., 33–34, 49–50

Decker, Michael, 274, 279, 366 (n. 21)

Declaration of Constitutional Principles, 49, 51, 110, 343 (n. 43)

Deep South states, 4, 6, 22, 40, 336 (n. 13); 1964 presidential election and, 100; 2008 presidential election and, 296

Defense of Marriage Act, 311–12, 313, 370 (n. 43)

Demagogues, 280–81, 282

Democratic National Conventions: 1948, 21–22; 1960, 68–69, 91; 1964, 99; 1968, 117, 120; 1972, 146; 1976, 166, 173, 354 (n. 17); 1984, 201; 1988, 224; 1992, 243; 1996, 267; 2000, 265; 2004, 275; 2008, 291–92; 2012, 287, 315, 316

Democratic Party, 34, 45, 51, 60, 195, 366 (n. 27); 1948 dissension between south and north, 21–23; 1948 gubernatorial campaign and, 16, 19–20, 338 (nn. 3, 10, 13–14); 1950 U.S. Senate elections and, 26, 28, 339 (n. 39); 1960 elections and, 72, 75, 76; 1964 presidential election and, 101; 1966 U.S. Senate elections and, 110; 1968 campaigns and, 117, 119, 120–21, 349 (n. 5); 1968 presidential election and, 121–24; 1972 elections and, 146–47, 148, 155, 156, 159; 1972 gubernatorial Democratic primaries and, 137, 141–42, 352 (n. 13); 1974

161, 206, 207; Southern Manifesto and, 49; Watergate and, 157, 159

Etheridge, Bob, 257, 258, 310, 314, 369 (n. 39)

Eure, Thad, 179, 189, 226, 356 (n. 40), 361 (n. 64)

Euripides, 280

Evangelical Christianity, 169, 279, 359 (n. 30); 1980 elections and, 214; 1984 U.S. Senate elections and, 214–15; 1986 U.S. Senate elections and, 221; 1996 gubernatorial election and, 252; 2002 U.S. Senate elections and, 272; 2008 presidential election and, 300; 2008 U.S. Senate elections and, 304; 2012 presidential election and, 317, 370 (n. 52); abortion issue and, 193, 283

Everett, Robinson, 241

Facebook, 303, 316

Faircloth, Lauch, 19, 31, 250; 1984 gubernatorial Democratic primaries and, 206, 207; 1986 U.S. Senate elections and, 221, 235; 1992 U.S. Senate elections and, 244, 246, 247, 360 (n. 48); 1998 U.S. Senate elections and, 260–61, 364 (nn. 2–3), 364–65 (n. 5); Hunt's administration and, 177, 206; as Republican, 235, 244, 271

Faison, Bill, 314

Falwell, Jerry, 221, 283

Family values, 252, 282

Farmer, James, 86

Faubus, Orval, 53, 64

Fayetteville, 4, 18, 43, 50, 66, 76, 107, 198, 225

Fayetteville State University, 126

Fayetteville Teachers' College, 45

Federal Bureau of Investigation, 111, 204, 349 (n. 45)

Federal Court of Appeals, 182

Feminism, 214, 289

Ferguson, James, 182

Ferraro, Geraldine, 201

Ferrell, Claude, 96–97, 347 (n. 19)

Fetzer, Tom, 173, 221, 276

Fifteenth Amendment, 56

Financial meltdown (2008), 6, 292

Finkelstein, Arthur, 202, 260

First Citizens Bank, 93, 95

Flaherty, David, 170, 174, 176

Fletcher, A. J., 61, 64, 65, 144, 154

Florida, 6, 38, 255, 267, 275, 316, 363 (n. 34), 370 (n. 51)

Folsom, James "Kissin' Jim," 15

"Food tax," 18, 80–82, 222, 345 (nn. 43, 45), 360 (n. 45)

"Food Tax Terry," 81, 345 (n. 45)

Ford, Gerald, 158, 184, 218; 1976 presidential election and, 173, 367 (n. 6); 1976 presidential Republican primaries and, 164–65, 188, 282, 360 (n. 53); 1976 Republican National Convention and, 166–67

Forrest, Dan, 315, 318

Forsyth County, 38, 100, 143, 153, 212, 235, 247. *See also* Winston-Salem

Fort Bragg, 13

Fountain, L. H., 145, 171, 194, 195

Fountain, Richard, 30, 75

"Fountain's Fishhook," 195

Fourteenth Amendment, 34, 35, 40, 46, 51, 56

Fourth Circuit Court of Appeals, 35, 47

Fowle, David, 44

Fox news, 283

*Frank Porter Graham and the 1950 Senate Race in North Carolina* (Pleasants and Burns), 25

"Freedom Democratic Party," 99

Freedom Riders, 86

Freeman, Franklin, 277

Friday, William, 31, 77, 113, 264, 332; 1964 Democratic gubernatorial primaries and, 92–93; 1992 gubernatorial election and, 229; higher education wars and, 106, 107; as president of state university system, 27, 54, 104–5, 108, 109, 125, 128, 129, 160–61, 199, 263, 348 (nn. 30, 35), 350 (n. 16)

Frye, Henry, 124

Funderburk, Betty, 257–58

Funderburk, David, 220–21, 249, 257–58, 360 (n. 53), 364 (n. 48)

Furniture industry, 79, 82, 170, 192, 222

Future Farmers of America, 169

Galifianakis, Nick, 155, 351 (nn. 2, 3); 1972 U.S. Senate Democratic primaries and, 138; 1972 U.S. Senate elections and, 148, 149–50, 151, 153, 156, 234, 326; 1974 U.S. Senate elections and, 163

Gallup, 316

Gantt, Harvey: 1990 U.S. Senate elections and, 229 37, 242, 252, 266, 298, 362 (nn. 6, 8–9, 15), 363 (n. 39); 1996 Senate elections and,

232; conservatism and, 153–54, 155–56, 161, 163, 185, 188, 198, 213, 214, 219, 282–83, 367 (n. 41); constituent service and, 201–2, 358 (n. 5); death of, 280; as demagogue, 213, 280–81, 366 (n. 33); Tom Ellis and, 144, 145, 148, 186, 202, 224, 229, 332; Sam J. Ervin Jr. and, 204, 281, 366 (n. 35); failing health and, 258, 259; governor term limits and, 180; higher education and, 160, 264; legacy, 280–84, 285–86, 328, 371 (n. 4); as "mass leader," 281–82; Panama Canal treaty and, 184, 185; race and, 204, 213–14, 230, 233, 280–84; Republican Party and, 158, 159, 188, 192, 218, 354 (n. 5); retirement, 270–71; Terry Sanford and, 220, 223, 244; as senator, 260–61, 278, 283–84, 287, 288, 289; social populism and, 185, 193, 254, 357 (n. 20); speaking skills, 216–17; white voters and, 153–56, 212, 213–14, 254, 281, 353 (n. 28); WRAL radio and, 28, 154; WRAL television and, 37, 96, 105, 130, 144, 154–55

Henderson County, 143, 174

*Henderson v. United States*, 34

Hendon, William, 192, 197

Henley, John, 107

Hertford County, 79

Higher education: boost in capital spending, 2000, 263–64, 365 (n. 7); colleges becoming universities and, 102–9, 126–27; consolidation and, 10–11; growth, 1960s, 102–3, 134, 136; Jim Holshouser and, 160; reorganization, 1971, 127–29; student life, 1969–72, 129–31; wars over, 102–9. *See also* Desegregation; University of North Carolina, Chapel Hill; University of North Carolina system

High Point, 6, 88

Hill, George Watts, 54, 86, 92–93, 104, 108, 128

Hispanics, 7, 269, 289

Hobby, Wilbur, 140, 141, 352 (n. 10)

Hodges, Luther, 81, 168, 185, 342 (n. 33), 344 (n. 28); 1952 lieutenant governor elections, 37; 1954 succession to governorship and, 44–45, 179; 1956 gubernatorial election and, 50, 170, 179; 1960 elections and, 60, 62, 66, 69, 70, 344 (n. 7); 1964 Democratic gubernatorial primaries and, 93; *Brown v. Board of Education* and, 45–46; business community and, 53–55,

343 (n. 52), 360 (n. 42); desegregation and, 47–48, 61; as governor, 50–51, 60, 62, 79, 82, 91, 113, 158, 345 (n. 42), 354 (n. 4); governor term limits and, 179; industry recruitment and, 54–55, 126, 328; legacy, 328; as lieutenant governor, 37, 44, 147, 340 (n. 14); as progressive, 84, 87, 93

Hodges, Luther, Jr., 185, 206

Hodgkins, Sarah, 176

Hoey, Clyde, 26, 29–30, 39, 41, 44

Hoffer, Eric, 281–82

Hoke County, 7, 234

Holding family, 93, 95

Holloman, Wayne, 188

Holly, Buddy, 135

Holshouser, Jim, 188, 217, 285, 332; 1972 gubernatorial election and, 148, 149, 150, 152, 153, 326; 1972 gubernatorial Republican primaries and, 143, 144, 145, 245; as governor, 158–62, 163, 164, 170, 218, 325; governor term limits and, 179, 180, 356 (n. 42); legacy, 328; Republican Party and, 158–59, 165, 218, 245, 354 (n. 5)

Hooper, Ruby, 207

Hoover, Herbert, 10, 11, 22, 38, 76, 120, 191, 337 (n. 24)

Hoover, J. Edgar, 204

Howell, Henry, 140, 352 (n. 10)

Hughes, Charles Evans, 9

*Human Events*, 189

Humphrey, Hubert: 1964 presidential election and, 99; 1968 Democratic primaries and, 117; 1968 presidential election and, 120–21, 122, 123, 124, 172, 235; civil rights and, 21, 120–21

Hunt, Carolyn, 176

Hunt, James Baxter, Jr., 2, 230, 277, 332, 347 (n. 21), 354 (n. 4); 1972 lieutenant governorship elections and, 146–48, 156, 181; 1976 gubernatorial Democratic primaries and, 159, 167–70, 171–72, 326, 355 (nn. 21–22); 1976 gubernatorial election and, 170, 174–75, 190, 194, 247; 1980 gubernatorial Democratic primaries and, 187; 1980 gubernatorial election and, 182, 183, 190, 194, 247; 1984 gubernatorial Democratic primaries and, 205, 206, 208, 213, 235, 358 (n. 15), 359 (n. 18); 1984 U.S. Senate elections and, 199, 201–5, 208, 209–12,

Mizell, Wilbur "Vinegar Bend," 124, 162
*Modern Age*, 189
Mondale, Walter "Fritz," 173, 200–201, 210, 216, 234, 235
Monroe, 13, 272, 332
Montgomery bus boycott, 51–52, 56
Moore, Dan K., 168, 349 (n. 5); 1964 gubernatorial Democratic primaries and, 92–97, 113, 346–47 (n. 9), 347 (nn. 10, 12, 19–20); 1964 gubernatorial election and, 99, 100, 102; as governor, 97, 103, 106, 107–9, 112–13, 135, 158, 349 (nn. 49–50), 354 (n. 4); governor term limits and, 179; higher education wars and, 107–9, 348 (n. 38); Ku Klux Klan and, 111
Moore, Richard, 249, 291, 294
Moore County, 261, 274
"Moral Monday" demonstrations, 328
Morgan, Richard, 274, 366 (n. 23)
Morgan, Robert, 30, 31, 61, 113, 167, 201, 358 (n. 16); 1960 elections and, 70, 344 (n. 10); 1964 elections and, 96; 1968 elections and, 139; 1972 gubernatorial Democratic primaries and, 139, 141, 159; 1974 U.S. Senate elections and, 139, 159, 163; 1980 U.S. Senate elections and, 188, 189–90, 191, 192, 194; as attorney general, 119, 127, 139, 159, 160, 163, 188, 207, 245, 358 (n. 16); higher education wars and, 106, 107; as U.S. Senator, 163, 184, 188, 192, 356 (n. 10)
Morganton, 41
Mormons, 317, 370 (n. 52)
Morrison, Cameron, 9, 10, 14, 30, 51, 78, 87
Morrow, Sarah, 176
Morton, Hugh, 180
Mountains of North Carolina: 1950 U.S. Senate race and, 30; 1952 presidential election and, 38, 76; 1956 presidential election and, 76; 1960 gubernatorial Democratic run-off primary and, 66, 67, 76; 1960 gubernatorial election and, 76; 1960 presidential election and, 71–72, 74, 76; 1964 gubernatorial Democratic primaries and, 94, 95, 97; 1964 gubernatorial election and, 100; 1964 presidential election and, 100, 101; 1968 presidential election and, 121–23; 1972 gubernatorial election and, 150, 152; 1972 presidential election and, 149; 1972 U.S. Senate elections and, 151, 153; 1976

presidential election and, 174; 1984 gubernatorial election and, 212; 1984 U.S. Senate elections and, 211, 212; 1986 U.S. Senate elections and, 223; 1988 presidential election and, 235; 1990 U.S. Senate elections and, 234, 235, 236; 1992 gubernatorial election and, 247; 1992 presidential election and, 247; 1992 U.S. Senate elections and, 247; 1996 presidential election and, 255; 1996 U.S. Senate elections and, 256; 2000 gubernatorial election and, 268; 2000 presidential election and, 267; 2002 U.S. Senate elections and, 272; 2004 gubernatorial election and, 277; 2004 presidential election and, 275, 276; 2008 gubernatorial election and, 304, 305; 2008 presidential election and, 296, 297; 2008 U.S. Senate elections and, 303; 2010 U.S. Senate elections and, 309; 2012 gubernatorial election and, 321; 2012 presidential election and, 317, 319; Amendment 1 (Defense of Marriage Act) referendum and, 313; geography of, 4–6; political affiliation and, 6; population, 1960s, 106, 348 (n. 34)
Munger, Mike, 294
Murdoch, Rupert, 283
Murphy School, 85, 346 (n. 53)
Muskie, Edmund, 121
Myrdal, Gunnar, 115
Myrick, Sue, 230, 244

Nader, Ralph, 139, 267, 275
Nash County, 30, 216, 226, 239
National Abortion Rights Action League, 233
National Association for the Advancement of Colored People (NAACP), 125, 328; 1960 gubernatorial Democratic primaries and, 62, 63, 64; *Brown v. Board of Education* and, 42, 47; redistricting and, 195, 239; segregation and, 47, 133, 337 (n. 33)
National Guard, 125, 131, 132
Native Americans, 7, 84, 114, 126, 234, 273
Neal, Stephen, 162
Neely, Chuck, 265, 268
Nesbit, Lynn, 81
New Bern, 159
New Deal, 12–13, 26, 32, 75, 101, 113, 339 (n. 28)
*New Frontiers*, 43
New Hanover County, 132

New technology for campaigns, 299–300, 302–3, 316, 368 (nn. 15, 24)

*New York Times*, 316

New York University, 106

Nineteenth Amendment, 10, 306

Nisbet, Lynn, 44

Nixon, Richard, 100, 173, 271, 348 (n. 26), 354 (n. 2); 1952 presidential election and, 37–38; 1960 presidential election and, 69, 70, 71, 72–73, 74, 75–76, 303; 1968 presidential election and, 119–20, 121, 122, 123–24, 148, 294, 296, 350 (n. 15); 1972 presidential election and, 137, 142, 146, 148–49, 150, 153, 157, 210, 218, 327; resignation of, 157, 162, 164, 204; Vietnam War and, 130; Watergate and, 157–58, 159, 162, 164

Northampton County, 149

North Carolina: 1916 presidential election and, 9; 1928 presidential election and, 10, 38, 59, 296; 1932 presidential election and, 11; 1936 presidential election and, 148; 1948 presidential election and, 22–23; 1952 presidential election and, 38–39, 72, 73, 76, 101, 123, 149, 174, 296; 1956 presidential election and, 51, 71, 72, 73, 76, 101, 123, 149, 174, 247, 296; 1960 presidential election and, 69, 70–77, 90, 100, 101, 123, 149, 174, 294; 1964 presidential election and, 99–102, 121, 123, 144, 148, 174, 294, 347 (n. 24), 347–48 (n. 25); 1968 presidential election and, 112, 120–24, 148, 153, 154, 155, 235, 245, 296, 327; 1972 elections and, 156, 353 (nn. 29–30); 1972 presidential Democratic primaries and, 138, 220; 1972 presidential election and, 137, 142, 148–49, 150, 153, 155, 210, 218, 235, 239, 296, 327; 1976 presidential Democratic primaries and, 166, 169, 220; 1976 presidential election and, 173, 174, 294, 327; 1976 presidential Republican primaries and, 164, 165, 166, 170, 188, 218, 282; 1980 presidential election and, 187, 190, 191–92, 193, 200, 216, 239, 282, 294; 1984 presidential Democratic primaries and, 201, 205; 1984 presidential election and, 200, 210, 216, 234, 239, 254; 1988 presidential election and, 224–25, 227, 235, 239, 254, 361 (n. 56); 1992 presidential Democratic primaries and, 243; 1992 presidential election and, 246, 247–48,

249, 255, 296, 363 (n. 34); 1996 presidential election and, 251, 254, 255, 256; 2000 presidential election and, 265, 267–68, 269, 295; 2004 presidential election and, 275–76, 277, 295, 296, 306, 366 (n. 24); 2008 presidential Democratic primaries and, 289, 290, 291; 2008 presidential election and, 287, 288, 294, 295–304, 306, 310, 312, 315, 320, 367 (n. 6), 368 (n. 25); 2008 presidential Republican primaries and, 291; 2012 presidential election and, 287, 312, 315, 316, 317, 318, 319, 320, 370 (nn. 50–51); blue moon elections, 248, 278; democracy in, 8–9, 323–24; economic indicators, 2013, 327–28; King's assassination, response to, 116–17; as peripheral southern state, 6, 336 (n. 13); U.S. affairs affecting, 2–3

North Carolina A&T State College, 45, 47–48, 58, 107

North Carolina Advisory Commission on Civil Rights, 84

North Carolina Association of Educators, 177, 178, 300–301

North Carolina Bar Association, 27

North Carolina Central University, 126, 277

North Carolina College for Negroes (Durham), 35, 102

North Carolina Constitution, 48, 158, 179–80, 310, 311

North Carolina Court of Appeals, 181

North Carolina court system, 82–83, 112

North Carolina Democratic Convention of 1954, 41

North Carolina Educators Association, 112, 141

North Carolina Fund, 83, 84

North Carolina General Assembly. *See* North Carolina House of Representatives; North Carolina Senate; North Carolina state legislature

North Carolina Good Neighbor Council, 87

North Carolina House of Representatives: 1962 elections and, 82; 1966 elections, 110; 1968 elections and, 124; 1972 elections and, 156, 194, 225, 262; 1974 elections, 162; 1976 elections, 175; 1978 elections, 185, 262; 1980 elections, 194; 1984 elections, 213; 1986 elections, 223; 1988 elections, 225–26, 227; 1990 elections, 234; 1992 elections, 246, 248; 1994 elections, 250, 258, 259, 260, 279, 366 (n. 29); 1996 elections, 256, 258, 260; 1998 elections, 260, 262; 2000 elections, 265, 266, 267, 268; 2002 elections, 273–74; 2004 elections, 277; 2006 elections, 279, 366 (n. 29); 2008 elections, 295; 2010 elections, 310; 2012 elections, 318, 320; 2013 outlook, 327; Appropriations Committee, 308; Jim Beatty, 218; Jim Black, 266, 269, 273, 274, 277, 279–80, 307, 366 (nn. 21–22); Clifton Blue, 98; Dan Blue, 271; Hargrove "Skipper" Bowles, 140; David Britt, 108; Harold Brubaker, 250; Linda Coleman, 315; Roy Cooper, 226; Leo Daughtry, 250; Michael Decker, 274; Defense of Marriage Act and, 312; Democratic Party and, 260, 272–73, 366 (n. 21); Bill Faison, 314; Finance Committee, 285, 308; David Flaherty, 170; "food tax" and, 81; Henry Frye, 124; Nick Galifianakis, 138; Tom Gilmore, 206; Phillip Godwin, 127; Jimmy Green, 167, 171, 206; Joe Hackney, 307; Jim Holshouser, 143; Joe Hunt, 79; Jim Johnson, 144; Sam Johnson, 127; Walter Jones Jr., 226, 242; Walter Jones Sr., 189; Paul Luebke, 285, 308; Joe Mavretic, 226, 228; Henry McKinley "Mickey" Michaux, 307–8; Richard Morgan, 274, 366 (n. 23); Thomas Pearsall, 16, 45; James Ramsey, 158, 167, 196; Liston Ramsey, 198, 225–26; range of members of, 1960s, 78–79; Republican Party and, 124, 213, 227, 250, 258, 259; revolt, 1989, 225–26, 228, 250, 361 (nn. 61–62); Carolyn Russell, 250; Willis Smith, 27; Paul Stam, 311; Thom Tillis, 310; I. T. "Tim" Valentine, 195

North Carolina Microelectronics Center, 198

North Carolina Press Association, 87

North Carolina School of Science and Mathematics, 178–79, 197, 356 (n. 39)

North Carolina Senate: 1928 elections, 213; 1960 elections, 77; 1962 elections and, 82; 1964 elections, 96; 1966 elections, 110; 1968 elections and, 124; 1972 elections and, 156, 194, 213, 225, 262; 1974 elections, 162; 1976 elections, 175; 1978 elections, 185, 262; 1980 elections, 194; 1984 elections, 212, 213; 1986 elections, 223; 1988

elections, 225; 1990 elections, 234; 1992 elections, 246, 248; 1994 elections, 250, 260; 1996 elections, 256, 260; 1998 elections, 260, 262; 2000 elections, 266, 268; 2002 elections, 273; 2004 elections, 277; 2006 elections, 279; 2008 elections, 295; 2010 elections, 310; 2012 elections, 318; 2013 outlook, 327; Gordon Allen, 158, 167; Patrick Ballantine, 276; Marc Basnight, 266, 268, 269, 277, 279, 307, 366 (nn. 27, 29); Phil Berger, 310; Hargrove "Skipper" Bowles, 140; William Copeland, 79; Walter Dalton, 314; Defense of Marriage Act and, 312; Democratic Party and, 250, 260; early 2000s and, 307, 369 (n. 32); "food tax" and, 81; Jimmy Green and, 198; Kay Hagan, 288, 291; Luther Hamilton, 108; John Henley, 107; higher education wars and, 106–7; James Baxter Hunt Jr. and, 159, 212; lieutenant governor powers and, 226, 361 (n. 63); lottery approval and, 279, 293; Brad Miller, 273; Billy Mills, 105; Robert Morgan, 61, 106, 107, 139; Tony Rand, 307; recession, 2009 and, 308; Republican Party and, 124, 213; Kenneth Royall, 127; Terry Sanford, 59; Sanford as governor and, 79–80; Ralph Scott, 80, 125, 127, 350 (n. 21); Malcolm Seawell, 60; Clarence Stone, 108; Thomas White, 128; George Wood, 168, 170

North Carolina State Baptist Convention, 49

North Carolina State Board of Higher Education, 107, 128, 129

North Carolina State College (Raleigh), 102, 103, 105, 107, 108, 128, 147, 209, 337 (n. 26)

North Carolina state legislature: 1890s Republican-Populist alliance, 81, 250; 1960 elections and, 72, 77; 1972 elections and, 156; 2008 elections and, 307, 325; 2010 elections and, 326–27, 328; 2012 elections and, 325, 328; blacks and women and, 198; *Brown v. Board of Education* and, 45, 46; budgets, 112, 126, 160, 163; chiropractic treatments and insurance and, 279–80; Coastal area land management act (CAMA), 160; Defense of Marriage Act, 311–12; Democratic Party and, 156, 168, 268–69, 310, 325, 365 (n. 13); Thad Eure and, 226, 361 (n. 64); governor term limits

and, 179, 180; higher education wars and, 106, 107–8, 109; lottery approval, 279, 293; minimum wage increase and, 81, 125; one-stop voting policies and, 301; Pearsall Plan and, 48; primary dates and, 164, 167, 243, 363 (n. 27); primary runoff abolition with 40 percent rule and, 242; recession and, 2009–10, 307–8, 311, 369 (n. 34); reorganization of higher education and, 1971, 127–29; Republican Party and, 250, 310–11, 314, 320, 325, 371 (n. 56); sales taxes and, 11–12, 80–82, 345 (nn. 43, 45); Sanford as governor and, 79–80, 81, 91, 346 (n. 6); Kerr Scott and, 23, 24, 36, 345 (n. 42); Robert W. "Bob" Scott and, 126–27, 350 (nn. 21–22); taxes and, 9, 10, 11, 53, 80, 126, 160, 218, 245, 311, 327, 328; University of North Carolina system and, 128–29, 160; women's rights and, 10, 162
—redistricting and: 1880s and 1890s, 239–40; after 1960 and, 106, 237, 348 (n. 34), 360 (n. 40); after 1970, 194; after 1980, 194–95; after 1990, 238–42, 269; after 2000, 265, 266, 270, 273, 277, 310, 365 (n. 10); after 2010, 310, 318, 328
*See also* Public education
North Carolina State University, 169, 206, 277, 309, 369 (n. 36)
North Carolina State University Faculty Club, 103
North Carolina Superior Court, 36, 45, 83, 92, 112
North Carolina Supreme Court, 42, 77–78, 80, 83, 112, 175, 190, 345 (n. 46)
North Carolina Teachers' Association, 47, 48
North Carolina Young Democratic Clubs, 43, 50, 59, 117, 147, 159, 206

Obama, Barack: 2008 presidential Democratic primaries and, 289–91; 2008 presidential election and, 291–92, 294, 295–303, 304, 306, 310, 312, 317, 362 (nn. 6–9), 368 (nn. 15, 18, 24–25); 2012 presidential election and, 315–18, 319, 370 (nn. 43, 50–51, 53); approval ratings, 309, 370 (nn. 46, 50); charter schools and, 310, 369 (n. 40); fundraising and, 215, 300; as president, 300, 307, 368 (n. 18)

Obama, Michelle, 316, 370 (n. 51)
Office of Economic Opportunity (OEO), 114
Office of Equal Educational Opportunity, 110
O'Herron, Ed, 168, 170
Olive, Hubert, 36, 37, 51, 340 (n. 13)
O'Neill, Thomas P. "Tip," 184
Onslow County, 252, 270
Orange County, 54, 117, 145, 149, 171, 212, 264, 307, 314; 2008 presidential election and, 295; 2012 presidential election and, 317, 318; Amendment 1 (Defense of Marriage Act) referendum and, 312; redistricting and, 194, 195. *See also* Chapel Hill
*Orange County Landmark*, 209
Outer south, 6, 336 (n. 13)
Oxford, 131, 132, 351 (nn. 28, 30)

Palin, Sarah, 292
Panama Canal, 184, 185, 192
Parent-Teacher Association (PTA), 48, 68
Parker, Hazel, 45
Parker, John J., 47
Parks, desegregation of, 85, 346 (n. 54)
Parks, Rosa, 51
Patterson, Jane, 177, 355 (n. 36)
Pearce, Gary, 176, 328
Pearsall, Elizabeth, 87
Pearsall, Thomas, 16, 45, 46, 86–87, 92–93, 97, 346 (n. 57)
Pearsall Plan, 48–49, 50, 59, 342 (n. 40), 343 (n. 4)
Pearson, Drew, 69
Pell, Joe, 176
Pembroke State College, 102
Pembroke State University, 126
Pender County, 16, 20, 37, 270
Perdue, Beverly, 293–94, 304–7, 325, 370 (n. 46); as governor, 183, 294, 304, 307, 308, 309, 314, 315, 369 (n. 31); as lieutenant governor, 279, 291, 293
Peripheral South states, 6, 336 (n. 13)
Perot, H. Ross, 243–44, 246, 247, 255, 363 (n. 28)
Person County, 167, 196
Petty, Richard, 271
Phillips, Kevin, 157, 354 (n. 2)
Phillips, Meg Scott, 279
Philpott, Cloyd, 79
Piedmont plateau: 1948 gubernatorial campaign and, 20; 1950 U.S. Senate race and,

367 (n. 6), 368 (nn. 15, 18, 24–25); 2008 Democratic primaries, 289–91, 367 (n. 5); 2012, 287, 312, 314, 315–18, 319, 370 (nn. 43, 50–51, 53); landslides, 190–91, 210, 246, 294; North Carolina as swing state, 287, 303, 315, 316, 320; Republican electoral vote lock, 227, 228, 258, 361 (n. 1)

Preyer, L. Richardson, 45, 206; 1964 Democratic gubernatorial primaries and, 93, 94–95, 96, 100, 113, 118, 148, 346–47 (n. 9), 347 (nn. 12, 19–21); 1968 U.S. House elections and, 124; 1980 U.S. House elections and, 192

Price, David, 249, 257, 318

Primaries, 9, 13, 336 (n. 18); North Carolina dates for, 164, 167, 243, 363 (n. 27); run-off primary abolition with 40 percent rule, 196–97, 242, 272. *See also* Governorships; Presidential elections; U.S. Senate

Pritchard, George, 21, 23, 24

Private schools, 48, 49, 112, 134, 293

Privette, Coy, 170

*Profiles in Courage* (Kennedy), 72

Progressives, 162, 171, 227, 257, 369 (n. 32); 1990 U.S. Senate elections and, 232; Charles Aycock, 3, 125; Hargrove "Skipper" Bowles, 140; Democratic Party in North Carolina and, 55, 59; O. Max Gardner, 12, 78, 337 (n. 27); Kay Hagan, 293; higher education and, 105, 264; Luther Hodges, 84, 87, 93; James Baxter Hunt Jr., 168; James Martin, 217, 285, 359 (n. 38); Pat McCrory, 291; preserving white supremacy, 3, 8, 12, 68; public education and, 2, 18, 264; Terry Sanford, 59, 78, 79, 84, 125, 206, 260, 326; Kerr Scott, 24, 78, 326

Prohibition, 10

Project Head Start, 84

Property taxes, 9, 11, 80

Protestants, 4, 69, 272, 279, 366 (n. 20). *See also* Baptists; Evangelical Christianity; Methodism; Presbyterians

Public education: 1960 gubernatorial Democratic primaries and, 60, 62, 64, 65, 66, 68; 1964 Democratic gubernatorial primaries and, 96–97, 347 (n. 19); 1972 Democratic gubernatorial primaries and, 141; Charles Aycock and, 7–8, 177, 264, 279; Better Roads and Schools and,

23–24; Community Schools Act and, 178; competency testing and, 177, 178, 355 (n. 38); desegregation and, 46, 48, 52–53, 109–10, 132, 133–34, 157, 342 (nn. 36–37, 40), 351 (n. 37); Mike Easley and, 269, 277, 279; equalization of, 307; eye exams and, 280; funding and, 11–12, 14, 109–10, 218, 337 (n. 35), 365 (n. 9); O. Max Gardner and, 10–11; growth, 1960s, 134, 135–36; "integrated" schools, 85, 109, 346 (n. 53); kindergartens, 127, 160; James Martin and, 218; North Carolina School of Science and Mathematics, 178–79, 197, 356 (n. 39); as progressive issue, 2, 18, 264; Republican Party and, 250, 310–11; School of the Arts, 83, 126–27, 178–79; segregation and, 36, 39–40, 42, 45–49, 50, 52–53, 84, 131, 342 (n. 36); teacher instructional supplies and, 177–78; teachers' salaries, 12, 17–18, 36, 60, 81, 112, 126, 127, 160, 269, 349 (n. 49); teaching positions, 311. *See also* Higher education; Hunt, James Baxter, Jr.; Sanford, Terry

Quakers, 58, 116

Quayle, Dan, 224

Race: 1948 gubernatorial campaign and, 19; 1950 U.S. Senate race and, 29, 31, 339 (n. 43); 1960 gubernatorial Democratic primaries and, 60–68; 1964 gubernatorial Democratic primaries and, 113; 1964 presidential election and, 102; 1972 U.S. Senate elections and, 282; 1976 gubernatorial Democratic primaries and, 172, 355 (n. 29); 1982 U.S. House Democratic primaries and, 196; 1984 U.S. Senate elections and, 203–5, 282, 358 (nn. 9, 14); 1988 gubernatorial election and, 225; 1990 U.S. Senate elections and, 229–37, 258, 282, 361 (n. 2); 1996 U.S. Senate elections and, 254, 258, 282, 363–64 (n. 45); 2008 presidential election and, 290, 367 (nn. 4–5); Democratic Party and, 91, 149, 235, 255; Helms and, 204, 213–14, 233, 280–84; poverty programs and, 114; quotas and, 233; redistricting, early 1990s and, 238–42. *See also* African Americans

Racial equality, 115, 131, 135, 183, 200; 1960

presidential election and, 75; 1972 Democratic gubernatorial primaries and, 139; 1976 gubernatorial Democratic primaries and, 172; 1984 U.S. Senate elections and, 203; black churches and, 196, 301, 368 (n. 19); congressional redistricting, early 1990s and, 240–41, 362 (n. 22); democracy in North Carolina and, 323–24; Hubert Humphrey and, 21, 120–21; Sanford and, 59, 77, 85, 86–89; Pat Taylor and, 139, 352 (nn. 5-6). *See also* African Americans; Desegregation; Voter registration; Voting rights

Racial unrest: desegregation of public schools and, 133–34; Duke University, 134–35; Durham, 1940s, 13; Oxford and, 131, 351 (nn. 28, 30); Wilmington and, 131–32

Racism, 8–9, 34; 1980s and, 203-4, 358 (n. 11); "black belt counties" and, 7, 55, 56, 79, 237; sales tax on food and, 81, 345 (n. 43); southern leaders and, 15, 40, 78, 214, 280; Truman and, 21, 338 (n. 17). *See also* African Americans; Ku Klux Klan; Segregation

Radio, 24, 30; 1960 gubernatorial primaries and, 64; 1968 elections and, 121; 1984 Senate elections and, 203, 215; 1990 U.S. Senate elections and, 232–33, 234; 2008 presidential election and, 302; *Brown v. Board of Education* and, 40, 47; WPTF radio, 49, 64, 343 (n. 43); WRAL radio, 28, 154

Raleigh, 6, 7, 13, 33, 34, 173, 177, 244, 275; 1948 gubernatorial campaign and, 16; 1984 U.S. Senate elections and, 212; 2008 presidential election and, 296; 2012 presidential election and, 318; growth, 1960s, 134; higher education and, 10, 54; radio and television of, 64; segregation and, 61. *See also* North Carolina State College; North Carolina State University; Urban population centers

*Raleigh News and Observer*, 11, 25, 28, 35, 68, 85, 168, 287, 293–94

Ramsey, James, 158, 167, 196

Ramsey, Liston, 198, 225–26, 361 (nn. 61-62)

Rand, Tony, 225, 307

Randolph County, 144, 174, 185, 250

Rankin, Ed, 39, 40, 45, 158, 341 (n. 24), 342 (n. 32)

Rasmussen, 316

Ready, Milton, 3

Reagan, Ronald, 227, 299, 328, 354 (n. 2), 358 (n. 4); 1976 presidential election and, 173; 1976 presidential Republican primaries and, 164, 165, 166, 170, 188, 218, 282, 360 (n. 53); 1976 Republican National Convention and, 166–67; 1980 presidential election and, 187, 190, 191–92, 193, 216, 239, 259, 282, 283, 294; 1984 presidential election and, 200, 208, 210, 212, 216, 239, 254, 283, 364–65 (n. 5); abortion issue and, 187, 193, 357 (n. 20); Atlantic coastal plain and, 223; conservatism and, 200, 214, 215; military spending and, 197, 200, 210, 282, 358 (n. 2); as president, 197, 199, 204, 205, 209, 210, 219, 222, 224, 271, 272; tax cuts and, 209, 248

"Red Shirt" attack, 8

Reed, Amos, 177

Referenda: 1961 capital improvements, bonds for, 82; amendment for private schools to avoid integration and, 49; Amendment 1 (Defense of Marriage Act), 312, 313, 370 (n. 43); Better Roads and Schools and, 24–25; bonds for capital spending on UNC system, 263–64; constitutional amendment on governorship terms, 180; state income taxes and, 9

Reform Party, 267

Regan, Donald, 219

Religion. *See* Baptists; Catholic Church; Evangelical Christianity; Methodism; Presbyterians; Protestants

Republican National Conventions: 1952, 166–67; 1960, 69, 70; 1964, 98–99; 1968, 119–20; 1976, 164–65, 166–67, 189, 218; 1980, 189; 1988, 224; 2000, 265; 2004, 275; 2008, 290; 2012, 315

Republican Party, 6, 10, 13, 354 (n. 2), 357 (n. 28); 1948 gubernatorial election, 21, 23; 1948 presidential election and, 22; 1950 U.S. Senate race and, 30, 31; 1952 elections and, 191; 1952 gubernatorial election and, 37, 341 (n. 15); 1956 gubernatorial election and, 50; 1960 gubernatorial election and, 70, 77; 1960 presidential election and, 75–76; 1962 North Carolina House elections and, 82; 1962 U.S. House elections and, 82; 1964 gubernatorial election and,

Ryan, Paul, 315, 370 (n. 51)

Safer, Morley, 181
Safire, William, 280
Sales taxes, 11–12, 16, 24, 162, 311, 327; on food, 18, 80–82, 222, 345 (nn. 43, 45), 360 (n. 45)
Salisbury, 271, 291
Sampson County, 73
Sanders, Charles, 251–52
Sand hills of North Carolina, 4. *See also* Atlantic coastal plain; Piedmont plateau
Sands, A. P. "Sandy," 249
Sanford, Betsee, 85
Sanford, Terry, 119, 125, 167, 248, 344 (n. 28); 1954 U.S. Senate Democratic primaries and, 43; 1956 gubernatorial election and, 50; 1960 gubernatorial Democratic primaries and, 59–63, 93, 94, 95, 169, 326, 344 (nn. 7, 10, 23); 1960 gubernatorial Democratic run-off primary and, 63–68, 94; 1960 gubernatorial election, 70, 71, 72, 73, 75, 76–77, 118, 140, 148, 221; 1960 presidential campaign and, 68–69, 344 (n. 25); 1964 Democratic gubernatorial primaries and, 93, 95, 96, 97, 98, 347 (nn. 19–21); 1964 presidential campaign and, 99; 1972 elections and, 141–42, 147–48; 1972 presidential Democratic primaries and, 138, 220; 1976 presidential Democratic primaries and, 164, 165, 220; 1984 gubernatorial Democratic primaries and, 207; 1986 U.S. Senate elections and, 220, 221–23, 235, 360 (nn. 48, 52, 54); 1992 U.S. Senate elections and, 244, 246, 247, 248, 251, 360 (n. 48), 363 (n. 33); beginning of political career and, 18, 31, 326; Civil Rights Act and, 91–92; death of, 259; Democratic Party and, 59, 68, 94, 180, 198; desegregation and, 59, 342 (n. 40), 343 (n. 4); Duke University and, 135, 164, 220, 246, 259; economic populism and, 168, 172; "food tax" and, 80–82, 222, 345 (nn. 43, 45), 360 (n. 45); as governor, 2, 77–89, 91–92, 113, 140, 222, 345 (nn. 42, 45–46, 50), 346 (n. 6), 354 (n. 4), 360 (n. 45); governor term limits and, 179; Helms and, 220, 223, 244; higher education and, 102–3, 104, 106, 107–8; Kennedy and, 68–69, 76–77, 84, 85, 90, 91; legacy, 259–60, 328, 371

(n. 4); as progressive, 59, 78, 79, 84, 125, 206, 260, 326; public education and, 79–82, 83–84, 112, 126, 135, 177, 178–79, 264, 279, 349 (n. 49), 357 (n. 29); racial equality and, 59, 77, 85, 86–89; Robert W. "Bob" Scott and, 117–18; as U.S. Senator, 223, 244; woman appointments and, 83, 345 (n. 46)
Sanford, Terry, Jr., 85
San Francisco State University, 129
Savannah, Ga., 131, 171, 217
Saxapahaw, 50
School of the Arts, 83, 126–27, 178–79
Scotland County, 66
Scott, Kerr, 22, 30, 97, 117, 126, 175, 177, 206, 248, 279, 338 (n. 13), 343 (n. 45); 1948 gubernatorial Democratic primaries and, 15–21, 326, 338 (n. 10), 355 (n. 21); 1948 gubernatorial election, 15, 21, 23; 1949 Senate appointment and, 25–26, 125; 1950 U.S. Senate race and, 26, 27, 28, 31, 339 (n. 37); 1952 gubernatorial election and, 36–37; 1954 U.S. Senate race and, 43–44, 59, 68; black and women appointees and, 36; death of, 50, 51; economic populism and, 23, 55, 78, 84; as governor, 15, 23–26, 36, 126, 139, 338 (n. 23), 340 (n. 12), 345 (n. 42); legacy, 328; roads and, 18, 23–25, 36, 257, 340 (n. 12); Southern Manifesto and, 49
Scott, "Miss Mary," 25
Scott, Ralph, 49, 80, 125, 127, 350 (n. 21)
Scott, Robert W. "Bob," 20, 93, 113, 177, 206, 279, 332, 347 (nn. 10, 21); 1968 gubernatorial Democratic primaries and, 117–19, 125; 1968 gubernatorial election and, 121, 124, 142, 143, 225; 1972 gubernatorial Democratic primaries and, 139, 140–41, 142; 1972 gubernatorial election and, 150; 1980 gubernatorial Democratic primaries and, 187; Democratic National Convention of 1968 and, 120; as governor, 124–26, 134, 135, 138, 139, 146, 350 (nn. 16, 18, 21–22); governor term limits and, 179; higher education and, 126–27, 128–29; James Baxter Hunt Jr. and, 186–87; as lieutenant governor, 97–98, 107, 118, 147; protest movements and, 131; tax increases and, 126, 160
Seabrook, J. W., 45
Seawell, H. F. "Cousin Chub," 10, 37

Seawell, Malcolm, 60, 61, 62, 63, 66, 93, 344 (n. 7)
Secular Coalition of America, 293
Segregation, 1, 15, 19, 323, 337 (n. 33); 1948 Democratic Convention and, 21, 22; 1950s and, 32, 33, 55–57, 340 (n. 1); 1950 U.S. Senate elections and, 29, 30, 31; 1954 U.S. Senate elections and, 43–44; 1960 gubernatorial Democratic primaries and, 60–68; 1964 Democratic gubernatorial primaries and, 92–97; 1972 Democratic gubernatorial primaries and, 139; beginning of end of, 34–35, 340 (nn. 7–8); buses and, 13, 51–52; bus stations, 52, 84, 86; churches and, 59, 131; hotels and motels, 87, 98; housing and, 171; Pearsall Plan and, 50, 59, 343 (n. 4); public places and, 84, 86, 98; public schools and, 36, 39–40, 42, 45–49, 50, 52–53, 84, 131, 342 (n. 26); restaurants, 58, 61, 86, 98; U.S. Army and, 13; "voluntary," 47–48, 52–53, 62, 64, 109, 112; White Citizens' Councils and, 112
"Separate but equal," 19, 21, 35, 40, 43, 340 (n. 7)
Shallcross, John, 110
Sharp, Susie Marshall, 36, 83, 345 (n. 46)
Shriver, Sargent, 146
Shuler, Heath, 278
Silver, Nate, 316
Simmons, Furnifold, 8, 9, 10, 11, 169, 336 (n. 16), 337 (n. 24)
Simmons, Gene "Magnolia Mouth," 185
Sitterson, Carlyle, 125, 350 (n. 16)
60 Minutes (CBS), 181
Smith, Alfred E., 10, 296, 337 (n. 24), 344 (n. 29)
Smith, Ellison D. "Cotton Ed," 280
Smith, Fred, 291
Smith, Mary, 125
Smith, McNeill, 185
Smith, William French, 199
Smith, Willis, 26–30, 31, 34, 39, 43, 51, 61, 65–66, 94, 326, 339 (n. 31), 363–64 (n. 45)
Smith v. Allwright, 13
Socialist Workers Party, 191
Social media, 316
Social populism, 168, 185, 193, 224, 254, 354 (n. 2), 357 (n. 20)
Soul City, 242
South Carolina, 6, 47, 120, 201, 205, 219, 224, 229, 261, 280, 336 (n. 13); 2008 Democratic

presidential primaries and, 290, 367 (n. 5); 2012 presidential election and, 318
Southern Association of Colleges and Schools, 108
Southern Conference for Human Welfare, 27
Southern Manifesto, 49, 51, 110, 343 (n. 43)
Southern Pilot, 145
Southern Politics in State and Nation (Key), 55, 237, 324
Southern Textile Bulletin, 27
Southport, 265, 276, 277
Sowers, Roy, Jr., 146
Spangler, C. D., Jr., 263
Sparkman, John, 38
Speaker Ban Law, 107–9
Speight, Marvin, 208
Spencer, Frank, 171
Spicely, Booker T., 13, 52
Stagflation, 184, 192
Stam, Paul, 311
Stanly County, 264
State Board of Education, 14, 36, 186
States' rights, 21, 61, 92, 96, 112
States' Rights Party, 22
Stevens, William, 163
Stevenson, Adlai E., 37, 38, 51, 76, 174, 191, 247
Stickley, John "Jack," 119
Stone, Clarence, 108
Strickland, Tommy, 168, 169, 170
Strong, Donald, 331
Suburbia, 33, 112, 247, 267, 270, 276, 295
Sugg, James, 159
Swain County, 212
Swann, James, 133
Swann v. Charlotte-Mecklenburg Board of Education, 133
Sweatt, Heman, 35
Sweatt v. Painter, 29, 35

Talmadge, Eugene, 15, 280–81
Talmadge, Herman, 40
Tarboro, 18, 45, 145, 194
Taxes: 1960 gubernatorial Democratic primaries and, 60, 63; 1960 gubernatorial election and, 76; 1984 gubernatorial election and, 209; 1984 U.S. Senate elections and, 216, 359 (n. 33); 1988 presidential election and, 224, 243; 2000 gubernatorial election and, 266; on cigarettes, 126; corporate, 11,

53, 80, 162; gasoline tax, 10, 126; James Baxter Hunt Jr. and, 252, 266, 363 (n. 40), 365 (n. 9); Hunt cuts to, 252, 266, 363 (n. 40), 365 (n. 9); income, 9, 11, 80, 162, 327, 345 (n. 40); James Martin and, 218, 245; Pat McCrory and, 327, 328; Beverly Perdue and, 307; property, 9, 11, 80; Reagan tax cuts, 209, 248; Republican Party and, 248, 250, 259; Franklin D. Roosevelt and, 38; reform, 9, 218, 327, 328. *See also* Sales taxes
Taylor, Charles, 278
Taylor, Frank, 39
Taylor, Hoyt Patrick, Sr., 23, 24
Taylor, Pat, 121, 139, 141–42, 149, 208, 352 (nn. 4–6)
Tea Party movement, 315
Technical colleges, 82, 83, 103, 141, 263, 264
Technology, 198, 201, 357 (n. 30)
Teel, Robert, 131
Television, 32, 40; 1960 gubernatorial primaries and, 64, 65; 1960 presidential campaign and, 71, 72–73; 1964 Democratic gubernatorial primaries and, 95, 97; 1984 U.S. Senate elections and, 193–94, 203, 205, 210, 215–16; 1986 U.S. Senate elections and, 222–23; 1990 U.S. Senate elections and, 231, 233–34, 362 (n. 11); 1998 U.S. Senate elections and, 261; 2000 gubernatorial election and, 265, 365 (n. 11); 2002 U.S. Senate elections and, 272; 2008 presidential election and, 302; 2012 presidential election and, 316; *Brown v. Board of Education* and, 47; civil rights demonstrations and, 52; Speaker Ban Law hearings and, 108; WZY television, 233. *See also* Campaign advertisements; WRAL television
Tennessee, 6, 38, 99, 243, 247, 255, 265, 267
Tennessee Valley Authority, 12, 101
Texas, 6, 38, 71, 73, 91, 101, 224
Textile industry, 78, 134, 140, 175, 306; 1960 gubernatorial Democratic primaries and, 68; 1980 elections and, 192; 1986 U.S. Senate elections and, 222; 1990 U.S. Senate elections and, 237; O. Max Gardner and, 11, 16; Frank Porter Graham and, 11, 26, 27, 337 (n. 26); Robin Hayes and, 252, 278; Luther Hodges and, 37; Benjamin Everett Jordan and, 50, 343 (n. 45), 351 (n. 1); segregation and, 55

Text messaging, 303, 368 (n. 24)
Thornburg, Lacy, 245
*Thornburg vs. Gingles*, 241
Thurmond, Strom, 22–23, 120, 219, 280, 358 (n. 5)
Tillis, Thom, 310
Title VI, 109, 186
Tobacco, 6, 16, 73, 111, 222; 1950s and, 32–33, 55, 340 (n. 2); 1964 presidential election and, 101; cigarette manufacturing and, 32–33, 126, 340 (n. 2); federal anti-smoking campaigns, 186, 255; federal price-support program, 32, 75, 186, 198; Gore's stance against, 267
Townsend, Nat, 95
*Transformation of Southern Politics, The* (Bass and De Vries), 162
Trigg, Harold, 36
Trinity College, 27. *See also* Duke University
Troxler, Steve, 320
Truman, Harry S., 21–23, 26, 28, 38, 39, 101, 191, 338 (n. 17)
Twenty-Sixth Amendment, 135
Two-party politics, 1–2, 323, 324–26, 371 (n. 1)
Tyson, David, 253–54
Tyson, Timothy, 3, 8

Umstead, John Wesley, 31, 39
Umstead, William B., 50, 79, 92, 113, 158; 1948 U.S. Senate elections and, 20, 25; 1950 U.S. Senate race and, 26, 27, 31; 1952 gubernatorial election and, 36–37, 38, 51, 340 (n. 13); *Brown v. Board of Education* and, 40, 42; death of, 44, 179, 342 (n. 31); as governor, 39, 40–42, 43, 44, 45, 342 (n. 32), 345 (n. 42)
Unemployment, 175, 184, 298, 316–17, 327
Union County, 270, 276
United Church of Christ, 132
United Forces for Education, 60, 68, 76, 79, 80
U.S. Army, segregation and, 13
U.S. Census Bureau, 237, 265
U.S. Congress: Congressional Black Caucus, 182; Medicare and, 113; North Carolina black representation and, 197, 238; Republican Party and, 259; Southern Manifesto and, 49; Voting Rights Act extension, 1982, 240, 362 (n. 22). *See also* U.S. House of Representatives; U.S. Senate
U.S. Constitution, 241; Equal Rights

White, Thomas, 128

White Citizens' Councils, 112

"White hands ad," 233, 237, 254, 362 (n. 11)

White supremacy, 55, 323, 324, 353 (n. 28); 1950 U.S. Senate race and, 28, 29, 326, 339 (n. 43); 1964 gubernatorial election and, 100; 1972 U.S. Senate primaries and, 138; Democratic Party and, 39, 138; direct democracy and, 8–9, 336 (n. 18); "progressives" and, 3, 8, 12, 68; voting rights and, 1, 13–14

White voters: 1956 presidential election and, 51; 1960 gubernatorial Democratic run-off primary and, 66, 73; 1960 presidential election and, 73; 1964 gubernatorial Democratic primaries and, 94, 96; 1964 gubernatorial election and, 100, 101; 1964 presidential election and, 101–2, 348 (n. 26); 1968 presidential election and, 121, 123; 1972 presidential election and, 149, 239; 1976 presidential election and, 174; 1980 presidential election and, 239; 1980 U.S. Senate elections and, 192–93; 1982 U.S. House Democratic primaries and, 196; 1984 presidential election and, 239, 254; 1984 U.S. Senate elections and, 212, 216, 223, 232, 298, 359 (n. 25); 1986 U.S. Senate elections and, 223; 1988 presidential election and, 225, 239, 254; 1990 U.S. Senate elections and, 231, 232, 234, 235, 237, 298; 1996 U.S. Senate elections and, 256, 298; 2000 gubernatorial election and, 265–66; 2000 presidential election and, 267; 2008 presidential election and, 296, 298; 2008 U.S. Senate elections and, 304; 2012 presidential election and, 318, 370 (n. 53); "Black Belt counties" and, 7, 55, 56, 79, 237; congressional redistricting, early 1990s and, 239, 362 (n. 20); electorate, 1960s, 84; evangelical Christianity and, 214, 359 (n. 30); Helms and, 153–56, 212, 213–14, 254, 281, 353 (n. 28); "law and order" and, 203, 358 (n. 10); liberal, 251–52; Barack Obama and, 290, 296, 298, 318, 367 (n. 4); Republican Party and, 200, 239, 254, 327, 357–58 (n. 1); Terry Sanford and, 220, 360 (n. 45); George Wallace and, 123, 153, 154, 155; white backlash and, 62, 63, 76, 88, 112, 153, 255; working-class Bible Belt and, 192–93, 357 (n. 18). See also Segregation

Wicker, Dennis, 250, 266

Wiggins, Norman, 244

Wilder, Douglas, 230

Wilkes County, 143, 144, 174

Williams, John A., 176

Williams, T. Harry, 281–82

Wilmington, 4, 13, 22, 24, 39, 50, 150, 270, 276; racial unrest and, 131–32, 181–83, 351 (n. 31)

Wilmington College, 107

Wilmington Ten, 132, 181–83, 202, 356 (n. 46)

Wilson, Henry Hall, 163

Wilson, Woodrow, 9

Wilson County, 146, 147, 159, 167, 212, 284

Winberry, Charles, 159

Windsor, Bob, 209, 210, 359 (n. 21)

Wingfield, Alvin, 43

Winston, Robert, 7

Winston-Salem, 6, 16, 24, 37, 49, 50, 83, 161; public schools and segregation and, 52–53, 109; tobacco and, 32–33, 340 (n. 2)

Winston-Salem State University, 126

Wolfe, Thomas, 4, 336 (n. 11)

Womble, Carlyle, Sandridge, and Rice, 284

Women, 8, 103, 306; 2008 elections and, 294–95, 304; Equal Rights Amendment, 161–62, 200; governorships, 294; North Carolina Supreme Court and, 83, 345 (n. 46); public office and, 138, 145–46, 176, 177, 271, 272–73, 306, 352 (n. 18), 355 (n. 36), 367 (n. 1)

Women's suffrage, 9–10, 323, 336 (nn. 20–21)

Wood, Beth, 294, 320

Wood, George, 168–69, 170

Works Progress Administration, 12

World War II, 13, 59, 78, 222

WPTF radio, 49, 64, 343 (n. 43)

WRAL radio, 28, 154

WRAL television, 37, 64, 65, 96, 105, 130, 144, 154–55

Wrenn, Carter, 164, 186, 189, 202, 213–14, 219, 234, 244, 253, 280, 332, 362 (n. 15)

Wright, Fielding, 22

Wright, Jeremiah, 290

Yadkin County, 143, 174

Yancey County, 212

Yates, Graem, 218

Young Republicans, 170

Young voters, 302–3, 368 (n. 25)